The Lighter Classics in Music

The Lighter Classics in Music

*A Comprehensive Guide to
Musical Masterworks in a Lighter Vein
by 187 Composers*

by David Ewen

Arco Publishing Company, Inc.

NEW YORK

Contents

❧❧ ❦❦

The Lighter Classics in Music

Joseph Achron

⋞⋞⋞ ⋟⋟⋟

JOSEPH ACHRON was born in Lozdzieje, Lithuania, on May 13, 1886. He attended the St. Petersburg Conservatory, where he studied the violin with Leopold Auer and theory with Anatol Liadov, graduating in 1904. After teaching at the Kharkov Conservatory for three years, he toured Russia, Europe and the Near East as a concert violinist for about six years, and settled permanently in the United States in 1925. Some of his most ambitious and significant compositions were written in this country. Among these were three violin concertos, two violin sonatas, the *Golem Suite* for orchestra and the *Stempenyu Suite* for violin and piano. Achron died in Hollywood, California, on April 29, 1943.

When Achron was twenty-five years old, and still living in Russia, he became a member of the music committee of the Hebrew Folk Music Society of St. Petersburg. Its aim was twofold: to encourage research in Hebrew music, and to direct the enthusiasm of gifted Russian composers toward the writing of Hebrew music. It was as a direct result of this association, and the stimulus derived from the achievements of this society, that in 1911 Achron wrote a popular composition in a Hebraic vein which to this day is his most famous piece of music. It is the *Hebrew Melody*, Op. 33, for violin and orchestra. The melodic germ of this composition is an actual synagogical chant, amplified by Achron into a spacious melody following several introductory measures of descending, brooding phrases. This melody is first given in a lower register, but when repeated several octaves higher it receives embellishments similar to those provided a synagogical chant by a cantor. The composition ends with the same descending minor-key phrases with which it opened. This *Hebrew Melody,* in a transcription for violin and piano by Leopold Auer, has been performed by many of the world's leading violin virtuosos.

Adolphe-Charles Adam

୰ଽ୰ଽ ଽ୶ଽ୶

ADOLPHE-CHARLES ADAM, eminent composer of comic operas, was born in Paris on July 24, 1803. He attended the Paris Conservatory, where he came under the decisive influence of François Boieldieu, under whose guidance he completed his first comic opera, *Pierre et Catherine,* first produced at the Opéra-Comique in Paris on February 9, 1829. His first major success, *Le Chalet,* was given on September 25, 1834, enjoying almost fifteen hundred performances in Paris before the end of the century. Adam subsequently wrote almost fifty other stage works in a light style. With Boieldieu and Auber he became founder and leading exponent of the opéra-comique. His most celebrated work in this genre was *Le Postillon de Longjumeau,* first given at the Opéra-Comique on October 13, 1836. This work was frequently heard in the United States in the 1860's and 1870's, but has since lapsed into obscurity. Adam was also a highly significant composer of ballets, of which *Giselle* is now a classic; of many serious operas; and of a celebrated Christmas song, "Noël," or "Oh, Holy Night" (*"Cantique de Noël: Minuit, Chrétiens"*), which has been transcribed for orchestra. In 1847, Adam founded his own theater—the Théâtre National—which a year later (with the outbreak of the 1848 revolution in France) went into bankruptcy. From 1849 on he was professor of composition at the Paris Conservatory. Adam died in Paris on May 3, 1856.

Giselle is one of the proudest achievements of French Romantic ballet. Through the years it has never lost its immense popularity. With choreography by Jules Perrot and Jean Coralli, it was introduced in Paris on June 28, 1841. Carlotta Grisi appeared in the title role. *Giselle* was an immediate triumph. Since then, the world's foremost ballerinas have appeared as Giselle, including Fanny Elssler, Taglioni, Pavlova, Karsavina, Markova, Danilova, Margot Fonteyn, and Moira Shearer.

"What is the secret charm of this ballet?" inquires the famous scenic designer, Alexander Benois. He goes on to answer: "It is mainly due to its simplicity and clearness of plot, to the amazingly impetuous spontaneity with which the drama is developed. There is barely time to collect one's thoughts before the heroine, who but a moment ago charmed everybody with her vitality, is lying stiff and cold and dead at the feet of the lover who deceived her. . . . It is deeply moving, and the magic of a true poet . . . consists in making us accept without question any absurdities he may choose to offer us. . . . No one is inclined to criticize while under the spell of this strange idyl."

The ballet text was the collaborative creation of Théophile Gautier, Vernoy de Saint-Georges, and Jean Coralli. Gautier had read a legend by Heinrich Heine in *De L'Allemagne* which described elves in white dresses (designated as "wilis") who died before their wedding day and emerged from their graves in bridal dress to dance till dawn. Any man an elf met was doomed to dance himself to death. Gautier, recognizing the ballet potentialities of this legend, decided to adapt it for Carlotta Grisi. He interested Vernoy de Saint-Georges in assisting him in making this ballet adaptation and Jean Coralli in creating some of the dance sequences. "Three days later," Gautier revealed in a letter to Heine, "the ballet *Giselle* was accepted. By the end of the week, Adam had improvised the music, the scenery was nearly ready, and the rehearsals were in full swing."

The ballet text finds Giselle as a sweet, carefree peasant girl. Betrayed by Albrecht, the Duke of Silesia, she goes mad and commits suicide. Her grave is touched by the magic branch of Myrtha, Queen of the Wilis. Giselle arises from the grave as a wili, and performs her nocturnal dance. Albrecht, who comes to visit her grave, is caught up by her spell and must dance to his doom.

A master of expressive and dramatized melodies, Adam here created a score filled with the most ingratiating tunes and spirited rhythms, all beautifully adjusted to the sensitive moods of this delicate fantasy. From this score the 20th-century English composer Constant Lambert extracted four melodic episodes which he made into a popular orchestral suite: "Giselle's Dance"; "Mad Scene"; "Pas de deux, Act 2"; and "Closing Scene."

From the repertory of Adam's operas comes a delightful overture, a favorite in the semi-classical repertory, even though the opera itself is rarely heard. It is the Overture to *If I Were King (Si j'étais roi)*. This comic opera was first performed in Paris on November 4, 1852; the libretto was by D'Ennery and Brésil. In Arabia, the fisherman, Zephoris, has managed to save the life of Nemea, beautiful daughter of King Oman. But Nemea is being pursued by Prince Kador, who does not hesitate to employ treachery to win her. Nemea is determined to marry none but the unidentified man who had saved her life. Eventually, the fisherman is brought to the palace, placed in command of the troops, and becomes a hero in a war against the Spaniards. Kador is sent to his disgrace, and Zephoris wins the hand of Nemea.

The oriental background of the opera permeates the atmosphere of the overture. A forceful introduction for full orchestra and arpeggio figures in harp lead to a skipping and delicate tune for first violins against plucked cello strings. The flutes and clarinets respond with a subsidiary thought. A crescendo brings on a strong subject for the violins against a loud accompaniment. After a change of tempo, another light, graceful melody is given by solo flute and oboes. The principal melodic material is then amplified with dramatic effect.

Richard Addinsell

ₑₛₑ ₑₛₑ

RICHARD ADDINSELL was born in Oxford, England, on January 13, 1904. After studying law at Oxford, he attended the Royal College of Music in London and completed his music study in Berlin and Vienna between 1929 and 1932. In 1933 he visited the United States, where he wrote music for several Hollywood films and for a New York stage production of *Alice in Wonderland*. He has since made a specialty of writing music for the screen, his best efforts being the scores for *Goodbye, Mr. Chips, Blithe Spirit, Dangerous Moonlight, Dark Journey,* and *Fire Over England*. During World War II he wrote music for several documentary films, including *Siege of Tobruk* and *We Sail at Midnight*.

Addinsell's most frequently played composition is the *Warsaw Concerto,* for piano and orchestra. He wrote it for the English movie *Dangerous Moonlight* (renamed in the United States *Suicide Squadron*). Anton Walbrook here plays the part of a renowned concert pianist who becomes an officer in the Polish air force during World War II and loses his memory after a crash. The *Warsaw Concerto,* basic to the plot structure, recurs several times in the film. It first became popular, however, on records, and after that with "pop" and salon orchestras. Though the composer's indebtedness to Rachmaninoff's Second Piano Concerto is pronounced, the *Warsaw Concerto* has enough of its own individuality and charm to survive. Structurally, it is not a concerto but a rhapsody. It opens with several massive chords, arpeggios, and scale passages in the piano. This dramatic opening leads to the sensitive and romantic principal melody, heard in the strings. Later on there appears a second lyric thought, but the rhapsodic character remains predominant. The composition ends with a final statement of the opening phrase of the first main melody.

Addinsell is also sometimes represented on semi-classical programs with a light-textured and tuneful composition called *Prelude and Waltz*, for orchestra. This also stems from a motion picture, in this case the British screen adaptation of Noel Coward's *Blithe Spirit*.

Isaac Albéniz

I S A A C   A L B É N I Z, one of Spain's most distinguished composers, was born in Camprodón, Spain, on May 29, 1860. He was a child prodigy who gave piano concerts in Spain after some spasmodic study in Paris with Marmontel. In 1868 he entered the Madrid Conservatory, but in his thirteenth year he ran away from home and spent several years traveling about in Puerto Rico, Cuba, and the United States, supporting himself all the while by playing the piano. He was back in Spain in 1875, and soon thereafter undertook music study seriously, first at the Brussels Conservatory and then at the Leipzig Conservatory. He settled in Paris in 1893, where he wrote his first important works, one of these being his first composition in a national Spanish idiom: the *Catalonia,* for piano and orchestra, in 1899. After 1900 he lived in his native land. From 1906 to 1909 he devoted himself to the writing of his masterwork, the suite *Iberia,* consisting of twelve pieces for the piano gathered in four volumes. *Iberia* is a vast tonal panorama of Spain, its sights and sounds, dances and songs, backgrounds. Albéniz died in Cambo-Bains, in the Pyrenees, on May 18, 1909.

Albéniz may well be regarded as the founder of the modern Spanish nationalist school in music. This school sought to exploit the rhythms and melodies and styles of Spanish folk music within serious concert works, thus providing a musical interpretation to every possible aspect of Spanish life.

Albéniz' first work in the national style is also one of his rare compositions utilizing an orchestra. It is the *Catalonia,* written in 1899, and introduced that year at a concert of the Société nationale de musique in Paris. This work is sometimes erroneously designated as a suite, but it is actually a one-movement rhapsody. A single theme, unmistakably Spanish, dominates the entire work. A brief rhythmic middle section for wind, percussion, and a single double bass provides contrast. This middle part is intended as a burlesque on a troupe of wandering musicians playing their favorite tune: the clarinet plays off key and the bass drum is off beat. The original dance melody returns to conclude the work.

Córdoba, a haunting nocturne, is the fourth and most famous number from the *Cantos de España,* a suite for the piano, op. 232. *Córdoba* is a vivid tone picture of that famous Andalusian city. Sharp chords, as if plucked from the strings of a guitar, preface an oriental-type melody which suggests the Moorish background of the city.

Fête Dieu à Seville, or *El Corpus en Sevilla (Festival in Seville)* is the third and concluding number from the first volume of *Iberia.* Besides its original version for the piano, this composition is celebrated in several transcriptions for orchestra, notably those by E. Fernández Arbós and Leopold Stokowski. This music depicts a religious procession in the streets of Seville on the Thursday after Trinity Sunday. At the head of the procession is the priest bearing the Host, or Blessed Sacrament, under a lavishly decorated canopy. As the procession moves, worshipers who crowd the streets improvise a religious chant.

Fête Dieu à Seville opens with a brusquely accented march melody, against which emerges an improvisational-type melody similar to those sung by worshipers in the street. The march melody and the improvised chant alternate, but it is the chant that is carried to a thunderous climax. Then this chant subsides and fades away into the distance, as the composition ends.

Navarra is a poignant tonal evocation for piano of the Spanish province below the Pyrenees. Albéniz never completed this work; it was finished after his death by Déodat de Séverac. This composition is perhaps best known in Fernández Arbós' transcription for orchestra. Against the provocative background of a jota rhythm moves a languorous and sensual gypsy melody.

Sevillañas (Seville) is the third number from *Suite española* for piano; it has become famous independent of the larger work and is often heard in transcription. The heart of the piece is a passionate song, typical of those heard in the haunts of Seville. As a background there is an incisive rhythm suggesting the clicking of castanets.

The Tango in D major, op. 165, no. 2, for piano, is not only the most famous one by Albéniz but one of the most popular ever written. With its intriguing flamenco-like melody and compelling rhythm it is Spanish to the core—the prototype of all tango music. The original piano version as written by the composer is not often heard. When it is performed on the piano, this tango is given in a brilliant but complex arrangement by Leopold Godowsky. But it is much more famous in various transcriptions, notably one for violin and piano by Fritz Kreisler, and numerous ones for small or large orchestras.

Triana is the third and concluding number from the second book of Albéniz' monumental suite for piano, *Iberia*. Triana, of which this music is a tonal picture, is a gypsy suburb of Seville. In the introduction, random phrases bring up the image of various attitudes and movements of Spanish dances. A triple-rhythmed figure leads to a light and graceful dance melody against a bolero rhythm. As the melody is developed and repeated it gains in intensity and is enriched in color until it evolves climactically with full force. A transcription for orchestra by Fernández Arbós is as famous as the original piano version.

Hugo Alfvén

⋖⋗ ⋘⋙

H U G O   A L F V É N   was born in Stockholm, Sweden, on May 1, 1872. His music study took place at the Stockholm Conservatory and, on government stipends, with César Thomson in Brussels, and in Germany and France. From 1910 to 1939 he was musical director and conductor of the student chorus at the Uppsala University. Alfvén was a nationalist composer of Romantic tendencies who wrote five symphonies together with a considerable amount of orchestral and choral music. He died in Faluns, Sweden, on May 8, 1960.

Midsummer Vigil (Midsommarvaka), op. 19 (1904), a Swedish rhapsody for orchestra, is his best known composition. It was produced as a ballet, *La Nuit de Saint-Jean,* in Paris on October 25, 1925, where it proved so successful that it was given more than 250 performances within four years. As a work for symphony orchestra it has received universal acclaim for its attractive deployment of national Swedish folk song idioms and dance rhythms. The music describes a revel held in small Swedish towns during the St. John's Eve festival. The work opens with a gay tune for clarinet over plucked strings. This is followed by a burlesque subject for bassoon. Muted strings and English horns then offer a broad, stately, and emotional folk song. Repeated by the French horns, this song is soon amplified by the strings. The tempo now quickens, and a rustic dance theme is given softly by the violins. The mood gradually becomes frenetic. The violins offer a passionate subject over a pedal point. A climax is finally reached as the revelry becomes unconfined.

Louis Alter

LOUIS ALTER was born in Haverhill, Massachusetts, on June 18, 1902, where he received his academic education in the public schools, and his initial instruction in music. Music study was completed with Stuart Mason at the New England Conservatory. In 1924 Alter came to New York, where for five years he worked as accompanist for Nora Bayes, Irene Bordoni and other stars of the stage; he also did arrangements for a publishing firm in Tin Pan Alley. Between 1925 and 1927 he wrote his first popular songs and contributed a few of them to Broadway productions. Since then he has written many song hits, as well as scores for Broadway musicals and Hollywood films. His best known songs include "A Melody from the Sky" and "Dolores," both of which were nominated for Academy Awards; also "Twilight on the Trail," such a favorite of President Franklin D. Roosevelt that the manuscript, together with a recording by Bing Crosby, repose in the Roosevelt Museum in Hyde Park, New York.

Alter has been successful in writing skilful compositions for piano and orchestra in which the popular element is pronounced, encased within a symphonic structure. Some of them are now staples in the symphonic-jazz repertory. His best compositions were inspired by the sights, sounds and moods of New York City.

Jewels from Cartier (1953), as the title indicates, was inspired not by New York but by one of the city's most famous jewelers when Alter was one day allowed to inspect its collection. In his suite, Alter attempts in eight sections to translate various jewels into tones. The first movement is "Emerald Eyes." Since many beautiful emeralds come from South America, this section emphasizes the rumba beat and other Latin-American rhythms. "The Ruby and the Rose" is a romantic ballad in which voices supplement the instruments of the orchestra. "Pearl of the Orient" consists of an oriental dance. "Black Pearl of Tahiti" exploits exotic Polynesian rhythms and its languorous-type melodies. "Diamond Earrings" is a swirling waltz while "Star Sapphire" is a beguine. In "Cat's Eye in the Night," the music suggests a playful kitten darting about in a room. The finale, "Lady of Jade," is in the style of Chinese processional music.

Manhattan Masquerade (1932) is the most dramatic of Alter's New York murals. It consists of a Viennese-type waltz played in fox-trot time, a suggestion on the part of the composer that Vienna and New York are not too far apart spiritually.

Manhattan Moonlight (1932) is, on the other hand, atmospheric. It opens with four chords in a nebulous Debussy vein. The core of the work is an extended melody for strings against piano embellishments. A light and frivolous mood is then invoked before the main melody returns in an opulent scoring.

Manhattan Serenade (1928) is the most famous of all Alter's instrumental works and the one that first made him known. He published it first as a piano solo, but soon rewrote it for piano and orchestra. Paul Whiteman and his orchestra made it popular in 1929 on records and in public concerts. This work is extremely effective in laying bare the nerves of the metropolis through syncopations, and jazz tone colorations. Its main melody is a plangent song to which, in 1940, Howard Johnson adapted a song lyric. *Manhattan Serenade* is often heard as background music on radio and television programs about New York.

Side Street in Gotham (1938) attempts to portray the city from river to river. The composition begins with a few notes suggesting "London Bridge Is Falling Down," which is later elaborated in a vigorous and amusing tempo; the reason this theme is here used is because it is referred to in the lyric of "The Sidewalks of New York." Some of the mystery of New York's side streets can also be found in this music.

Leroy Anderson

LEROY ANDERSON is one of America's most successful and best known composers of light orchestral classics. He was born in Cambridge, Massachusetts, on June 29, 1908. His early musical training took place at the New England Conservatory, after which he studied the bass and organ with private teachers. In 1929 he was graduated from Harvard *magna cum laude,* and one year after that he received there his Master's degree in music on a Naumberg Fellowship. For the next few years he served as organist and choirmaster in Milton, Massachusetts; as a member of the music faculty at Radcliffe College; and as director of the Harvard University Band. In 1935 he became a free-lance conductor, composer and arranger in Boston and New York. As orchestrator for the Boston Pops Orchestra, for which he made many orchestral arrangements over a period of several years, Anderson completed his first original semi-classical composition, *Jazz Pizzicato,* successfully introduced by the Boston Pops Orchestra in 1939. Since then the Boston Pops Orchestra has introduced most of Anderson's compositions, many of which proved exceptionally popular in concerts throughout the country and on records. Anderson has also appeared frequently as guest conductor of important American symphony orchestras and has conducted his own compositions with his orchestra for records. In 1958, his first musical comedy, *Goldilocks,* was produced on Broadway.

Beyond possessing a most ingratiating lyric invention and a consummate command of orchestration, Anderson boasts an irresistible sense of humor and a fine flair for burlesque. He is probably at his best in programmatic pieces in which extra-musical sounds are neatly adapted to and often serve as a background for his sprightly tunes—ranging from the clicking of a typewriter to the meowing of a cat.

Blue Tango is the first strictly instrumental composition ever to achieve first place on the Hit Parade. For almost a year it was the leading favorite on juke boxes, and its sale of over two million records represents Anderson's healthiest commercial success. Scored for violins, this music neatly combines an insistent tango rhythm with a sensual melody in a purple mood. *Bugler's Holiday* is a musical frolic for three trumpets. *A Christmas Festival* provides a colorful orchestral setting to some of the best loved Christmas hymns, including "Joy to the World," "Deck the Halls," "God Rest Ye Merry Gentlemen," "Silent Night," "Jingle Bells," and "Come All Ye Faithful."

Fiddle-Faddle is a merry burlesque-escapade for the violins, inspired from a hearing of Paganini's *Perpetual Motion;* this, then, is a modern style "Perpetual Motion." In *Horse and Buggy,* the music nostalgically evokes a bygone day with a sprightly, wholesome tune presented against the rhythms of a jogging horse. The *Irish Suite* was commissioned by the Eire Society of Boston, and is a six-movement adaptation of six of Thomas Moore's *Irish Melodies.* They are: "The Irish Washerwoman," "The Minstrel Boy," "The Rakes of Mallow," "The Wearing of the Green," "The Last Rose of Summer," and "The Girl I Left Behind Me." *Jazz Legato* and *Jazz Pizzicato* are studies in contrasting moods and dynamics. The *Jazz Pizzicato* consists of a jazz melody presented entirely by plucked strings; its companion piece is a broader jazz melody for bowed strings. *Plink, Plank, Plunk* also makes effective use of pizzicato strings, this time attempting to simulate the sounds suggested by the descriptive title. *Saraband* brings about the marriage between the very old and very new in musical styles. The old classical dance in slow triple time and accented second beat is exploited with a quickening of tempo and with modern rhythmic and melodic embellishments.

In *Sleigh Bells,* jangling sleighbells and the sound of a cracking whip, provide a delightful background to a jaunty tune that has the bite and sting of outdoor winterland. This piece has become something of a perennial favorite of the Christmas season. In *The Syncopated Clock,* the rhythm of a clicking grandfather's clock, presented by percussion instruments in a modern rhythm, is placed against a bouncy, syncopated melody. This number has become popular as theme music for the CBS-TV "Early Show." *The Trumpeter's Lullaby* is a sensitive melody with the soothing accompaniment of a lullaby.

The Typewriter permits members of the percussion section to imitate the incisive, rigid rhythm of a functioning typewriter, punctuated by the regular tinkle of the bell to provide the warning signal that the carriage has come to the end of a line. Against this rhythm moves a vivacious message in strings. *The Typewriter* was played in the motion picture *But Not for Me,* starring Clark Gable, released in 1959. In *The Waltzing Cat,* an imaginary cat dances gracefully to a waltz melody made up mainly of meows.

Daniel François Auber

DANIEL FRANÇOIS ESPRIT AUBER, genius of opéra-comique, was born in Caen, Normandy, France, on January 29, 1782. In his youth he lived in London, where he studied both the business of art, in which he hoped to engage, and music. There he wrote several songs which were heard at public entertainments. After returning to France and settling in Paris in 1804, he gave himself up completely to music. Two minor stage works with music were privately performed between 1806 and 1811 before his first opera received its première performance: *Le Séjour militaire* in 1813. His first success came seven years after that with *La Bergère châtelaine.* From then on he was a prolific writer of both light and grand operas, many to texts by Eugène Scribe. *La Muette de Portici* in 1828 was a triumph, and was followed by such other major successes *Fra Diavolo* (1830), *Le Cheval de bronze* (1835), *Le Domino noir* (1837) and *Les Diamants de la couronne* (1841). His last opera, *Rêves d'amour,* was completed when he was eighty-seven. Auber was one of France's most highly honored musicians. From 1842 until his death he was director of the Paris Conservatory, and in 1857 he was made by Napoleon III Imperial Maître de Chapelle. Auber died in Paris on May 12, 1871.

With Adam and Boieldieu, Auber was one of the founding fathers of the opéra-comique. He was superior to his two colleagues in the lightness of his touch, surpassing wit, and grace of lyricism. But Auber's charm and gaiety were not bought at the expense of deeper emotional and dramatic values; for all their lightness of heart, his best comic operas are filled with pages that have the scope and dimension of grand opera. As Rossini once said of him, Auber may have produced light music, but he produced it like a true master.

Overtures to several of his most famous operas are standards in the light-classical repertory.

The Black Domino (*Le Domino noir*), text by Eugène Scribe, was introduced in Paris on December 2, 1837. The central character is Lady Angela, an abbess, who attends a masked ball where she meets and falls in love with Horatio, a young nobleman. Numerous escapades and adventures follow before Angela meets up again with her young man. Now released from her religious vows by the Queen, Angela is free to marry him.

In the overture, a loud outburst for full orchestra emphasizes a strongly rhythmic theme. A staccato phrase in the woodwind and a return of the initial strong subject follow. This leads into a light dancing motive for the woodwind. Another *forte* passage is now the bridge to a melodious episode in the woodwind. A change of key brings on a gay bolero melody for clarinets and bassoons in octaves. After this idea is amplified, a jota-like melody is given by the full orchestra. The closing section is a brilliant presentation of a completely new jota melody.

The Crown Diamonds (*Les Diamants de la couronne*) was first produced in Paris on March 6, 1841, when it scored a major success. But it enjoyed an even greater triumph when it was first performed in England three years after that; from then on it has remained a great favorite with English audiences. The text, by Eugène Scribe and Saint-Georges, is set in 18th-century Portugal where the Queen assumes the identity of the leader of a gang of counterfeiters and uses the crown diamonds to get the money she needs to save her throne. When Don Henrique falls into the unscrupulous hands of these counterfeiters, the

Queen saves his life and falls in love with him. The throne is eventually saved, and the crown jewels retrieved. The Queen now can choose Don Henrique as her husband.

The overture opens with a sustained melody for the strings that is dramatized by key changes. A rhythmic passage leads to a martial subject for the brass. Several other vigorous ideas ensue in the brass and woodwind. After their development there comes a lyrical string episode which, in turn, leads into a second climax. Contrast comes with a lyrical idea in the strings. A loud return of the first martial subject in full orchestra marks the beginning of a spirited conclusion.

Fra Diavolo was an immediate success when first given in Paris on January 28, 1830; it has remained Auber's best known comic opera. It has even received burlesque treatment on the Hollywood screen in a comedy starring Laurel and Hardy. The text by Eugène Scribe has for its central character a bandit chief by the name of Fra Diavolo who disguises himself as an Italian Marquis. He flirts with a lady of noble birth, hides in the bedroom of Zerlina, the inn-keeper's daughter, and is finally apprehended by Zerlina's sweetheart, the captain of police.

This popular overture opens with a *pianissimo* drum roll, the preface to a march tune for strings. The march music is extended to other instruments, and as the volume increases it gives the impression of an advancing army. It attains a *fortissimo* for full orchestra, then subsides. The overture ends with several sprightly melodies from the first act of the opera.

The Mute of Portici (La Muette de Portici)—or, as it is sometimes called, *Masaniello*—is a grand opera that contributed a footnote to the political history of its times. First performed in Paris on February 29, 1828, it had profound repercussions on the political situation of that period, and it is regarded by many as a significant influence in bringing on the July Revolution in Paris in 1830. When first performed in Brussels the same year, it instigated such riots that the occupying Dutch were ejected from that country and Belgium now achieved independence.

The text by Eugène Scribe and Germain Delavigne is based on an episode from history: a successful Neapolitan revolt against the Duke of Arcos, headed by Tommaso Anello in 1647. In the opera, Masaniello assumes Anello's part, and toward the end of the opera after the insurrection is smothered, he is assassinated.

The overture begins with stormy music in full orchestra. After the tempo slackens, a sensitive melody is presented by clarinets and bassoons in octaves. The main section of the overture now unfolds, its main theme divided between the strings and the woodwind. After a *fortissimo* section for full orchestra, a second important melody is heard in the woodwind and violins. The two main subjects are recalled and developed. The overture closes with a coda in which percussion instruments are emphasized.

Johann Sebastian Bach

JOHANN SEBASTIAN BACH was born in Eisenach, Germany, on March 21, 1685. He was the most significant member of a family that for generations had produced professional musicians. His career can be divided into three convenient periods. The first was between 1708 and 1717 when, as organist to the Ducal Chapel in Weimar, he wrote most of his masterworks for organ. During the second period, from 1717 to 1723, he served as Kapellmeister to Prince Leopold in Coethen. During this period he wrote most of his major works for orchestra, solo instruments, and chamber-music ensembles. The last period took place in Leipzig from 1723 until his death where he was cantor of the St. Thomas Church. In Leipzig he produced some of his greatest choral compositions. Towards the end of his life he went blind and became paralyzed. He died in Leipzig on July 28, 1750.

As the culmination of the age of polyphony, Johann Sebastian Bach's masterworks are, for the most part, too complex and subtle for popular appeal. But from his vast and incomparable outpout of concertos, sonatas, suites, masses, passions, cantatas, and various compositions for the organ and for the piano, it is possible to lift a few random items of such melodic charm and simple emotional appeal that they can be profitably exploited for wide consumption. In these less complicated works, Bach's consummate skill at counterpoint, and his equally formidable gift at homophonic writing, are always in evidence.

The *Air* is one of Bach's most famous melodies, a soulful religious song for strings. It can be found as the second movement of his Suite No. 3 in D major for orchestra, but is often performed apart from the rest of the work. August Wilhelmj transcribed this music for violin and piano, calling it the *Air on the G String*. This transcription has been severely criticized as a mutilation of the original; Sir Donald Francis Tovey described it as a "devastating derangement." Nevertheless, it has retained its popularity in violin literature, just as the original has remained a favorite in orchestral music.

Come Sweet Death (Komm, suesser Tod) is a moving chorale for voice and accompaniment: a simple and eloquent resignation to death. It does not come from any of Bach's larger works but can be found in Schemelli's collection (1736). It has become extremely popular in orchestral transcriptions by Leopold Stokowski and Reginald Stewart, but is also sometimes heard in arrangements for various solo instruments and piano, as well as for the organ.

Jesu, Joy of Man's Desiring (Jesu bleibt meine Freude) is probably Bach's best known and most frequently performed chorale: a stately melody introduced by, then set against, a gracefully flowing accompaniment. This composition comes from the church cantata No. 147, *Herz und Mund und Tat und Leben*. Various transcriptions have popularized this composition, notably that for piano by Myra Hess, for organ by E. Power Biggs, and for orchestra by Lucien Caillet.

The *Prelude in E major* is a vigorous and spirited piece of music whose rhythmic momentum does not relax from the first bar to the last. It appears as the first movement of the Partita No. 3 in E major for solo violin. It is perhaps even better known in transcription than in the original version, notably in those for violin and piano by Robert Schumann and Fritz Kreisler, for solo piano by Rachmaninoff, and for orchestra by Stokowski, Riccardo Pick-Mangiagalli, Sir Henry J. Wood, and Lucien Caillet.

The *Siciliano* is a beautiful, stately song—the first movement of the Sonata No. 4 in C minor for violin and accompaniment. Stokowski has made a fine transcription for orchestra.

The Wise Virgins is a ballet-suite comprising six compositions by Bach drawn from his literature for the church and transcribed for orchestra by the eminent British composer, Sir William Walton. It was used for a ballet produced at Sadler's Wells in 1940. Frederick Ashton's choreography drew its material from the parable of the Wise and Foolish Virgins in the 25th chapter of the Gospel According to St. Matthew;

but this parable is seen through the eyes of the Italian Renaissance painters. "Ashton," wrote Arnold Haskell, "has provided the perfect meeting place for music and painting. The inspiration was pictorial . . . it is equally musical. The movement and unfolding of the narrative follow directly from the Bach music so brilliantly arranged and orchestrated by William Walton."

All six movements of the suite are so lyrical and emotional that their impact on listeners is immediate. The first movement, "What God Hath Done Is Rightly Done" comes from the opening chorus of a cantata of the same name, No. 99 (*Was Gott tut das ist wohlgeben*). A lively melody is first shared by strings and woodwind and then given fanciful embellishments. A strong chorale melody for the brass is then given prominent treatment. The second movement, "Lord, Hear My Longing" is a chorale from the *Passion According to St. Matthew* which is here given the treatment of an organ chorale-prelude with a tenderly expressive chorale melody in woodwind amplified by strings. The third movement, "See What His Love Can Do" is an expansive melody for strings and woodwind against a flowing accompaniment; this music is derived from Cantata No. 85, *Ich bin ein guter Hirt*. This is followed by "Ah, How Ephemeral," a dramatic page for full orchestra highlighting a chorale for brass taken from Cantata No. 26, *Ach, wie fluechtig*. The fifth section is the most famous. It is "Sheep May Safely Graze" ("*Schafe koennen sicher weiden*") from the secular Cantata No. 208, *Was mir behagt*. An introductory recitative for solo violin leads to a swaying melody for the woodwind. The lower strings then present a pastoral song which soon receives beautiful filigree work from other parts of the orchestra. The swaying subject for woodwind closes the piece. Sir John Barbirolli also made an effective orchestral transcription of this composition, while Percy Grainger arranged it for solo piano, and Mary Howe for two solo pianos. The finale of the suite is "Praise Be to God," which is also the finale of Cantata No. 129, *Gelobet sei der Herr, mein Gott*. This is vigorous music that is an outpouring of pure joy.

Michael Balfe

ᴇᴥᶾᴥᶾ ᶾᴥᶾᴥ

MICHAEL WILLIAM BALFE was born in Dublin, Ireland on May 15, 1808. The son of a dancing master, Michael was only six when he played the violin for his father's classes. In 1823, Balfe came to London where he studied the violin and composition with private teachers and earned his living as violinist and singer. Additional study took place in Italy in 1825, including singing with Bordogni. Between 1828 and 1833 he appeared as principal baritone of the Italian Opera and several other French theaters in Paris. In 1835, he initiated an even more successful career as composer of English operas, with *The Siege of Rochelle,* produced that year in London. He continued writing numerous operas, producing his masterwork, *The Bohemian Girl,* in 1843. Between 1846 and 1856 Balfe traveled to different parts of Europe to attend performances of his operas. In 1864 he left London to retire to his estate in Rowney Abbey where he died on October 20, 1870.

The Bohemian Girl is a classic of English opera. It was first produced at Drury Lane in London on November 27, 1843, when it enjoyed a sensational success. It was soon translated into French, German and Italian and was extensively performed throughout Europe. The libretto, by Alfred Bunn, was based on a ballet-pantomime by Vernoy de Saint-Georges. The setting is Hungary in the 18th century, and its heroine is Arline, daughter of Count Arnheim who, as a girl, had been kidnapped by gypsies and raised as one of them. She is falsely accused by the Count's men of stealing a valuable medallion from the Count's palace and is imprisoned. Appearing before the Count to ask for clemency, she is immediately recognized by him as his daughter.

Melodious selections from this opera are frequently heard. The most famous single melody is "I Dream'd That I Dwelt in Marble Halls" which Arline sings in the first scene of the second act as she recalls a dream. "The Heart Bowed Down," the Count's song in the fourth scene of the second act as he gazes longingly on a picture of his long lost daughter, and "Then You'll Remember Me," a tenor aria from the third act are also familiar.

Hubert Bath

৵৳৵৳ ৡ৵ৡ৵

HUBERT BATH was born in Barnstaple, England, on November 6, 1883. He attended the Royal Academy of Music in London, after which he wrote his first opera. For a year he was conductor of an opera company that toured the world. After 1915 he devoted himself mainly to composition. Besides his operas, tone poems, cantatas and various instrumental works he wrote a considerable amount of incidental music for stage plays and scores for the motion pictures. He died in Harefield, England, on April 24, 1945.

The *Cornish Rhapsody,* for piano and orchestra, is one of his last compositions and the most famous. He wrote it for the British motion picture *Love Story,* released in 1946, starring Margaret Lockwood and Stewart Granger. Lockwood plays the part of a concert pianist, and the *Cornish Rhapsody* is basic to the story which involves the pianist with a man in love with another woman. The rhapsody begins with arpeggio figures which lead to a strong rhapsodic passage in full chords. A bold section is then contrasted by a gentle melody of expressive beauty, the heart of the composition. A cadenza brings on a return of the earlier strong subject, and a recall of the expressive melody in the orchestra to piano embellishments. The composition ends with massive passages and strongly accented harmonies.

Ludwig van Beethoven

❧❧ ☙☙

LUDWIG VAN BEETHOVEN was born in Bonn, Ger-
many, on December 16, 1770. He received his earliest musical training
in his native city where he early gave strong evidence of genius. He published his first works when he was eleven, and soon thereafter was performing publicly on the organ, cembalo, and the viola. He also disclosed a phenomenal gift at improvisation. He established permanent
residence in Vienna in 1792. Three years later he made there his first
public appearance, and from then on began to occupy a high position in
Viennese musical life as a piano virtuoso. His fame as a composer soon
superseded that of virtuoso as he won the support of Vienna's aris-
tocracy. He entered upon a new creative phase, as well as full maturity,
beginning with 1800, when his first symphony was introduced in
Vienna. His creative powers continually deepened and became enriched
from that time on. As he restlessly sought to give poetic and dramatic
expression to his writing he broke down the classical barriers so long
confining music and opened up new horizons for style and structure.
Meanwhile, in or about 1801 or 1802, he realized he was growing deaf,
a discovery that swept him into despondency and despair, both of which
find expression in a unique and remarkable document known as the
Heiligenstadt Testament. Deafness led to personal idiosyncrasies and
volatile moods which often tried the patience of even his closest friends,
but it did not decrease the quantity of his musical production nor pre-
vent him from achieving heights of creative expression achieved by few,
if any. He died in Vienna on March 26, 1827 after having ushered in a
new age for music with his symphonies, concertos, sonatas, string quartets, and masterworks in other categories including opera and choral
music.

The grandeur of expression, the profundity of thought, and the independence of idiom we associate with Beethoven is not to be found in
his lighter music which, generally speaking, is in a traditional mold,
pleasing style, and in an inviting lyric vein. This is not the Beethoven
who was the proud democrat, whose life was a struggle with destiny,

and who sought to make music the expression of his profoundest concepts. This is rather, another Beethoven: the one who liked to dance, though he did it badly; who flirted with the girls; and who indulged in what he himself described as "unbuttoned humor."

Beethoven wrote twelve *Contredanses (Contretaenze)* in 1801–1802. These are not "country dances" as the term *"contretaenze"* is sometimes erroneously translated. The Contredanse is the predecessor of the waltz. Like the waltz it is in three-part form, the third part repeating the first, while the middle section is usually a trio in contrasting mood. In 1801–1802, when Beethoven wrote his *Contredanses,* he was already beginning to probe deeply into poetic thought and emotion in his symphonies, sonatas, and concertos. But in the *Contredanses* the poet becomes peasant. This is earthy music, overflowing with melodies of folk-song vigor, and vitalized by infectious peasant rhythms. The *Contredanse* No. 7 in E-flat major is particularly famous; this same melody was used by the composer for his music to the ballet *Prometheus,* for the finale of his *Eroica Symphony,* and for his Piano Variations, op. 35. The key signatures of the twelve *Contredanses* are: C major, A major, D major, B-flat major, E-flat major, C major, E-flat major, C major, A major, C major, G major and E-flat major.

A half dozen years before he wrote his *Contredanses* Beethoven had completed a set of twelve *German Dances (Deutsche Taenze)*. The form, style, and spirit of the *German Dance* is so similar to the *Contredanse* that many Austrian composers used the terms interchangeably. Beethoven's early *German Dances,* like the later *Contredanses,* are a reservoir of lively and tuneful semi-classical music with an engaging earthy quality to the melodies and a lusty vitality to the rhythms.

Few Beethoven compositions have enjoyed such universal approval with budding pianists, salon orchestras, and various popular ensembles as the *Minuet in G.* It is not too far afield to maintain that this is one of the most famous minuets in all musical literature. Beethoven wrote it originally for the piano; it is the second of a set of six minuets, written in 1795, but published as op. 167. It is even more celebrated in its many different transcriptions than it is in the original. The composition is in three-part form. The first and third parts consist of a stately classical melody; midway comes a fast-moving trio of contrasting spirit.

The first movement of the *Moonlight Sonata* is also often heard in varied transcriptions for salon or "pop" orchestras. The *Moonlight Sonata* is the popular name of the piano sonata in C-sharp minor, op. 27, no. 2 which Beethoven wrote in 1801 and which he designated as

Sonata quasi una fantasia mainly because of the fantasia character of this first movement. The poetic and sensitive mood maintained throughout the first movement—with a romantic melody of ineffable sadness accompanied by slow triplets—is the reason why the critic Rellstab (and *not* the composer) provided the entire sonata with the name of "Moonlight." To Rellstab this first movement evoked for him a picture of Lake Lucerne in Switzerland at night time, gently touched by the moonlight. The fact that Beethoven dedicated the sonata to Countess Giulietta Guicciardi, with whom he was then in love, leads to a legend that he wrote this music to express frustrated love, but this was not the case. Another myth about this first movement is that Beethoven improvised this music while playing for a blind boy, as moonlight streamed into the window of his room; after he had finished playing he identified himself to the awe-stricken youngster. It was the opinion of the eminent critic, Henry E. Krehbiel, that the sonata was inspired by a poem, *Die Beterin* by Seume, describing a young girl kneeling at an altar begging for her father's recovery from a serious illness; angels descend to comfort her and she becomes transfigured by a divine light.

Beethoven wrote two *Romances* for violin and orchestra: in F major, op. 50 (1802) and G major, op. 40 (1803). Rarely do we encounter in Beethoven's works such a fresh, spontaneous and entirely unsophisticated outpouring of song—a song that wears its beauty on the surface—as in these two compositions. The two *Romances* are companion pieces and pursue a similar pattern. Each opens with the solo violin presenting the main melody (in the F major accompanied by the orchestra, in the G major, solo). Each then progresses to a pure outpouring of lyricism followed by virtuoso passages for the solo instrument. In each, violin and orchestra appear to be engaging in a gentle dialogue.

The *Turkish March (Marcia alla turca)* is one of several numbers (the fourth) comprising the incidental music to a play by Kotzebue, *The Ruins of Athens (Die Ruinen von Athen)*, op. 113 (1811). The production of this play with Beethoven's music was intended for the opening of a theater in Pesth on February 9, 1812. The *Turkish March* is in the pseudo-Turkish melodic style popular in Vienna in the early 19th century, and it employs percussion instruments such as the triangle which the Viennese then associated with Turkish music. The march, with its quixotic little melody, begins softly, almost like march music heard from a distance. It grows in sonority until a stirring climax is achieved. Then it dies out gradually and ebbs away in the distance. Leopold Auer made a famous transcription for violin and piano, while

Beethoven himself transcribed it for piano, with six variations, op. 76 (1809).

Vincenzo Bellini

VINCENZO BELLINI was born in Catania, Sicily, on November 3, 1801. Born to a musical family, he received music instruction in childhood, and while still very young started composing. He then attended the San Sebastiano Conservatory in Naples; during his stay there he completed a symphony, two masses, and a cantata among other works. He made his bow as opera composer with *Adelson e Salvini,* introduced at the Conservatory in 1825. He continued writing operas after that, and having them produced in major Italian opera houses with varying degrees of success. *I Capuleti e i Montecchi,* given in Venice in 1830, was a triumph. Then came the two operas by which Bellini is today most often represented in the repertory: *La Sonnambula* and *Norma,* both produced in 1831. In 1833 he came to Paris where he completed his last opera, *I Puritani,* given in Paris in 1835. He was at the height of his fame and creative powers when he died in Puteaux, near Paris, on September 23, 1835, at the age of thirty-four, a victim of intestinal fever.

Bellini was the genius of opera song. His fresh, pure lyricism—perfect in design and elegant in style—elevates his greatest operas to a place of significance. His masterwork is *Norma,* introduced at La Scala in Milan on December 26, 1831, where it was at first a failure. The libretto by Felice Romani was based on a tragedy by L. A. Soumet. In Gaul, during the Roman occupation, in or about 50 B.C., Norma, high priestess of the Druids, violates her vows by secretly marrying the Roman proconsul, Pollione, and bearing him two sons. Pollione then falls in love with Adalgisa, virgin of the Temple of Esus. Unaware that Pollione is married, Adalgisa confides to Norma she is in love with him.

With Pollione's infidelity now apparent, he is brought before Norma for judgment. She offers him the choice of death or the renunciation of Adalgisa. When Pollione accepts death, Norma confesses to her people that, having desecrated her vows, she, too, must die. Moved by this confession, Pollione volunteers to die at her side in the funeral pyre.

The overture is famous. Loud dramatic chords in full orchestra are succeeded by a soft *lento* passage. A strong melody is then presented by flutes and violins against an incisive rhythm. There follows a graceful, sprightly and strongly accented tune in the strings. Both melodies are then amplified, dramatized, and repeated; particular emphasis is placed on the delicate, accented tune. The overture then proceeds to an energetic conclusion.

One vocal episode from *Norma* is also extremely popular and is often heard in orchestral transcriptions. It is Norma's aria, *"Casta diva,"* surely one of the noblest soprano arias in all Italian operatic literature. It comes in the first act and represents Norma's prayer for peace, and her grief that the hatred of her people for the Roman invaders must also result in their hatred for her husband, Pollione, the Roman proconsul.

Ralph Benatzky

RALPH BENATZKY was born in Moravské-Budejovice, Bohemia, on June 5, 1884. He acquired his musical training in Prague and with Felix Mottl in Munich, after which he devoted himself to light music by composing operettas. While residing at different periods in Vienna, Berlin, and Switzerland, he wrote the scores for over ninety operettas and 250 motion pictures, besides producing about five thousand songs. His most successful operettas were *The Laughing Triple Alliance, My Sister and I, Love in the Snow, Axel at the Gates of Heaven,* and *The White Horse Inn.* He came to live in the United

States in 1940, but after World War II returned to Europe. He died in Zurich on October 17, 1957.

The White Horse Inn (Im weissen Roess'l) is not only Benatzky's most celebrated operetta, but also one of the most successful produced in Europe between the two world wars, and possibly the last of the great European operettas. It was first performed in Berlin in 1930, after which it enjoyed over a thousand performances in Europe. Its première in America in 1936 (the book was adapted by David Freedman, lyrics were by Irving Caesar, William Gaxton and Kitty Carlisle starred) was only a moderate success. The operetta book of the original—freely adapted by Erik Charell and Hans Mueller, from a play by Blumenthal and Kadelburg—is set in the delightful resort of St. Wolfgang on Wolfgangsee in Austria, in the era just before World War I. Leopold, headwaiter of *The White Horse Inn,* is in love with its owner, Frau Josepha, who favors the lawyer, Siedler. In a fit of temper she fires Leopold, but upon learning that Emperor Franz Josef is about to pay the inn a visit, she prevails upon him to stay on. Leopold makes a welcoming speech to the Emperor, during which his bitter resentment against Frau Josepha gets the upper hand. Later on, when Frau Josepha confides to the Emperor that she is in love with Siedler, he urges her to consider Leopold for a husband. Leopold then comes to Josepha with a letter of resignation, which she accepts, but only because she is now ready to give him a new position, as her husband.

Selections from this tuneful operetta include the main love song, *"Es muss ein wunderbares sein,"* the ditty *"Zuschau'n kann ich nicht,"* and the lively waltz, *"Im weissen Roess'l am Wolfgangsee."*

It is mainly the worldwide popularity of this operetta (even more than the natural beauty of Wolfgangsee) that brings tourists each year to the White Horse Inn at St. Wolfgang, for a sight of the operetta's setting, and to partake of refreshments on the attractive veranda overlooking Wolfgangsee. The inn is now generously decorated with pictures in which the two main songs of the operetta are quoted, supplemented by a portrait of Benatzky. Souvenir ashtrays also carry musical quotations from the operetta.

Arthur Benjamin

ARTHUR BENJAMIN was born in Sydney, Australia, on September 18, 1893. His music study took place at the Royal College of Music in London. After serving in World War I, he became professor at the Sydney Conservatory, and in 1926 he assumed a similar post with the Royal College of Music in London. Meanwhile in 1924 he received the Carnegie Award for his *Pastoral Fantasia,* and in 1932 his first opera, *The Devil Take Her,* was produced in London. For five years, beginning with 1941, he was the conductor of the Vancouver Symphony. He has written notable concertos, a symphony, and other orchestral music, together with chamber works and several operas including *A Tale of Two Cities* which won the Festival of Britain Prize following its première in 1953. He also wrote a harmonica concerto for Larry Adler. Though many of his compositions are in an advanced style and technique, Benjamin was perhaps best known for his lighter pieces, particularly those in a popular South American idiom. He died in London on April 10, 1960.

The *Cotillon* (1939) is a suite of English dances derived from a medley entitled *The Dancing School,* published in London in 1719. Presented by Benjamin in contemporary harmonic and instrumental dress, these tunes—popular in England in the early 18th century—still retain their appeal. A short introduction, built from a basic motive from the first dance, leads to the following episodes with descriptive titles: "Lord Hereford's Delight" for full orchestra; "Daphne's Delight" for woodwind and strings; "Marlborough's Victory," for full orchestra; "Love's Triumph" for strings; "Jig It A Foot" for full orchestra; "The Charmer" for small orchestra; "Nymph Divine" for small orchestra and harp solo; "The Tattler" for full orchestra; and "Argyll" for full orchestra. A figure from the final tune is given extended treatment in the coda.

Benjamin's best known piece of music is the *Jamaican Rumba* (1942). This is the second number of *Two Jamaican Pieces* for orchestra. A light staccato accompaniment in rumba rhythm courses nimbly through the piece as the woodwinds present a saucy melody, and the strings a countersubject. Consecutive fifths in the harmony, a xylophone in the orchestration, and the changing meters created by novel arrangement of notes in each measure, provide particular interest. The *Jamaican Rumba* has been transcribed for various solo instruments and piano as well as for piano trio.

The *North American Square Dances,* for two pianos and orchestra (1955), is a delightful treatment of American folk idioms. The work comprises eight fiddle tunes played at old-time square dances. The native flavor is enhanced in the music by suggestions and simulations of feet-stamping, voice calling, and the plunking of a banjo. In the Introduction there appear fragments of the first dance; these same fragments return in the coda. There are eight sections: Introduction and "Heller's Reel"; "The Old Plunk"; "The Bundle Straw"; "He Piped So Sweet"; "Fill the Bowl"; "Pigeon on the Pier"; "Calder Fair"; and "Salamanca" and "Coda." The fourth and seventh dances are in slow tempo, while all others are fast.

Robert Russell Bennett

ROBERT RUSSELL BENNETT was born in Kansas City, Missouri, on June 15, 1894. He began his music study in Kansas City: piano with his mother; violin and several other instruments with his father; and harmony with Carl Busch. While still a boy he wrote and had published several compositions. He came to New York in 1916, worked for a while as copyist at G. Schirmer, then during World War I served for a year in the United States Army. After the war he spent several years in Paris studying composition with Nadia Boulanger; during this period he was twice the recipient of a Guggenheim Fellowship. In 1926–1927 he received honorable mention for his first symphony, in a contest sponsored by *Musical America;* in 1930 he received two awards from RCA Victor, one for *Sights and Sounds,* an orchestral tone poem, the other for his first successful and widely performed work, the symphony *Abraham Lincoln.* Since then Bennett has worked fruitfully in three distinct areas. As a composer of serious works he has produced several operas (including *Maria Malibran*), symphonies and other significant orchestral compositions. As an orchestrator for the Broadway theater, he has been involved with some of the foremost stage productions of our times including musicals by Rodgers and Hammerstein, Jerome Kern, Cole Porter, and Lerner and Loewe, and many others. He has also written compositions of a more popular nature, compositions which, while fully exploiting the resources of serious music, are nevertheless filled with popular or jazz materials. Among the last are his effective symphonic adaptations of music from George Gershwin's *Porgy and Bess; Oklahoma!* and *South Pacific* of Rodgers and Hammerstein; and *Kiss Me Kate* of Cole Porter. In each instance, the main melodies are brilliantly orchestrated and skilfully combined into an integrated synthesis so that each becomes a coherent musical composition.

The *March,* for two pianos and orchestra, (1930) makes delightful use of jazz melodies and rhythms. There are here four connected movements, each in march time. The first movement, in a vigorous style, leaps from one brief motive to another without any attempt at development. In the second, a sustained melody, first for solo oboe and later for the piano with full orchestra, is placed against a shifting rhythm. The third is a serious recitative culminating in an episode in which the classic funeral march is given sophisticated treatment. The fourth movement begins with a *marche mignonne* and concludes with a forceful, at times overpowering, statement of the funeral-march theme of the third movement.

While the *Symphony in D* (1941) is scored for symphony orchestra and has been played by many leading American orchestras, it is music with its tongue in the cheek, and is consistently light and humorous. This symphony was written to honor the Brooklyn Dodger baseball team (that is, when they were still in Brooklyn)—ironically enough an ode to a colorful team by a composer who has been a lifelong rooter of its most bitter rival, the New York Giants (once again, when they were still at the Polo Grounds). There are four brief movements. The first, subtitled "Brooklyn Wins," "means to picture the ecstatic joy of the town after the home team wins a game," as the composer has explained. This is followed by a slow (*Andante lamentoso*) movement, appropriately designated as "Brooklyn Loses"—music filled with "gloom and tears, and even fury." The third movement, a scherzo, is a portrait of the club's then (1941) president, Larry MacPhail, and his pursuit of a star pitcher. "We hear the horns' bay call—then we hear him in Cleveland, Ohio, trying to trade for the great pitcher, Bob Feller. He offers Prospect Park and the Brooklyn Bridge as an even trade, but the Cleveland management says 'No' in the form of a big E-flat minor chord. After repeated attempts we hear the hunting horns again, as he resumes the hunt in other fields." The finale is a choral movement, and like that of Beethoven's Ninth Symphony, an ode to joy. "It is purely fictitious, this text, but it speaks for itself. The subtitle of this finale is 'The Giants Come to Town.' "

Bennett has written two delightful orchestral compositions derived from the songs of Jerome Kern. One is *Symphonic Study,* a synthesis of some of Kern's best-loved melodies, and *Variations on a Theme by Jerome Kern.* Both of these compositions are discussed in the section on Kern. Bennett's symphonic treatment of George Gershwin's *Porgy and Bess,* entitled *Symphonic Picture,* is commented upon in the Gershwin section, specifically with *Porgy and Bess;* Bennett's symphonic treatment of the music of Cole Porter's *Kiss Me Kate,* and of *Oklahoma!* and *South Pacific* is spoken of in the sections devoted to Cole Porter and Richard Rodgers, respectively. Bennett has also orchestrated, and adapted into a symphonic suite, the music from Richard Rodgers' *Victory at Sea,* described in the Richard Rodgers section.

Hector Berlioz

HECTOR BERLIOZ was born in Côte-Saint-André, France on December 11, 1803. As a young man he was sent to Paris to study medicine, but music occupied his interests and he soon abandoned his medical studies to enter the Paris Conservatory. Impatient with the academic restrictions imposed upon him there, he left the Conservatory to begin his career as a composer. From the very beginning he set out to open new horizons for musical expression and to extend the periphery of musical structure. His first masterwork was the *Symphonie fantastique*, inspired by his love for the Shakespearean actress, Harriet Smithson. It was introduced in Paris in 1830, a year in which Berlioz also won the Prix de Rome. In his later works, Berlioz became one of music's earliest Romantics. He was a bold innovator in breaking down classical restraint; he helped extend the dramatic expressiveness of music; he was a pioneer in the writing of program music and in enriching the language of harmony, rhythm, and orchestration. Among his major works are the *Requiem, Harold in Italy* for viola solo and orchestra, the *Roman Carnival Overture*, the dramatic symphony *Romeo and Juliet*, and *The Damnation of Faust*. Berlioz married Harriet Smithson in 1833. It proved to be a tempestuous affair from the outset, finally ending by mutual consent in permanent separation. From 1852 until his death Berlioz was a librarian of the Paris Conservatory. He was active throughout Europe as a conductor and was a trenchant writer on musical subjects; among his books is a volume of *Memoirs*. He died in Paris on March 8, 1869.

The compositions by which Berlioz is most often heard on semiclassical programs are three excerpts from *The Damnation of Faust:* "The Dance of the Sylphs" (*"Danse des sylphes"*); "The Minuet of the Will-o'-the-Wisps" (*"Menuet des feux-follets"*), and "Rakóczy March" (*"Marche hongroise"*).

The Damnation of Faust, op. 24, described by the composer as a "dramatic legend," took many years for realization. It was based on a French translation of Goethe's *Faust,* published in 1827. A year later, Berlioz completed a musical setting of eight scenes as part of an ambitious project to prepare a huge cantata based on the Faust legend. He did not complete this project until eighteen years after that. Upon returning to it, he revised his earlier material, and wrote a considerable amount of new music. This work was first performed in oratorio style in Paris on December 6, 1846 and was a fiasco. It was given a stage presentation in Monte Carlo in 1903. Since then it has been performed both in concert version and as an opera.

"The Dance of the Sylphs" is graceful waltz music, its main melody assigned to the violins. It appears in the second part of the "legend." Faust is lulled to sleep by sylphs who appear in his dream in a delicate dance which brings up for him the image of his beloved Marguerite.

"Minuet of the Will-o'-the-Wisps" comes in the third part of the legend. Mephisto summons the spirits and the will-of-the-wisps to encircle Marguerite's house. The dance tune is heard in woodwind and brass. After the trio section, the minuet melody is repeated twice, the second time interrupted by chords after each phrase. The "Rakóczy March" is based on an 18th-century Hungarian melody. It is logically interpolated into the Faust legend by the expedience of having Faust wander about in Hungary. A fanfare for the brass leads to the first and main melody, a brisk march subject begun quietly in the woodwind. It gains in force until it is exultantly proclaimed by full orchestra. A countersubject is then heard in strings. After the march melody returns, it again gains in volume until it is built up into an overpowering climax.

Leonard Bernstein

LEONARD BERNSTEIN was born in Lawrence, Massachusetts, on August 25, 1918. Early music study took place with private piano teachers, and subsequently with Helen Coates and Heinrich Gebhard. He was graduated from Harvard in 1939 after which he attended the Curtis Institute of Music (a pupil of Fritz Reiner in conducting) and three summer sessions of the Berkshire Music Center as a student and protégé of Serge Koussevitzky. He made a sensational debut as conductor with the New York Philharmonic in 1943, appearing as a last-minute substitute for Bruno Walter who had fallen ill. Since that time he has risen to the front rank of contemporary symphony conductors, having led most of the world's leading organizations, and being appointed music director of the New York Philharmonic in 1958. As a serious composer he first attracted attention with the *Jeremiah Symphony* in 1944, which was performed by most of America's leading orchestras, was recorded, and received the New York City Music Critics Award. He subsequently wrote other major works for orchestra as well as the scores to successful ballets, an opera, and several Broadway musical comedies that were box-office triumphs; the last of these included *On the Town* (1944), *Wonderful Town* (1953) and *West Side Story* (1957). Bernstein has also distinguished himself as a musical commentator and analyst over television, concert pianist, and author.

Whether writing in a serious or popular vein Bernstein consistently reveals himself to be a master of his technical resources, endowed with a fine creative imagination, a strong lyric and rhythmic gift, and a restless intelligence that is ever on the search for new and fresh approaches in his writing. High on the list of favorites in the semi-classical repertory are the orchestral suites he adapted from his two popular and successful ballets.

Facsimile, choreography by Jerome Robbins, was introduced in New York in 1946. The ballet scenario revolves around three lonely people—a woman and two men—who find only frustration and disenchantment after trying to find satisfactory personal relationships. The orchestral suite from this vivacious score, vitalized with the use of popular melodies and dance rhythms, is made up of four parts. I. "Solo." The principal musical material here is found in a solo flute. This is a description of a woman standing alone in an open place. II. "Pas de Deux." Woman meets man, and a flirtation ensues to the tune of a waltz. The scene achieves a passionate climax, and is followed by a sentimental episode, romanticized in the music by a subject for muted strings and two solo violins and solo viola. The love interest dies; the pair become bored, then hostile. III. "Pas de trois." The second man enters. This episode is a scherzo with extended piano solo passages. A triangle ensues between the two men and one woman, there is some sophisticated interplay among them, and finally there ensue bitter words and misunderstandings. IV. "Coda." The two men take their departure, not without considerable embarrassment.

Fancy Free was Bernstein's first ballet, and it is still his most popular one; he completed his score in 1944 and it was introduced by the Ballet Theater (which had commissioned it) on April 18 of that year. It was a success of major proportions, received numerous performances, then became a staple in the American dance repertory. It is, wrote George Amberg, "the first substantial ballet entirely created in the contemporary American idiom, a striking and beautifully convincing example of genuine American style." The scenario, by Jerome Robbins, concerned the quest of girl companionship on the part of three sailors on temporary shore leave. Bernstein's music, though sophisticated in its harmonic and instrumental vocabulary, is filled with racy jazz rhythms and idioms and with melodies cast in a popular mold. The orchestral suite is made up of five parts: "Dance of the Three Sailors"; "Scene at the Bar"; "Pas de deux"; "Pantomime"; "Three Variations" (Galop, Waltz, Danzon) and Finale.

When this Suite was first performed, in Pittsburgh in 1945, with Bernstein conducting, the composer provided the following description of what takes place in the music. "From the moment the action begins, with the sound of a juke box wailing behind the curtain, the ballet is strictly Young America of 1944. The curtain rises on a street corner with a lamppost, side street bar, and New York skyscrapers tricked out with a crazy pattern of lights, making a dizzying background. Three sailors explode onto the stage; they are on shore leave in the city and on the prowl for girls. The tale of how they meet first one girl, then a second, and how they fight over them, lose them, and in the end take off after still a third, is the story of the ballet."

Fancy Free was expanded into a musical-comedy by Betty Comden and Adolph Green, for which Bernstein wrote his Broadway score. Called *On the Town* it started a one-year Broadway run on December 28, 1944, and subsequently was twice revived in off-Broadway productions, and was made into an outstanding screen musical.

Georges Bizet

GEORGES BIZET was born in Paris on October 25, 1838. Revealing a pronounced gift for music in early childhood he was entered into the Paris Conservatory when he was only nine. There—as a pupil of Marmontel, Halévy, and Benoist—he won numerous prizes, including the Prix de Rome in 1857. In that year he also had his first stage work produced, a one-act opera, *Le Docteur miracle*. After his return from Rome to Paris he started to write operas. *Les Pêcheurs de perles* (*Pearl Fishers*) and *La jolie fille de Perth* were produced in Paris in 1863 and 1867 respectively. Success came in 1872 with his first Suite from the incidental music to Daudet's *L'Arlésienne*. After that came his masterwork, the opera by which he has earned immortality: *Carmen*, introduced in Paris two months before his death. Bizet died in Bougival, France, on June 3, 1875.

His gift for rich, well-sounding melodies, and his feeling for inviting harmonies and tasteful orchestration make many of his compositions ideal for programs of light music, even salient portions of *Carmen*.

Agnus Dei is a vocal adaptation (to a liturgical Latin text) of the intermezzo from Bizet's incidental music to *L'Arlésienne*. It is also found as the second movement of the *L'Arlésienne Suite No. 2*. A dramatic dialogue between forceful strings and serene woodwinds leads into a spiritual religious song.

The *Arlésienne Suite, No. 1* is made up of parts from the incidental music, which Bizet wrote for the Provençal drama of Alphonse Daudet, *The Woman of Arles (L'Arlésienne)*. The play, with Bizet's music consisting of twenty-seven pieces, was given at the Théâtre du Vaudeville in Paris in 1872. Out of this score the composer selected four excerpts and assembled them into an orchestral suite, which has become his most celebrated instrumental composition, and his first success as a composer. A knowledge of the plot and characters of the Daudet play is by no means essential to a full appreciation of Bizet's tuneful suite.

The first movement, "Prelude," begins with a march melody based on an old French Christmas song. This is subjected to a series of variations. After the march tune has been repeated vigorously by the full orchestra there appears a pastoral interlude, scored originally for saxophones, but now usually heard in clarinets. This, in turn, is succeeded by a passionate song for strings, with brass and woodwind accompaniment. The second movement is a "Minuet," whose principal theme is a brisk and strongly accented subject. In the trio section, the clarinet appears with a flowing lyrical episode. As the violins take this material over they become rapturous; the harp and woodwind provide intriguing accompanying figures. A brief *"Adagietto"* comes as the third movement. This is a sensitive romance for muted strings. In the finale, "Carillon," we get a picture of a peasant celebration of the Feast of St. Eloi. The horns simulate a three-note chime of bells which accompanies a lively dance tune, first in strings, then in other sections of the orchestra. A soft interlude is interposed by the woodwind. Then the lively dance reappears, once again to be accompanied by vigorous tolling bells simulated by the horns.

There exists a second suite made up of four more numbers from the incidental music to *L'Arlésienne*. This was prepared after Bizet's death by his friend, Ernest Guiraud. This second suite is rarely played, but its second movement, "Intermezzo," is celebrated in its liturgical version as *"Agnus Dei"* (which see above). The other movements are Pastorale, Minuet and Farandole.

If the name of Bizet has survived in musical history and will continue to do so for a long time to come, it is surely because of a single masterwork—his opera *Carmen*. This stirring music drama—based on the famous novel of Prosper Mérimée, adapted for Bizet by Meilhac and Halévy—never fails in its emotional and dramatic impact. Carmen is the seductive gypsy girl who enmeshes two lovers: the bull fighter Escamillo, and the sergeant, Don José. Both she and Don José meet a tragic end on the day of Escamillo's triumph in the bull ring. The background to this fatal story of love and death is provided by the Spanish city of Seville—its streets, bull ring, taverns, and nearby mountain retreat of smugglers.

Carmen was introduced at the Opéra-Comique on March 3, 1875. Legend would have us believe it was a fiasco, and further that heartbreak over this failure brought about Bizet's premature death two months after the opera was first heard. As a matter of historic truth, while there were some critics at that first performance who considered the text too stark and realistic for their tastes, *Carmen* did very well, indeed. By June 18th it enjoyed thirty-seven performances. At the start of the new season of the Opéra-Comique it returned to the repertory to receive its fiftieth presentation by February 15, 1876. It was hailed in Vienna in 1875, Brussels in 1876, and London and New York in 1878. Many critics everywhere were as enthusiastic as the general public, and with good reason. For all the vivid color of Spanish life and backgrounds, and all the flaming passions aroused by the sensual Carmen, were caught in Bizet's luminous, dramatic score.

The Prelude to *Carmen* represents a kind of resumé of what takes place in the opera, and with some of its musical material. It opens with lively music for full orchestra describing the festive preparations in Seville just before a bull fight. After a sudden change of key, and several chords, the popular second-act song of Escamillo, the bullfighter, is first given quietly in strings, then repeated more loudly. Then there is heard an ominous passage against quivering strings which, in the opera, suggests the fatal fascination exerted by Carmen on men. This is repeated in a higher register and somewhat amplified until a dramatic chord for full orchestra brings this episode, and the overture itself, to a conclusion.

The Prelude to Act II is constructed from a motive of an off-stage unaccompanied little song by Don José in the same act praising the dragoons of Alcala. The Prelude to Act III is actually an entr'acte, a gentle little intermezzo which Bizet originally wrote for *L'Arlésienne.* The Prelude to Act IV is also an entr'acte, this time of dramatic personality. The brilliant and forceful music is based upon an actual Andalusian folk song and dance; it sets the mood for the gay festivities in a public square on the day of a gala bull-fight with which the fourth act opens.

It is sometimes a practice at concerts of semi-classical or pop music to present not merely one of the four orchestral Preludes but also at other times salient musical episodes from the opera, arranged and assembled into fantasias or suites. These potpourris or suites are generally made up of varied combinations of the following excerpts. From Act I: the "Changing of the Guard"; Carmen's seductive and extremely popular aria, the Habanera (*"L'amour est un oiseau rebelle"*), which was not by Bizet but borrowed by him from a song by Sebastian Yradier (see Yradier); the duet of Micaëla and Don José, *"Qui sait de quel démon";* and Carmen's Séguidille, *"Près des remparts de Séville."* From Act II: "The March of the Smugglers,"; Carmen's *"Chanson bohème";* the rousing Toreador Song of Escamillo; and Don José's poignant "Flower Song" to Carmen, *"La fleur que tu m'avais jetée."* From Act III: Carmen's Card Song, *"En vain pour éviter";* and Micaëla's celebrated Air, *"Je dis que rien ne m'épouvante".* From Act IV: the Chorus, March, and Finale.

Utilizing many of these selections, Ferruccio Busoni and Vladimir Horowitz each prepared striking concert fantasias for solo piano; Pablo de Sarasate, for violin and piano; and Franz Waxman for violin and orchestra for the motion picture, *Humoresque,* starring John Garfield.

Children's Games (Jeux d'enfants) is a delightful suite of twelve pieces for piano (four hands) for and about children. Bizet wrote it in 1871, but shortly afterwards orchestrated five of these numbers and assembled them into a suite, op. 22. The first movement is a march entitled "Trumpeter and Drummer" (*"Trompette et tambour"*) music punctuated by trumpet calls and drum rolls, accompanying a troop of soldiers as it approaches and then disappears into the distance. This is followed by a tender berceuse for muted strings, "The Doll" (*"La Poupée"*). The third movement is "The Top" (*"La Toupie"*), an impromptu in which the violins simulate the whirr of a spinning top while the woodwinds introduce a jolly dance tune. The fourth movement, "Little Husband, Little Wife" (*"Petit mari, petite femme"*) is a quiet little dialogue between husband and wife, the former represented by first violins, and the latter by the cellos. The suite ends with "The Ball" ("Le Bal"), a galop for full orchestra.

The *Danse bohèmienne* is a popular orchestral episode that comes from a comparatively unknown (and early) Bizet opera, *La jolie fille de Perth,* introduced in Paris in 1867. This vital dance music appears in the second act, but it is also often borrowed by many opera companies for the fourth act ballet of *Carmen.* The harp leads into, and then accompanies, a soft, sinuous dance melody for the flute. The tempo rapidly quickens, and the mood grows febrile; the strings take over the dance melody in quick time, and other sections of the orchestra participate vigorously.

La Patrie Overture, op. 19 (1873) is music in a martial manner. A robust, strongly rhythmed march tune is immediately presented by the full orchestra. After some amplification it is repeated softly by the orchestra. The second main theme is a stately folk melody first given by the violins, clarinets and bassoons, accompanied by the double basses. This new subject receives resounding treatment in full orchestra and is carried to a powerful climax. After a momentary pause, a third tune is heard, this time in violas and cellos accompanied by brasses and double basses, and a fourth, in violas, clarinets and English horn with the muted violins providing an arpeggio accompaniment. Then the stirring opening march music is recalled and dramatized. The overture ends in a blaze of color after some of the other themes are brought back with enriched harmonies and orchestration.

This music was written for a play of the same name by Sardou.

Luigi Boccherini

LUIGI BOCCHERINI was born in Lucca, Italy, on February 19, 1743. After studying music with various private teachers in Rome, he gained recognition as a cellist both as a member of theater orchestras in Lucca and later on tour throughout Europe in joint concerts with Filippo Manfredi, violinist. He served as court composer in Madrid from 1785 to 1787, and from 1787 until 1797 for Friedrich Wilhelm II of Prussia. His last years were spent in Madrid in poverty and poor health, and he died in that city on May 28, 1805.

Boccherini, a contemporary of Haydn, was a prolific composer of symphonies, concertos, and a considerable amount of chamber music which were all-important in helping to develop and crystallize a classical style of instrumental writing and in establishing the classic forms of instrumental music.

Despite the abundance of his creation in virtually every branch of instrumental music, and despite the significance of his finest works, Boccherini is remembered today by many music lovers mainly for a comparatively minor piece of music: the sedate *Minuet* which originated as the third movement of the String Quintet in E major, op. 13, no. 5. Transcribed for orchestra, and for various solo instruments and piano, (even for solo harpsichord) this light and airy Minuet has become one of the most celebrated musical examples of this classic dance form.

Several of Boccherini's little known melodies from various quintets and from his Sinfonia No. 2 in B-flat were used by the contemporary French composer, Jean Françaix, for a ballet score, from which comes an enchanting little orchestral suite. The ballet was *The School of Dancing (Scuola di Ballo)*, with book and choreography by Leonide Massine; it was introduced by the Ballet Russe de Monte Carlo in Monte Carlo in 1933. The book was set in the dancing school of Professor Rigadon. The professor tries to palm off one of his backward pupils on an impresario, while withholding his star; in the end all pupils leave him in disgust. The suite is in four parts. The first consists of *"Leçon"* and *"Menuet"*; the second, *"Larghetto,"* *"Rondo,"* and *"Dispute"*; the third, *"Presto,"* *"Pastorale,"* and *"Danse allemande"*; the last, *"Scène du notaire"* and *"Finale."* An unidentified program annotator goes on to explain: "An occasional stern note in the *'Leçon'* and strong chords in the *'Menuet'* suggest the teacher. The violin and bassoon play a duet which very clearly pictures the inept pupil. Further atmosphere is furnished by a guitar-like accompaniment heard on the harp from time to time. One is soon acquainted with the characters who reappear in the various sections. The *'Larghetto'* closely resembles a movement in one of Haydn's symphonies, which suggests a tempting line of speculation. The orchestration of the *'Rondo'* and the syncopation of the *'Danse allemande'* are noteworthy."

François Boieldieu

⋘⋙ ⋘⋙

FRANÇOIS-ADRIEN BOIELDIEU, genius of opéra-comique, was born in Rouen, France, on December 16, 1775. After studying music with Charles Broche, Boieldieu became a church organist in Rouen in his fifteenth year. Two years later his first opera, *La fille coupable,* was successfully given in the same city. In 1796 he came to Paris where from 1797 on his operas began appearing in various theaters, climaxed by his first major success, *Le Calife de Bagdad* in 1801. In 1798 he was appointed professor of the piano at the Paris Conservatory. From 1803 until 1811 he lived in Russia writing operas for the Imperial theaters and supervising musical performances at court. After returning to Paris in 1811, he reassumed his significant position in French music. From 1817 to 1826 he was professor of composition at the Paris Conservatory, and in 1821 he was made Chevalier of the Legion of Honor. All the while he kept on writing operas and enjoying considerable popularity. His most significant work was the opéra-comique, *La Dame blanche,* a sensation when introduced in Paris in 1825. Ill health compelled him to abandon his various professional activities in 1832. Supported by an annual government grant, he withdrew to Jarcy where he spent the last years of his life devoting himself mainly to painting. He died there on October 8, 1834. Boieldieu, with Adam and Auber, was one of the founders of French comic opera, and his best works are still among the finest achieved in this *genre.*

The Overture to *The Caliph of Bagdad (Le Calife de Bagdad)* is Boieldieu's most famous piece of music. The opera was a triumph when introduced at the Opéra-Comique in Paris on September 16, 1801. The libretto, by Saint-Just, is set in Bagdad where Isaaum is a benevolent Caliph, but given to mischievous pranks and tricks, including parading around the city in various disguises. Once, as an army officer, he meets and makes love to Zeltube. Her mother, suspicious of him, orders his arrest. When the Caliph reveals himself, he also discloses his intentions were honorable and that he intends making Zeltube his bride.

The overture opens with a mellow song for strings. When the tempo changes, a sprightlier tune is heard in strings and brought to a forceful climactic point. The music now assumes a dramatic character after which a new subject, again in a sensitive lyrical vein, is offered by the strings.

The Overture to *La Dame blanche* (*The White Lady*) is also popular. *La Dame blanche* is the composer's greatest work in the opéra-comique form. It was received with such sensational acclaim when introduced in Paris on December 10, 1825 that, temporarily at any rate, the sparkling comic operas of Rossini (then very much in vogue) were thrown into a shade. In time, *La Dame blanche* received universal acceptance as a classic in the world of opéra-comique. Between 1825 and 1862 it enjoyed over a thousand performances in Paris; by World War I, the total passed beyond the fifteen hundred mark. The libretto, by Eugène Scribe, is based on two novels by Sir Walter Scott, *The Monastery* and *Guy Mannering*. The setting is Scotland, and the "white lady" is a statue believed to be the protector of a castle belonging to the Laird of Avenel. The castle is being administered by Gaveston who tries to use the legend of the white lady for his own selfish purposes, to gain possession of the family treasures. Anna, Gaveston's ward, impersonates the white lady to help save the castle and its jewels for the rightful owner.

The vivacious overture is made up of several of the opera's principal melodies. The introduction begins with a motive from the first-act finale, and is followed by the melodious and expressive "Ballad of the White Lady." The Allegro section that follows includes the drinking song and several other popular arias, among these being the ballad of "Robin Adair" which appears during the hero's first-act revery and as a concert piece in the third act.

Giovanni Bolzoni

GIOVANNI BOLZONI was born in Parma, Italy, on May 14, 1841. He attended the Parma Conservatory, then achieved recognition as a conductor of operas in Perugia and Turin. In 1887 he became director of the Liceo Musicale in Turin. Bolzoni wrote five operas, a symphony, overtures, and chamber music, but all are now in discard. He died in Turin on February 21, 1919.

About the only piece of music by Bolzoni to survive is a beguiling little Minuet which comes from an unidentified string quartet and which has achieved outstanding popularity in various transcriptions, including many for salon orchestras with which it is a perennial favorite.

Carrie Jacobs Bond

CARRIE JACOBS BOND, whose art songs are among the most popular by an American, was born in Janesville, Wisconsin, on August 11, 1862. Coming from a musical family, she was given music instruction early, and made appearances as a child-prodigy pianist. After marrying Dr. Frank L. Bond, a physician, she went to live in Chicago where her husband died suddenly, leaving her destitute. For a while she earned a living by renting rooms, taking in sewing, and doing other menial jobs. Then she began thinking of supplementing this meager income with the writing of songs. To issue these compositions, she formed a modest publishing firm in New York with funds acquired from her New York song recital; for a long time her office was in a hall bedroom. Her first publication, just before the end of the century, was *Seven Songs,* which included "I Love You Truly" and "Just a Wearyin' For You," each of which she subsequently published as separate pieces. In 1909 she achieved a formidable success with the famous ballad, "The End of a Perfect Day," of which more than five million copies of sheet music were sold within a few years. Her later songs added further both to her financial security and her reputation. She was invited to give concerts at the White House, received awards for achievement in music from various organizations, and was singled out in 1941 by the Federation of Music Clubs as one of the two out-standing women in the field of music. She died in Hollywood, Cali-fornia, on December 28, 1946.

Carrie Jacobs Bond knew how to write a song that was filled with sentiment without becoming cloying, that was simple without becoming ingenuous, and which struck a sympathetic universal chord by virtue of its mobile and expressive lyricism. Besides "I Love You Truly," "Just a Wearyin' for You" and "The End of a Perfect Day," her most famous songs included "His Lullaby," "Life's Garden," "I've Done My Work," and "Roses Are in Bloom." Her songs are so popular that they have been often heard in various transcriptions for salon orchestras and band.

Alexander Borodin

A L E X A N D E R   B O R O D I N was born in St. Petersburg, Russia, on November 11, 1833. He was trained in the sciences, having attended the Academy of Medicine in St. Petersburg and in 1858 receiving his doctorate in chemistry. He continued after that to devote himself to scientific activities, both in and out of Russia. He produced several sig-nificant papers and, from 1859 to 1862, served on an important scien-tific mission.

He had also received some musical training in his boyhood. In 1862 he began to direct his energies with equal vigor to music as well as to science. He soon joined four colleagues (Mussorgsky, Balakirev, Cui, and Rimsky-Korsakov) in forming a national school of composition henceforth identified as "The Mighty Five" or "The Russian Five." Like the other members of this group, Borodin concerned himself with the creation of a national Russian musical art, well grounded in Rus-sian folk song and dance, Russian culture and history. In this style he produced three symphonies, the folk opera *Prince Igor*, two string quartets, and various operas and instrumental compositions. He differed from the other members of the "Russian Five" by his partiality to Oriental melodies, harmonies, rhythms, and instrumental colors, and by his preference for exotic subjects. Borodin died in St. Petersburg on February 27, 1887.

In the Steppes of Central Asia (1880) is a popular tone poem for orchestra, one of several *tableaux vivants* ("living pictures") commissioned from various composers to honor the 25th anniversary of the reign of Czar Alexander II. Each *tableau vivant* was intended to portray an incident from the Russian past, or a picture of a Russian scene. Borodin prepared his own programmatic note to explain his music; it appears in the published score. "Over the uniformly sandy steppes of Central Asia come sounds of a peaceful Russian song. Along with them are heard the melancholy strains of Oriental melodies, then the stamping of approaching horses and camels. A caravan, accompanied by Russian soldiers, traverses the measureless waste. With full trust in its protective escort, it continues its long journey in a carefree mood. Onward the caravan moves. The songs of the Russians and those of the Asiatic natives mingle in common harmony. The refrains curl over the desert and then die away in the distance."

The peaceful Russian song is given by the clarinet, while the "melancholy strains of Oriental melodies" is an expressive song for English horn. These two melodies are the core of a composition that is free in form.

The *Nocturne* (*Notturno*) is a haunting, poetic song for strings, the third movement of the composer's String Quartet No. 2 in D major (1885). It is often heard apart from the rest of the work, particularly in various transcriptions for orchestra, or for violin and piano. In 1953, furnished with lyrics and adapted into a popular song by Robert Wright and George "Chet" Forrest, it was heard in the Broadway musical *Kismet* as "This Is My Beloved" and became an outstanding hit.

The *Polovtsian Dances* come from *Prince Igor,* a folk opera with libretto by Vladimir Stassov based on an old Russian chronicle. It was introduced at the Imperial Opera in St. Petersburg in 1890. The setting is 12th-century Central Asia where a Tartar race, known as the Polovtzi, capture Prince Igor and his son, Vladimir. Though captives, Prince Igor and his son are regaled by the leader of the Tartars with a lavish feast and Oriental dances. It is at this point in the opera (Act 2) that the popular *Polovtsian Dances* appear. They are exciting aural experiences because of their primitive rhythms, exotic Oriental melodies, and flaming instrumental colors. One of the dances is a poignant melody for flute and oboe; another is a dance of savage men in which the main melody in clarinet is set against a sharply accented phrase of four descending notes; a third is barbaric, a syncopated melody for strings accompanied by crash of cymbals; a fourth is a haunting Oriental song divided by violins and cellos. This last melody was used by Robert Wright and George "Chet" Forrest for their popular song hit of 1953, "Stranger in Paradise," in their Broadway musical, *Kismet*. The concluding dance is again in a savage manner. A passionate melody is begun by the woodwind and carried on by the strings, while receiving a vigorous horn accompaniment.

Felix Borowski

ᴥᶑᴥᶑ ᶑᴥᶑᴥ

FELIX BOROWSKI was born in Burton, England, on March 10, 1872. He received his musical training at the Cologne Conservatory and with private teachers in England. In 1897 he settled in the United States where he later became a citizen. From 1897 to 1916 he was professor of harmony and counterpoint at Chicago Musical College, and from 1916 to 1925 its president. His career in music criticism began in 1905. From 1907 to 1917 he was music critic of the Chicago *Record-Herald* and from 1942 until his death, of the Chicago *Sun*. He was also program annotator for the concerts of the Chicago Symphony from 1908 on, some of these annotations being published in the books, *Standard Concert Guide* and *Encyclopedia of the Symphony*. Borowski died in Chicago, Illinois, on September 6, 1956.

As a composer, Borowski produced three symphonies, three string quartets, several ballet-pantomimes, various tone poems and other instrumental compositions. His major works are now rarely given, but his smaller salon pieces have retained their popularity through the years.

The best of these are the *Adoration,* for violin and piano, the *La Coquette* and *Valsette* for piano, all transcribed for orchestra. All three pieces are in simple song structure and unashamedly Romantic in their lyricism and emotional content. The uninhibited sentimentality of *Adoration* has made that piece a particular favorite.

Johannes Brahms

JOHANNES BRAHMS was born in Hamburg, Germany, on May 7, 1833. He received instruction in music from his father, Otto Cossel, and Eduard Marxsen. At fourteen he gave his first public concert as pianist, in which he introduced one of his own compositions. In 1853 he toured with the Hungarian violinist, Eduard Reményi, as his accompanist. During this period he met and aroused the interest of such notable musicians as Joachim, Liszt, and Schumann. The last of these was one of the first to give Brahms public recognition, through a glowing article in the *Neue Zeitschrift fuer Musik.* After a considerable amount of travel in Germany and Austria, and after holding various musical positions, Brahms established himself permanently in Vienna in 1863. The promise he had shown in his early piano and chamber music became fully realized with his first piano concerto in 1857, the *German Requiem* written between 1857 and 1868, and the first symphony completed in 1876. In his later orchestral, piano, and chamber music he assumed a position of first importance in the German Romantic movement, the spokesman for absolute music, the genius who succeeded in combining respect for classical discipline and tradition with the Romanticist's bent for emotion, poetry, and flexible thought. Brahms died in Vienna on April 3, 1897.

The supreme craftsmanship, mature thought, and profound feelings of Brahms' music do not lend themselves to popular consumption. Occasionally, though not frequently, he chose to give voice to a lighter mood, as he did in his ever-popular *Hungarian Dances*. In such music, as in his more ambitious works, he is always the master of form and style, and a powerful and inventive creator.

The *Cradle Song* (*Wiegenlied*) is Brahms' universally loved art song, one of the most famous lullabies ever written. It is the fourth in a collection of five songs, op. 49 (1868). Its lyric is a folk poem (*"Guten Abend, Gute Nacht"*). In its many and varied transcriptions, this lullaby has become an instrumental favorite.

The *Hungarian Dances* was originally published in 1869 in two volumes for four-hand piano. The first book contained dances Nos. 1 through 5, while the second book had Nos. 6 through 10. Brahms took special pains to point out that these melodies were not his own, but were adaptations. On the title page there appeared the phrase "arranged for the piano." Brahms further refused to place an opus number to his publication as another indication that this was not original music; and in a letter to his publisher, Simrock, he explained he was offering this music "as genuine gypsy children which I did not beget but merely brought up with bread and milk."

Despite Brahms' open candor about the origin of these melodies, a storm of protest was sounded by many newspapers and musicians accusing Brahms of plagiarism. Fortunately, the general public refused to be influenced by this unjust accusation. The two volumes of *Hungarian Dances* were a formidable success, the greatest enjoyed by Brahms up to that time.

In 1880, Brahms issued two more volumes of *Hungarian Dances,* still for four-hand piano. Book 3 had dances Nos. 11 through 16, and Book 4, Nos. 17 through 21. This time many of the melodies were original with Brahms, even if modeled after the style and idiosyncrasies of actual Hungarian folk dances and gypsy melodies.

The *Hungarian Dances* are most popular in transcriptions for orchestra. Brahms himself transcribed Dances Nos. 1, 3, and 10; Andreas Hellen, Nos. 2, 4, and 7; Dvořák, Nos. 7 through 21; and Albert Parlow, the rest. Walter Goehr and Leopold Stokowski also made transcriptions of several of these dances for orchestra. In addition, Brahms adapted Book 1 for piano solo, and Joachim all the dances for violin and piano.

The dances range from sentimental to passionate moods. They abound with abrupt contrasts of feeling and dynamics; they are often vital with vertiginous rhythms and changing meters. These gypsy melodies, both the gay and the sad, warm the heart like Tokay wine; the pulse of the rhythm is similarly intoxicating. As Walter Niemann wrote

of these dances: "They are pure nature music, full of unfettered, va-
grant, roving spirit, and a chaotic ferment, drawn straight from the
deepest well springs of music by children of Nature. It seems impossible
to imprison them in the bonds of measure, time, and rhythm, to con-
vert their enchantingly refreshing uncivilized character, their wild
freedom, their audacious contempt for all order into a civilized modera-
tion and order."

Yet Brahms was able to discipline this music with modern techniques
without robbing it either of its personality or popular appeal. "He has
maintained," continues Niemann, "and preserved the essential, individual genuine features of gypsy music in his musical idiom: the dances
sound like original Hungarian folk music . . . and for this reason they
delight and enchant everybody: the amateur by their natural quality,
the specialist by their art."

The most famous of these dances is the fifth in F-sharp minor, its passionate, uninhibited dance melody released at once by the strings against
a strong rhythm.

The following are some other popular dances.

No. 1, in G minor. A slow and languorous dance unfolds in strings,
and then is contrasted by a slight, tripping theme in woodwind; a second languorous dance melody follows in the strings.

No. 6 in D-flat major. A slow syncopated melody begins sensually
but soon gains in tempo and volume; a second arresting dance tune is
then offered by strings against strong chords in the rest of the orchestra.

No. 7 in A major. This dance opens with a vivacious melody in
strings, but through most of the piece a comparatively restrained mood
is maintained.

No. 12 in D minor. The first dance melody is presented in a halting
rhythm by the woodwind against decorative figures in the strings. This
is followed by two other dance tunes, the first in strings with trimmings
in the woodwind, and the second in full orchestra.

No. 19 in B minor and No. 21 in E minor. Both are fleet and graceful
both in melody and rhythm.

The *Waltz in A-flat major,* a graceful dance which is given without
any introduction or coda, originated as a piece for piano duet: the
fifteenth of a set of sixteen such waltzes op. 39 (1865). All of Brahms'
waltzes reveal their Viennese identity in their charm and lightness of
heart. Some are derivative from the waltzes of Johann Strauss II, but
the one in A-major is more in the character of a Schubert Laendler
than a Strauss waltz, though it does boast more delicacy and refinement

than we usually find in peasant dances. David Hochstein's transcription for violin and piano is in the concert violin repertory.

Charles Wakefield Cadman

⚜︎⚜︎ ⚜︎⚜︎

CHARLES WAKEFIELD CADMAN was born in Johns-town, Pennsylvania, on December 24, 1881. As a boy he played the organ in a church near Pittsburgh, and wrote a march that was published. His main music study took place with private teachers: Leo Oehmler, Luigi von Kunits, and Emil Paur. From 1908 to 1910 he was the music critic of the Pittsburgh *Dispatch*. Meanwhile, a meeting in 1902 with the lyric writer Nellie Richmond Eberhart, turned him to the writing of songs in which he achieved his initial outstanding successes as composer. Some of these were inspired by the American Indian. Later researches in the field of American-Indian ceremonials and music led him to write his opera *Shanewis*, produced by the Metropolitan Opera in 1918, as well as several significant instrumental works including the *Thunderbird Suite* and *To a Vanishing Race*. From 1917 until his death he lived in California where he wrote several major orchestral and chamber-music works, but none in the American-Indian idiom with which he became famous. He died in Los Angeles on December 30, 1946.

The *American Suite,* for strings (1938), is an engaging piece of music in which Cadman makes use of several different American folk idioms. In the first movement he borrows his melodies from the tribal music of Omaha Indians. In the second movement we hear Negro folk tunes indigenous to South Carolina. And in the third movement, two old fiddle tunes are effectively employed, "Sugar in the Gourd," and "Hoop-de-den-do."

"At Dawning" is one of Cadman's two most famous songs. It sold millions of copies of sheet music and records, and has been translated into many languages. Though originally published in 1906, it reposed forgotten and unknown on the shelves of the publisher (Oliver Ditson) until John McCormack sang it at one of his recitals in 1909 and was given an ovation. "At Dawning" was transcribed for violin and piano by Fritz Kreisler.

Dark Dancers of Mardi Gras, for orchestra with piano, (1933), is one of Cadman's most popular symphonic compositions. The composer explains: "The work takes its name from the Negro side of the Mardi Gras, though no Negro themes are used. The Negroes of New Orleans have a Mardi Gras of their own. The fantasy is supposed to reflect the fantastic, the grotesque, the bizarre spirit of the carnival. The original theme goes into a major key in the central section, and might represent the romantic feeling of the King and Queen, and the Court in carnival fashion."

"From the Land of the Sky-Blue Water" is the second of Cadman's two outstandingly successful songs. It is one of four songs with lyrics by Nellie Richmond Eberhart appearing in *American-Indian Songs,* op. 45, a cycle which was published in Boston in 1909 and in the same year received a prize in a contest sponsored by the Carnegie Institute. This song was first swept to national fame by the prima donna, Lillian Nordica, in her song recitals. It soon entered the repertory of virtually every leading concert singer in America. Fritz Kreisler transcribed it for violin and piano.

Lucien Caillet

LUCIEN CAILLET was born in Dijon, France on May 22, 1891. After attending the Dijon Conservatory he came to the United States in 1918 and settled first in Pennsylvania, and later in California. He has distinguished himself by his skilful symphonic transcriptions of compositions by Johann Sebastian Bach, Mussorgsky, and others. In his own works he frequently makes skilful use, and astute adaptations, of some famous pieces of popular music.

The *Fantasia and Fugue on Oh, Susanna!* (1942) for orchestra has for its point of departure the famous song of Stephen Foster, "Oh, Susanna!" Caillet's composition begins with a preface: a tutti for orchestra which quotes the melody only partly. This leads into a fantasia section featuring the solo string quartet and presenting a quiet version of the melody. A fugue follows, the germ of the "Susanna" melody found in first and second violins in unison.

In *Pop Goes the Weasel* for orchestra (1938) Caillet brings the full resources of his harmonic and instrumental skill to a famous American folk tune. "Pop Goes the Weasel" is a Western two-part melody, long a favorite of country fiddlers since before the Civil War. After presenting this melody, Caillet subjects it to intriguing variations, sometimes with comic effect.

Alfredo Catalani

A L F R E D O   C A T A L A N I was born in Lucca, Italy, on June 19, 1854. After receiving preliminary instruction in music from his father he was allowed to enter the Paris Conservatory without examinations. He concluded his music study at the Milan Conservatory, where in 1886 he succeeded Ponchielli as professor of composition. In 1880 he had his first opera, *Elda,* produced in Turin. He continued to confine himself to the stage, his most successful operas being *Loreley* in 1890, and *La Wally* in 1892. In his own time, and shortly thereafter, his operas were outstandingly successful in Italy. Today they are remembered almost exclusively because of some orchestral excerpts. Catalani died in Milan on August 7, 1893.

The most popular episodes from Catalini's two most famous operas are dances often performed by salon orchestras. "The Dance of the Waves" (*Danza delle ondine*) and "The Waltz of the Flowers" (*Valzer dei fiori*) appear in *Loreley,* an opera introduced in Turin in 1890. In this opera the action takes place on the banks of the Rhine. Walter, about to marry Anna, is loved by the orphan girl, Loreley. When Loreley learns she is about to lose her beloved, she calls upon the nymphs and the sprites of the Rhine to help her; throwing herself into the river, she becomes one of them. During the wedding ceremonies, Loreley appears and entices Walter away from his bride. Anna dies of grief; and Walter meets his doom in the Rhine, to which he is helplessly drawn through enticements by the sprites and by Loreley.

"The Dance of the Waves" takes place in the last act. After Anna's funeral procession passes by, Walter comes to the edge of the Rhine, grief-stricken. Out of the waters come the sprites to dance seductively before Walter and to beckon him on into the river. "The Waltz of the Flowers" is a graceful, even gentle, dance performed in the second act, during the wedding ceremonies of Walter and Anna.

"The Waltz of the Kiss" (*Valzer del bacio*) is a segment from *La Wally,* Catalani's most famous opera, which was such a particular favorite of Arturo Toscanini that not only did he conduct it frequently in Italy but he also named his son after its heroine. *La Wally* was introduced at La Scala in Milan in 1892. The text, by Luigi Illica, was based on a novel by Wilhelmine von Hillern. The setting is 19th century Switzerland where Wally and Hagenbach are in love, and meet their death in an avalanche; all the while Wally is being sought after by Gellner, whom she detests. The "Waltz of the Kiss" is a caressing piece of music from the second act which accompanies a dance by Wally and Hagenbach, in which they first discover they are in love and yield to passionate kissing while the hateful Gellner watches.

Otto Cesana

OTTO CESANA was born in Brescia, Italy, on July 7, 1899. He came to the United States in boyhood and studied music with private teachers. After working in Hollywood, where he wrote a considerable amount of music for motion pictures, he came to New York to become arranger for Radio City Music Hall, and for several important radio programs. In his own music he has been particularly successful in using within large forms popular American elements, at times folk idioms. In a more serious attitude he has produced half a dozen symphonies and various concertos for solo instruments and orchestra.

Negro Heaven for orchestra is one of his more popular attempts to use an American folk idiom within a symphonic mold. He explains: "Here follows a musical interpretation of the fluctuating moods that seize the colored man—now gay, now sad, always, however migrating towards carefreeness and abandon, as exemplified in the return of the first subject, which is soon followed by one of those superlative moods, a Negro in the throes of nostalgia."

Swing Septet (1942), for string orchestra, guitar and percussion is in three short movements, the first in sonata form, and the last two in three-part song form. "The chief purpose," says the composer, "is to give the string players an opportunity to compete with the ad lib boys who, while they improvise the wildest phrases imaginable, are 'floored' whenever an approximation of that material is set down on paper."

Emmanuel Chabrier

ᥫᦇᥫᦇ ᦇᥣᦇᥣ

EMMANUEL CHABRIER was born in Ambert, France, on January 18, 1841. He was trained as a lawyer; from 1862 to 1880 he was employed at the Ministry of the Interior in Paris. But he had also received a sound musical training with private teachers. Composition began for him in earnest in the 1870's, with two of his operettas receiving performances in Paris between 1877 and 1879. In 1879 he made a pilgrimage to Germany to hear Wagner's music dramas whose impact upon him proved so overwhelming that he finally decided to give up his government work and concentrate on music. Returning to Paris in

1880 he published the *Pièces pittoresques* for piano. Following a visit to Spain he produced in 1883 his first major work for orchestra and realized with it his first major success as a composer—the rhapsody *España*. He also wrote two operas, *Gwendoline* produced in 1886, and *Le Roi malgré lui* introduced one year later. Some of his best writing was for the piano and included such distinguished works as the *Habanera*, *Bourrée fantasque*, and *Trois valses romantiques*. Chabrier became a victim of paralysis in the last two years of his life, and just before his death he began losing his sanity. He died in Paris on September 13, 1894.

While in his operas he revealed his profound indebtedness to the Wagnerian idiom, Chabrier was at his best either in music that interpreted Spain or to which he brought a natural bent for laughter, gaiety, and the grotesque.

España, an orchestral rhapsody, is his most famous composition, as popular in the semi-classical literature as it is in the symphonic repertory. Chabrier wrote it in 1883 after a Spanish holiday, and its première in Paris on November 4 of that year was a sensation. This rhapsody is built from three principal subjects, two borrowed from Spanish folk melodies, and one Chabrier's own. A nervous rhythm in plucked strings leads to a strongly accented malagueña, first heard in the wind instrument. Different sections take it over before soaring strings arrive with a lyrical jota melody. Chabrier's own theme, a stately subject for trombones, is then heard, set against the background of the malagueña melody. The French waltz-king, Waldteufel, used Chabrier's themes from *España* for one of his most famous waltzes, also entitled *España*.

The *Joyeuse marche* (1888) reveals the composer in one of his satirical moods. Chabrier wrote it at first as a piano composition to be used for a sight-reading class at the Bordeaux Conservatory. It proved too difficult to fulfil this function, and Chabrier decided to orchestrate it, calling it *Joyeuse marche* and presenting it as one of his more serious endeavors. The music is in a burlesque style, believed to be a musical description of drunken musicians staggering home after a festive evening. The work opens with an orchestral flourish, following which the oboe offers a capricious subject. This gaiety is maintained in the lively second theme for the violins.

The *Suite pastorale* (1880) is an orchestral adaptation of four of the ten piano pieces in *Pièces pittoresques*. In the first, "*Idylle*," a beautiful melody is accompanied by plucked strings. The second, "*Danse villageoise*" is a country dance in which the lively dance tune is first heard in clarinets. The third piece, *"Sous bois"* has a pastoral character, while the concluding number, *"Scherzo-Valse"* is a protracted piece of pulsating music.

George Chadwick

GEORGE WHITEFIELD CHADWICK was born in Lowell, Massachusetts, on November 13, 1854. Most of his music study took place in Germany. When he was being graduated from the Leipzig Conservatory in 1879, his overture *Rip Van Winkle* received its première performance. He then studied organ and composition with Rheinberger in Munich. After returning to the United States in 1880, he became a teacher of harmony and composition at the New England Conservatory, rising to the post of director in 1897. He was also active for several years as director of the Worcester Music Festival. He died in Boston on April 4, 1931.

Chadwick was a prolific composer of symphonies, concertos, and various other orchestral and choral works. He never freed himself from the influence of German Romanticism, with which he had been infected during his student days. He wrote with a sure craftsmanship, usually filling his classical structures with winning melodies and often lush harmonies and orchestration.

Two compositions for orchestra are of particular popular appeal: *Jubilee* and *Noël*. Both are movements from the *Symphonic Sketches* (1895) which received its world première in Boston in 1908. (The other two movements, the third and fourth, are "Hobgoblin" and "A Vagrom Ballad.") *Jubilee* is a vigorous tonal picture of a carnival. A spirited melody is loudly presented by the full orchestra and is elaborated upon. A second virile subject is then presented by bass clarinet, bassoons, violas and cellos. Following a lively return of the opening carnival theme, the woodwind and horns appear with a lyrical subject. The music then gains in vitality until it comes to a rousing conclusion with a coda built from the carnival motive.

Noël has been described as "a little Christmas song." It is a haunting orchestral nocturne in which a serene Yuletide melody is offered by the English horn.

Cécile Chaminade

CÉCILE CHAMINADE was born in Paris on August 8, 1857. Music study took place in Paris with Marsick and Godard among others. In 1875 she launched her career as concert pianist by touring Europe in programs that often included her own compositions. At her American debut, on November 7, 1908, she appeared as soloist with the Philadelphia Orchestra in a performance of her own *Concerstueck*. She wrote many other ambitious works including a symphony, two orchestral suites, and ballets. She died in Monte Carlo on April 18, 1944.

Though Chaminade staked her future as composer on her larger, serious works for orchestra and the ballet stage, she is today remembered almost exclusively for her slight morsels of the salon variety. Most of these originated as compositions for the piano; her piano music numbers about two hundred works including arabesques, etudes, impromptus, valse-caprices, and so forth. *Automne,* a sentimental melody, and *Sérénade espagnole,* in a pseudo-Spanish style, come from her piano music: *Automne* from the *Concert Etudes,* op. 35. It has been transcribed for popular orchestra by Melachrino. *Sérénade espagnole* has been adapted for violin and piano by Fritz Kreisler. Chaminade's most popular piece, *Scarf Dance,* comes from a ballet, *Callirhoë,* produced in Marseilles in 1888. It is often heard in its original orchestral version and in various transcriptions for solo piano, and solo instrument and piano.

Gustave Charpentier

❧❧ ❧❧

GUSTAVE CHARPENTIER was born in Dieuze, France, on June 25, 1860. He received his musical training in the Conservatories in Lille and Paris, winning the Prix de Rome in 1881. During his stay in Rome he wrote *Impressions of Italy* for orchestra, with which he realized his first success upon its première performance in Paris in 1892. Charpentier's fame, however, rests securely on a single opera, *Louise,* a triumph when introduced in Paris on February 2, 1900, and since become recognized as one of the major achievements of the French lyric theater. A sequel, *Julien* (1913), was a failure. From 1913 on, Charpentier wrote almost nothing more, living a Bohemian existence in the Montmartre section of Paris where he died on February 18, 1956.

Impressions of Italy, a suite for orchestra (1890) is a nostalgic picture of five Italian scenes. The first movement is "Serenade," in which is described a picture of young men emerging from a bistro at midnight, singing love songs under the windows of their girl friends. "At the Fountain" depicts girls parading with dignified steps near a waterfall by a ravine; from the distance come the sounds of a shepherd's tune. "On Muleback" tells of evening as it descends on the Sabine Mountains. The mules trot along, and there rises the song of the muleteer followed by the sweet love song of girls riding in their carts to the village. "On the Heights" presents noontime on the heights overlooking Sorrento. All is peace, though the toll of bells can be heard from a distance. The finale is a musical tribute to a great city, "Naples." In this music we see the crowds of the city, the parading bands. A tarantella is being danced in the streets. The strains of a sentimental folk song drift in from the quay. Evening falls, and fireworks electrify the sky.

Frédéric Chopin

❧❧ ❧❧

FRANÇOIS FRÉDERIC CHOPIN, genius of music for the piano, was born in Zelazowa Wola, Poland, on February 22, 1810. He began to study the piano at six. One year later he made his first public appearance and wrote his first piece of music. His later music study took place privately with Joseph Elsner and at the Warsaw Conservatory from which he was graduated with honors in 1829. In that year he visited Vienna where he gave two successful concerts of his works. He left Poland for good in 1830, settling permanently in Paris a year after that. He soon became one of the most highly regarded musicians in France, even though he gave only a few public concerts. In 1837 he first met the writer, George Sand, with whom he was involved emotionally for about a decade, and under whose influence he composed some of his greatest music. Always sensitive in physique and of poor health, Chopin suffered physically most of his adult life. He died in Paris on October 17, 1849 and was buried in Père Lachaise.

Chopin produced 169 compositions in all. Practically all of them are for the piano, and most within the smaller forms. In writing for the piano he was an innovator who helped change the destiny of piano style and technique. He is often described as the poet of the keyboard, by virtue of his sensitive and deeply affecting lyricism (usually beautifully ornamented), his always exquisite workmanship, and his profound emotion. Many of his works are nationally Polish in expression.

The Etude in E major, op. 10, no. 3 (1833) is one of two of Chopin's most famous works in the etude form. While an etude is essentially a technical exercise, Chopin produced twenty-seven pieces for piano which, though they still probe various technical problems, are nevertheless so filled with poetic thought and musical imagination that they belong in the realm of great art and must be numbered with his most significant compositions. That in E major is one of his most beautiful melodies, a soulful song rather than a technical exercise; Chopin himself regarded this as one of his most inspired pages. One of the many transcriptions of this composition existing is for the voice.

The so-called *Revolutionary Etude*—C minor, op. 10, no. 12 (1833)—was inspired by the tidings received by Chopin while he was traveling from Vienna to Paris that Warsaw had fallen to the Russians. His first impulse was to rush back home and join in the battle. He was dissuaded from doing this by his family, and instead he sublimated his intense patriotic feelings by writing a fiery piece of national music, full of the spirit of defiance. Since then this etude has become as inextricably associated with Poland and its national aspirations and ideals as, for example, is Sibelius' *Finlandia* with Finland. This etude was repeatedly played over the Polish radio when Nazi Germany first attacked Poland in 1939, a continual inspiration to the defenders of Warsaw; it was the last piece of music played over the Polish radio before the Germans took over.

In the Fantaisie-Impromptu in C-sharp minor, op. 66 (1834), Chopin makes a structural compromise between the forms of the fantasy and the impromptu. In doing so, he produced one of his best known melodies, a melody that appears after a fast bravura opening. This is a flowing sentimental song that was used for the popular American tune, "I'm Always Chasing Rainbows."

The *Funeral March* is surely the most celebrated funeral music ever written. It is found as the third movement of the Sonata No. 2 in B-flat minor, for piano, op. 35 (1839). In various arrangements, especially for orchestra, for band and for organ, this music has accompanied the dead to their final resting place in every part of the civilized world. In three-part form, the first section consists of a slow, mournful march. In the middle trio a more reflective mood is projected, almost like a kind of gentle recollection of the dead and the good he had performed. The opening mournful tread returns after this trio to bring the composition to its conclusion.

The fifty-five Mazurkas are among the most national of Chopin's compositions, those in which he most fervently expressed his strong feelings about his native land. The Mazurka is a Polish dance in 3/4 time, somewhat slower in tempo than the waltz, and highly varied in rhythm and emotion. In Chopin's Mazurkas we find, on the one hand, brief mood pictures, and on the other, a fiery romantic temperament which expresses itself in rapid and at times abrupt alternations of feeling from the gay to the melancholy, from the energetic to the pensive. One of the most beautiful of the Mazurkas is that in A minor, op. 17, no. 4 (1833), of which Stokowski made an excellent orchestral arrangement. One of the most dramatic is that in B-flat minor, op. 24, no. 4

(1835) orchestrated by Stokowski, Auber, among others. Two other Chopin Mazurkas that have been orchestrated are found in *Les Sylphides* (see below): that in D major, op. 33, no. 2 (1838) and C major, op. 67, no. 3 (1835).

Chopin wrote nineteen Nocturnes, each one a slow, poetic and atmospheric piece of "night music." "Chopin loved the night," wrote James Gibbons Huneker, "and its soft mysteries, and his nocturnes are true night pieces, some with agitated, remorseful countenance, others seen in profile only, while many others are whisperings at the dusk." The most celebrated of Chopin's Nocturnes is that in E-flat major, op. 9, no. 2 (1833), truly a "whispering at the dusk." This is a beautiful, romantic song that begins without preliminaries. As this spacious melody unfolds, it acquires even new facets of beauty through the most exquisite embellishments. Among the many transcriptions that have become popular, besides those for orchestra, is one for violin and piano by Pablo de Sarasate, and another for cello and piano by David Popper.

There are two Chopin Polonaises that are particularly favored by audiences everywhere. One is the *Heroic,* the other the *Military.* Chopin was especially successful in endowing artistic dimensions and significance to this old courtly folk dance which is technically characterized by its syncopations and accents on the half beat. He wrote twelve for piano. The *Heroic,* in A-flat major, op. 53, no. 6 (1842) is fiery music, its first robust theme being the reason why the entire work has been designated as "heroic." This main melody was borrowed for the American popular song, "Till the End of Time," a big hit in 1945. (Sigmund Spaeth has pointed up the interesting fact that while "Till the End of Time" was at the head of the "Hit Parade" in 1945, the polonaise itself from which this song was derived was in fifteenth place, "competing with all the light and serious music of the world." And one of the reasons why the Polonaise suddenly became so popular was because it was featured prominently in the screen biography of Chopin released that year, *A Song to Remember.*) The *Military Polonaise,* in A major, op. 40, no. 1 (1839) is one of Chopin's most commanding pieces of music. Both principal themes have a pronounced military character, though the second is somewhat more subdued and lyrical than the first. Glazunov's transcription for orchestra, for the ballet *Chopiniana,* is one of several adaptations.

Of Chopin's twenty-six Preludes, two should be singled out for their enormous popular appeal. Chopin's Preludes are brief compositions suggesting a mood or picture, but at the end leaving the impression with the listener that much more could be spoken on that subject. These Preludes, as Robert Schumann wrote, "are sketches, the beginnings of studies, or, if you will, ruins; eagles' pinions, wild and motley and pell-mell. But in every piece we find, in his own pearly handwriting, 'this is by Frederic Chopin'; even in his pauses we recognize him by his agitated breathing." There are twenty-four pieces in op. 28 (1839), each one in one of the keys of the major or minor scale, beginning with C major and A minor, and concluding with F major and D minor. The most popular is that in A major, one of the shortest in the group, a sixteen-bar melody in two short sentences; this is not only one of Chopin's simplest lyrical thoughts, but also one of his most eloquent. Among the orchestral transcriptions is the one found in the ballet *Les Sylphides* (see below).

The second of Chopin's most popular Preludes is the so-called *Raindrop,* in D-flat major, op. 28, no. 15. Some of the depression experienced by Chopin during a miserable stay in Majorca with George Sand —where he was plagued by illness, bad weather, and the antagonism and suspicions of his neighbors—can here be found. The melody is a somber reflection, through which is interspersed a repetitious figure that seems to suggest the rhythm of falling raindrops, the reason why this piece acquired its familiar nickname. The belief that Chopin was inspired to write this music by listening to the gentle sound of falling rain on the roof of his Majorca house is apocryphal.

Les Sylphides, one of the most popular works in the classic ballet repertory, makes extensive use of some of Chopin's best-known compositions for the piano, orchestrated by Stravinsky, Alexander Tcherepnine, Glazunov, and Liadov. With choreography by Michel Fokine it was first presented by Diaghilev's Ballet Russe de Monte Carlo in Paris on June 2, 1909 with Pavlova, Karsavina, and Nijinsky as principal dancers. There is no story line to this ballet. In place of characters there are only dancers dressed in long white dresses, and a danseur in black and white velvet. In place of an actual plot there is only atmosphere and mood. A subdued, introspective overture (Prelude in A major, op. 28, no. 7) leads to the rise of the curtain on an ancient ruin within a secluded wood. Girls in white are transfixed in a tableau; then they begin dancing to the strains of the Nocturne in A-flat, op. 32, no. 2. After that come various dances to the following Chopin compositions: Waltz in G-flat, op. 70, no. 1; Mazurka in C major, op. 67, no. 3; Mazurka in D major, op. 33, no. 2; a repetition of the opening A major Prelude; Waltz in A-flat, op. 69, no. 1, the *L'adieu;* a repetition of the opening

A major Prelude; Waltz in C-sharp minor, op. 64, no. 2; Waltz in E-flat, op. 18, the *Grande valse brilliante.*

Chopin's fourteen waltzes are the last word in aristocratic elegance and refinement of style; they are abundant with the most beguiling lyrical ideas. Perhaps the best loved of all these waltzes is that in C-sharp minor, op. 64, no. 2 (1847). The waltz opens without preliminaries with music of courtly grace; two other equally appealing subjects follow. The so-called *Minute Waltz*—in D-flat major, op. 64, no. 1 —is one of the shortest of Chopin's compositions for the piano. The term "minute" does not refer to the sixty seconds supposedly required for its performance (actually that performance takes less than a minute) but to the French term, *"minute"* meaning "small."

Eric Coates

ERIC COATES, one of England's most highly esteemed and widely performed composers of light music, was born in Hucknall, England, on August 27, 1886. While attending the Royal Academy of Music in London, where he specialized in the viola under Lionel Tertis, he supported himself by playing in several of London's theater orchestras. Upon graduating from the Academy, Coates became violist with several string quartets, including the Hambourg String Quartet with which he toured South Africa in 1908. From 1912 to 1918 he was first violist of the Queen's Hall Orchestra. Meanwhile, in 1911 he realized his first success as composer of light music when his *Miniature Suite* was introduced at a Promenade Concert; after 1920 he devoted himself almost completely to composition, producing ballets, rhapsodies, suites, marches, and so forth, that were heard around the world. In 1930, his valse-serenade *Sleepy Lagoon* achieved a phenomenal success in London; with lyrics by Jack Lawrence and in a popular-song arrangement by Dr. Albert Sirmay, it made in 1942 seventeen appearances on the American "Hit Parade," twice in first place. Coates appeared as guest conductor throughout the music world, visiting the United States in 1946 and 1955, on both occasions conducting concerts of his music over the radio networks. In 1957 he became president of the British Light Music Association. He died in Chichester, England, on December 21, 1957.

In *Four Centuries,* a suite for orchestra (1941), Coates created a four-movement work, each of which was in a musical style of a different century. The first movement is a fugue, the second pavane, the third Valse, and the last is called "Jazz."

London Suite (1932), for orchestra, is one of his best known works inspired by the city dearest to his heart. As he himself wrote: "My best inspiration is to walk down a London street and a tune soon comes to me. When I can think of nothing I walk down Harley Street and there is a lamp post. Every time I catch sight of it a tune comes to my mind. That lamp post has been my inspiration for years." The most celebrated movement of his suite is the stirring "Knightsbridge March," one of the most popular marches by an Englishman, perhaps second only in universal appeal to Elgar's *Pomp and Circumstance.* It has been used as the theme music for a program on the BBC, and when first used the radio station was swamped with over twenty thousand letters asking for its identification. Two other highly familiar movements from this suite are "Westminster" and "Covent Garden." The former is a "meditation," introduced by the chiming of bells of the Westminster clock and followed by tunes both gay and pensive suggesting different moods of people strolling in London streets below. The second is a tarantella, a lively dance recalling the fact that the famous opera house, Covent Garden, has also distinguished itself for the performances of comic and light operas.

The Three Bears is a realistic tonal picture of the famous fairy tale of Goldilocks and the three bears. An expressive *Andante* section is intended to depict the query of the three bears, "Who's been sitting in my chair?" In the gentle waltz section that follows, Goldilocks goes to sleep in the small bear's bed. A vigorous fast section demonstrates how the three bears discover Goldilocks and chase her wildly. They finally give up the pursuit, go home in good humor, while Goldilocks returns to her grandmother to tell her of her adventure that day.

In *The Three Elizabeths* (1944), Coates provides sensitive lyrical portraits of three English queens, Queen Elizabeth I, the Virgin Queen; Elizabeth, the Queen mother, widow of King George VI; and Elizabeth II.

Peter Cornelius

❦❦❦ ❦❦❦

PETER CORNELIUS was born in Mayence, Germany, on December 24, 1824. After studying theory with Dehn in Berlin from 1845 to 1852 he became a passionate advocate of the "music of the future" as promulgated by Liszt and Wagner. It was Liszt who introduced Cornelius' comic opera, *The Barber of Bagdad,* in Weimar in 1858; Liszt was finally forced to resign his conducting post in Weimar because of the hostility of the audiences to this masterwork. From 1865 on Cornelius lived in Munich where he was reader to King Ludwig II and professor of harmony at the Royal Conservatory. He died in Mayence on October 26, 1874. He was a composer of operas and songs, but is today remembered almost exclusively for *The Barber of Bagdad,* one of the most delightful comic operas in the German repertory.

The Barber of Bagdad (Der Barbier von Bagdad)—whose world première took place in Weimar on December 15, 1858, Liszt conducting— has an amusing text written by the composer himself. The plot concerns a rendezvous between Nureddin and Margiana, daughter of the Caliph; Nureddin's friend, the barber of Bagdad, stands guard. This amatory adventure is brightened by a series of episodes and accidents in which Nurredin (mistaking his friend for the Caliph) seeks refuge in a chest in which he almost suffocates. All turns out well in the end. The Caliph offers his parental blessings to Nureddin and Margiana.

The overture is famous. Its main melody is a chromatic Oriental subject which represents the barber. Another significant episode is the theme with which the overture opens: a tender melody for woodwind and muted strings. These two ideas, and several subsidiary ones derived from the opera score, are developed with considerable good humor and merriment until a dramatic conclusion is realized in the coda.

Noel Coward

ᘒᘒ ᘒᘒ

N O E L C O W A R D, one of England's most brilliant and versatile men of the theater in the 20th century, was born in Teddington, on December 16, 1899. He made his stage debut in 1911 in a fairy play, and for the next few years appeared regularly in various other productions. His career as performer was interrupted by military service during World War I. After the war he decided upon a career as writer. His first major success came with the play *The Vortex,* in 1924. From then on he wrote dramas and comedies which placed him in the front rank of contemporary playwrights. But his achievements in the theater do not end here. He has also distinguished himself as an actor, night-club entertainer, producer, lyricist, composer, and on occasion even as a conductor. He wrote the texts, lyrics, and the music to several musical productions, the most famous of which is the operetta, *Bitter Sweet* in 1929. Other musicals by Coward include *Year of Grace* (1928), *Words and Music* (1932) *Conversation Piece* (1934) and *After the Ball* (1954). Out of some of these have come such celebrated Coward songs as "Mad About the Boy," "Mad Dogs and Englishmen," "Some Day I'll Find You" and "I'll Follow My Secret Heart." An anthology of fifty-one Noel Coward songs from his various musical productions called *The Noel Coward Song Book* was published in New York in 1953. Never having received any musical training, Coward can play the piano only in a single key, and must call upon the services of an amanuensis to get his melodies down on paper.

Bitter Sweet is his most famous musical, first produced in London on July 18, 1929, and in New York on November 5, 1929. It was twice adapted for motion-pictures, the first time in 1933 in England, and the second time in 1940 in the United States in a production starring Jeanette MacDonald and Nelson Eddy. In *Bitter Sweet,* Noel Coward made a conscious effort at writing a romantic, sentimental, nostalgic operetta in the style so long favored in Vienna; indeed it was a hearing of a recording of Johann Strauss' *Die Fledermaus* that proved to be the immediate stimulus in the writing of his text. The setting is for the most part Vienna, and the time the 1880's. Sari, an English girl, is about to marry an English man of means when she suddenly decides to elope with Carl, a music teacher. They go to live in Vienna. Carl comes to his sudden death in a duel, after which Sari continues to live in Vienna where she becomes a famous singer. In her old age, after an absence of half a century, she returns to London.

Three melodies from *Bitter Sweet* have become extremely popular. The first is a nostalgic waltz, "I'll See You Again," from the first act, the love song of Sari and Carl; the song recurs again in the third act, and its closing measures serve to bring the play to a dramatic conclusion. "Zigeuener," also sung by Sari is, as its name suggests, in the gypsy style so favored by the Viennese public. The third famous melody from *Bitter Sweet* is "If Love Were All."

"I'll Follow My Secret Heart" comes from *Conversation Piece*, first produced in London on February 16, 1934, and in New York the same fall. The setting of this sentimental and nostalgic operetta is the English resort town of Brighton in 1811 where Paul, a duke turned adventurer, and Melanie, a Parisian chanteuse, are involved in a stormy romance that ends happily. As sung by Yvonne Printemps in London, "I'll Follow My Secret Heart" was the pivot on which the story rotated, and the main reason for this operetta's enormous success.

César Cui

CÉSAR CUI was born in Vilna, Russia, on January 18, 1835. He was graduated as an engineer from the St. Petersburg Engineering Academy in 1857; following that he served for many years as a topographer, as an authority on fortifications, and as an engineering professor. All the while his principal avocation was music, which he had studied from childhood on. Between 1864 and 1900 he was active as music critic for various Russian newspapers and journals. As a composer, he belonged to the nationalist group known as the "Russian Five" or "Mighty Five," but unlike his distinguished colleagues (Balakirev, Rimsky-Korsakov, Mussorgsky and Borodin) his influence proved far greater than his music. He wrote many operas and large orchestral works, but none have remained alive in the repertory. He was probably at his best in miniature for the piano, and in his songs. He died in St. Petersburg on March 24, 1918.

It is with one of his miniatures that his name is still remembered. This piece is the *Orientale,* a composition originally for violin and piano, the ninth number in a suite of twenty-four pieces collectively entitled *Kaleidoscope,* op. 50. The principal melody is in oriental style, introduced and then accompanied by a persistent rhythm (which in the original version is produced by plucked strings, while the melody itself is first given by the piano. This melody is soon taken over by the violin.) Transcriptions for orchestra have made this a salon favorite.

Claude Debussy

ACHILLE-CLAUDE DEBUSSY, father of musical Impressionism, was born in St. Germain-en-Laye, France, on August 22, 1862. From 1873 to 1884 he attended the Paris Conservatory where he was both a rebellious and a brilliant student. He won many prizes, including the Prix de Rome in 1884. In the compositions written in Rome under the provisions of the Prix he already revealed his independence of thought and unorthodoxy of style. After returning from Rome to Paris he became influenced not only by the Impressionist movement in French art and the Symbolist movement in French literature but also by the iconoclastic musical approaches and idioms of Erik Satie. Debussy now began to develop his own techniques and mannerisms and to crystallize his highly personal style. His first masterworks appeared between 1892 and 1893: the orchestral prelude, *The After-*

noon of a Faun (L'Après midi d'un faun), and his string quartet. With later works for orchestra and for solo piano—and with his remarkable opera, *Pelleas and Melisande,* introduced at the Opéra-Comique on April 30, 1902—he brought musical Impressionism to its highest technical development and to its most advanced stage of artistic fulfillment. He became the musical poet of the most subtle suggestions, elusive moods, and delicate impressions. A victim of cancer, Debussy suffered severely in the closing years of his life. He died in Paris on March 25, 1918, on a day when the city was being bombarded by the Germans during World War I. Because of the war, his death passed unnoticed except by a handful of friends.

Debussy's greatest works are, to be sure, too complex in technique and too subtle in style to enjoy ready consumption by the general public. But a few of his compositions have a wide appeal because their charm and sensitivity are easily comprehended, even at first hearing. One of these is the delightful piano suite, *Children's Corner* (1908) written by the composer for the delight of his little daughter, Chou-Chou. In it Debussy evokes the imaginative world of the child; but he also produces unsophisticated descriptive music that is readily appreciated by the very young. Debussy used English rather than French titles for this work because he wished to suggest the kind of stories and games that involve an English governess and a French child. André Caplet's orchestration of this suite is famous.

There are six brief movements. The first, "Doctor ad Parnassum," is a satire on young pianists and their struggles with five-finger exercises. This is followed by "Jimbo's Lullaby," a tender lullaby crooned by a child to his toy elephant named Jimbo. In the third movement, "Serenade for a Doll," the child turns from his pet elephant to his pet doll to croon to it a sensitive serenade. "The Snow Is Falling" is a tone picture of a snowfall, seen by a child from his window. "The Little Shepherd" is a pastoral piece of music. The most famous movement of the suite is the last one, "Golliwogg's Cakewalk" in which the composer exploits the style and rhythm of a Negro dance popular in America in the 19th century, the cakewalk. In this movement, the composer maliciously interpolates a fragment from the Prelude of Wagner's *Tristan and Isolde.*

The beloved *Clair de Lune (Moonlight)* is probably the composer's most celebrated melody. This is a poetic, sensitive evocation of the peace and beauty of a moonlight light. It comes from his *Suite bergamasque* for piano (1890), where it can be found as the third of four movements. Orchestral transcriptions have made this piece of music world-famous.

The Girl With the Flaxen Hair (*La Fille aux cheveux de lin*) is an exquisite portrait, in the composer's most felicitous impressionist style. It is the eighth number of his Preludes for the piano, Book I (1910), and like *Clair de lune* is often heard in various orchestral transcriptions; Arthur Hartmann's adaptation for violin and piano is also familiar.

The *Petite Suite* (*Little Suite*) for piano duet (1889) is early Debussy, more in the Romantic vein of Delibes than in the provocative idiom Debussy later made famous. As orchestrated by Henri Busser it is in the repertory of many salon and pop orchestras. There are four short movements. The first, *"En Bateau"* (*"In a Boat"*) is particularly popular. In the orchestration a gentle barcarolle melody for flute suggests the gentle course of the boat in a placid lake. This is followed by turns by a vigorous episode and a passionate section, both of them for the strings. The flute then restores placidity, and the opening sensitive melody returns in the violins. *"Cortège"* ("March") is a pert little march tune shared by the woodwind and strings. *"Menuet"* is of classic grace while the finale, *"Ballet,"* has a compelling rhythmic vigor.

Rêverie (1890) is a brief, atmospheric piece for the piano which has became a favorite with Americans because in 1938 it was adapted into the popular song, "My Reverie."

Léo Delibes

❧❧ ❧❧

LÉO DELIBES was born in St. Germain-du-Val, France, on February 21, 1836. After attending the Paris Conservatory from 1848 on, he became an accompanist for the Théâter Lyrique and organist of the Church of St.-Jean et St.-François in Paris in 1853. Between 1855 and 1865 he wrote a dozen operas, none of them successful. In 1865 he was appointed chorusmaster of the Grand Opéra where he was encouraged to write music for ballet; the first of these was *La Source* in 1866 (renamed *Naila* when later given in Vienna). His most successful ballets were *Coppélia* in 1870 and *Sylvia* in 1876, both still vital in the repertory. In 1873 his most important opéra-comique, *Le Roi l'a Dit,* was introduced by the Opéra-Comique; Delibes' most important opera, *Lakmé,* was first performed on April 14, 1883 by the Paris Opéra. Meanwhile, in 1881, Delibes was appointed professor of composition at the Conservatory. Three years after that he became a member of the French Academy. He died in Paris on January 16, 1891.

Delibes is often described as the creator of modern ballet music. He was the first composer to write symphonically for the dance, to bring to ballet music the fullest creative and technical resources of the skilled serious composer. Thus he opened a new field of compositions which later composers (Tchaikovsky, Stravinsky, and Ravel among many others) cultivated with fertility. The elegance of Delibes' style, the caressing warmth of his lyricism, the richness of his harmonic and rhythmic language, the delicacy of his orchestration endow his ballet music with interest even when it is divorced from its choreography.

Coppélia is a staple in the classic ballet repertory. It was introduced at the Paris Opéra on May 25, 1870, choreography by A. Saint-Léon, and scenario by C. Nuitter and A. Saint-Léon based upon *The Sandman,* a story by E. T. A. Hoffmann. *Coppélia* is the first successful ballet to utilize the subject of a doll become human. Coppélia is a doll created by Dr. Coppélius. She comes to life and gets out of control. Franz, thinking she is human, falls in love with her. But when he realizes she is but a doll he becomes reconciled with his former sweetheart, Swanilda.

Delibes' score is one of the earliest in ballet to make successful use of such folk dances as the Mazurka and the Czardas; because of his success in this direction, many later composers of ballet music were encouraged to follow suit.

An orchestral suite adapted from the score never ceases to delight audiences at both symphonic and semi-classical concerts. It opens with the *"Valse lente,"* a suave waltz to which Swalinda dances as she strives to attract the attention of Coppélia, of whom she is jealous. This is followed by the "Mazurka," a gay episode danced by a group of villagers after Franz has mistaken Coppélia for a human and salutes her. The "Ballade" then comes as a pensive interlude; to this music Swalinda puts a stalk of wheat to her ear, following a long existing superstition, to discover if Franz has been faithful to her. When the answer is in the negative, she breaks the stalk savagely before his very eyes. *"Theme Slave Varié"* is danced by Swalinda; this section comprises a tuneful Polish melody and five variations. The stately and at times fiery "Czardas" which concludes the first act is a corybantic in which all villagers join. *"Valse de la poupée"* (or "Dance of the Doll") is probably the most familiar musical number in the entire ballet, an elegant waltz danced by Swalinda as she assumes the dress, and imitates the actions, of Coppélia.

The *Naila Waltz* (or *Pas des Fleurs*) was written by Delibes in 1867 as an intermezzo for the revival in Paris of Adolph Adam's opera *Le Corsaire*, in Paris. When Delibes' early ballet, *La Source*, was introduced in Vienna as *Naila*, this waltz was interpolated into the production. A short, vigorous introduction for full orchestra and several notes in the basses lead to the lilting waltz melody in strings, with the woodwinds soon joining in. Ernst von Dohnányi made an effective transcription of this waltz for the piano.

Le Roi l'a dit (*The King Said So*) is an opéra-comique with libretto by Edmond Gondinet, introduced at the Opéra-Comique in Paris on May 24, 1873. The plot revolves around a peasant boy whom a Marquis is trying to pass off before the king as his own son. The peasant makes the most of this situation to the continual embarrassment and chagrin of the Marquis who finally manages to get rid of him by marrying him off to a maid with whom the boy is in love.

The popular overture to this light opera opens with a brisk march in full chords. A gracious little melody then unfolds in the strings. After a return of the march music in a more subdued vein, a romantic song is offered by the clarinets against plucked strings. The music now grows livelier as a principal thought is given by chattering strings and woodwind. Extended use is now made of the first graceful melody. The opening march is at last recalled to bring the overture to a boisterous end.

The second of Delibes' famous ballets, *Sylvia*, was introduced at the Paris Opéra on June 14, 1876. The choreography was by Louis Mérante, and the text by Jules Barbier and Baron de Reinach. The classical subject is derived from mythology. Aminta, a shepherd, comes to a sacred grove seeking a huntress he had once seen there. She is Sylvia, who soon appears with her nymphs. She is later captured by Orion, the black huntsman. But her escape is effected by Eros, and she and Aminta are reunited in love.

Like *Coppélia, Sylvia* has a popular orchestral suite adapted from the ballet score. After a brief Prelude comes *"Les Chasseresses"* ("The

Huntresses"), sprightly music with which Sylvia and her nymphs make their first appearance; to its rhythmic strains they dance before a statue of Eros. A gentle "Intermezzo" follows, describing the nymphs as they rest near a stream. In the *"Valse lente"* Sylvia dances to a graceful musical episode. The "Barcarolle" highlights a saxophone solo; to this background music appears a ship bearing Eros, disguised as a pirate. The most celebrated single number in the entire suite comes next, the "Pizzicato," a delicate dance performed by Sylvia disguised as a slave. The *"Cortège de Bacchus"* ("March of Bacchus") is the dynamic music with which a bacchanalian rite is being celebrated.

Gregore Dinicu

GREGORE DINICU, who was born in Bucharest, Rumania, on April 5, 1889, is a gypsy violinist who became popular in leading Rumanian cabarets and restaurants. In 1939 he visited the United States, scoring a major success with his gypsy orchestra at the New York World's Fair. His *Hora Staccato,* for violin and piano (or violin and orchestra)—a virtuoso piece of folk character—is his only composition to become famous outside Rumania. Jascha Heifetz, the famous virtuoso, heard Dinicu play it in Rumania and was so delighted with it that he transcribed it, and popularized it both at his concerts and on records. The Hora is an exciting Rumanian folk dance with lively rhythms and a vertiginous melody that shifts flexibly from major to minor or modal scales. These traits are all found in Dinicu's electrifying *Hora Staccato.*

Gaetano Donizetti

GAETANO DONIZETTI was born in Bergamo, Italy, on November 29, 1797. His early music study took place in Bergamo and Naples and was completed at the Liceo Filarmonico in Bologna. Despite his strong bent not only for music but also for art, literature, and architecture, he aspired for a military career. While serving in the Austrian army he completed his first opera, *Enrico di Borgogna,* introduced in Venice in 1818. Success came four years after that in Rome with *Zoraide di Granata.* Now exempted from further military duty, Donizetti was able to devote himself entirely to composition. Between 1822 and 1829 he wrote twenty-three operas. In 1830 he achieved renown throughout Europe with *Anna Bolena,* introduced in Milan. In the five succeeding years he produced two masterworks by which he is still represented in the operatic repertory: *L'Elisir d'amore* in 1832 and *Lucia di Lammermoor* in 1835. From 1837 to 1839 he was the director of the Naples Conservatory. In 1839 he went to live in Paris where he wrote and had produced several highly successful operas including *The Daughter of the Regiment* and *La Favorita* in 1840 and *Don Pasquale* in 1843. Soon after this he returned to his native city where he was stricken by a mental disorder and for a time confined to an asylum. He died in Bergamo on April 8, 1848.

The facility with which Donizetti wrote his sixty-seven operas is apparent in the easy flow of his lovable melodies and in the spontaneity of his aurally agreeable harmonies. He also possesses a fine theatrical gift, and much of his best music combines delightful lyricism and affecting emotion with dramatic force.

The Daughter of the Regiment (La Fille du régiment, or *La figlia del reggimento)* was first performed at the Opéra-Comique in Paris on February 11, 1840. The French libretto by Jean François Bayard and Vernoy de Saint-Georges was translated into Italian by the composer. The setting is Tyrol in 1815, then being invaded by Napoleon's troops. Marie is the *vivandière* (canteen manager) of the 21st Regiment of the French army. In love with Tonio, who is suspected by the French of being a spy, she is able to prevail on the troops to save his life. But Marie is soon compelled to be separated from both Tonio and the French soldiers when it is discovered that she is the long lost niece of the Countess of Berkenfeld and must return with her aunt to her castle. The Countess wants Marie to marry the Duke of Crackenthorp. When the French troops, with Tonio among them, storm the Berkenfeld castle and want to reclaim Marie, the Countess now reveals that Marie is not her niece but her daughter and thus must obey her wishes. However, the French soldiers finally prevail on the Countess to permit Marie to marry Tonio.

The most popular selections from this tuneful, and occasionally martially stirring opera are: Marie's moving tribute to her regiment (*"Ah, chacun le sait, chacun le dit"*) and her tender farewell as she is about to leave for Berkenfeld (*"Il faut partir, mes bons compagnons"*) and a spirited French war song to victory (*"Rataplan"*) all from the first act; and from the second act, Marie's moving aria (*"Par le rang, et l'opulence*), the orchestral entr'acte *"Tyrolienne,"* and the dramatic paean to France (*"Salut à la France"*) with which the opera ends.

Don Pasquale is a classic in the literature of opera buffa. It received its première in Paris on January 3, 1843; its libretto (by the composer and Giacomo Ruffini) is based on a libretto created by Angelo Anelli for another opera. The central character is an old bachelor who objected to the marriage of his young nephew with a beautiful widow, Norina. To teach him a lesson, Norina puts on a disguise, involves the old man in a mock marriage, and then tortures him with her shrewish ways. Pasquale finally becomes so relieved to discover that he has merely been the victim of an intrigue, rather than a catastrophic marriage, that he does not hesitate any longer to give Norina and his nephew his consent to their marriage.

In the case of *Don Pasquale* its overture is heard far more often than potpourris of principal sections. It opens with heavy descending chords which lead into an opulent song for cellos, soon assumed by horns and the woodwind. The heart of the overture is a saucy melody for strings. The music now becomes dramatized with transitional material, but a new gay melody is offered by the woodwind and strings. The main string melody and the succeeding sprightly tune are recalled to finish the overture in a gay mood.

L'Elisir d'amore (*The Elixir of Love*) like *Don Pasquale,* is a delightful comic opera, one of the most effervescent ever written. It received its first performance in Milan on May 12, 1832. The libretto, by Felice

Romani, was based on Eugène Scribe's *Le Philtre*. Nemorino, in love with Adina who rejects him, purchases a love elixir from the quack, Dr. Dulcamara. But a sudden inheritance from his uncle, which forthwith makes Nemorino extremely popular with the girls, proves even more potent in winning Adina's love than the potion itself.

Orchestral selections from his gay opera include one of the best loved tenor arias in the operatic repertory. It is *"Una furtiva lagrima,"* a soulful song by Nemorino in the second act with which he hopes to console Adina when he sees her jealousy suddenly aroused by the fact that he had become the favorite of the village girls. Other familiar episodes include a merry comic number *"Udite, Udite"* in which Dr. Dulcamara boasts of the power of his potions, and a beautiful aria, *"Quanto è bella,"* in which Nemorino discloses his love and longing for Adina, both in the first act.

Lucia di Lammermoor is Donizetti's most famous grand opera, and the title role has been favored by the world's foremost coloratura sopranos. The libretto, by Salvatore Cammarano, was based on the Sir Walter Scott romance, *The Bride of Lammermoor*. The opera was first performed in Naples on September 26, 1835. Lucia, sister of Lord Ashton, is in love with Edgar; but in planning to have her marry the wealthy Lord Arthur Bucklaw, Lord Ashton uses lies and wiles to convince her sister that Edgar does not love her. On the day of the signing of the marriage contract between Lucia and Bucklaw, Edgar invades the Lammermoor castle and curses its family. Maddened by her grief, Lucia kills her husband soon after the wedding, and then dies. When Edgar learns that Lucia has loved him all the time, he commits suicide.

The favorite selections from this opera include one of the most famous ensemble numbers in all opera, the sextet *"Chi mi frena."* It is sung in Act 2, Scene 2, by Lucia, Edgar, Bucklaw, Raimond, Ashton and Alisa after Edgar had invaded the Lammermoor castle and witnessed the signing of the marriage contract between Lucia and Bucklaw. Each of the characters here gives voice to his or her personal reaction to this dramatic situation: Lucia speaks of her despair at the treachery of her brother; Edgar wonders why he does not commit an act of vengeance; Lord Ashton is led to sympathy at his sister's despair; Lucia's companion, Alisa, and Bucklaw hope that bloodshed might be averted; and Raimond, a chaplain, invokes divine help.

Another highly popular excerpt from the opera offered in orchestral potpourris includes Lucia's "Mad Scene" from Act 3, Scene 2 (*"Ardon gl'incensi"*). Dressed in a white gown, Lucia appears and mistakes her brother for her beloved Edgar, who she believes has come to marry her. Then she entreats those around her to place a flower on her grave and not to weep at her death (*"Spargi d'amaro pianto"*).

Several other selections often played include Lucia's lyrical cavatina from Act 1, Scene 2 (*"Quando rapita in estasi"*) as she thinks of her beloved Edgar; the love duet of Lucia and Edgar from the same scene (*"Verrano a te sull'aure"*); and the wedding music from Act 3, Scene 1 that precedes the "Mad Scene" (*"D'immenso giubilo"*).

Franz Drdla

FRANZ DRDLA was born in Saar, Moravia on November 28, 1868. He attended the Conservatories in Prague and Vienna, winning at the latter place first prize in violin playing and the medal of the Gesellschaft der Musikfreunde. After serving for several years as a violinist in the orchestra of the Vienna Court Opera, he toured Europe as a concert violinist. From 1923 to 1925 he lived in the United States, making many concert appearances. He died in Bad Gastein, Austria, on September 3, 1944.

Drdla's most famous compositions are slight but lyrical pieces for the violin, of which he wrote over two hundred fifty. His most famous composition is the *Souvenir,* with its familiar upward skip in the main melody and its broad sentimental middle section in double stops. In a similarly sentimental and gentle melodic vein (they might aptly be described as instrumental songs) are the *Romance, Serenade in A* (No. 1), and *Vision.* All are familiar to violin students, and to lovers of light classics in transcriptions for orchestra.

Riccardo Drigo

❧❧ ☙☙

RICCARDO DRIGO was born in Padua, Italy, on June 30, 1846. He first became famous as conductor of orchestral concerts at the Imperial Theater in St. Petersburg. After World War I, he continued his activities as conductor in his native city. He died there on October 1, 1930.

Drigo was the composer of ballets and operas, none of which have survived. He is today remembered almost exclusively for two slight but well loved items. One is the melodically suave *Serenade,* popular in every conceivable transcription. It comes out of a ballet entitled *I milioni d'Arlecchino (Harlequin's Millions)* and consequently is sometimes known as the *Harlequin's Serenade.* The other is *Valse bluette,* an elegant waltz melody, which the composer originally wrote for salon orchestra, but which is in the violinist's repertory by virtue of a famous transcription.

Arcady Dubensky

❧❧ ☙☙

ARCADY DUBENSKY was born in Viatka, Russia, on October 15, 1890. After being graduated from the Moscow Conservatory in 1909 he played the violin in the orchestra of the Moscow Opera. In 1921 he came to the United States, where he later became a citizen. He served as violinist of the New York Symphony Society, and after that of the New York Philharmonic Orchestra, until his retirement in 1953.

Dubensky had written many works for orchestra, whose sound technique and fresh approaches command respect. One or two of these are of popular appeal without sacrificing sound musical values. Of particular interest is the *Stephen Foster Suite* for orchestra (1940), in which Dubensky quotes five Stephen Foster songs: "My Old Kentucky Home," "Jeanie With the Light Brown Hair," "Some Folks," "I See Her Still in My Dreams," and "Camptown Races." The composer goes on to explain: "The first part represents to me a beautiful summer evening in the country. From far away I hear a choir, coming gradually closer and then fading into the distance. It sings to me the wonder song, 'My Old Kentucky Home.' The second part is built around 'Jeanie With the Light Brown Hair.' Here the melody is given to a tenor solo, with a soft, gentle orchestral accompaniment beginning with a short introduction. The last two parts are for orchestra. The fourth part centers around the song 'I See Her Still In My Dreams.' It is a dreamy song, and I have given it the character of an intermezzo played by string orchestra, muted. If this movement is played in slow tempo, and pianissimo, it sounds not at all realistic but like the dream it portrays. The fifth part, 'Camptown Races' is the focal point of the suite. The theme is treated in a number of different keys and always in a different character. Sometimes it is delicate and graceful, and sometimes rude and robust, but always it is gay."

Paul Dukas

PAUL DUKAS was born in Paris, France, on October 1, 1865. After attending the Paris Conservatory, where he won prizes in counterpoint and fugue as well as the second Prix de Rome, he served as music critic for several Parisian journals. From 1910 to 1912 he was professor of orchestration at the Paris Conservatory, and from 1927 until his death its professor of composition. His first successful work was a concert overture, *Polyecute,* introduced in Paris in 1892. His Symphony in C major, first heard in 1897, enhanced his reputation while his orchestral scherzo, *The Sorcerer's Apprentice,* also introduced in 1897, made him famous. Being exceptionally fastidious and self-critical, Dukas did not produce many compositions, but the best of these are works so aristocratic in technique and subtle in musical content that they make a direct appeal only to sophisticated music lovers. These works include the opera *Ariane et Barbe-bleue,* first performed in Paris on May 10, 1907; the ballet, *La Péri,* introduced in Paris on April 22, 1912; and some piano music. Towards the end of his life, Dukas destroyed several of his earlier works deeming them unsuitable for survival. He was one of France's most revered musicians. He was made Chevalier of the Legion of Honor in 1906, and in 1918 elected a member of the *Conseil de l'enseignement supérieur* at the Paris Conservatory. He died in Paris on May 17, 1935.

The Sorcerer's Apprentice (L'Apprenti sorcier), scherzo for orchestra (1897), is Dukas' most famous composition, the one that made him known throughout the world of music. It is so witty, so vivid in its pictorial writing that it has become a favorite of both the very young and the mature. The program, which the music follows with amazing literalness, comes from Goethe's ballad *Der Zauberlehrling* which, in turn, was adapted from a famous folk tale. The story goes something like this: An apprentice to a magician has come upon his master's secret formula for turning a broom into a human being and making it perform human tasks. The apprentice decides to try out this incantation for himself while the master is away, and watches with amazement as the broom acquires human powers. He orders the broom to fetch water, a command meekly obeyed. Pail after pail of water is carried into the magician's shop by the broom until the place is rapidly being inundated. The apprentice now tries to arrest the water-fetching activity of the broom, but he does not know the proper incantation to achieve this, or to strip the broom of its human powers. In terror, the apprentice attacks the broom with a hatchet. The broom, split into two brooms, now becomes two humans performing the ritual of bringing water into the den. In despair, the apprentice cries out for his master who arrives in time to bring the broom back to its former inanimate state, and to restore order.

The atmosphere of mystery and peace prevailing in the magician's den is created in the opening measures with a descending theme for muted violins, while different woodwinds give a hint of the principal subject, a roguish tune describing the sorcerer's apprentice; this subject finally appears in the double bassoon, and is then repeated by the full orchestra. The call of trumpets suggests the incantation pronounced by the apprentice; a brisk theme for bassoons against plucked strings describes the parade of the broom back and forth as it brings the water; and arpeggio figures in the orchestra depict the water itself. The music then portrays the mounting terror of the apprentice as he is unable to arrest the march of the broom. After an overwhelming climax, at which point the apprentice splits the broom into two with a hatchet, the saucy march tune is doubled to inform us that two brooms are now at work. A shriek in the orchestra simulates the panic-stricken call of the apprentice. After the master arrives and sets things in order, the music of the opening measures is repeated to suggest that once again the magician's den is pervaded by peace and mystery.

The Sorcerer's Apprentice was made into an animated motion picture by Walt Disney, the Dukas music performed on the sound track by the Philadelphia Orchestra under Stokowski; it was part of a program collectively entitled *Fantasia* which came to New York on November 13, 1940.

Antonin Dvořák

ANTONIN DVOŘÁK was born in Muehlhausen, Bohemia, on September 8, 1841. As a boy he studied the violin with the village schoolmaster. He subsequently attended the Organ School in Prague. After completing his studies, he played in various orchestras in Prague, including that of the National Theater from 1861 to 1871 where he came under the influence of Smetana, father of Bohemian national music. Dvořák first attracted interest as a composer with *Hymnus,* a choral work introduced in 1873. Two years later he won the Austrian State Prize for a symphony, and in 1878 he became famous throughout

Europe with the *Slavonic Dances*. In 1883 he was appointed organist of the St. Adalbert Church in Prague. From 1892 to 1895 he was the director of the National Conservatory in New York. During this period he was influenced in his compositions by the folk music of the American Negro and Indian. From 1901 until his death he was director of the Prague Conservatory. He died in Prague on May 1, 1904.

A prolific composer of operas, symphonies, chamber and piano music, and songs, Dvořák stood in the forefront of the Romantic composers of the late 19th century and among the leading exponents of Bohemian national music. He was gifted with an expressive melodic gift, a strong and subtle rhythmic pulse, and an inventive harmonic language. Whatever he wrote was charged with strong emotional impulses, whether he used the style of Bohemian folk music or those of the American Negro and American Indian.

The *Carnival Overture* (*Carneval*), written in 1891, is one of three overtures planned by the composer as a cycle to portray "three great creative forces of the Universe—Nature, Life, and Love." A unifying element among them was a melody intended to describe the "unchangeable laws of Nature." Eventually, Dvořák abandoned this plan and published the three overtures separately, calling them *In Nature* (*In der Natur*), op. 91, *Carnival*, op. 92, and *Othello*, op. 93.

Dvořák himself provided a description of the music of *Carnival Overture*. He aimed to describe "a lonely, contemplative wanderer reaching the city at nightfall where a carnival of pleasure reigns supreme. On every side is heard the clangor of instruments, mingled with shouts of joy and the unrestrained hilarity of the people giving vent to their feelings in songs and dances." The overture begins with a lively section portraying the gayety of the carnival. A subdued melody in the violins brings relaxation, but the hubbub soon returns. Another gentle episode depicts a pair of lovers in a secluded corner; the principal melodic material in this part is offered by the solo violin, and by the English horns and flutes. The brilliant opening material returns. It is with this spirit of revelry that the overture ends.

The *Humoresque* in G-flat major is the seventh in a set of eight *Humoresques* for piano (1894). This delightful, elegant piece of music in three-part song form has been transcribed not only for orchestra but for every possible instrument or combinations of instruments, and is undoubtedly the most popular composition by the composer. It was Fritz Kreisler, the famous violin virtuoso, who helped make the work so famous. Kreisler visited Dvořák in 1903 and asked him for some music. Dvořák showed him a pile of compositions, most of it completely unknown. Among these was the G-flat major *Humoresque*. Kreisler transcribed it for violin and piano, introduced it at his concerts, later recorded it, and made it universally popular. As we know it today the *Humoresque* is not the way Dvořák intended it to sound. Dvořák wanted it to be a light, whimsical piece of music, a "humoresque," in fast tempo. Kreisler transcribed it in a slower tempo and more sentimental mood; and it is in this style that *Humoresque* is now known and loved.

The *Indian Lament* is one of several compositions by Dvořák influenced by the idioms of American-Indian music. While serving as director of the National Conservatory in New York, he paid a visit to the town of Spillville, Iowa. There three Iroquois Indians visited him and entertained him with authentic Indian music. Dvořák was so taken with this strange and haunting lyricism, and the primitive rhythms, that he wrote several major works incorporating these idioms. One was a Sonatina in G major for violin and piano, op. 100 (1893). Its slow movement is a delicate song embodying the intervallic peculiarities of authentic American-Indian music. Fritz Kreisler edited this movement and named it *Indian Lament,* the version in which it has become famous. Gaspar Cassadó transcribed this movement for cello and piano.

Dvořák's *Largo* is the second movement of his Symphony No. 5 in E minor better known as the *Symphony from the New World* (1893). This is the symphony written by Dvořák during his visit to the United States as director of the National Conservatory. One of his students was Harry T. Burleigh, who brought to his attention the music of the Negro Spiritual. These melodies moved Dvořák so profoundly that he urged American composers to use the style, technique and personality of these Negro songs as the basis for national American music. As if to set an example, Dvořák wrote several compositions in which his own melodic writing was strongly influenced by the Negro Spiritual. The most significant of these was his symphony, which received its world première in the United States (at a concert of the New York Philharmonic Orchestra on December 15, 1893, Anton Seidl conducting). The main spacious, poignant melody of the Largo movement—given by English horn over string harmonies after a few preliminary chords—so strongly simulates the personality of a Negro Spiritual that it was long thought that Dvořák was indulging in quotation. This is not true; the melody is Dvořák's own. Many transcriptions of this melody exist. One is the familiar song, "Goin' Home," lyrics by William Arms Fisher (also one of Dvořák's pupils); another is a composition for violin and piano by Fritz Kreisler called *Negro Spiritual Melody;* a third is an adaptation for salon orchestra by Sigmund Romberg.

This Largo movement has two other melodies besides the basic one in the Negro-Spiritual style. One is heard in flute and oboe, and the second in the oboe.

The *Scherzo Capriccioso,* in D-flat major, op. 66 (1883) is one of the composer's liveliest and most dynamic larger works for orchestra, but in an idiom that is neither Bohemian nor American. It is in two sections. The first is the Scherzo, opening with an energetic subject for horns that is a kind of a motto theme for the entire work. The principal melody that follows is stated by full orchestra; after that comes a waltz-like tune for violins. The second part of the composition, a trio, is introduced by an expressive melody for English horn. A secondary theme then comes in the strings and wind. The principal idea of the first section now receives extended treatment before the second theme of the second part returns in a modified form. The work ends with a coda in which effective use is made of the opening motto subject.

Dvořák achieved international fame for the first time with the first set of eight *Slavonic Dances,* op. 46, published in 1878. He had been recommended to the publisher Simrock by Brahms; it was the publisher who suggested to Dvořák that he write Slavonic dances similar to the Hungarian dances which Brahms had made so popular. Dvořák wrote his first set for piano four-hands; but these instantly proved so successful that Simrock prevailed on Dvořák to orchestrate them. In 1886, Dvořák wrote a second set of eight *Slavonic Dances,* op. 72, once again both for four-hand piano and for orchestra. Though the melodies and harmonic schemes in all these dances are Dvořák's, they have caught the essence of the Slavonic folk song and dance, and to such a degree that their authentic national character has never been questioned. Karel Hoffmeister wrote: "Something of the Slavic character speaks in every phrase of them—the stormy high-spirited mood of the Furiants; the whimsical merriment, the charm, the touch of coquettry, the ardent tenderness of the lyrical passages."

The following are among the best known of these dances:

C major, op. 46, no. 1. A chord sustained through one measure is followed by a whirlwind presto passage. After a sudden pianissimo we hear a second rhythmic melody. Music of a more serene character appears in flute and strings after a change of key. A force climax is evolved to set the stage for the return of the opening whirlwind subject.

E minor, op. 46, no. 2. A poignant melody is here contrasted with a dynamic rhythmic section. Fritz Kreisler transcribed this dance for violin and piano.

A-flat major, op. 46, no. 6. A dance melody with a strong rhythmic impulse is the opening subject. Pianissimo chords lead to a new virile subject, but there soon comes a decisive change of mood with two expressive melodies. This dance, however, ends dynamically.

G minor, op. 46, no. 8. This is one of the gayest of the Slavonic dances, alive in its electrifying changes of dynamics and tonality.

E minor, op. 72, no. 2. This is one of the best loved of all these dances, a song of rare sensitivity and sadness, only temporarily alleviated by the more optimistic music of the middle section. Fritz Kreisler transcribed it for violin and piano.

A-flat major, op. 72, no. 8. Here, as in the preceding E minor dance, the emphasis is on tender, elegiac song in strings. A dramatic middle section provides some relief, but the gentle moodiness of the opening section soon returns. Fritz Kreisler transcribed it for violin and piano.

Songs My Mother Taught Me is one of Dvořák's most celebrated songs. It is one of seven gypsy songs, based on Slavonic-gypsy folk idioms, gathered in op. 55 (1880); the lyrics are by Adolf Heyduk. This nostalgic, delicate melody has enjoyed numerous transcriptions, including one for violin and piano by Fritz Kreisler, and another for cello and piano by Alfred Gruenfeld.

Sir Edward Elgar

SIR EDWARD ELGAR was born in Broadheath, near Worcester, England on June 2, 1857. He studied the organ with his father, and the violin with Adolf Pollitzer in London. In 1885 he succeeded his father as organist of St. George's Church in Worcester. Two years after his marriage to Alice Roberts, which had taken place in 1889, he with-

drew to Malvern where he lived the next thirteen years, devoted completely to serious composition. Several choral works were performed at
various English festivals before Elgar achieved outstanding success, first
with the *Enigma Variations* for symphony orchestra, introduced in
London in 1899, and then with his oratorio, *The Dream of Gerontius,*
whose première took place in Birmingham in 1900. From then on Elgar
assumed a position of first importance in English music by virtue of his
two symphonies, vast amount of orchestral, choral and chamber music,
and songs. He was generally regarded one of the most significant English composers since Purcell in the 17th century. Elgar was knighted in
1904, appointed Master of the King's Music in 1924, and made a
baronet in 1931. He died in Worcester, England, on February 23, 1934.

It is not difficult to understand Elgar's enormous popularity. Together with an elegant sense of structure and style, and a consummate
musicianship, he had a virtually inexhaustible fund of ingratiating
lyricism. His best works are conceived along traditional lines. They are
Romantic in concept, and poetic in content. These qualities—and with
them a most ingratiating sentiment—are also found in his semi-classical
pieces.

The *Bavarian Dances,* for orchestra, come from *The Bavarian Highlands,* a set of choral songs based on Bavarian folk songs adapted by
Elgar's wife, Alice, and set for chorus with piano and orchestra, op. 27
(1895). Three folk tunes were subsequently adapted by the composer
for orchestra. Collectively called *Bavarian Dances,* the individual dances
were subtitled by the composer "The Dance," "Lullaby," and "The
Marksman." These dances were first introduced in London in 1897 and
have since enjoyed universal acceptance in some cases for their peasant
rhythmic vigor, and in others for their atmospheric charm.

The *Cockaigne Overture (In London Town),* for orchestra, op. 40
(1901) describes London "as represented by its parks and open spaces,
the bands marching from Knightsbridge to Buckingham Palace, Westminster with its dignified associations of Church and State," in the
words of Sir George Grove. The composer himself revealed he wanted
to portray in his music the sights witnessed by a pair of lovers as they
stroll through the city. The hubbub of the city is depicted in the opening measures, following by an intensely romantic section highlighted by
a broad melody for strings, reflecting the feelings of the lovers as they
stop off momentarily to rest in a public park. They continue their walk,
hear the approaching music of a brass band, then enter a church where
organ music is being played. The lovers continue their walk. The ani-

mated life of the city streets once again is reproduced, and the earlier romantic melody telling of their emotional ardor for each other is repeated.

In the South (Alassio), a concert overture for orchestra, op. 50 (1904) was written one Spring while the composer was vacationing in southern Europe. This work reflects Elgar's intense love of Nature. The following quotation appears in the published score: "A land which *was* the mightiest in its old command and *is* the loveliest; wherein were cast the men of Rome. Thou are the garden of the world." The overture opens with a gay tune for clarinets, horns, violins and cellos. It receives vigorous treatment and enlargement before a pastoral section is given by the woodwind and muted strings, a description of a shepherd and his flock. The overture then alternates between stress and tranquillity, with great prominence being given to the shepherd's melody. A viola solo then leads to the recapitulation section.

Pomp and Circumstance is a set of five marches for symphony orchestra, op. 39. The composers wanted these marches to provide such music with symphonic dimensions in the same way that dance music (polonaise or waltz, etc.) acquired artistic stature at the hands of Chopin, among others. The phrase "pomp and circumstance" comes from Shakespeare's *Othello*. The five marches are in the keys of D major, A minor, C minor, G major, and C Major. The first two were written in 1901; the third, in 1905; the fourth in 1907; and the fifth in 1930. The most famous of these is the second in A minor, one of Elgar's most frequently performed compositions, and music as often identified with the British Empire as "God Save the King." It opens in a restless, vigorous vein and erupts into a spacious melody for strings which Laurence Housman subsequently set to lyrics ("Land of Hope and Glory"). Elgar once again used this same melody in his *Coronation Ode* for King Edward VII in 1902. The opening brisk, restless music is recalled after a full statement of the melody.

The first in D major has a vigorous introduction after which unison strings come forth with a robust march tune. The opening introduction is subsequently used as a transition to the trio in which a soaring melody is set against a uniform rhythmic beat.

The fourth in G major, known as "Song of Liberty," is also familiar. Once again the opening consists of spirited march music, and once again the heart of the composition is a broad and stately melody for the strings. This melody receives extended treatment which culminates with a rousing statement by the full orchestra.

Salut d'amour, for chamber orchestra, op. 12 (1889) is a nostalgic and sentimental piece of music in three-part song form that has become a salon favorite. It is also famous in a transcription for violin and piano.

Duke Ellington

~~~~

EDWARD KENNEDY "DUKE" ELLINGTON was born in Washington, D.C. on April 29, 1899. His career as a popular musician began in his adolescence when he performed jazz pieces on the piano in an ice-cream parlor in Washington, and after that formed his own jazz group. In 1923 he came to New York where he soon thereafter formed a jazz band which performed at the Kentucky Club in Harlem. Discovered by Irving Mills, the publisher, Ellington was booked for the Cotton Club where he remained several years and established his fame as an outstanding exponent of real jazz—as pianist, conductor of his orchestra, composer, and arranger. He has since joined the all-time greats of jazz music, acclaimed in night clubs, on the Broadway stage and Hollywood screen, over the radio, on records, and in triumphant tours throughout the music world.

As a composer Ellington is famous for his popular songs ("Mood Indigo," "Sophisticated Lady" and so forth) and short instrumental jazz pieces (*Black and Tan Fantasy, Creole Rhapsody, East St. Louis Toodle-oo,* etc.) All this falls within the province of either popular music or jazz, and for this reason cannot be considered here.

Ellington has also produced a rich repertory of larger works for orchestra which have a place in the permanent library of semi-classical music in the same way that Gershwin's larger works do. Skilfully utilizing the fullest resources of jazz techniques, styles, and idioms, Ellington has created in these larger works an authentically American music. He himself prefers to consider many of these works as "Negro music" rather than jazz; nevertheless, in their blues harmonies, jazz colorations, and melodic and rhythmic techniques these works represented jazz music at its very best.

Perhaps the most distinguished of these symphonic-jazz works is *Black, Brown and Beige,* an extended work which Ellington introduced with his orchestra in Carnegie Hall, New York, in 1943, and which he described as a "tonal parallel of the Negro in America." The first movement, "Black," is a musical picture of the Negro at work, singing at his labors on the docks and levees in the slavery period before the Civil War. An alto saxophone solo brings on a plangent Spiritual, "Come Sunday." The second movement, "Brown," represents the wars in which Negroes have participated. A tenor solo sings an eloquent blues of the unsettled condition of the Negro after the Civil War. The contemporary Negro is the inspiration for the finale, "Beige," utilizing jazz idioms and styles in portraying the period of the Twenties, Thirties and Forties. Many facets of Negro life are drawn in brief musical episodes, including the Negro church and school, and the Negro's aspiration towards sophistication. The work ends on a patriotic note, prophesying that the Negro's place in the American way of life is secure.

Georges Enesco

GEORGES ENESCO was born in Liveni, Rumania, on August 19, 1881. He studied the violin at the Conservatories of Vienna and Paris, winning highest honors in both places. Following the completion of his studies in 1899, he launched a successful career both as concert violinist and as composer. For several years he was the court violinist to the Queen of Rumania, besides making outstandingly successful appearances on the concert stage throughout Europe. His debut as composer took place in Paris before his sixteenth birthday, with a concert devoted entirely to this own works. Success came in 1901 with his *Rumanian Rhapsody No. 1.* Enesco also distinguished himself as a conductor. When he made his American debut—on January 2, 1923 with the Philadelphia Orchestra in New York City—it was in the triple role of violinist, conductor, and composer. After World War I, Enesco divided his residence between Paris and his native Rumania while touring the music world. He made his last American appearance in 1950 on the occasion of the 60th anniversary of his debut as violinist; once again he appeared in the triple role of violinist, conductor and composer. He suffered a stroke in Paris in July 1954 and died there on May 4, 1955. After his death, his native village, and a street in Bucharest, were named after him.

Enesco was Rumania's foremost twentieth-century composer. His major compositions range freely over several different styles from nationalism, to neo-classicism, to ultra-modernism. But the works with which he first gained world fame, and which have since had the widest circulation, are those in a national Rumanian style, with Oriental-like melodies and propulsive rhythms all modeled after the exotic folk songs and dances of the Rumanian gypsies.

In such a style are his two Rumanian rhapsodies for orchestra: No. 1 in A major, op. 11, no. 1 (1901); No. 2 in D major, op. 11, no. 2 (1902). The first rhapsody is the one played more often. It opens with a languorous subject for clarinet which is soon assumed by other woodwind, then by the strings and after that (in a quickened tempo) by the full orchestra. A passionate gypsy tune follows in the strings; and this is succeeded by an abandoned dance melody in first violins and the woodwind, and an Oriental-type improvisation in solo flute. Now the mood becomes more frenetic, with a rapid succession of whirling folk-dance tunes and rhythms that are carried to a breathtaking climax. Relaxation finally comes with a gentle Oriental melody in clarinet, but this is only a passing phase. The rhapsody ends in a renewed outburst of vitality.

In comparison to the first, the second rhapsody is an emotionally reserved piece of music. After a solemn declaration by the strings, there comes an equally sober and restrained folk song in the strings. The dark mood thus projected becomes further intensified with a theme for English horn against tremolo strings and continues throughout most of the rhapsody, except for a brief interpolation of a vigorous dance melody by the solo viola.

Leo Fall

❧❧ ❦❦

LEO FALL was born in Olmuetz, Austria, on February 2, 1873. The son of a military bandmaster, he early received music instruction from his father. Then, after attending the Vienna Conservatory, he conducted theater orchestras in Berlin, Hamburg, and Cologne. An opera, *Paroli,* was unsuccessfully produced in Berlin before Fall settled permanently in Vienna to devote himself to the writing of those charming operettas in an abundantly lyric vein and graceful, sophisticated manner which the Austrian capital favored. His greatest successes were *The Dollar Princess* in 1907, *The Rose of Stamboul (Die Rose von Stambul)* in 1916, and *Madame Pompadour* in 1923. He died in Vienna on September 15, 1925.

Fall's most famous operetta is *The Dollar Princess (Die Dollarprinzessin)*, selections from which are often given on salon programs. *The Dollar Princess*—book by A. M. Willner and F. Gruenbaum based upon a comedy by Gatti-Trotha—was introduced in Vienna on November 2, 1907. Its first American performance took place on September 6, 1909 at the Knickerbocker Theater in an adaptation by George Grossmith, Jr. Some songs by Jerome Kern were interpolated into the New York production. The "dollar princess" is the heroine of the operetta: Alice Couder, pampered daughter of a New York coal magnate who goes in pursuit of Freddy. When at a lavish party at the Couder mansion she brazenly announces her intention of marrying Freddy without previously consulting him, he leaves her in disgust, and goes off to Canada where he becomes a successful business man. He cannot forget Alice, however. He brings the Couders to Canada on a pretext of discussing with the father a business deal, when he confesses his love to Alice, who no longer is brazen or arrogant.

A Viennese operetta must by necessity have a major waltz number, and *The Dollar Princess* is no exception; *"Will sie dann lieben treu und heiss"* from Act 1, is the most important melody of the operetta. When other selections from this operetta are given they invariably include also the lilting title song from Act 2, and the seductive little duet *"Wir tanzen Ringelreih'n hin einmal und her."*

Manuel de Falla

❧❧ ☙☙

MANUEL DE FALLA, Spain's most significant twentieth-century composer, was born in Cádiz on November 23, 1876. After studying music with private teachers in his native city, and with J. Tragó and Felipe Pedrell in Madrid, he completed in 1905 *La Vida breve,* a one-act opera that received first prize in a competition for native Spanish operas sponsored by the Academia de Bellas Artes. From 1907 to 1914 he lived in Paris where he absorbed French musical influences and became a friend of Debussy and Ravel. In 1914 he was back in his native land; from 1921 to 1939 he lived a retiring existence in Granada, devoting himself to serious composition. He left his native land in 1939 because of his disenchantment with the Franco regime which he had originally favored. Until his death on November 14, 1946, he lived in seclusion in Alta Gracia, in the province of Córdoba, in Argentina.

Falla's art is deeply embedded in the soil of Spanish folk songs and dance. His major works, which number a mere handful, are all evocations of the spirit of Spain in music which, though never a direct quotation from Spanish sources, is nevertheless Spanish to the core in details of melody, harmony, and rhythm. His principal works include a harpsichord concerto, *Nights in the Gardens of Spain* (*Noches en los jardines de España*) for piano and orchestra, the ballet *El Amor brujo,* and the opera *The Three-Cornered Hat* (*El sombrero de tres picos*).

In Falla's most effective national idiom are two popular Spanish dances. The *Ritual Fire Dance* (*Danza ritual del fuego*) is the seventh section from the ballet, *El Amor brujo* (1915). Trills with the searing intensity of hot flame lead into a languorous Spanish melody for the oboe, behind which moves an irresistible rhythm. This is followed by a second subject more intense in mood, loudly proclaimed by unison horns and after that repeated quietly by muted trumpets. Throughout, this dance has an almost savage ferocity, the music continually punctuated by piercing chords; the dance is finally brought to a frenetic conclusion. The composer himself made a highly effective transcription of this dance for solo piano, and Gregor Piatigorsky for cello and piano.

The *Spanish Dance No. 1* comes from the second act of the opera, *La Vida breve,* with which Falla first achieved recognition. An impulsive rhythmic opening serves as the background for a bold and sensual gypsy melody for horns and strings. The piece ends with rich chords for full orchestra. Fritz Kreisler made a fine transcription of this dance for violin and piano.

Gabriel Fauré

GABRIEL-URBAIN FAURÉ was born in Pamiers, France, on May 12, 1845. His music study took place in Paris with Niedermeyer and Saint-Saëns. After that he served as organist in Rennes and Paris, and held the important post of organist at the Madeleine Church in Paris from 1896 on. In 1896 he also became professor of composition at the Paris Conservatory where, from 1905 until 1920, he was director. In 1909 he was elected member of the Académie des Beaux Arts, and in 1910 made Commander of the Legion of Honor. In the last years of his life he suffered from deafness. He died in Paris on November 4, 1924.

Fauré was one of France's major composers, creator of a considerable library of piano and chamber music as well as works for symphony orchestra which included *Pelleas and Melisande,* a suite (1898) and the *Ballade* for piano and orchestra (1881). His music is filled with classic beauty, serenity, and a most delicate sensibility and thus makes an appeal only to a highly cultivated music lover. But a few of his works have such melodic charm and appealing moods that they cannot fail to cast a spell even on the untrained listener.

Après un rêve is a song, the first in a set of three published as op. 7 (1885), lyrics by Romain Bussine. Exquisite in its sensitive lyricism, this melody has become popular in many transcriptions, some for orchestra, one for violin and piano by Mischa Elman, and another for cello and piano by Pablo Casals.

Dolly (1893–1896) is a suite of six pieces for children which the composer originally wrote as a piano duet for Dolly Bardac, daughter of a woman who later became Debussy's wife. Henri Rabaud orchestrated this suite in 1906, and it was first performed in connection with a ballet staged at the Théâtre des Arts in Paris. In this music the composer looks back on childhood and the world of the child with poetic insight and occasionally a gentle sense of humor; in this respect this suite is not unlike *Children's Corner* of Debussy. It opens with "Berceuse," a gentle melody for the woodwind, which Jacques Thibaud arranged for violin and piano. This is followed by "Mi-a-ou," a little quartet for muted trumpets. A flute solo dominates *"Le Jardin de Dolly,"* while *"Kitty Valse"* is a light and vivacious waltz tune. In *"Tendresse"* the melody is first heard in strings. A tranquil middle section presents the solo oboe above a harp accompaniment. The closing movement, *"Le Pas espagnol"* is gay and brilliant music that pays homage to Chabrier, composer of *España.*

The *Pavane,* for orchestra, op. 50 (1887) is music of stately, classic beauty over which hovers the Hellenic spirit so often found in Fauré's most significant works. Against an insistent rhythm, the flute offers the haunting refrain of the Pavane. This dance melody is soon shared by the other woodwind, after which it unfolds completely in violins and the woodwind, other strings providing a rhythmic pizzicato accompaniment. A transition in the strings then leads us back to the graceful mood and the gentle lyricism of the Pavane melody.

The same subdued and classic repose we find in the *Pavane* distinguishes another of Fauré's popular compositions, the *Sicilienne,* for cello and piano, op. 78 (1898). Transcriptions for orchestra of this composition are even more famous than the original version.

Friedrich Flotow

FRIEDRICH FREIHERR VON FLOTOW was born in Teutendorf, Mecklenburg, on April 26, 1812. He was descended from a family that traced its nobility back several centuries. After studying music in Paris with Anton Reicha and Johann Pixis between 1828 and 1830, he wrote his first opera, *Peter und Katharina*. Success came first with *Alessandro Stradella* introduced in Hamburg in 1844, and was solidified in 1847 with the opera by which he is still remembered, *Martha*. From 1856 to 1863 he was Intendant of the Schwerin Court Theater. He went into retirement in 1880 and died in Darmstadt, Germany, on January 24, 1883.

The ebullient melodies with which Flotow flooded his operas made him extremely popular in his day. This same joyous lyricism keeps the overtures to *Alessandro Stradella* and *Martha* fresh in the orchestral repertory.

Alessandro Stradella—introduced in Hamburg on December 30, 1844 —was based on a romantic episode in the life of a 17th century opera composer; the libretto was by Wilhelm Friedrich. Stradella elopes with Leonora, whose guardian hires assassins to kill the composer. But Stradella's singing has such an effect on the assassins that they are incapable of murdering him. They let him go, and in the end the guardian himself is moved to forgive the composer and sanction his union with Leonora.

The overture opens with a solemn chant for the brass (Stradella's song in the last act). Vigorous transitional material leads to a robust song for full orchestra which is soon repeated expressively by the strings. A sprightly tune for strings (the bell chorus of the second act) is given prominent treatment and developed climactically. The mood now alternates between lightness and gaiety with an occasional intrusion of a strong dramatic effect.

Martha received its première in Vienna on November 25, 1847. The libretto, by Friedrich Wilhelm Riese was based on a ballet-pantomime by Vernoy de Saint-Georges. "Martha" is Lady Harriet in disguise as a servant girl for the sake of an amusing escapade; and the opera is concerned with her amatory adventures with Lionel, and that of her maid with Plunkett, at the Richmond fair. The complications that ensue when the men discover this deception are eventually happily resolved.

The overture begins with a slow introduction which leads into a *Larghetto* section where considerable attention is paid to the main melody of the quintet at the close of the third act, *"Mag der Himmel euch vergeben."* The tempo quickens as the lively country dances of the opera are presented. A crescendo reaches towards a fortissimo restatement of the main theme of the third-act quintet, and the overture ends with a brief and energetic coda.

Salon orchestras often present potpourris of this opera's main melodies. Two are always dominant in such potpourris. "The Last Rose of Summer" (*"Qui sola, vergin rosa"*)—an aria sung by the heroine in the second act—is a melody familiar to all; it is not by Flotow, but from an old Irish song, "The Groves of Blarney," set to a poem by Thomas Moore. The second famous melody from *Martha* is the beautiful tenor aria from the third act, *"M'Appari,"* in which Lionel expresses his grief when he feels he has lost Martha for good.

Stephen Foster

STEPHEN COLLINS FOSTER, America's foremost song composer, was born in Lawrenceville, near Pittsburgh, Pennsylvania on July 4, 1826. He received no formal musical training. *Tioga Waltz*, in 1841, was his first piece of music to get performed. About a year after that, Foster published his first song, "Open Thy Lattice, Love." His initial success came with "Oh, Susanna!" for which he received only $100. But "Oh, Susanna!" became so popular soon after its publication in 1848 that it became the theme song (with improvised lyrics) of the Forty Niners on their way to California. Beginning with 1848 he wrote songs for Ed Christy's Ministrels—at first allowing some of them to appear as Christy's own creations. It was within the context of the minstrel show that such permanent Foster favorites as "Camptown Races" and "Old Folks at Home" were first performed. Both songs were outstandingly successful and, because of a favorable contractual arrangement with a New York publisher, Foster was earning handsome royalties. Now feeling financially secure, Foster married Jane Denny McDowell in 1850, a relationship that was unhappy almost from the beginning. In 1860 Foster came to New York with the hope of further-ing his career as a composer. But by now he was virtually forgotten by the public, and publishers paid him only a pittance for his last songs, many of them mostly hack pieces. Always disposed towards alcohol,

Foster now became a habitual drunkard, living in the most abject poverty in a miserable room on the Bowery. He died at Bellevue Hospital on January 13, 1864.

Foster was the composer of numerous songs which in various orchestral arrangements are basic to the repertory of every salon or pop orchestra. His greatest songs were inspired by the Negro; they are the eloquent expressions of Northern sentiment about slavery in the South. Foster's most famous Negro songs are: "Old Folks at Home" (or "Swanee River"), "Massa's in de Cold, Cold Ground," "My Old Kentucky Home," and "Ol' Black Joe."

When Foster first wrote "Old Folks at Home" his inspiration was an obscure Florida River by the name of "Pedee." But while writing his song he thought "Pedee" not sufficiently euphonious for his purpose. He went to a map of Florida to find another river, came upon "Suwanee" which he contracted to "Swanee."

Foster was also successful in the writing of sentimental ballads. Here his most important songs were "Jeanie With the Light Brown Hair" (written for and about his wife), and "Beautiful Dreamer."

Besides orchestral adaptations of individual songs, Foster's music is represented on orchestral programs by skilful suites, or ingenious symphonic transcriptions of individual songs, by other composers. Arcady Dubensky's *Stephen Foster Suite* is discussed in the section on Dubensky, and Lucien Caillet's *Fantasia and Fugue on "Oh, Susanna!"* in the Caillet section. Other composers to make symphonic use of Foster's melodies are: Mario Castelnuovo-Tedesco (*Humoresques on Foster Themes*); Morton Guild (*Foster Gallery*); and Alan Shulman (*Oh, Susanna!*).

Rudolf Friml

RUDOLF FRIML was born in Prague, Czechoslovakia, on December 7, 1879. He received his musical training at the Prague Conservatory, after which he toured Europe and America as assisting artist and accompanist for Jan Kubelik, the noted violin virtuoso. In 1906, Friml established permanent residence in the United States, making several appearances as concert pianist, twice in the performance of his own Concerto in B-flat. He now published piano pieces, instrumental numbers, and songs which attracted the interest of two publishers, Gus Schirmer and Max Dreyfus. When, in 1912, Victor Herbert stepped out of an assignment to write the music for the operetta *The Firefly*, both Schirmer and Dreyfus recommended Friml as his replacement. *The Firefly* made Friml famous. Until 1934 he continued writing music for the Broadway stage, achieving further triumphs with *Rose Marie* in 1924, *The Vagabond King* in 1925, and *The Three Musketeers* in 1928. After 1934, Friml concentrated his activity on motion pictures in Hollywood.

Friml belongs with those Broadway composers of the early 20th century whose domain was the operetta modelled after German and Austrian patterns. As long as the operetta was popular on the Broadway stage, Friml remained a favorite, for his ingratiating melodies, pleasing sentimentality, winning charm, and strong romantic flair were in the best traditions of the operetta theater. But when the vogue for operettas died down and the call came for American musicals with native settings and characterizations, realistic approaches, and a greater cohesion between text and music, Friml's day was over. He has produced nothing of significance since the middle 1930's, and very little of anything else. But the music he wrote for his best operettas has never lost its appeal.

The Firefly, book and lyrics by Otto Harbach, was introduced in New York on December 2, 1912. The plot concerned a little Italian street singer by the name of Nina (enchantingly played by Emma Trentini). She disguises herself as a boy to get a job aboard a yacht bound for Bermuda, and is first accused and then cleared of the charge of being a pickpocket. Many years later she reappears as a famous prima donna when she is finally able to win the wealthy young man with whom she had fallen in love while working on the yacht.

Orchestral potpourris from *The Firefly* always include three of the songs Emma Trentini helped to make famous: "Giannina Mia," "The Dawn of Love" and "Love is Like a Firefly." The melodious duet, "Sympathy," is also popular.

The Donkey Serenade, now regarded as one of the favorites from *The Firefly* score, was not in the original operetta when it was produced on Broadway. Friml wrote it in collaboration with Herbert

Stothart for the motion picture adaptation of the operetta released in 1937 and starring Jeanette MacDonald and Allan Jones. This appealing Spanish-type melody is set against an intriguing rhythm suggesting the jogging movement of a donkey; this rhythm precedes and closes the number, which has become as celebrated in an instrumental version as it is as a song with lyrics by Chet Forrest and Bob White.

Rose Marie, book and lyrics by Otto Harbach and Oscar Hammerstein II, came to Broadway on September 2, 1924 where it remained for more than a year. The rest of the country became acquainted with this lovable operetta at that time by means of four road companies. The setting is the Canadian Rockies, and the love interest involves Rose Marie and Jim, the latter falsely accused of murder. The Canadian Mounted Police, headed by Sergeant Malone, help to clear Jim and to bring the love affair of Rose Marie and Jim to a happy resolution. Selections in orchestral adaptations most often heard from this operetta include two of Friml's most famous songs, the title number and "Indian Love Call"; a third delightful song was found in "Totem Tom Tom." *Rose Marie* was adapted for motion pictures three times, once in a silent version.

The Vagabond King had for its central character the French vagabond poet of the 15th century, François Villon, who is made king for a day. This musical was based on the romance of J. H. McCarthy, *If I Were King,* adapted by Brian Hooker. *The Vagabond King,* which opened on September 21, 1925, was one of Friml's greatest successes, mainly because of such rousing numbers as "The Song of the Vagabonds," the caressing waltz melody "Waltz Huguette," and the love song "Only a Rose," all often heard in orchestral adaptations. *The Vagabond King* was made into motion pictures twice, most recently in 1956 starring Kathyrn Grayson and Oreste.

Julius Fučík

❧❧ ☙☙

JULIUS FUČÍK was born in Prague, Czechoslovakia, on July 18, 1872. He was a pupil of Antonin Dvořák in composition. After playing the bassoon in the German Opera in Prague in 1893, he became band-master of the 86th and 92nd Austrian Regiments in which he won re-nown throughout Europe. He died in Leitmeritz, Czechoslovakia, on September 25, 1916. Fučík wrote numerous dance pieces and marches for band. The most popular of these is the stirring march, *Entrance of the Gladiators,* which became popular throughout the world and is still frequently played by salon orchestras as well as bands.

Sir Edward German

❧❧ ☙☙

SIR EDWARD GERMAN was born Edward German Jones in Whitchurch, England, on February 17, 1862. He attended the Royal Academy of Music in London where, in 1895, he was elected Fellow. Meanwhile, in 1888–1889 he became the musical director of the Globe Theater in London. The incidental music he wrote there that year for Richard Mansfield's production of *Richard III* proved so popular that Sir Henry Irving commissioned him to write similar music for his own presentation of *Henry VIII.* German subsequently wrote incidental music for many other plays including *Romeo and Juliet* (1895), *As You Like It* (1896), *Much Ado About Nothing* (1898) and *Nell Gwynn* (1900). He also produced a considerable amount of concert music, including two symphonies and various suites, tone poems, rhapsodies, and a march and hymn for the Coronation of George V in 1911. German was knighted in 1928, and in 1934 he received the Gold Medal of the Royal Philharmonic Society. He died in London on November 11, 1936.

German is most famous for his incidental music for the stage. He combined a graceful lyricism with a consummate skill in orchestration. He also possessed to a remarkable degree the capacity of simulating the archaic idioms of old English music of the Tudor and Stuart periods. Thus the greatest charm of his writing lies in its subtle atmospheric recreation of a bygone era; but a lightness of touch and freshness of material are never sacrificed.

Of his incidental music perhaps the most famous is that for Shakespeare's *Henry VIII,* introduced at the Lyceum Theater in London in 1892 in Sir Henry Irving's production. German's complete score consists of an overture, five entr'actes, a setting of the song "Orpheus and his Lute" and other pieces. But what remain popular are three delightful old English dances from the first act; the style and spirit of old English music are here reproduced with extraordinary effect. The three are: "Morris Dance," "Shepherd's Dance," and "Torch Dance."

The best sections of his incidental music to Anthony Hope's *Nell Gwynn,* produced at the Prince of Wales Theater in 1900, also are revivals of old English dances: "Country Dance," "Merrymaker's Dance," and "Pastoral Dance." Other delightful dances, often in an old English folk style, are found in his incidental music to *As You Like It* ("Children's Dance," "Rustic Dance," and "Woodland Dance") and *Romeo and Juliet* ("Pavane" and "Torch Dance").

German also wrote several operettas, the most famous being *Merrie England,* text by Basil Hood, first performed at the Savoy Theater in London on April 2, 1902. The setting is Elizabethan England, and the plot involves the love affair of Sir Walter Raleigh and the Queen's Maid of Honor which upsets Queen Elizabeth since she herself has designs on Sir Walter. German's score is filled with the most delightful old world jigs, country dances, glees, and melodies imitating the style of old-time madrigals. In addition, there is here an impressive patriotic song ("The Yeomen of England"), Queen Elizabeth's effective air ("O Peaceful England"), a rousing drinking song by Sir Walter Raleigh, a poignant ballad by the Maid of Honor, and an equally moving love duet by the Maid of Honor and Sir Walter Raleigh. Because of its effective music, rich with English flavors, *Merrie England* has survived as one of the most popular

English operettas of the 20th century, and has often been revived in London.

Among German's many concert works for orchestra one of the most famous is the *Welsh Rhapsody* (1902). This is a skilful symphonic adaptation of Welsh tunes, the last of which ("Men of Larech") is utilized by the composer to bring his rhapsody to a powerful culmination. The other Welsh folk songs used earlier by the composer in this rhapsody are "Loudly Proclaim O'er Land and Sea," "Hunting the Hare," "Bells of Aberdorry" and "David of the White Rock."

George Gershwin

❧❧ ☙☙

GEORGE GERSHWIN was born in Brooklyn, New York on September 26, 1898. Though he received serious musical training in piano from Charles Hambitzer, and in harmony and theory from Edward Kilenyi, he early set his sights on popular rather than serious music. When he was fifteen he found a job as song plugger and staff pianist in Tin Pan Alley where he soon began writing songs. The first to get published was "When You Want 'Em You Can't Get 'Em" in 1916; in the same year another of his songs, "The Making of a Girl" appeared for the first time on the Broadway stage, in *The Passing Show of 1916*. Gershwin's first complete score for Broadway was *La, La, Lucille,* and his first smash song hit was "Swanee," both in 1919. Between 1920 and 1924 Gershwin wrote the music for five editions of the George White *Scandals* where he first demonstrated his exceptional creative gifts; his most famous songs for the *Scandals* were "I'll Build a Stairway to Paradise" and "Somebody Loves Me." For one of the editions of the *Scandals* he also wrote a one-act Negro opera to a libretto by Buddy De Sylva—originally called *Blue Monday* but later retitled *135th Street.*

Late in 1923, Paul Whiteman, the orchestra leader, commissioned

Gershwin to write a symphonic work in a jazz style for a concert Whiteman was planning for Aeolian Hall, in New York. That jazz composition—introduced on February 12, 1924—was the *Rhapsody in Blue* with
which Gershwin achieved world renown, and which once and for all
established the jazz idiom and jazz techniques as significant material for
serious musical deployment. From then on, until the end of his life,
Gershwin continued to write concert music in a popular style—growing
all the time in technical assurance, in the command of jazz materials,
and in the inventiveness of his melodic, rhythmic, and harmonic writing. In the eyes of the world he assumed a position of first significance
among American composers. For the symphony orchestra he wrote the
Piano Concerto in F, *An American in Paris, Cuban Overture, Variations on I Got Rhythm,* and the *Second Rhapsody;* for solo piano, the
three piano preludes; for the stage his monumental folk opera, *Porgy
and Bess.*

While devoting himself to the concert field, Gershwin did not neglect
the popular Broadway theater. He produced a library of remarkable
songs for such productions as *Lady Be Good* (1924), *Oh Kay!* (1926),
Funny Face (1927), and *Girl Crazy* (1930). The best of these included
"Fascinating Rhythm," "Lady Be Good," "Someone to Watch Over
Me," "Clap Yo' Hands," " 'S Wonderful," "I Got Rhythm," "Embrace-
able You," and "But Not for Me." The lyrics for these and other
Gershwin song classics were written by his brother, Ira.

In 1930 Gershwin revealed a fresh bent for mockery and satire, together with a new skill for more spacious musical writing than that
required for a song, in *Strike Up the Band,* a satire on war. These qualities in Gershwin's music came to full ripeness in 1931 with the political
satire *Of Thee I Sing!,* the first musical ever to win the Pulitzer Prize
for drama.

In 1931, Gershwin wrote his first original score for motion pictures,
Delicious. When he returned to Hollywood in 1936 he settled there
permanently and wrote the music for several delightful screen musicals,
among these being *Damsel in Distress, Shall We Dance,* and *The Goldwyn Follies.* The songs he wrote for the last-named revue (they included
"Love Walked In" and "Love Is Here to Stay") were the last pieces of
music he was destined to write. He died in Hollywood, California on
July 11, 1937, a victim of a cystic tumor on the right temporal lobe of
the brain. His screen biography, *Rhapsody in Blue,* was produced in
1945. In 1951, the screen musical, *An American in Paris* (whose score
included several of Gershwin's songs as well as the tone poem that gave

this picture its title) received the Academy Award as the best picture of the year. *Porgy and Bess* was adapted for motion pictures, in a Samuel Goldwyn production, in 1959.

It would be difficult to overestimate Gershwin's importance in American music. To the popular song he brought the technical skill of a consummate musician, endowing it with a rhythmic, melodic and harmonic language it had rarely before known. By that process he often lifted it to the status of true art. To serious music he contributed the vitality and the spirit—as well as the techniques and idioms—of American popular music; serious musicians throughout the world were inspired by his example to create a serious musical art out of the materials of American popular music. Since his untimely death, his artistic stature has grown in all parts of the civilized world. There will be few today to deny him a place of honor among America's foremost composers.

An American in Paris is a tone poem for symphony orchestra inspired by a European vacation in 1928. It received its world première in New York on December 13, 1928, Walter Damrosch conducting the New York Philharmonic Orchestra. In this music the composer describes the nostalgia of an American tourist for home, and his experiences as he strolls along the boulevards of Paris. It opens with a "walking theme," a sprightly little tune for strings and oboe; our American is beginning his stroll. As he walks he hears the piercing warnings of taxi horns: Gershwin's score calls for the use of actual Parisian taxi horns. The American passes a café, and stops for a moment to listen to the sounds of a music-hall melody, presented by the trombones. Then he resumes his stroll, as a second walking subject is heard in the clarinet. A solo violin (which Deems Taylor interpreted as a young lady accosting our tourist!) provides a transition to two main melodies in both of which the American's growing feeling of homesickness finds apt expression. The first is a blues melody for muted trumpets; the second a Charleston melody for two trumpets. The blues melody receives climactic treatment in full orchestra. After a hasty recollection of the second walking theme, the composition comes to a vigorous conclusion. As Mr. Taylor goes on to explain, the tourist now decides "to make a night of it. It will be great to get home, but meanwhile, this is Paris!"

The Concerto in F, for piano and orchestra, was the immediate consequence of Gershwin's phenomenal success with the *Rhapsody in Blue*. The Concerto was commissioned in 1925 by the New York Symphony Society and its conductor, Walter Damrosch. They introduced it in Carnegie Hall, on December 3, 1925, with the composer as soloist. This work, like its eminent predecessor, is in a jazz style; but unlike the first version of the *Rhapsody in Blue* it boasts Gershwin's own orchestration. (From this time on Gershwin would always prepare his own orchestrations for his serious concert music.) There are three movements. The first (*Allegro*) begins with a Charleston theme shared by the woodwind and timpani. The main body of this movement is given over to a spicy jazz tune first heard in the bassoon and after that in full orchestra; to a tender melody for solo piano; and to a lilting waltz for strings with decorative treatment by the piano. The second movement (*Andante con moto*) is lyrical throughout, and at times subtly atmospheric and poetic. Muted trumpet, against harmonies provided by three clarinets, set the romantic stage for the felicitous lyrical thoughts that ensue: a brisk, jazzy, strikingly rhythmic idea for the piano; and a broad, sensual melody for strings. This movement ends in the same sensitive atmospheric mood with which it began. In the finale (*Allegro con brio*) dynamic forces are released. Main themes from the first two movements are recalled with a particularly effective recapitulation of the second theme of the first movement in the strings.

The *Cuban Overture* was written in 1932 after a brief visit to Havana and was introduced at the Lewisohn Stadium in New York, Albert Coates conducting, on August 16, 1932. This is a concert overture for orchestra utilizing native percussion Cuban instruments. The work has three sections played without interruption. The first consists of two melodies, a Cuban theme in strings followed by a second lyrical subject which is placed against the contrapuntal background of fragments from the first Cuban theme. A solo clarinet cadenza leads to the middle section which is a two-voice canon. The ensuing finale makes considerable use of earlier thematic material and ends with an electrifying presentation of a fully projected rumba melody in which prominent use is made of Cuban percussion instruments (cuban stick, bondo, gourd, and maracas).

The folk opera, *Porgy and Bess,* was Gershwin's last work in the field of serious music—and his greatest. It took Gershwin over two years to write his opera, a period during which he spent some time in the opera's setting of Charleston, South Carolina, absorbing not only local color but also native Negro music whose style he skilfully assimilated into his own writing. He completed his opera in the summer of 1935; on September 30 its world première took place in Boston; and on October 10, it began its New York run. It cannot be said that either critics or audiences were fully aware at the time that they were hearing a masterwork. Some of the Boston and New York scribes found things to admire in the opera, but most of them were highly critical. Olin Downes said "it does not utilize all the resources of the operatic composer or pierce very often to the depths of the pathetic drama." Lawrence Gilman found Gershwin's emphasis on the popular element a disturbing blemish while Viril Thomson did not hesitate at the time to refer to it as "a fake." The run of 124 performances in New York (followed by a three-month tour) represented a box-office failure.

Gershwin himself remained convinced he had written a work of first importance, but regrettably he did not live to see his faith in his opera justified beyond his wildest hopes or aspirations. Revived in New York in 1941 it had an eight-month run, the longest of any revival in Broadway history. More important still, many critics revised earlier estimates. Virgil Thomson now spoke of it as "a beautiful piece of music and a deeply moving play for the lyric theater." Olin Downes said that Gershwin had here "taken a substantial step, and advanced the cause of native opera." The New York Music Critics Circle singled it out as the most important musical revival of that season.

But still greater triumphs awaited the opera. In 1952, a Negro cast toured Europe under the auspices of the State Department. Before that tour was over, several years later, the opera had been heard throughout Europe, the Near East, in countries behind the Iron Curtain, the Soviet Union and Latin America. Everywhere it enjoyed acclaim realized by few contemporary operas anywhere. There were not many dissenting voices in the universal judgment that *Porgy and Bess* was one of the most significant operas of the twentieth century, and certainly one of the most popular. And its popularity was further enhanced by the stunning production given it by Samuel Goldwyn in motion pictures in 1959.

The text of the opera was based on the play *Porgy*, by Dorothy and Du Bose Heyward, produced by the Theater Guild in New York in 1927, which in turn had been adapted from Du Bose Heyward's novel of the same name. The opera text and lyrics were written by Du Bose and Dorothy Heyward with several additional lyrics by Ira Gershwin. The tragic love affair of the cripple, Porgy, and Bess, a lady of easy virtue, is set in the Negro tenement, Catfish Row, in Charleston, South Carolina. Porgy has found true happiness with Bess for the first time in his life. When Crown, Bess' old sweetheart returns to claim her, Porgy kills him but manages to elude the law after having been detained a while. Upon returning to Catfish Row he discovers that his Bess had succumbed to the lure of dope, and the gay life in New York offered her by Sportin' Life. Heartbroken, Porgy jumps in his goat cart to follow Bess to New York and try to bring her back.

The main melodic sections of the opera have provided the material for several delightful suites. The most famous is *A Symphonic Picture* by Robert Russell Bennett, commissioned by Fritz Reiner, the conductor of the Pittsburgh Symphony in 1942. Bennett created out of the score an integrated tone poem faithful to Gershwin's own harmonic and orchestral intentions. The tone poem (or suite) is made up of the following sequences in the order of their appearance: Scene of Catfish Row with the peddler's calls; Opening Act II; "Summertime" and Opening of Act I; "I Got Plenty of Nuttin' "; Storm Music; "Bess, You Is My Woman Now"; "It Ain't Necessarily So" and the finale, "Oh Lawd I'm On My Way."

George Gershwin himself prepared an orchestral suite from his opera score in 1936, and conducted it in performances with several major American orchestras in 1936–1937. This manuscript, long forgotten, was found in the library of Ira Gershwin, and was revived in 1959 by Maurice Abravanel and the Utah Symphony. Now named *Catfish Row*, to distinguish it from other suites prepared by other musicians, it had five sections: "Catfish Row," "Porgy Sings," "Fugue," "Hurricane," and "Good Morning, Brother."

Beryl Rubinstein transcribed five of the principal melodies from the opera for piano, and Jascha Heifetz for violin and piano.

The three piano *Preludes* are famous not only in their original version but also in transcriptions for symphony orchestra. The first prelude, in B-flat major, is rhythmically exciting, highlighting the basic elements of the tango and the Charleston. The second, in C-sharp minor, is the most famous of the set. This is an eloquent three-part blues melody. The concluding prelude, in E-flat major, once again like the first one has greater rhythmic than melodic interest, a lively expression of uninhibited good feelings. Besides transcriptions for orchestra by Roy Bargy, Gregory Stone and several others, these preludes have been adapted for violin and piano by Heifetz, for trumpet and piano by Gregory Stone, and for saxophone and piano by Sigurd Rascher.

The *Rhapsody in Blue* was Gershwin's first work for symphony orchestra and it is the composition with which he first won fame, fortune, and artistic significance. It was commissioned by Paul Whiteman for an all-American music concert planned by that bandleader for Aeolian Hall, New York, on February 12, 1924. With the composer at the piano, the *Rhapsody* appeared as the tenth and penultimate number of a long program, but it was the work that gave Whiteman's concert its main interest and significance. The critics the following day were divided in their opinion. On the one hand, Henry T. Finck considered it superior to the music of Schoenberg and Milhaud; equally high words of praise came from Gilbert W. Gabriel, William J. Henderson, Olin Downes, Deems Taylor, and Carl van Vechten. In the opposite camp stood Pitts Sanborn and Lawrence Gilman who described the work as "meaningless repetition" and "trite, feeble, and conventional."

But the opposing opinions notwithstanding, the *Rhapsody in Blue* immediately became one of the most famous pieces of serious music by an American. It was transcribed for every possible instrument or groups of instruments; it was adapted several times for ballet; it was used in a motion picture. Royalties from the sale of sheet music and records brought in a fortune. Through the years it has never lost its popularity; it is still one of the most frequently performed American symphonic works.

Its prime significance rests in the fact that it decisively proved that it was possible to produce good music within ambitious structures utilizing idioms and techniques of American jazz. The *Rhapsody in Blue* was by no means the first composition to do so; it was preceded by works by Erik Satie, Stravinsky, and Milhaud among others. But due to its enormous popular appeal it was the most influential composition of all in convincing the world's foremost composers that jazz could be used with serious intent. Undoubtedly it was largely as a result of the triumph of the *Rhapsody in Blue* that world-famous composers like William Walton, Constant Lambert, Maurice Ravel, Kurt Weill and Paul Hindemith among many others produced serious jazz music.

Much has been said about its diffuseness of structure, and the inept way its material is developed. But for all its faults, the *Rhapsody in Blue* remains a vital, dynamic and at times an inspired piece of music. It is filled with wonderful lyricism; its rhythmic cogency is irresistible; its identity is completely American.

The work opened with an ascending seventeen-note slide by the clarinet which culminates in the saucy, first theme. A transition in the wind instrument leads to another brisk, jaunty idea for piano. After some development, and several ascending chords in the piano we get to the heart of the rhapsody and to one of the most famous melodies in all contemporary symphonic music: a spacious, rhapsodic song for the strings. The full orchestra repeats it. Two earlier themes are now briefly recalled, the first theme by the full orchestra, the second by the piano.

A brief, dramatic coda brings the rhapsody to an exciting conclusion.

For the Paul Whiteman concert of 1924, Ferde Grofé provided the orchestration from a two-piano version handed him by the composer. Gershwin later prepared his own orchestration, and it is this version that is now given by all the major symphonic organizations.

The *Second Rhapsody* for orchestra succeeded the more popular *Rhapsody in Blue* by eight years; it was first performed by the Boston Symphony under Koussevitzky on January 29, 1932. Gershwin originally called this work *Rhapsody in Rivets* because the opening measures present a strongly rhythmic subject in solo piano suggesting riveting. This "rivet theme" is then taken over by the full orchestra, after which we hear a rumba melody. These ideas are then developed. A piano cadenza brings on a spacious melody, first in strings, and then in brass. All this material is amplified before the rhapsody is swept to an exciting end.

This rhapsody was the outgrowth of a six-minute sequence written by the composer for the motion picture, *Delicious*. The sequence was intended to describe the sights and sounds of a city. In the picture only one of the six minutes of this music was retained, but Gershwin liked the rest of it well enough to expand it into a major symphonic work.

The *Variations on I Got Rhythm,* for piano and orchestra, was written for a tour of one-night stands made by Gershwin throughout the United States in all-Gershwin programs. Its first performance took place in Boston on January 14, 1934. The main subject is a famous Gershwin song, "I Got Rhythm" which Ethel Merman made famous in the musical comedy *Girl Crazy*. The symphonic work begins with a four-note ascending phrase from the first measure of the song's chorus, presented by solo clarinet. The theme is then taken over by solo piano and after that by full orchestra, after which the entire chorus is presented by the piano. In the ensuing variations the composer changes not only the basic structure of the song, melodically and rhythmically, but also its mood and feeling, traversing the gamut of emotion from melancholy to spirited gaiety.

Still another remarkably effective symphonic adaptation of "I Got Rhythm" was made by Morton Gould, and introduced by him with his orchestra over the CBS radio network in 1944.

Gershwin wrote two marches, both with satirical overtones, which are often given at "pop concerts." Each was meant for a musical comedy. "Strike Up the Band" comes from the musical comedy of the same name, produced on January 14, 1930 starring Clark and McCullough.

This was a stinging satire on war and international diplomacy, with America embroiled in a conflict with Switzerland over the issue of chocolates. The march, "Strike Up the Band," helps deflate some of the pomp and ceremony of all martial music.

"Wintergreen for President" comes from *Of Thee I Sing*, the epoch-making satire on politics in Washington, D.C., first produced on December 26, 1931. "Wintergreen for President" is the music accompanying a political torchlight parade whose illuminated signs read "Even Your Dog Loves Wintergreen" and "A Vote for Wintergreen Is a Vote for Wintergreen" and so on. The march music carries over the satirical implications of this procession by quoting such tunes as "Hail, Hail the Gang's All Here," "Tammany," "A Hot Time in the Old Town Tonight" and "Stars and Stripes Forever." This music even carries a hasty recollection of Irish and Jewish music to suggest that Wintergreen is a friend of both these people.

Gershwin's greatest songs are often performed in orchestral transcriptions at all-Gershwin concerts and other "pop performances," sometimes singly, and sometimes in various potpourris. Besides songs already mentioned in the first part of this section, Gershwin's greatest ones include the following: "Bidin' My Time" from *Girl Crazy;* "I've Got a Crush On You" from *Strike Up the Band;* "Let's Call the Whole Thing Off" from *Shall We Dance;* "Liza" from *Show Girl;* "The Man I Love," originally meant for *Lady Be Good* but never used there; "Mine" from *Let 'Em Eat Cake;* the title song from *Of Thee I Sing;* "Soon" from *Strike Up the Band;* "That Certain Feeling" from *Tip Toes;* and "They Can't Take That Away From Me" from *Shall We Dance.* Among those who have written orchestral medleys of Gershwin's songs are Nathan van Cleve, Fred von Epps, Claude Thornhill, David Broekman, Irving Brodsky, George B. Leeman, and Nathaniel Finston.

Henry F. Gilbert

❧❧ ❧❧

HENRY FRANKLIN BELKNAP GILBERT was born in Somerville, Massachusetts, on September 26, 1868. He attended the New England Conservatory, and studied composition privately with Edward MacDowell, before playing the violin in various theaters. For many years music was a secondary pursuit as he earned his living in a printing establishment, a real-estate agent, factory foreman, and finally an employee in a music-publishing firm. A hearing in Paris of Gustave Charpentier's opera, *Louise,* proved such an overpowering experience that it inspired him to devote himself henceforth to music alone. In 1902 he helped found in America the Wa-Wan Press which promoted nationalism in American music and published Gilbert's first works. In these a strong emphasis was placed by the composer upon American folk music and American folk idioms. In 1903 he wrote *Humoresque on Negro Minstrel Tunes.* After that came his famous *Comedy Overture on Negro Themes* (1905), the symphonic ballet *The Dance in Place Congo* (1906), the *Negro Rhapsody* (1913), and *Indian Sketches* (1921). Here native elements were skilfully fused into a style that was Romantic to produce music that remains appealing for its freshness and vitality. Towards the end of his life, Gilbert was an invalid. Nevertheless, in 1927, he traveled to Germany in a wheel-chair to attend a performance of his *Dance in Place Congo* at the Festival of the International Society for Contemporary Music in Frankfurt. He died in Cambridge, Massachusetts, on May 19, 1928.

The *Comedy Overture on Negro Themes* (1905) is one of Gilbert's most frequently performed compositions. It is made up of five sections played without interruption. The composer goes on to explain: "The first movement is light and humorous, the theme being made from two four-measure phrases taken from Charles L. Edwards' book *Bahama Songs and Stories.* . . . This is followed by a broader, and somewhat slower, phrase. I have here used the only complete Negro tune which occurs in the piece . . . formerly used as a working song by roustabouts and stevedores on the Mississippi River steamboats in the old days. . . . Next comes a fugue. The theme of this fugue consists of the first four measures of the Negro Spiritual 'Old Ship of Zion.' . . . It is given out by the brass instruments and interspersed with phrases from the roustabouts' song. . . . After this a short phrase of sixteen measures serves to reintroduce the comic element. There is a repetition of the first theme and considerable recapitulation, which leads finally to the development of a new ending or coda, and the piece ends in an orgy of jollity and ragtime."

Dance in Place Congo (1906) is both a ballet and a tone poem for orchestra. Its first version was a pantomime ballet, but soon thereafter the composer adapted his score into a composition for orchestra. The tone poem—describing the barbaric revels on a late Sunday afternoon of slaves in Place Congo, a section on the outskirts of New Orleans—opens in a dark mood which achieves a climax with an outcry in the orchestra. At this point a bamboula melody is heard in full orchestra. It is permitted to gain in intensity until it acquires barbaric ferocity. When the passions are spent, a beautiful romantic section unfolds, occasionally interrupted by a recall of the bamboula theme. Various Negro songs and dances are then presented over an insistent rhythm. The somber mood of the opening is brought back to conclude the composition.

The Indian Sketches for orchestra (1921) presents several facets of American-Indian life. "They are," explains the composer, "for the most part not musical pictures of definite incidents so much as they are musical mood pictures." There are six sections. The first, a prelude, is music of savage power. This is followed by the subjective music of the "Invocation," a prayer or supplication of the Great Spirit. "Song of the World" briefly develops a cry of the Kutenai Indians, and "Camp Dance" is a scherzo portraying the lighter side of Indian life. "Nocturne" is a romantic description of the dark forests alive with the distant sounds of birds and animals. The suite concludes with the "Snake Dance," suggested by a prayer dance for rain of the Hopi Indians in Arizona.

Don Gillis

🙠🙢 🙠🙢

D O N G I L L I S was born in Cameron, Missouri, on June 17, 1912. He was graduated from Christian University at Fort Worth, Texas in 1936, after having engaged in various musical activities including the direction of a band and a symphony orchestra, and the writing of two musical comedies produced at the University. Following the completion of his education he became a member of the faculty of Christian University and Southwest Baptist Seminary; served as a trombonist and arranger for a Fort Worth radio station; and played the trombone in the Fort Worth Symphony. In 1944 he became a producer for the National Broadcasting Company in New York, taking charge of many important programs including those of the NBC Symphony.

As a composer of symphonies and other orchestral compositions Gillis reveals a refreshing sense of humor as well as a delightful bent for whimsy, qualities which make some of his works ideal for programs of light music. He has often drawn inspiration and materials from American folk music and jazz, consistently producing music that combines sound musical values with sound entertainment. "My feeling," he has said, "is that music is for the people and the composer's final aim should be to reach them. And since the people whistle and sing, I should like them to whistle and sing my music." Thus Gillis aims for simplicity, sincere emotions, and sheer fun. "I have tried to write so that there will be a feeling of enjoyment in the fun of the thing."

Portrait of a Frontier Town, a suite for orchestra (1940), is a tuneful composition consisting of five short movements. The title of each of these provides the clue to the programmatic content of the music. The first, "Chamber of Commerce," portrays the activities of such an organization in a typical American town. "Where the West Begins" tells of the opening of the West through two significant musical subjects, the first for strings, and the second for oboe, flute, and clarinet. "Ranch House Party" is described in the score as "brightly—in a gay manner." A jovial melody first given by the full orchestra gives prominent attention to percussion instruments. This is followed by a mood picture,

"Prairie Sunset" in which the English horn, answered by the clarinet, presents the main melody. The suite concludes with "Main Street Saturday Night," in which gaiety and abandon alternate with suggestions of nostalgia.

Symphony No. 5½ (1947), is one of the composer's wittiest works which he himself subtitled as "a symphony for fun." It consists almost entirely of jazz melodies, some treated in burlesque fashion; the work also quotes some famous melodies in a facetious manner. The four movements have whimsical titles: "Perpetual Emotion," "Spiritual?", "Scherzophrenia" and "Conclusion."

Alberto Ginastera

ALBERTO GINASTERA was born in Buenos Aires, Argentina, on April 11, 1916. He was graduated with honors from the National Conservatory in his native city where, in 1953, he became professor. In 1946 he visited the United States remaining a year on a Guggenheim Fellowship. Ginastera's music combines musical elements native to Argentina with modern techniques and idioms, and includes ballets, chamber music, a *Pastoral Symphony* and other works for orchestra, and pieces for the piano.

The *Dances* from the ballet, *Estancia* (1941) is among his most popular works. The ballet, choreography by George Balanchine, was first introduced by the Ballet Caravan. It describes life on an "estancia," an Argentine ranch, tracing the activities of its principal character through a single day from dawn of one day to dawn of the next. The orchestral dances are rich in native melodies and rhythms, presenting the various dance sequences in "stylized version." Two dances are especially popular: "Dance of the Wheat" and "Malambo."

Alexander Glazunov

ᴥᴥᴥ ᴥᴥᴥ

ALEXANDER GLAZUNOV was born in St. Petersburg, Russia, on August 10, 1865. As a boy he studied music privately while attending a technical high school. At fifteen he became a pupil of Rimsky-Korsakov in harmony, counterpoint and orchestration. Such was his progress that only one year later he completed a gifted symphony which was performed in St. Petersburg in 1882 and acclaimed by several eminent Russian musicians. Between that year and 1900, Glazunov produced most of the works which won him renown not only in Russia but throughout the rest of the music world: symphonies, string quartets, numerous shorter orchestral works, and compositions in a lighter style. Here he was the traditionalist who placed reliance on palatable melodies, sound structures, and heartfelt emotion. For these reasons much of what he has written falls gracefully into the light-classic category. After 1914 he wrote little, nothing to add to his stature. Meanwhile he achieved renown first as professor then as director of the St. Petersburg Conservatory. He also made successful appearances as conductor following his debut at the Paris Exposition in 1899; his first appearance in the United States took place in Detroit on November 21, 1929. In 1928, Glazunov left his native land for good, and from then until his death on March 21, 1936 his home was in Paris.

The *Carnival Overture,* or *Carnaval,* op. 45 (1894) is a brilliant picture of a festival. It opens with a lively dance melody in violins and woodwind. This is followed by a more stately melody in woodwind and violins against a counter-melody in cellos and bassoons. A brief transition leads to the main body of the overture built out of two basic ideas. The first is a gay dance tune in flutes and clarinets; the second provides a measure of contrast through a more reflective subject for oboes, clarinets, horns, and cellos.

From the Middle Ages—a suite for orchestra, op. 79 (1902)—evokes the settings and backgrounds of the middle ages in four sections. The first is a "Prelude," portraying a castle by the sea, the home of two lovers. Death plays the violin in the second movement, a "Scherzo";

he urges the people to dance to his abandoned fiddling. In the third part, "Serenade," a troubadour sings his tune. The suite ends with "The Crusaders," in which soldiers are marching off to war, while priests chant a solemn blessing.

The original title of *Ouverture solennelle,* op. 73 (1901) was *Festival Overture;* the music throughout has a festive character. After preliminary chords, woodwind and horns present a subject soon taken over and amplified by the strings. The main part of the overture begins with an expressive and soulful melody for the violins. The second theme is first given by the clarinets against a vigorous accompaniment. After the first theme receives elaboration, the overture concludes with a forceful coda.

The orchestral suite *Raymonda,* op. 57a, comes from the score to a ballet with choreography by Marius Petipa; it was introduced in St. Petersburg on January 17, 1898. The composer's first work for the stage, this ballet has for its central character the lovely Raymonda, betrothed to a knight. After the knight has gone off to join the Crusade and fight the Saracens, Raymonda is wooed by a Saracen. When she rejects him he makes an attempt to abduct her. Just then the knight returns, and slays the culprit. The lovers thus reunited, are now able to celebrate their nuptials.

The orchestral suite is a staple in the light-classical repertory. It consists of the following sections: I. "Introduction." Raymonda's sorrow at the absence of her lover. A scene in Raymonda's castle where pages indulge in athletics. II. *"La Traditrice."* The dance of pages and maidens. III. *"Moderato."* Fanfares announce the arrival of a stranger. Joy and general animation. As Raymonda enters, girls throw flowers in her path. IV. *"Andante."* Raymonda is playing the lute outside the castle in the moonlight. Raymonda dances. VI. "Entr'acte; *Valse fantastique."* Raymonda dreams she is in fairyland with her beloved. VII. *"Grand Pas d'action."* At a feast given by Raymonda at her castle the Saracen appears, woos her, and is spurned. VIII. "Variation." Raymonda defies the Saracen, who now tries to dazzle her with his wealth. IX. "Dance of the Arab Boys." "Dance of the Saracens." X. "Entr'acte." The triumph of love and the festivities attending the nuptials.

Scènes de ballet, suite for orchestra, op. 52 (1894) is made up of eight parts. The first, *"Préamble,"* has an extended introduction to a main section in which the main subject is given by the violins. "Marionettes," offers a lively theme for piccolo and glockenspiel with which this section opens and closes; midway comes a trio with main theme in first violins. The third part is a "Mazurka" for full orchestra. The fourth is a "Scherzo," its principal idea in muted strings and woodwind. An expressive melody for cellos and violins is the heart of the fifth section, *"Pas d'action,"* while the sixth, *"Danse orientale"* is a sensuous, exotic dance melody set against the insistent beats of a tambourine. The ensuing *"Valse"* begins with an introduction following which the main waltz melody is presented by the violins. The suite concludes with a dashing "Polonaise" for full orchestra.

The orchestral suite, *The Seasons,* op. 67—like that of *Raymonda*—comes from a ballet score. The ballet—choreography by Marius Petipa—was first performed in St. Petersburg in 1900. The scenario interprets the four seasons of the year in four scenes and an apotheosis. First comes Winter and her two gnomes; they burn a bundle of faggots, whose heat causes Winter to disappear. Spring now arrives with Zephyr, Birds and Flowers. All of them join in a joyous dance. When Summer comes he is in the company of the Spirit of the Corn. Various flowers perform a dance, then fall exhausted on the ground. Satyrs and fauns, playing on pipes, try to recapture the Spirit of the Corn who is protected by the flowers. In the Autumn scene, Bacchantes perform a dance in the company of the Seasons. The Apotheosis presents an idyllic scene with stars shining brightly in the sky.

The orchestral suite adapted from the ballet score by the composer for concert purposes is one of his best known compositions. It consists of the following sections: I. "Winter: Introduction; The Frost; The Ice; The Hail; The Snow." II. "Spring." III. "Summer: Waltz of the Cornflowers and Poppies; Barcarolle; Variation; Coda." IV. "Autumn: Bacchanale—Petit Adagio. Finale—The Bacchantes and Apotheosis."

The *Valse de concert* Nos. 1 and 2, D major and F major respectively, opp. 47 and 51, are among the composer's most delightful shorter pieces. The first waltz, written in 1893, begins with a brief introduction after which the principal waltz melody is heard first in violas and clarinets, and subsequently in violins. A second theme is then offered by the clarinets against plucked strings, after which the first waltz reappears. The second waltz came one year after the first. This also has a short introduction in which the main waltz melody is suggested. This melody is finally given by the strings. While other thematic material occasionally intrudes, the main waltz subject dominates the entire composition.

Reinhold Glière

❧❧ ❦❦

REINHOLD GLIÈRE was born in Kiev, Russia, on January 11, 1875. He was graduated from the Moscow Conservatory in 1900. After two years in Berlin, he returned to his native land to become professor of composition at the Kiev Conservatory; from 1914 to 1920 he was its director. After 1920 he was a member of the faculty of the Moscow Conservatory. Glière's most famous works are his third symphony (named *Ilia Mourometz*) introduced in Moscow in 1912, and the ballet, *The Red Poppy*. But he wrote many other works—orchestral, chamber, and vocal, as well as ballets. On two occasions he received the Stalin Prize: in 1948 for his fourth string quartet, and two years later for his ballet, *The Bronze Horseman*. He died in Moscow on June 23, 1956.

Two excerpts from the Soviet ballet, *The Red Poppy,* are perhaps the composer's best known compositions. The ballet was first presented in Moscow on June 14, 1927 with extraordinary success. Its setting is a port in China where coolies are exploited. When a Soviet ship comes to port, its captain falls in love with a Chinese girl, Tai-Hao. She is ultimately killed by the port commander while she is trying to escape from China on the Soviet ship. Her last words urge the Chinese to fight for their liberty, and she points to a red poppy as a symbol of their freedom.

The most celebrated single excerpt from this ballet is the *Russian Sailors Dance,* for orchestra, with which the third act comes to a whirlwind conclusion. The main melody is a simple Russian tune that appears first in lower strings. It is then subjected to a series of variations, and is permitted to gain momentum through acceleration of tempo and expanding sonorities until an orgiastic climax is reached. Less popular, but still often performed, is the "Dance of the Chinese Girls" from the same ballet. A repeated descending interval leads to an Oriental dance in the pentatonic scale; in this dance percussion instruments and the xylophone are used prominently and with telling effect.

Michael Glinka

MICHAEL GLINKA was born to prosperous landowners in Novosspaskoye, in Smolensk, Russia, on June 1, 1804. His academic education took place at a private school in St. Petersburg, while he studied music with Carl Meyer, Carl Boehm and John Field. From 1824 to 1827 he worked in the office of the Ministry of Communications in St. Petersburg. Further music study then took place in Italy and Germany. After returning to his native land in 1834, he was fired with the ambition of writing a national Russian opera. That opera was *A Life for the Tsar,* produced in 1836, an epoch-making work since it is the foundation upon which all later Russian national music rests. Glinka's second national opera, *Ruslan and Ludmila,* produced in 1842, successfully carried on the composer's national ideals further. In the last years of his life Glinka traveled a great deal, spending considerable time in Paris, Warsaw, and Spain. He died suddenly in Berlin, Germany, on February 15, 1857.

It is impossible to overestimate Glinka's significance in Russian music. His national operas were the source from which the later nationalists, the "Russian Five" derived their direction and inspiration.

In *Jota aragonesa,* a "caprice brilliant" for orchestra (1845) Glinka is stimulated by Spanish rather than Russian folk music. This is the first Russian composition to make serious use of Spanish folk idioms. It was written during the composer's visit to Spain in 1845 where he was fascinated by Spanish folk songs and dances. Within a fantasy form, Glinka poured melodies and dance rhythms closely modeled after the Spanish in which the background, culture, and geography of that colorful country have been fixed.

Kamarinskaya (1848), also for orchestra, is a fantasy in the field in which Glinka was both an acknowledged master and a significant pioneer—Russian folk music. This composition is based on two Russian folk songs heard by the composer in Warsaw: "Over the Hills, the High Hills" (which appears in strings following a brief introduction), and a dance tune, "Kamarinskaya" (first heard in violins).

The most popular excerpts from Glinka's national opera, *A Life for the Tsar,* are the overture, and the Mazurka and Waltz, for orchestra. The opera—libretto by Baron von Rosen—was first performed in St. Petersburg on December 9, 1836. The action takes place in Poland and Russia in 1612. During the struggle between Russia and Poland, Romanov becomes the new Czar of Russia, and Ivan Susanin, a peasant, is the hero who saves Russia and the Czar. The love interest involves Ivan's daughter, Antonida, and Bogdan Sabinin.

The overture opens with a stately introduction dominated by a melody for the oboe. A spirited melody brings on the main section. After this melody is developed, a second theme is offered by the clarinets. Both ideas are discoursed upon briefly, and they are given further amplification in the coda.

The Mazurka and Waltz appear at the close of the second act, climaxing a festive celebration held in the throne room of Sigismund III of Poland in his ancient castle. The Waltz comes first. Two principal waltz melodies are given by the woodwind and repeated by strings; a third waltz tune is then heard in brass, and soon taken over by the strings. The Waltz is immediately followed by the Mazurka. After a dignified introduction, a vigorous Mazurka melody unfolds. This leads to a second dance tune, first heard in the woodwind and cellos; but the first Mazurka melody soon reappears in the full orchestra. A third lively dance melody is then presented by the strings.

Ruslan and Ludmila also contributed a lively overture to the orchestral repertory. This opera, with libretto by the composer and several others based on a Pushkin poem, was first heard in St. Petersburg on December 9, 1842. Ruslan is a knight who is a rival of Ratmir for the love of Ludmila. Ludmila is abducted by the dwarf Tchernomor, and after Ruslan has saved her, Ludmila's father blesses his future son-in-law.

Vigorous chords lead to a dashing melody in violins, violas and woodwinds. A more lyrical second theme, almost folk-song in character, is then heard in violas, cellos and bassoons. Both themes are given a vigorous development in which the sprightly character of the overture is never allowed to lose its brisk pace or vitality.

Christoph Willibald Gluck

CHRISTOPH WILLIBALD GLUCK was born in Eras-bach, Upper Palatinate, on July 2, 1714, the son of a forester on the estate of Prince Lobkowitz. Gluck received his early music instruction in his native country from local teachers. He then earned his living playing the violin and cello in rural orchestras. In 1736 he came to Vienna where soon thereafter he began to serve as chamber musician for Prince Lobkowitz. After a period of study and travel in Italy he returned to Vienna, now to become one of its most influential musi-cians. In Vienna he had produced several of his early operas, all of them in the traditional Italian style of that period. But he soon drew away from the stilted conventions of the Italian opera to achieve a fusion of music and drama new to opera, as well as dramatic truth, simplicity, and directness of emotional appeal. His works in this new style, with which a new epoch in opera was launched, included *Orfeo ed Euridice* in 1762, *Alceste* in 1767, and *Iphigénie en Aulide* in 1774, the last written for the Paris stage. After living in Paris from 1773 to 1779, Gluck returned to Vienna to remain there the rest of his life. During his last years he was an invalid. He died in Vienna on November 15, 1787.

Gluck was a giant in the early history of opera. With Rameau, he was a pioneer in establishing music drama as opposed to formal Italian opera. *Orfeo ed Euridice,* produced in Vienna on October 5, 1762—with which Gluck first set forth his new ideas and theories about opera—is the earliest opera to have survived in the permanent repertory.

A delightful *Ballet Suite,* adapted by Felix Mottl from various orches-tral dances from several of Gluck's greatest operas, is an orchestral work by which the composer is most often represented on semi-classical as well as symphonic programs. This suite includes the following: "Dance of the Blessed Spirits" from *Orfeo ed Euridice;* "Air gai" and *"Lento"* from *Iphigénie en Aulide;* and two old baroque dances, the "Musette" and "Sicilienne" from *Armide.*

The "Dance of the Blessed Spirits" is one of the loveliest of all

Gluck's melodies, and one of the most famous from 18th century opera. This is a beatific song mainly for flute solo and strings, describing Elysium, to which Orfeo has come in search of his wife, Eurydice. Fritz Kreisler's transcription for violin and piano is entitled *Mélodie*. Sgambati arranged it for piano solo, and Gruenfeld for cello and piano.

Benjamin Godard

BENJAMIN LOUIS GODARD was born in Paris on August 18, 1849. After attending the Paris Conservatory, he received in 1878 a municipal prize for an orchestral work, besides having his first opera produced. He wrote several operas after that, winning fame with *Jocelyn* in 1888. He also wrote a considerable amount of chamber and orchestral music, in which his fine, sensitive lyricism is evident. He died in Cannes, France, on January 10, 1895.

Among his more familiar works is the *Adagio pathétique*. This started out as a piece for violin and piano, the third of a set of compositions in op. 128. It was orchestrated by Ross Jungnickel in 1910, and is most popular in this version. This is music notable for its expressive emotion; its lyricism at times has a religious stateliness.

The most famous single piece of music by Godard, however, is the "Berceuse" from his opera, *Jocelyn*. With libretto by Paul Armand and Silvestre and Victor Capoul—based on a poem by Lamartine—*Jocelyn* was introduced in Brussels on February 25, 1888. The setting is France during the French Revolution, and concerns the love of Jocelyn, a young priest, for the daughter of a nobleman. After many inner struggles, Jocelyn decides to remain true to his calling and give up his beloved. They meet for the last time at her deathbed to which Jocelyn has been summoned to administer absolution. The "Berceuse" is a tender aria by Jocelyn (*"Cachés dans cet asile"*) in which he calls upon angels to protect his loved one.

Leopold Godowsky

LEOPOLD GODOWSKY was born in Soshly, near Vilna, Poland, on February 13, 1870. A prodigy pianist, he attended the Berlin High School for Music, after which he made his American debut in Boston in 1884. Additional study took place in Paris with Saint-Saëns. Godowsky then launched his career as a mature concert pianist with performances throughout the world of music. He achieved international renown not only as a virtuoso but also as a teacher of the piano, at the Chicago Conservatory and the Vienna Academy. His concert career ended in 1930 when he was stricken by a slight paralysis of the hand. As a composer, Godowsky was most famous for his suites for the piano, the most famous being *Triakontameron, Java,* and *Renaissance.* He also produced a library of remarkable transcriptions for the piano. He died in New York City on November 21, 1938.

Though Godowsky was a sophisticated composer of highly complex piano works, he did succeed in producing at least one number that became an international "hit." It was the *Alt Wien (Old Vienna),* a sentimental, nostalgic piece of music on whose title page appears the following quotation: "Whose yesterdays look backwards with a smile through tears." *Alt Wien* is the eleventh number in *Triakontameron* (1920), a suite in six volumes described by the composer as "thirty moods and scenes in triple measure." The immense popularity of *Alt Wien* is proved by its many and varied transcriptions: for salon orchestra; band; violin and piano (by Heifetz); three-part woman's chorus; dance orchestra; marimba and piano; and even a popular song adapted by David Saperton to lyrics by Stella Ungar.

Edwin Franko Goldman

EDWIN FRANKO GOLDMAN was born in Louisville, Kentucky, on January 1, 1878. He came from a distinguised musical family. His uncles were Franko and Nahan Franko, both prominent in New York as conductors, violinists, and pioneers in the presentation of free concerts. Goldman attended the National Conservatory in New York, specializing in the cornet. After completing his training with Jules Levey, he served for ten years as solo cornetist of the Metropolitan Opera orchestra. In 1911 he organized his first band. Seven years later he founded the famous Goldman Band which from then on gave free concerts in New York and Brooklyn public parks, and elsewhere on tour. Under his direction it became one of the outstanding musical organizations of its kind in the country, presenting a remarkable repertory of popular music, light classics, and band transcriptions of symphonic and operatic compositions. Goldman conducted his band until his death, which took place in New York on February 21, 1956. He was succeeded by his son, Richard Franko Goldman, who for many years had served as his father's assistant.

For his concerts Goldman wrote over a hundred marches which have won him recognition as John Philip Sousa's successor. The best of the Goldman marches won immediate success for their robust tunes and vigorous beat. These include: "Central Park," "Children's March," "On the Campus," "On the Farm," and "On the Mall."

The "Children's March," is actually an adaptation for band of several children's tunes including "Three Blind Mice," "Jingle Bells," and "Here We Go Round the Mulberry Bush," presented in march time.

Karl Goldmark

❧❧ ❧❧

KARL GOLDMARK was born in Keszthely, Hungary, on May 18, 1830, the son of a cantor. Demonstrating unusual talent on the violin, he was sent to Vienna in 1844. There he studied with Leopold Jansa, then attended the Vienna Conservatory. His musical education was brought to an abrupt halt by the revolution of 1848. For many years after that, Goldmark earned his living by teaching music, playing in theater orchestras, and writing criticisms. He first came to the fore as a composer with a concert of his works in Vienna on March 20, 1857. Success followed eight years later with the première of his concert overture, *Sakuntala*. From then on, Goldmark occupied an esteemed position in Viennese music by virtue of many distinguished works that included the opera *The Queen of Sheba*, the *Rustic Wedding Symphony*, and various shorter works for orchestra, as well as numerous compositions for chorus, the piano, and chamber-music groups. He died in Vienna on January 2, 1915.

Throughout his life he remained true to the Germanic-Romantic tradition on which he was nurtured. His writing was always vital with emotion, at times to the point of being sensual; it overflowed with luxurious melody and harmony. Most of the works by which he is remembered, while of the serious concert-hall variety, are light classics because of their charm and grace and pleasing melodic content.

The *Bacchanale* for orchestra is in Goldmark's identifiable sensual style. This is an episode from his most famous opera, *The Queen of Sheba* (*Die Koenigen von Saba*), libretto by Solomon Herman Mosenthal based on the Old Testament story of the love of the Queen of Sheba for Assad. The opera was successfully introduced in Vienna on March 10, 1875. The *Bacchanale* takes place at the beginning of Act 3 in which a sumptuous reception honors the Queen of Sheba. This dynamic piece of music is especially interesting for its Oriental melodies and lush orchestral colors.

In Spring (*Im Fruehling*), op. 36 (1889), is a concert overture for orchestra echoing the composer's emotional reaction to the vernal season. The first main theme, in first violins accompanied by other strings, is given without any preliminaries. The second theme in violins is more bucolic, the woodwind suggesting bird calls in the background. Both themes are discussed and stormy episodes ensue. After the return of the two main themes the overture ends with a brilliant coda.

The *Rustic Wedding Symphony (Laendliche Hochzeit)*, op. 26 (1876) is a programmatic composition for orchestra in five movements. The first is a "Wedding March" in which the main melody (given in fragments in the lower strings) is subjected to thirteen variations. The second movement is a "Bridal Song," a lovely tune mainly for oboe in which the first-movement march subject occasionally intrudes in the background in the basses. This is followed by the third-movement "Serenade," its main subject being a spacious melody mainly for the violins. The fourth movement, "In the Garden," depicts the walk of two lovers in a garden as they exchange tender sentiments. The symphony ends with a vital "Dance," in which the main theme receives fugal treatment.

The concert overture for orchestra, *Sakuntala,* op. 13 (1865)—with which the composer achieved his first major success and which is still one of his most popular works—was based on the celebrated story of Kalidasa. Sakuntala is the daughter of a water nymph who is raised by a priest as his own daughter. The King falls in love with her and marries her, giving her a ring which will always identify her as his wife. A powerful priest, seeking revenge against Sakuntala, effects a loss of memory in the king, who now no longer recognizes her as his wife. To complicate matters further, Sakuntala has lost her ring while washing clothes in a sacred river. After being repudiated by the king as a fraud, Sakuntala returns to her water-nymph mother. The king's memory is restored when the ring is found, and he is overwhelmed with grief at his loss of Sakuntala.

A somber introduction is highlighted by a rippling subject in lower strings and bassoons suggesting the water which was Sakuntala's original abode and to which she finally returns. After a change of tempo, clarinets and cellos in unison offer a beautiful love melody. This is followed by a hunting theme in first violins and oboes while the second violins and violas present a fragment of the love song as a countersubject. After this material has been amplified into a loud and dramatic climax there comes still a third idea, in oboes and English horn against chords in harp and arpeggios in strings. In a free fantasia section some of this material is reviewed after which the coda offers the hunting theme, and after that the love melody. A climax is realized with the hunting theme bringing the overture to a dramatic ending.

Rubin Goldmark

ᴥᴥᴥ ᴥᴥᴥ

R U B I N G O L D M A R K, nephew of Karl, was born in New York City on August 15, 1872. After studying music with private teachers in New York, he attended first the Vienna Conservatory in Austria, and after that the National Conservatory in New York where one of his teachers was Antonin Dvořák. His primary energy was directed to teaching. For six years he was the director of the Colorado College Conservatory, and from 1924 until his death head of the composition department at the Juilliard School of Music in New York. As a composer, Goldmark is most often remembered for the *Negro Rhapsody* and the *Requiem* for orchestra, the latter inspired by Lincoln's Gettysburg Address. Goldmark died in New York City on March 6, 1936.

It is with the *Negro Rhapsody* (1923) that Goldmark is most often represented on concert and semi-classical concerts. As its title suggests the work is made up of Negro melodies. After a slow introduction, the cellos and violas in unison offer the strains of "Nobody Knows De Trouble I'd Seen." Before long, the basses are heard in "O Peter, Go Ring Dem Bells." The main section of the rhapsody begins with a variation of "Nobody Knows De Trouble I'd Seen" and a repeat of "O Peter." The violins then engage "Oh Religion, I See Fortune," and the English horn is heard in "Sometimes I Feel Like a Motherless Child. After the solo cello quotes two measures of "Oh, When I Come to Die," the last Negro melody of the rhapsody appears. This melody comes from an untitled song found by Goldmark in a magazine, a tune sung by Tennessee Negroes while working on the river.

François Gossec

❧❧ ☙☙

FRANÇOIS JOSEPH GOSSEC was born in Vergniès, Bel-
gium, on January 17, 1734. After receiving some music instruction in
his native town, he came to Paris in 1751, and three years after that was
attached to the musical forces employed by La Pouplinière. For these
concerts, Gossec wrote many symphonies and chamber-music works. He
later worked in a similar capacity for the Prince de Conti. In 1770 he
founded the Concerts des Amateurs, in 1773 became director of the
Concert Spirituel, and from 1780 to 1785 was conductor at the Paris
Opéra. When the Paris Conservatory was established in 1795 Gossec
became Inspector and professor of composition. In the same year he also
became a member of the newly founded Institut de France. During the
French Revolution he wrote many works celebrating events growing
out of that political upheaval, allying himself with the new regime.
He lived to a ripe old age, spending the last years of his life in retirement in Passy. He died in Paris on February 16, 1829.

Gossec was a significant pioneer of French orchestral and chamber
music, though little of his music is remembered. What remains alive,
however, is a graceful trifle: the Gavotte, one of the most popular pieces
ever written in that form. This music comes from one of his operas,
Rosina (1786); a transcription for violin and piano by Willy Burmeister
is famous.

Louis Gottschalk

৶৳৶ৼ ৡৢ৶ৡৢ৶

LOUIS MOREAU GOTTSCHALK was born in New Orleans on May 8, 1829. His music study took place in Paris where he specialized in the piano. He gave many successful concerts as pianist in France, Switzerland and Spain before returning to the United States in 1853. He then began the first of many tours of the country, to become the first significant American-born piano virtuoso. At his concerts he featured many of his own works; his reputation as a composer was second only to that as virtuoso. He was on tour of South America when he was stricken by yellow fever. He died in Rio de Janeiro on December 18, 1869.

Gottschalk was the composer of numerous salon pieces for the piano, enormously popular in his day—a favorite of young pianists everywhere. One of these pieces is "The Banjo," familiar on semi-classical programs in orchestral arrangements. In his music Gottschalk often employed either Spanish or native American idioms.

The contemporary American composer, Ulysses Kay, used several of Gottschalk's piano pieces for a ballet score, *Cakewalk*. This ballet, with choreography by Ruthanna Boris based on the minstrel show, was introduced by the New York City Ballet in New York on June 12, 1951. The dancers here translate the routines of the old minstrel show into dance forms and idioms. An orchestral suite, derived from this ballet score, has five sections: "Grand Walkaround," in which the performers strut around the stage led by the interlocutor; "Wallflower Waltz," music to a slow, sad dance performed solo by a lonely girl; "Sleight of Feet," a rhythmic specialty accompanying feats of magic performed by the Interlocutor; "Perpendicular Points," a toe dance performed by the two end men, one very tall, the other very short; and "Freebee," an exciting dance performed by the girl, as other performers accompany her dance with the rhythm of clapping hands.

Morton Gould

❧❧ ❧❧

MORTON GOULD was born in New York City on December 10, 1913. He received a comprehensive musical education at the Institute of Musical Art in New York, at New York University, and privately (piano) with Abby Whiteside. After completing these studies, he played the piano in motion-picture theaters and vaudeville houses and served as the staff pianist for the Radio City Music Hall. He was only eighteen when the Philadelphia Orchestra under Stokowski introduced his *Chorale and Fugue in Jazz,* his first successful effort to combine classical forms and techniques with modern popular American idioms. In his twenty-first year he started conducting an orchestra for radio, and making brilliant transcriptions of popular and semi-classical favorites for these broadcasts. During the next two decades he was one of radio's outstanding musical personalities, his programs enjoying important sponsorship. During this period he wrote many works for orchestra which have been performed by America's foremost symphony orchestras. He also wrote the scores for several successful ballets (including *Interplay* and *Fall River Legend*), as well as music for Broadway musical comedies and motion pictures.

Like Gershwin, Gould has been a major figure in helping make serious music popular by writing ambitious concert works which make a skilful blend of serious and popular musical elements. Gershwin came to the writing of serious concert works after apprenticeship in Tin Pan Alley; Gould, on the other hand, came to popular writing after an intensive career in serious music. Thus he brings to his more popular efforts an extraordinary technique in composition, advanced thinking in orchestration, harmony, counterpoint, and rhythm. Yet there is nothing pedantic about his writing. Many of his works are such consistent favorites with audiences because they are the creations of a consummate musician without losing popular appeal. Few have been more successful than Gould in achieving such a synthesis between concert and popular music.

American Salute (1942) is a brilliant orchestral adaptation of the famous American popular song by Patrick Gilmore, "When Johnny

Comes Marching Home." Though written during the Civil War, this robust marching song became most popular during the Spanish American War with which it is today most often associated. Gould prepared this composition during World War II for an all-American music concert broadcast over the Mutual radio network on February 12, 1942. "I have attempted," Gould explained, "a very simple and direct translation in orchestral idiom of this vital tune. There is nothing much that can be said about the structure or the treatment because I think it is what you might call 'self-auditory.'"

The *American Symphonette No. 2* is one of several works for orchestra in the sinfonietta form in which Gould made a conscious effort to fuse classical structure with elements of popular music. The composer's purpose, as he explained, was "entertainment, in the better sense of the term." The most famous movement is the middle one, a "Pavane," often played independently of the other movements. It is particularly favored by school orchestras, and has also been adapted for jazz band. The old and stately classical dance of the Pavane is here married to a spicy jazz tune jauntily presented by the trumpet; there are here overtones of a gentle sadness. The first and last movements of this Symphonette abound with jazz rhythms and melodies, respectively marked "Moderately Fast, With Vigor" and "Racy."

The *Cowboy Rhapsody* (1944) started out as a composition for brass band, but was later adapted by the composer for orchestra. This is a rhapsodic treatment of several familiar and less familiar cowboy tunes including "Old Paint," "Home on the Range," "Trail to Mexico" and "Little Old Sod Shanty." The composer here attempted "a program work that would effectively utilize the marvelous vigor and sentiment of these unusual songs."

Family Album (1951) is one of two suites in which Gould evokes nostalgic pictures of the American scene and holidays through atmospheric melodies. (The other suite is *Holiday Music,* written in 1947.) The composer explains that the music of both these suites is so simple and direct in its pictorial appeal that it requires no program other than the titles of the respective movements to be understood and appreciated; nor is any analysis of the music itself called for. *Family Album,* for brass band, is made up of five brief movements: "Outing in the Park," "Porch Swing on a Summer Evening," "Nickelodeon," "Old Romance" and "Horseless Carriage Gallop." *Holiday Music,* for orchestra, also has five movements: "Home for Christmas," "Fourth of July," "Easter Morning," "The First Thanksgiving," and "Halloween."

Interplay is a ballet with choreography by Jerome Robbins introduced in New York in 1945. The score is an adaptation of the composer's *American Concertette,* for piano and orchestra, written for the piano virtuoso, José Iturbi. The text of the ballet contrasts classic and present-day dances; Gould's music is a delightful contrast between old forms and styles, and modern or popular ones. *Interplay,* as the concert work is now called, has four movements, each of popular appeal. The first, "With Drive and Vigor," was described by the composer as "brash." It has two sprightly main themes and a brief development. This is followed by a "Gavotte" in which the composer directs "a sly glance to the classical mode." The third movement is a "Blues," "a very simple and, in spots, 'dirty' type of slow, nostalgic mood." The finale, "Very Fast" brings the composition to a breathless conclusion through unrelenting motor energy.

Latin-American Symphonette, for orchestra (1941) is the fourth of Gould's sinfoniettas using popular idioms. The three earlier ones exploit jazz, while the fourth consists of ideas and idioms indigenous to Latin America. Each of the four movements consists of a stylized Latin-American dance form: "Rumba," "Tango," "Guaracha," and "Conga."

In *Minstrel Show* (1946) Gould tried to bring to orchestral music some of the flavor of old time minstrel-show tunes and styles. There are no borrowings from actual minstrel shows. All the melodies are the composer's own, but they incorporate some of the stylistic elements of the original product. "The composition," Gould goes on to say, "alternates between gay and nostalgic passages. There are characteristic sliding trombone and banjo effects, and in the middle of the piece the sandpaper blocks and other percussion convey the sounds and tempo of a soft-shoe dance. The score ends on a jubilant note."

Yankee Doodle Went to Town, like the *American Salute,* is the presentation of a popular American tune in modern orchestration and harmony. The tune in this case is, to be sure, "Yankee Doodle," probably of English origin which made its first appearance in this country in 1755. The general belief is that it was used by a certain Richard Shuchburg, a British Army soldier, to poke fun at the decrepit colonial troops. For two decades after that the tune was frequently heard in the Colonies as the means by which British soldiers could taunt Colonials. Once the Revolution broke out, however, the colonists used "Yankee Doodle" as its favorite war song, and it was sung lustily by them when Cornwallis surrendered at Yorktown. Gould's orchestration emphasizes some of the humorous elements in the song, while giving it some freshness and vitality through his fine sense for orchestral color and striking harmonizations.

Charles Gounod

ৡৢৡ ৡৣৡ

CHARLES FRANÇOIS GOUNOD was born in Paris on June 17, 1818. He received his academic education at the Lycée St. Louis, and his musical training at the Paris Conservatory with Halévy and Lesueur among others. In 1839 he won the Prix de Rome. During his stay in Italy he became interested in church music and completed several choral works. He turned to opera after returning to Paris, his first work for the lyric stage being *Sapho,* successfully produced at the Paris Opéra in 1851. From then on, for many years, he concentrated mainly on opera, winning world renown in 1859 with *Faust.* In 1870 he visited London where he conducted orchestral and choral concerts. During the last years of his life he devoted himself for the most part to the writing of religious music. Gounod died in Paris on October 18, 1893. He is most famous for his operas, and most specifically for *Faust,* though *Mireille* (1864) and *Roméo et Juliette* (1867) have also been highly acclaimed and frequently given. Gounod was a composer who conveyed to his music sensitive human values. He was a melodist of the first order, his lyricism enhanced in its expressiveness through his subtle feeling for orchestral and harmonic colors.

The *Ave Maria,* while originally a song, is famous in transcriptions for solo instruments and also for orchestra. The interesting feature of this work is the fact that Gounod wrote this spiritual, deeply moving melody to the famous prayer in Latin, against an accompaniment comprising the music (without any change whatsoever) of Bach's Prelude in C major from the *Well-Tempered Clavier.* The marriage of melody and accompaniment is so ideal it is difficult to realize that each is the work of a different composer from a different generation.

Gounod's masterwork, the opera *Faust,* is surely one of the most celebrated works of the French lyric theater. Many of its selections are deservedly popular. The opera—libretto by Jules Barbier and Michel
Carré based on the poetic drama of Goethe—was first performed in
Paris on March 19, 1859. Strange to report, it was originally a failure
with both audience and critics. Not until it was revived in Paris in 1869
did the opera finally win favor; from this point it went on to conquer the world. One of the reasons for this permanent, if somewhat be-
lated, success, is the sound theatrical values of the libretto. The opera is
consistently excellent theater, rich with emotion, pathos, drama, pomp
and ceremony. The story, of course, is that of the celebrated Faust
legend. Faust makes a pact with the devil, Mephistopheles, to trade his
soul for the return of his youth. As a young man, Faust makes love to
Marguerite. When she becomes a mother she kills her child. Faust
comes to her prison cell to entreat her to escape, but she does not seem
to understand him. After her punishment by death, Faust is led to his
own doom by Mephistopheles.

Perhaps the most famous single excerpt from the opera is the rousing
Soldier's Chorus ("Gloire immortelle des nos aïeux") from Act 4, Scene
3. The soldiers, returning from the war, sing out their joy on coming
home victorious. This episode is celebrated in transcriptions either for
orchestra or for brass band. Almost as popular is the captivating Waltz
in Act 2. In the opera it is sung and danced by villagers during a celebration in the public square *("Ainsi que la brise légère")*; this excerpt
is also familiar in transcription.

The Walpurgis Night Ballet Music from *Faust,* though generally
omitted from the performances of the opera itself, has become a concert favorite. This music is given in Paris during the first scene of the
last act. The classic queens—Helen, Phryne and Cleopatra—and their
attendants are called upon to dance to distorted versions of several of
the opera's beloved melodies. There are here seven dances of which
six appear in the score only with tempo markings: *Waltz, Adagio,
Allegretto, Moderato maestoso, Moderato con moto, Allegretto,* and
Allegro vivo.

When an orchestral potpourri from the opera is given by semi-
classical orchestra, it includes some other beloved excerpts: Marguerite's "Jewel Song" *("Je ris de me voir"),* in which she speaks her joy
in finding the casket of jewels secretly placed for her in her garden by
Faust; the rousing *Kermesse* or Fair Music that opens the second act,
"Vin ou bière"; Mephistopheles' cynical comment on man's greed for

gold, *"Le Veau d'or";* Faust's hymn of love for Marguerite, *"O belle enfant! je t'aime";* the "Chorus of Swords" (*"De l'enfer qui vient émousser"*), a vibrant exhortation by the young men of the village who, sensing they are in the presence of the devil, raise their swords in the form of a cross to confound him.

The *Funeral March of a Marionette* (*Marche funèbre d'une marionnette*) is a delightful piece originally written for the piano in 1873, and after that transcribed by the composer for orchestra. Gounod had hopes to make it the first movement of a piano suite. When he failed to complete that suite, he issued the march as a separate piece of music in the now-famous orchestral version. The opening march music tells of the procession of pallbearers to a cemetery as they carry a dead marionette. A brighter spirit is induced as the pallbearers stop off at an inn. Then the procession continues. The funereal atmosphere of the closing measures speaks of the ephemeral nature of all life, even the life of a marionette.

The opera *Mireille*—libretto by Barbier and Carré based on Mistral's poem, *Mirèio*—is not often performed. But this is not true of its overture. The opera was first performed in Paris on March 19, 1864. The story revolves around the tragic love affair of the Provençal girl, Mireille, and the basket-weaver, Vincent. The overture opens with a slow introduction in which a stately idea is offered by the woodwind. In the main body, the principal melody is heard in the strings while the subsidiary theme is first presented by the violins. After both ideas are amplified, a crescendo section leads to the triumphant reappearance of the first theme in the full orchestra. The overture ends with a short but spirited coda.

Out of the opera *Roméo et Juliet* comes a most charming waltz. The opera was introduced in Paris on April 27, 1867. The libretto, once again by Barbier and Carré, was based on the Shakespeare tragedy. The waltz opens the first act, a ballroom scene in the Capulet palace honoring Juliet. Against the lilting strains of this music, the guests perform an eye-filling dance.

Percy Grainger

⋙⋙ ⋘⋘

PERCY ALDRIDGE GRAINGER was born in Melbourne, Australia on July 8, 1882. After receiving some piano instruction from his mother he was sent to Germany in his twelfth year to continue his music study with James Kwast and Ferruccio Busoni. In 1900 he made his debut as concert pianist in London, following which he made an extended tour of Great Britain, New Zealand, Australia, and South Africa. A meeting with Grieg, in 1906, was a significant influence in Grainger's artistic development. Grieg infected the young man with some of his own enthusiasm for folk music. The result was that Grainger now began to devote himself to research in the English folk music of the past. His orchestral and piano arrangements of many of these folk tunes and dances, between 1908 and 1912, were responsible for bringing them to the attention of the music world. In 1915, Grainger made his debut as pianist in the United States. He has lived in America since that time, devoting himself to concert work, lecturing and teaching, besides composition. Grainger died in White Plains, New York, on February 20, 1961.

In his own music, Grainger reveals the impact that his studies in English music made upon him: in his partiality to modal writing, to the contrapuntal technique, to placid lyricism. But it is in his fresh arrangements of old English songs and dances that Grainger is most famous. "Even when he keeps the folk songs within their original dimensions," says Cyril Scott, "he has a way of dealing with them which is entirely new, yet at the same time never lacking in taste."

Brigg Fair is a plaintive melody of pastoral character from the district of Lincolnshire. It was used by the contemporary British composer, Frederick Delius, as the basis for his orchestral rhapsody of the same name (dedicated to Grainger).

The bucolic and ever popular *Country Gardens* is a "Mock Morris," the "Mock Morris" being an old English dance popular during the reign of Henry VII and since then associated with festivities attending May Day. Grainger's original transcription was for piano solo, and only later did he adapt it for orchestra.

Handel in the Strand is a lively clog dance. *Irish Tune from County Derry* is better known as the *Londonderry Air,* a poignant melody now known to us through numerous versions other than that originally made famous by Grainger. The piece, designated as a Mock Morris, is one of a series in a collection entitled *Room Music Tit Bits.* "No folk music tune-stuffs at all are used herein," says the composer. "The rhythmic cast of the piece is Morris-like, but neither the build of the tunes nor the general layout of the form keeps to the Morris dance shape."

The lively *Molly on the Shore* was first written for piano before being adapted by the composer for orchestra. *Shepherd's Hey* is a Mock Morris and consists of four tunes, two fiddle tunes and two folk songs.

Of Grainger's own compositions three are of general interest. The *Children's March* (1917) was written during World War I for the United States Army Band. "This march," says the composer, "is structurally of a complicated build, on account of the large number of different themes and tunes employed and of the varied and irregular interplay of many contrasted sections. Tonally speaking, it is a study in the blend of piano, wind, and percussion instruments."

Passacaglia on Green Bushes has two versions. One is for small orchestra, and the other for a large one. This composition is built around the folk melody "Green Bushes" which remains unchanged in key, line, and rhythm throughout the work (except for eight measures of free passage work near the beginning, and forty measures at the end). Against this melody move several folk-like melodies of Grainger's own invention.

Youthful Suite for orchestra is made up of five sections. Part of this work was completed in 1902, and part in 1945. The first movement, "Northern March," derives its character from the melodic and rhythmic traits of the folk music of North England and Scotland. The main melody here acquires its folk-song character through the use of the flat-seventh minor scale. "Rustic Dance" achieves an exotic quality through the employment of an unusual variant of the F major chord. "Norse Digger" is a somber lament in which is mourned the passing of a dead hero, possibly from an Icelandic saga. "Eastern Intermezzo" has an Oriental cast. The repeated use of drum beats and the virile rhythms were inspired by a reading of a description of the dance of the elephants in *Toomal of the Elephants* from Kipling's Jungle Book. This suite ends with a formal "English Waltz."

Enrique Granados

ENRIQUE GRANADOS was born in Lérida, Spain, on July 27, 1867. After completing his music study at Conservatories in Barcelona and Madrid, and privately with Charles de Bériot in Paris, he earned his living playing the piano in Spanish restaurants. In 1898, his first opera was produced in Madrid, *Maria del Carmen*. The national identity of this music was to characterize all of Granados' subsequent works and place him among the most significant of Spanish national composers. His most famous composition is *Goyescas*, a remarkable series of piano pieces inspired by the paintings of Goya; the composer later adapted this music for an opera, also called *Goyescas*, which received its world première in New York at the Metropolitan Opera on January 28, 1918. Granados came to the United States to attend this performance, after which he visited Washington, D.C. to play the piano for President Wilson at the White House. He was aboard the ship *Folkstone*, sailing from Folkstone to Dieppe, when it was torpedoed by a German U-Boat during World War I on March 24, 1916, bringing him to his death.

In their rhythmic and harmonic vocabulary, Granados' best music is unmistakably Spanish. Perhaps his most famous single piece of music is an orchestral "Intermezzo" from the opera *Goyescas*. He wrote it after he had fully completed his score to the opera because the directors of the Metropolitan Opera filled the need of an instrumental interlude. This sensual Spanish melody is as famous in various transcriptions (including one for cello and piano by Gaspar Cassadó) as it is in its original orchestral version.

Twelve *Spanish Dances*, for piano, op. 37 (1893) are also popular. The most frequently performed of these is the fifth in E minor named *Andaluza* (or *Playera*). Fritz Kreisler transcribed it for violin and piano, one of numerous adaptations. The sixth in D major is also familiar—*Rondalla Aragonesa*, a jota, transcribed for violin and piano by Jacques Thibaud.

Edvard Grieg

৵৽৽৶ ৡ৵ৡ৶

EDVARD HAGERUP GRIEG, Norway's greatest com-
poser, was born in Bergen on June 15, 1843. Revealing unusual talent
for music as a boy, he was sent to the Leipzig Conservatory in 1858.
He remained there several years, a pupil of Plaidy, Moscheles, and
Reinecke among others. In 1863 he returned to his native land where
several of his early compositions were performed. He then lived for
several years in Copenhagen. There he met and became a friend of two
musicians who interested him in Scandinavian music and musical
nationalism: Niels Gade and Rikard Nordraak. Under their guidance
and stimulation Grieg began writing music in a national style, beginning with the *Humoresques* for piano, op. 6, which he dedicated to
Nordraak. Grieg also became a sponsor of Scandinavian music and
composers by helping Nordraak organize a society for their benefit. In
1866, Grieg helped arrange in Oslo the first concert ever given over
entirely to Norwegian music; a year later he helped found the Norwegian Academy of Music. He also served as a conductor of the Harmonic Society, an important influence in presenting Scandinavian
music.

After marrying Nina Hagerup in 1867, Grieg settled in Oslo to
assume an imperial position in its musical life. He also achieved worldwide recognition as a composer through his violin Sonata in F major,
the A major piano concerto, and the incidental music to Ibsen's *Peer
Gynt*. He was the recipient of many honors both from his native land
and from foreign countries. His sixtieth birthday was honored as a
national Norwegian holiday. From 1885 on Grieg lived in a beautiful
villa, Troldhaugen, a few miles from Bergen. Music lovers made pil-
grimages to meet him and pay him tribute. His remains were buried
there following his sudden death in Bergen on September 4, 1907.

Its national identity is the quality that sets Grieg's music apart from
that of most of the other Romanticists of his day. Though he rarely
quoted folk melodies or dance tunes directly, he produced music that
is Norwegian to its core. In his best music he speaks of Norway's geog-

raphy, culture, people, backgrounds, holidays, and legends in melodies and rhythms whose kinship with actual folk music is unmistakable.

The *Holberg Suite* for string orchestra, op. 40 (1885)—or to use its official title of *From Holberg's Time*—was written to honor the bicentenary of Ludvig Holberg, often called the founder of Danish literature. The composer also adapted this music for solo piano. Bearing in mind that the man he was honoring belonged to a bygone era, Grieg wrote a suite in classical style and with strictly classical forms; but his own romantic and at times national identity is not sacrificed. The first movement is a "Prelude," a vigorous movement almost in march time. This is followed by three classical dances—"Sarabande," "Gavotte," and "Musette." The fourth movement temporarily deserts the 17th and 18th centuries to offer a graceful "Air" in the manner of a Norwegian folk song, but the classical era returns in all its stateliness and grace in the concluding "Rigaudon."

In Autumn, a concert overture for orchestra, op. 11 (1865, revised 1888) was Grieg's first effort to write symphonic music. This composition is a fresh and spontaneous expression of joy in Nature's beauties. The principal melody is a song written by Grieg in 1865, "Autumn Storm." This material is preceded by an introduction and followed by a coda in which a happy dance by harvesters is introduced.

The *Lyric Suite* for orchestra, op. 54 (1903) is an adaptation by the composer of four numbers from his *Lyric Pieces,* for piano—a set of sixty-six short compositions gathered in ten volumes, each a delightful miniature of Norwegian life. The first of the four episodes in the *Lyric Suite* is "Shepherd Lad," scored entirely for strings, music in a dreamy mood whose main romantic melody has the character of a nocturne. "Rustic March" (or "Peasant March"), for full orchestra, has for its principal thought a ponderous, rhythmic theme first given by the clarinets. The third movement is a poetic "Nocturne" whose main melody is presented by the first violins. The suite ends with the popular "March of the Dwarfs" in the grotesque style of the composer's "In the Hall of the Mountain King" from *Peer Gynt.* This movement alternates a sprightly fantastic march tune (first heard in the violins) with an expressive melody for solo violin.

The *Norwegian Dance No. 2* is the second of a set of four folk dances originally for piano four hands and later transcribed by the composer for orchestra, op. 35 (1881). This second dance, in the key of A minor, is probably the composer's most famous composition in a national idiom. It is in three parts, the flanking section consisting of a sprightly rustic dance tune, while the middle part is faster and more vigorous contrasting music. The other somewhat less familiar, but no less beguiling, *Norwegian Dances* are the first in D minor, the third in G major, and the fourth in D major.

The *Peer Gynt Suite No. 1,* for orchestra, op. 46 (1876) consists of four numbers from the incidental music for the Ibsen drama, *Peer Gynt,* produced in Oslo in 1876. Ibsen's epic is a picaresque drama about a capricious and at times spirited Norwegian peasant named Peer, and his fabulous adventures, some of them amatory. He abducts the bride, Solveig, then deserts her; as an outlaw he roams the world; when he returns home he finds Solveig still believing in him and through that belief he comes upon salvation.

The first movement of Suite No. 1 is a bucolic picture, "Morning," in which a barcarolle-type melody is prominent. This is followed by a tender elegy for muted strings, "Ase's Death," Ase being Peer Gynt's mother. A capricious, sensual dance follows, "Anitra's Dance," a mazurka-like melody with an Oriental identity. The final movement, "In the Hall of the Mountain King" is a grotesque march built from a four-measure phrase which grows in volume and intensity until it evolves into a thunderous fortissimo.

Grieg prepared a second suite from his incidental music for *Peer Gynt,* op. 55. Only one movement from this set is popular, "Solveig's Song," a haunting Norwegian song for muted strings portraying Solveig, the abducted bride who thereafter remains forever faithful to Peer Gynt. This is the final movement of a suite whose preceding movements are "Ingrid's Lament," "Arabian Dance," and "Peer Gynt's Homecoming."

Sigurd Jorsalfar, a suite for orchestra, op. 56 (1872, revised 1892) also comes from the incidental music to a play, in this case a historical drama of the same name by Bjørnstjerne Bjørnson, produced in Oslo in 1872. The central character is the twelfth-century Norwegian king, Sigurd, who joins the Crusades to fight heroically against the Saracens. There are three movements to this suite. The first "Prelude" is subtitled "In the King's Hall," and has three distinct sections. In the first of these the main thought is a theme for clarinets and bassoons against plucked strings; in the second, a trio, the most prominent melody is that for flute imitated by the oboe; the third part repeats the first. The second movement is "Intermezzo" or "Borghild's Dream." This is serene music alternated by an agitated mood. The finale is "March of Homage" in which trumpet fanfares and a loud chord for full orchestra set the stage for the main theme, in four cellos. This same theme is later proclaimed triumphantly by the full orchestra. Midway there appears a trio in which the first violins offer the main melody.

Two Elegiac Melodies, for string orchestra, op. 34 (1880) are adaptations of two of the composer's most famous songs found in op. 33, "Heartwounds" and "The Last Spring," lyrics by A. O. Vinje. Both melodies are for the most part in a somber mood. The first is in a comparatively fast time while the second is in slow tempo.

Two Northern Melodies, for string orchestra, op. 63 (1895) is, as the title indicates, in two sections. The first, "In the Style of a Folksong," offers its main melody in the cellos after a short introduction. The second, "The Cowherd's Tune," begins with a slow, simple tune and ends with a delightful peasant dance.

The Broadway operetta, *Song of Norway,* was not only based upon episodes in the life of Grieg but also makes extensive use of Grieg's music. The book is by Milton Lazarus based on a play by Homer Curran, and the lyrics and music are by Robert Wright and George Forrest. The operetta opened on Broadway on August 21, 1944 (Lawrence Brooks played Grieg, and Helena Bliss his wife, Nina) to accumulate the impressive run of 860 performances. Since the operetta has become something of a classic of our popular theater through frequent revivals —and since its music is sometimes heard on concerts of semi-classical music—it deserves consideration. The story centers mainly around the love affair of Grieg and Nina Hagerup, and their ultimate marriage; it also carries the composer from obscurity to world fame. Wright and Forrest reached into the storehouse of Grieg's music for their songs. "Strange Music," which became a popular-song hit in 1944 and 1945, is based on one of Grieg's *Lyric Pieces* for piano, *Wedding Day in Troldhaugen.* "I Love You" is based on Grieg's famous song of the same name (*"Ich liebe Dich"*) which he actually wrote to express his love for Nina; the lyric was by Hans Andersen, and the song appeared in a set of four collected in op. 5 (1864). Musical episodes from Grieg's G major Violin Sonata, the *Peer Gynt Suite, Norwegian Dance No. 2,* the A minor Piano Concerto, and some of the piano pieces provided further material for popular songs and ballet music.

Ferde Grofé

୶ଌ୵ଌୗ ଌ୵ଌ୵

FERDE GROFÉ was born Ferdinand Rudolph Von Grofé in New York City on March 27, 1892. He began to study the violin and piano early. During his adolescence he became a member of the viola section of the Los Angeles Philharmonic. While engaged in serious music he started playing with jazz ensembles. Before long he formed one of his own, for which he made all the arrangements, and whose performances attracted considerable interest among jazz devotees. Paul Whiteman was one of those who was impressed by Grofé's brand of jazz. In 1919 he hired Grofé to play the piano in, and make all the arrangements for, the Paul Whiteman Orchestra. Grofé worked for Whiteman for a dozen years, a period during which he prepared most of the arrangements used by Whiteman, including that of George Gershwin's historic *Rhapsody in Blue* at its world première in 1924. In 1924, Grofé wrote his first symphonic composition in a jazz style, *Broadway at Night.* One year later, came the *Mississippi Suite,* his first success. In 1931 he scored a triumph with the *Grand Canyon Suite,* still his most celebrated composition. After 1931, Grofé toured the country as conductor of his own orchestra, making numerous appearances in public and over the radio. From 1939 to 1942 he taught orchestration at the Juilliard School of Music in New York and in 1941 he began an eight-year contract with the Standard Oil Company of California to conduct the San Francisco Symphony over the radio. Grofé has also written music for motion pictures and special works for industry.

With Gershwin, Grofé has been an outstanding composer of symphonic music utilizing jazz and other popular styles and idioms. He is distinguished for his remarkable skill at orchestration, which frequently employs non-musical devices for special effects—for example, a typewriter in *Tabloid,* pneumatic drills in *Symphony in Steel,* a bicycle pump in *Free Air,* shouts and door-banging in *Hollywood Suite,* and the sound of bouncing bowling balls in *Hudson River Suite.*

The *Grand Canyon Suite* (1931), Grofé's most significant composition as well as the most famous, is an orchestral description in five movements of one of America's natural wonders. The first movement, "Sunrise," opens with a timpani roll to suggest the break of dawn over the canyon. The main melody depicting the sunrise itself is heard in muted trumpet against a chordal background. As the movement progresses, the music becomes increasingly luminous, until the sun finally erupts into full resplendence. "The Painted Desert" is an atmospheric tone picture. Nebulous chords suggest an air of mystery before a sensual melodic section unfolds. "On the Trail" is the most popular movement of the suite, having for many years been expropriated as the identifying theme-signature for the Philip Morris radio program. An impulsive, restless rhythm brings us a picture of a jogging burro. A cowboy tune is then set contrapuntally against this rhythm. In "Sunset" animal calls precede a poignant melody that speaks about the peace and serenity that descend on the canyon at sunset. "Cloudburst" is the concluding movement in which a violent storm erupts, lashes the canyon with its fury, and then subsides. Tranquillity now returns, and the canyon is once more surrounded by breathless and quiet beauty.

The *Hudson River Suite* (1955) was written for André Kostelanetz, the conductor, who introduced the work in Washington, D.C. This music provides five different aspects of the mighty river in New York, and its associations with American history. The river itself is described in the opening movement, "The River." This is followed by a portrait of Henry Hudson. The colonial times and the land of Rip Van Winkle are discussed in the third movement, "Rip Van Winkle," while in "Albany Night Boat," a delightful account is given of New York in years gone by, when a holiday trip on the boat was a favorite pastime of New York couples. The suite ends with "New York" a graphic etching of the metropolis along the Hudson.

The *Mississippi Suite* (1925)—like its eminent successor, the *Grand Canyon Suite*—was written for Paul Whiteman, who introduced it in Carnegie Hall. The first movement, "Father of the Waters" has a melody of an American-Indian identity representing the river. In "Huckleberry Finn," the character of the boy is suggested by a jazz motive in the tuba, later amplified into a spacious jazz melody for strings. "Old Creole Days" highlights a Negro melody in muted trumpet soon taken over by different sections of the orchestra. The closing movement is the suite's best known section and the composer's own favorite among his compositions. Called "Mardi Gras" it is a lively and colorful picture of carnival time in New Orleans. A rhythmic passage with which the movement opens serves as the preface to an eloquent melody for strings.

David Guion

⤦⤦⤦ ⤦⤦⤦

DAVID WENDELL FENTRESS GUION was born in Ballinger, Texas, on December 15, 1895. He received his musical training at the piano with local teachers and with Leopold Godowsky in Vienna. After returning to the United States he filled several posts as teacher of music in Texas, and from 1925 to 1928 taught piano at the Chicago Music College. Early in the 1930's he appeared in a cowboy production featuring his own music at the Roxy Theater in New York and soon thereafter made weekly broadcasts over the National Broadcasting Company network. A David Guion Week was celebrated throughout Texas in 1950.

He is best known for his skilful arrangements and transcriptions of Western folk songs and Negro Spirituals, some of which first became famous in his versions. His orchestral adaptation of "The Arkansas Traveler" has long been a favorite on "pop" concerts. A familiar legend helped to dramatize this American folk song to many. A traveler caught in the rain stops outside an Arkansas hut where an old man is playing part of a folk tune on his fiddle. Upon questioning him the traveler learns that the old fiddler does not know the rest of the song, whereupon the stranger takes the fiddle from him and completes it. The two then become devoted friends.

Even more famous is David Guion's arrangement of "Home on the Range," in 1930. It is not quite clear who actually wrote this song. It was discovered by John A. Lomax who heard it sung by a Texan saloon keeper, recorded it, and published it in his 1910 edition of *Cowboy Songs*. Only after Guion had arranged it did it become a national favorite over the radio, its popularity no doubt immensely enhanced by the widely circulated story that this was President Franklin D. Roosevelt's favorite song.

Guion's concert arrangement for full orchestra of "Turkey in the Straw" is also of interest. This folk tune—sometimes known as "Zip Coon"—first achieved popularity on the American musical stage in the era before the minstrel show. It was published in Baltimore in 1834 and first made popular that year by Bob Farrell at the Bowery Theater. After that it was a familiar routine of the black-faced entertainer, George Washington Dixon. Several have laid claim to the song, but it is most likely derived from an English or Irish melody.

Other arrangements and transcriptions by Guion include "Nobody Knows De Trouble I've Seen," "Oh, Bury Me Not on the Lone Prairie," "Ride Cowboy Ride," "Short'nin' Bread," and "Swing Low, Sweet Chariot."

Guion has also written several compositions of his own in which the folk element is pronounced. One of these is named *Alley Tunes,* three musical scenes from the South. Its most famous movement is the last, "The Harmonica Player," but the earlier two are equally appealing for their homespun melodies and vigorous national identity: "Brudder Sinkiller and His Flock of Sheep" and "The Lonesome Whistler." Another pleasing orchestral composition by Guion is a waltz suite entitled *Southern Nights.*

Johan Halvorsen

JOHAN HALVORSEN was born in Drammen, Norway, on March 15, 1864. After attending the Stockholm Conservatory he studied the violin with Adolf Brodsky in Leipzig and César Thomson in Belgium. In 1892 he returned to his native land. For many years he was the distinguished conductor of the Oslo National Theater. His admiration of Grieg (whose niece he married) directed him toward musical nationalism, a style in which many of his most ambitious works were written. He was the composer of three symphonies, two rhapsodies, a festival overture, several suites, and a number of peasant dances all for orchestra. He died in Oslo on December 4, 1935.

The *Andante religioso*, in G minor, for violin and orchestra, is a richly melodious and spiritual work which has gained recognition with semi-classical orchestras. But Halvorsen's most popular composition is the *Triumphant Entry of the Boyars*, for orchestra. The boyar or boyard was a military aristocrat of ancient Russia, a tyrant as notorious for his cruelty as for his extravagant way of life. Halvorsen's vigorous, colorful march has an Oriental personality. It opens with a stirring march subject for clarinet against a drone bass in cellos and double basses, and it highlights a fanfare for trumpets and trombones.

George Frederick Handel

GEORGE FREDERICK HANDEL was born in Halle, Saxony, on February 23, 1685. After studying the organ in his native city he settled in Hamburg where he wrote, and in 1705 had produced, his first operas, *Almira* and *Nero*. A period of travel and study in Italy followed, during which he was influenced by the Italian instrumental music of that period. In 1770 he was appointed Kapellmeister in Hanover. In 1712 he settled permanently in England where in 1727 he became a British subject and Anglicized his name. He became one of England's giant figures in music, first as a composer of operas in the Italian style, and after that (when the vogue for such operas died out) as a creator of oratorios. For several years he was the court composer for Queen Anne and royal music master for George I. In 1720 he was appointed artistic director of the then newly organized Royal Academy of Music. In the last years of his life he suffered total blindness, notwithstanding which fact he continued giving public performances at the organ, conducting his oratorios, and writing music. He died in London on April 14, 1759 and was buried in Westminster Abbey.

Handel was a prolific composer of operas, oratorios, orchestral music, concertos for solo instruments and orchestra, sonatas, compositions for harpsichord, and chamber works. He was greatest in his religious music, in the deservedly world-famous oratorio *Messiah,* and in such somewhat less familiar but no less distinguished works as *Judas Maccabaeus, Samson, Solomon,* and *Israel in Egypt.* His greatest music is on such a consistently high spiritual plane, is filled with such grandeur of expression, and reveals such extraordinary contrapuntal skill that it does not easily lend itself to popular consumption. But one passage from the *Messiah* is particularly famous, and especially popular with people the world over; it is probably the most celebrated single piece of music he ever wrote, and while originally for chorus and orchestra, is familiar in innumerable transcriptions for orchestra or for band. It is the sublime "Hallelujah Chorus," about which the composer himself said when he finished writing it: "I did think I did see all Heaven before me, and the great God himself." This grandiose choral passage, a miracle of contrapuntal technique, is undoubtedly the climactic point of the entire oratorio. When the *Messiah* was first heard in London on March 23, 1743 (a little less than a year after its world première which took place in Dublin, Ireland, on April 13, 1742) the awesome immensity of this music made such an impression on King George II, in the audience, that he rose spontaneously in his seat and remained standing throughout the piece. The audience followed their king in listening to the music in a standing position. Since then it has been a custom in performances of *Messiah* for the audience to rise during the singing of the "Hallelujah Chorus."

The *Harmonious Blacksmith* is Handel's best known composition for the harpsichord. This is the fourth movement of a harpsichord suite, No. 5 in E major, which the composer wrote in 1720; but most frequently it is played apart from the rest of the movements as a self-sufficient composition. The title *Harmonious Blacksmith* was created not by the composer but by a publisher in Bath, England, when in 1822 he issued the fourth movement of the suite as a separate piece of music. There happened to be in Bath a blacksmith who often sang this Handel tune and who came to be known in that town as the "harmonious blacksmith." The Bath publisher recognized the popular appeal of a title like "Harmonious Blacksmith" and decided to use it for this music. The story that Handel conceived this tune while waiting in a blacksmith's shop during a storm is, however, apocryphal. The *Harmonious Blacksmith* begins with a simple two-part melody which then undergoes five equally elementary variations.

The *Largo,* so familiar as an instrumental composition in various transcriptions, is really an aria from one of Handel's operas. It was a tenor aria *("Ombrai mai fu")* from *Serse* (1738) in which is described the beauty of the cool shade of a palm tree. In slower tempo it has become, in its instrumental dress, a broad, stately melody of religious character with the simple tempo marking of *Largo* as its title.

The *Water Music* (1717) is a suite for orchestra made up of charming little dances, airs and fanfares written for a royal water pageant held on the Thames River in London on July 19, 1717. A special barge held the orchestra that performed this composition while the musicians sailed slowly up and down the river. The king was so impressed by Handel's music that he asked it be repeated three times. In its original form, this suite is made up of twenty pieces, but the version most often heard today is an adaptation by Sir Hamilton Harty in which only six movements appear: Overture, Air, Bourrée, Hornpipe, Air, and Fanfare.

Joseph Haydn

FRANZ JOSEPH HAYDN was born in Rohrau, Austria, on March 31, 1732. From 1740 to 1749 he was a member of the choir of St. Stephen's in Vienna, attending its school for a comprehensive musical training. For several years after that he lived in Vienna, teaching music, and completing various hack assignments, while pursuing serious composition. In 1755 he was appointed by Baron Karl Josef Fuernberg to write music for and direct the concerts at his palace; it was in this office that Haydn wrote his first symphonies and string quartets as well as many other orchestral and chamber-music works. From 1758 to 1760 he was Kapellmeister to Count Ferdinand Maximilian Morzin. In

1761 Haydn became second Kapellmeister to Prince Paul Anton Esterházy at Eisenstadt, rising to the post of first Kapellmeister five years after that. Haydn remained with the Esterházys until 1790, a period in which he arrived at full maturity as a composer. His abundant symphonies, quartets, sonatas and other compositions spread his fame throughout the length and breadth of Europe. After leaving the employ of the Esterházys, Haydn paid two visits to London, in 1791 and again in 1794, where he directed orchestral concerts for which he wrote his renowned *London* symphonies. At the dusk of his career, Haydn produced two crowning masterworks in the field of choral music: the oratorios *The Creation* (1798) and *The Seasons* (1801). Haydn died in Vienna on May 31, 1809.

Haydn was an epochal figure during music's classical era. He helped to establish permanently the structures of the symphony, quartet, sonata; to arrive at a fully realized homophonic style as opposed to the contrapuntal idiom of the masters who preceded him; and to arrive at new concepts of harmony, orchestration, and thematic development. He helped pave the way for the giants who followed him, most notably Mozart and Beethoven, who helped carry the classical era in music to its full flowering. To his musical writing Haydn brought that charm, grace, stateliness, beauty of lyricism that we associate with classicism, and with it a most engaging sense of humor and at times even a remarkable expressiveness. Most of Haydn's music belongs to the serious concert repertory. He did write some music intended for the masses— mainly the Contredanses, German Dances and Minuets which, after all, was the dance music of the Austrian people in Haydn's time. Haydn's *German Dances* and Minuets are especially appealing. The former was the forerunner of the waltz, but its melodies and rhythms have a lusty peasant quality and an earthy vitality; the latter was the graceful, sedate dance of the European court. Twelve of Haydn's *German Dances* and twelve of his Minuets (the latter called *Katherine Menuetten*) were written in the closing years of his life and published in 1794; they were intended for the court ball held at the Redoutensaal in Vienna where they were introduced on November 25, 1792. The *German Dances* here have sobriety and dignity, and are often filled with Haydn's remarkable innovations in melodic and harmonic writing; the Minuets are consistently light and carefree in spirit.

The *Gypsy Rondo*—often heard in various transcriptions, including one for violin and piano by Fritz Kreisler—comes from the Piano Trio No. 1 in G major, op. 73, no. 2 (1795) where it is the concluding movement (Rondo all' ongarese). It is in Hungarian style, vivacious in rhythmic and melodic content; it is for this reason that Haydn himself designated this music "in a gypsy style" and Kreisler's transcription bears the title of *Hungarian Rondo.*

Of Haydn's more than one hundred symphonies the one occasionally given by pop orchestras is a curiosity known as the *Toy Symphony.* Actually we now know that Haydn never really wrote it, but it was the work of either Mozart's father, Leopold, or Haydn's brother, Michael. But it was long attributed to Joseph Haydn, and still is often credited to him. This little symphony in C major, which is in three short movements, was long believed to have been written by Haydn during his visit to Berchtegaden, Bavaria, in 1788 where he became interested in toy instruments. The symphony uses numerous toy instruments (penny trumpet, quail call, rattle, cuckoo, whistle, little drum, toy triangle, and so forth) together with three orthodox musical instruments, two violins and a bass.

Joseph Haydn was also the composer of Austria's national anthem, "*Gott erhalte Franz den Kaiser.*" He was commissioned to do so in 1797 by the Minister of the Interior to help stir the patriotic ardor of Austrians; it was first performed in all Austrian theaters on the Emperor's birthday on February 12, 1797. The Emperor was deeply impressed by the anthem. "You have expressed," he said, "what is in every loyal Austrian heart, and through your melody Austria will always be honored." Haydn himself used the same melody in one of his string quartets: as the slow second movement in which it receives a series of variations. It is for this reason that this quartet, in C major, op. 76, no. 3, is popularly known as the *Emperor Quartet.*

Victor Herbert

VICTOR HERBERT was born in Dublin, Ireland, on February 1, 1859. He received a sound musical training at the Stuttgart Conservatory, following which he studied the cello privately with

Bernhard Cossmann in Baden-Baden. For several years after that he played the cello in many German and Austrian orchestras. His bow as a composer took place with two ambitious works, a suite and a concerto, both for cello and orchestra. They were introduced by the Stuttgart Symphony (the composer as soloist) in 1883 and 1885 respectively. After marrying the prima donna, Therese Foerster, in 1886, Herbert came to the United States and played the cello in the Metropolitan Opera orchestra, his wife having been engaged by that company. He soon played the cello in other major American orchestras besides conducting symphonic concerts, concerts of light music, and performances at important festivals. In 1893 he succeeded Patrick S. Gilmore as bandleader of the famous 22nd Regiment Band, and from 1898 to 1904 he was principal conductor of the Pittsburgh Symphony. After 1904 he was the conductor of his own orchestra.

Herbert won world renown as a composer of operettas for which he produced a wealth of melodies that have never lost their charm or fascination for music lovers. His first produced operetta, *Prince Ananias,* in 1894 was a failure. But one year later came *The Wizard of Oz,* the first of a long string of stage successes Herbert was henceforth to enjoy. From then on, until the end of his life, Herbert remained one of Broadway's most productive and most significant composers. Many of his operettas are now classics of the American musical stage. Among these are: *The Fortune Teller* (1898), *Babes in Toyland* (1903), *Mlle. Modiste* (1905), *The Red Mill* (1906) and *Naughty Marietta* (1910). A facile composer with an extraordinary technique at orchestration and harmonization, and a born melodist who had a seemingly inexhaustible reservoir of beautiful tunes, Herbert was a giant figure in American popular music and in the music for the American popular theater. He died of a heart attack in New York City on May 26, 1924.

Victor Herbert produced a considerable amount of concert music—concertos, symphonies, suites, overtures—most of which has passed out of the more serious repertory. A few of these concert works have enough emotional impact and melodic fascination to enjoy a permanent status in the semi-classical repertory. Potpourris from the scores of his most famous operettas—and orchestral transcriptions of individual songs from these productions—are, of course, basic to any pop or semi-classical orchestra repertory. For Herbert's greatest songs from his operettas are classics, "as pure in outline as the melodies of Schubert and Mozart" according to Deems Taylor.

Al Fresco is mood music which opens the second act of the operetta, *It Happened in Nordland* (1904). Herbert had previously written and published it as a piano piece, using the pen-name of Frank Roland, in order to test the appeal of this little composition. It did so well in this version that Herbert finally decided to include it in his operetta where it serves to depict a lively carnival scene.

The American Fantasia (1898) is a brilliantly orchestrated and skilfully contrived fantasy made up of favorite American national ballads and songs. It is the composer's stirring tribute to the country of his adoption. The ballads and songs are heard in the following sequence: "Hail Columbia," "Swanee River," "The Girl I Left Behind Me," "Dixie," "Columbia the Gem of the Ocean." This composition comes to an exciting finish with "The Star-Spangled Banner" in a Wagnerian-type orchestration.

The operetta *Babes in Toyland,* which opened in New York on October 13, 1903, was an extravaganza inspired by the-then recent success on Broadway of *The Wizard of Oz.* Herbert's operetta drew its characters from fairy tales, *Mother Goose,* and other children's stories, placing these characters in a rapid succession of breath-taking scenes of spectacular beauty. The complicated plot concerned the escape of little Jane and Alan from their miserly uncle to the garden of Contrary Mary. They then come to Toyland where they meet the characters from fairy tales and Mother Goose, and where toys are dominated by the wicked Toymaker whom they finally bring to his destruction. Principal musical numbers from this score include the delightful orchestral march, "March of the Toys," and the songs "Toyland" and "I Can't Do the Sum."

Dagger Dance is one of the most familiar pieces in the semi-classical repertory in the melodic and rhythmic style of American-Indian music. It comes from Herbert's opera *Natoma,* whose première took place in Philadelphia on February 25, 1911. This spirited Indian dance music appears in the second act, at a climactic moment in which Natoma, challenged to perform a dagger dance, does so; but during the performance she stabs and kills the villain, Alvarado.

The Fortune Teller whose New York première took place on September 26, 1898, is an operetta that starred Alice Neilsen in the dual role of Musette, a gypsy fortune teller, and Irma, a ballet student. Against a Hungarian setting, the play involves these two girls in love affairs with a Hungarian Hussar and a gypsy musician. Hungarian characters and a Hungarian background allowed Herbert to write music generously spiced with Hungarian and gypsy flavors, music exciting for its sensual appeal. The most famous song from this score is "Gypsy Love Song," sometimes also known as "Slumber On, My Little Gypsy Sweetheart," sung by Sandor, the gypsy musician, in tribute to Musette.

Indian Summer: An American Idyll (1919) is a tone picture of Nature which Herbert wrote in two versions, for solo piano, and for orchestra. Twelve years after the composer's death, Gus Kahn wrote lyrics for its main melody, and for fourteen weeks it was heard on the radio Hit Parade, twice in the Number 1 position.

The Irish Rhapsody for orchestra (1892) is one of several concert works in which Herbert honored the country of his birth. This work is built from several familiar Irish ballads found by the composer in Thomas Moore's *Irish Melodies,* published in 1807. "Believe Me if All These Endearing Young Charms" comes immediately after a harp cadenza. This is followed by a variation of "The Rocky Road to Dublin," "To Ladies' Eyes," "Thamma Hulla," "Erin, Oh Erin," and "Rich and Rare Were the Gems She Wore." An oboe cadenza then serves as the transition to "St. Patrick's Day." The rhapsody ends with "Garry Owen" set against "Erin, Oh Erin" in the bass.

Mlle. Modiste, introduced in New York on December 25, 1905, is the operetta in which Fritzi Scheff, once a member of the Metropolitan Opera, became a star of the popular musical theater. This is also the operetta in which she sang the waltz with which, for the rest of her life, she became identified, "Kiss Me Again." Fritzi Scheff was cast as Fifi, an employee in a Parisian hat shop. Her lowly station precludes her marriage to the man she loves, Capt. Etienne de Bouvray. An American millionaire becomes interested in her, and provides her with the funds to pursue her vocal studies. Fifi then becomes a famous opera star, thereby achieving both the fame and the fortune she needs to gain Capt. Etienne as a husband.

Early in this operetta, Fifi tries to demonstrate her talent as a singer by performing a number called "If I Were On the Stage," in which she offers various types of songs, including a polonaise, a gavotte, and a waltz. The waltz part was originally intended by Herbert as a caricature of that kind of dreamy, sentimental music and consisted of the melody of "Kiss Me Again" which he had written some time earlier, in 1903. On opening night the audience liked this part of the number so well, and was so noisy in its demonstration, that Herbert decided to feature it separately and prominently in his operetta, had new sentimental lyrics written for it, and called it "Kiss Me Again." This, of course, is the most celebrated single number from this operetta, but several others are equally appealing notably one of Herbert's finest marches, "The Mascot of the Troop," another waltz called "The Nightingale and the Star," and a humorous ditty, "I Want What I Want When I Want It."

The operetta, *Naughty Marietta*—first New York performance on November 7, 1910—was set in New Orleans in 1780 when that city was under Spanish rule. The noble lady, Marietta (starring the prima donna, Emma Trentini) had come to New Orleans from Naples to avoid an undesirable marriage. There she meets, falls in love with, and after many stirring adventures wins, Captain Dick Warrington. A basic element of this story is a melody—a fragment of which has come to the heroine in a dream. Marietta promises her hand to anybody who could give her the complete song of which this fragment is a part, and it is Dick Warrington, of course, who is successful. This melody is one of Herbert's best loved, "Ah, Sweet Mystery of Life." Other favorites from *Naughty Marietta* are "I'm Falling in Love With Someone," "Italian Street Song" the serenade " 'Neath the Southern Moon," and the march, "Tramp, Tramp, Tramp."

Pan Americana (1901) is a composition for orchestra described by Herbert as a *"morceau caractéristique."* He wrote it for the Pan American Exposition in Buffalo in 1901 (where President McKinley was assassinated). The three sections are in three different popular styles, the first in American-Indian, the second in ragtime, and the third in Cuban or Spanish.

Punchinello and *Yesterthoughts* (1900) are two evocative tone pictures originally for piano from a suite of pieces describing the natural beauties of scenes near or at Lake Placid, New York. Herbert orchestrated both these numbers.

The Red Mill, which came to New York on September 24, 1906, was an operetta starring the comedy team of Fred Stone and David Montgomery in a play set in Holland. They are two Americans stranded and penniless at an inn called "The Sign of the Red Mill." When they discover that little Gretchen is in love with Capt. Doris van Damm and refuses to marry the Governor to whom she is designated by her parents, they come to her assistance. After numerous escapades and antics they help her to win her true lover who, as it turns out, is the heir to an immense fortune. The following are its principal musical episodes: the main love duet, "The Isle of Our Dreams,"; "Moonbeams"; and the comedy song, "Every Day Is Ladies' Day for Me."

The *Suite of Serenades,* for orchestra (1924) was written for the same Paul Whiteman concert of American music at Aeolian Hall on February 12, 1924 in which Gershwin's *Rhapsody in Blue* was introduced. This is a four movement suite which represented Herbert's only attempt to write directly for a jazz orchestra, and parts of it are characterized by jazz scoring and syncopations. Herbert wrote a second version of this suite for symphony orchestra. In the four movements the composer skilfully simulates four national styles. The first is Spanish, the second Chinese, the third Cuban, and the fourth Oriental.

Another familiar orchestral suite by Herbert is the *Suite Romantique* (1901). Herbert's vein for sentimental melody is here generously tapped. The four movements are mood pictures named as follows: *"Visions," "Aubade"* (a beautiful solo for the cellos), *"Triomphe d'amour"* (a glowing love duet), and *"Fête nuptiale."*

The Woodland Fancies, for orchestra (1901) also consist of four evocative and pictorial mood pictures, this time inspired by the Adirondack mountains where Herbert maintained a summer home and which he dearly loved. Here the four movements are entitled: "Morning in the Mountains," "Forest Nymphs," "Twilight," and "Autumn Frolics."

There are individual songs from several other Herbert operettas that are part of the semi-classical repertory in orchestral transcriptions. Among these are: "The Angelus" and the title song from *Sweethearts* (1913); "I Love Thee, I Adore Thee" which recurs throughout *The Serenade* (1897); "A Kiss in the Dark" from *Orange Blossoms* (1922); "Star Light, Star Bright," a delightful waltz from *The Wizard of the Nile* (1895); and "Thine Alone" from the Irish operetta, *Eileen* (1917).

Ferdinand Hérold

꿎꿎 ꙸꙸ

LOUIS JOSEPH FERDINAND HÉROLD was born in Paris on January 28, 1791. He began to study music when he was eleven. From 1805 to 1812 he attended the Paris Conservatory where his teachers included Adam and Méhul. In 1812 he received the Prix de Rome. Following his three-year stay in Rome he settled in Naples where he was pianist to Queen Caroline and had his first opera, *La Gioventù di Enrico,* produced in 1815. After returning to his native city he completed a new opera, *Charles de France,* which was successfully produced in 1816 at the Opéra-Comique in Paris where, from this time on, all his operas were given. Hérold wrote many serious operas before turning to the field in which he earned his importance and popularity, the opéra-comique. His first work in this genre was *Marie* in 1826; his most successful, *Zampa,* in 1831. He also enjoyed a triumph with his last opéra-comique, *Le Pré aux clercs,* produced in 1832. Hérold died of consumption in Paris on January 19, 1833 before reaching his forty-second birthday.

About all that has survived from Hérold's most famous opera, *Zampa,* is its overture, a semi-classical favorite everywhere. *Zampa*—libretto by Mélesville—was introduced at the Opéra-Comique in Paris on May 3, 1831. The hero, Zampa, is the leader of a band of pirates who invade an island. He meets Camille and compels her to desert her lover and marry him. During the marriage festivities the pirate leader mockingly tries to place a ring on the finger of a statue. The statue suddenly comes to life and brings Zampa to his doom by drowning.

The overture opens with a robust subject for full orchestra (derived from the pirates' chorus of the first act). A brief pause separates this section from a slower one in which timpani rolls and loud chords in the wind precede a stately melody for wind instruments. After some development, in which the mood becomes dramatic, two new subjects are heard: the first is a sensitive melody for clarinet against plucked strings, and the second is a soaring song for the violins.

Jenö Hubay

JENÖ HUBAY was born in Budapest, Hungary, on September 15, 1858. His father, a professor of the violin at the Budapest Conservatory, gave him his first violin lessons. Jenö made his public debut as violinist when he was eleven, then completed his violin studies with Joachim in Berlin and with Vieuxtemps in Belgium. In 1886 he was appointed professor of the violin at the Budapest Conservatory, and from 1919 to 1934 he was its director. Hubay was one of Europe's most eminent violinists, violin teachers, and performers of chamber music, the last with the Hubay Quartet which he founded. He died in Vienna on March 12, 1937.

Hubay was the composer of several operas, four symphonies, four violin concertos, and many pieces for the violin. He was at his best when he drew both his inspiration and materials from Hungarian folk music. Perhaps his best known work is a set of fourteen pieces for violin and orchestra collectively known as *Scènes de la Csárda,* or *Hungarian Czardas Scenes.* The czardas is a popular Hungarian folk dance in duple time characterized by quick syncopations, and exploiting alternating slow and rapid passages. These *Scènes* are often presented as orchestral compositions. The fourth, *Hejre Kati,* is the most popular of the group, a piece of music electrifying for its rhythmic momentum. The second, known as *Hungarian Rhapsody,* and the fifth, *Waves of Balaton,* are also familiar. Besides their rhythmic vitality these compositions are of interest for their sensual melodies, and dramatic contrasts of tempo and mood.

From Hubay's most famous opera, *The Violin Maker of Cremona,* comes a sensitively lyrical "Intermezzo," for orchestra. Hubay wrote this one-act opera in 1894, and it was introduced in Budapest the same year. The text by Francois Coppé and Henri Beauclair concerns a violin-making contest in Ferrari, Italy, in which the prize is the beautiful girl, Giannina. A hunchback, Filippo, makes the best violin, but he generously permits Giannina to marry Sandro, the man she really loves. A transcription of the "Intermezzo" for violin and piano is popular in the repertory and bears the title of the opera. The Intermezzo had also been adapted by Stoll as a composition for voice and orchestra under the name "Lonely Night."

Engelbert Humperdinck

ENGELBERT HUMPERDINCK was born in Sieburg, Germany, on September 1, 1854. He attended the Cologne Conservatory where his teachers included Hiller (who was the first to recognize his talent), Jensen and Gernsheim. After winning the Mozart Scholarship of Frankfort in 1876, Humperdinck continued his music study in Munich with Franz Lachner and Rheinberger. In Munich he published his first important composition, a *Humoreske* for orchestra (1880). In 1881, he received the Meyerbeer Prize and in 1897, the Mendelssohn Prize, both for composition. Between 1885 and 1887 he was professor of the Barcelona Conservatory in Spain and in 1890 he became professor at Hoch's Conservatory in Frankfort, and music critic of the *Frankfurter Zeitung*. He achieved his greatest success as a composer with the fairy opera, *Hansel and Gretel,* produced in Weimar in 1893. After 1896, Humperdinck devoted himself exclusively to composition, and though he wrote several fine operas none was able to equal the popularity of his fairy-opera. He died in Neustrelitz, Germany, on September 27, 1921.

Hansel and Gretel scored a sensational success in its own day; and, in ours, it is the only opera by which Humperdinck is remembered. Following its première in Weimar, Germany, on December 23, 1893, it was performed within a year in virtually every major German opera house. In 1894 it came to London, and in 1895 to New York. The text by Adelheid Wette (Humperdinck's sister) is based on the Ludwig Grimm fairy tale familiar to young and old throughout the world.

The overture, and two orchestral episodes, are often performed outside the opera house. The Overture is made up of several melodies from the opera beginning with the so-called "prayer melody," a gentle song for horns and bassoons. A rhythmic passage then describes the spell effected by the witch on the children. After this comes the lovable third-act melody in which the children are awakened by the dewman. The happy dance of the children from the close of the opera leads back to the opening prayer with which the overture comes to a gentle conclusion.

The *Dream Pantomime* comes in the second act and is an orchestral episode in which is described the descent of the fairies who provide a protective ring around the children, alone and asleep in the deep forest. The *Gingerbread Waltz* (*Knusperwalzer*) from Act 3 is the joyous music expressing the children's delight after they have succeeded in pushing the witch inside the oven and burning her to a crisp.

Among Humperdinck's many works for symphony orchestra one is occasionally performed by semi-classical or pop orchestras. It is the *Moorish Rhapsody* (1898) written for the Leeds Festival in England. The first movement, "Tarifa—Elegy at Sunrise" reflects the sorrow of a shepherd over the decay of the Moorish people. "Tangiers—A Night in a Moorish Café" is a coffee-house scene highlighted by the sensual chant of a café singer. The suite concludes with "Tetuan—A Rider in the Desert," depicting a desert ride with a view of Paradise in the distance. To carry into his music an Oriental atmosphere, Humperdinck modeled some of his principal themes after actual Moorish melodies, such as the second theme of the first movement for English horn, and the main melody for woodwind in the second movement.

Jacques Ibert

JACQUES IBERT was born in Paris on August 15, 1890. He attended the Paris Conservatory between 1911 and 1919, with a hiatus of several years during World War I when he served in the French Navy. In 1919 he won the Prix de Rome. While residing in the Italian capital he wrote a symphonic work with which he scored his first major success, the suite *Escales,* introduced in Paris in 1924. From 1937 to 1955 he was director of the Academy of Rome. During this period he also served for a while as director of the combined management of the Paris Opéra and Opéra-Comique.

Ibert has written many works in virtually every form, which have placed him in the front rank of contemporary French composers. Many of these compositions are in a neo-classical idiom. Occasionally, however, he has made a delightful excursion into satire. It is with one of the latter works, the *Divertissement* for orchestra (1930) that he has entered the semi-classical repertory, though to be sure this composition is also frequently given at symphony concerts. The *Divertissement* begins with a short Introduction in which the prevailing mood of levity is first introduced. Then comes the *"Cortège."* A few introductory bars suggest two march themes, the first in strings, and the second in trumpet. After that appears a loud quotation from Mendelssohn's "Wedding March" from his *A Midsummer Night's Dream Suite*. The "Nocturne" is a dreamy little melody which precedes a delightful "Waltz" and a breezy "Parade." The finale is in the style of an Offenbach can-can, with the piano interpolating some impudent dissonant harmonies.

Michael Ippolitov-Ivanov

MICHAEL IPPOLITOV-IVANOV was born in Gatchina, Russia, on November 19, 1859. He was graduated from the St. Petersburg Conservatory in 1882 where he was a pupil in composition of Rimsky-Korsakov. From 1882 to 1893 he was associated with the Tiflis Music School, first as teacher, then as director. In 1893 he was appointed professor of composition at the Moscow Conservatory on Tchaikovsky's recommendation, and from 1906 to 1922 he served as its director. He also distinguished himself as a conductor of opera in Moscow. He died in that city on January 28, 1935.

Ippolitov-Ivanov's best music profited from his intensive researches into Caucasian folk music. His principal works have assimilated many of the Oriental melodic and rhythmic idioms of songs and dances from that region. His most popular work of all is the *Caucasian Sketches* for orchestra, op. 10 (1895). The first movement, "In the Mountain Pass," brings up the picture of a mountain scene. Horn calls are here used prominently. "In the Village," opens with a cadenza for English horn and proceeds to a beautiful melody for viola set against a persistent ⅜ rhythm. "In the Mosque" dispenses with the strings while describing an impressive religious ceremony. The suite ends with the stirring "March of the Sirdar," a "sirdar" being an Oriental potentate.

Ivanovici

ও৳ও৳ ৡৡৡ

Neither Ivanovici's first name nor details of his life are known. He was born in Banat, Rumania, in 1848, distinguished himself as a bandleader in his native country, and died in Bucharest on April 1, 1905. For his band concerts he wrote many popular concert numbers. One of these is the concert waltz, *The Waves of the Danube (Donauwellen)*, written in 1880, and achieving from the first phenomenal popularity throughout Europe. The main waltz melody of this set of waltzes was expropriated by Al Dubin and Dave Franklin for the American popular song "The Anniversary Song," (lyrics by Saul Chaplin), which was effectively used in the motion picture *The Jolson Story* in 1946, sung on the sound track by Jolson himself.

Armas Järnefelt

ও৳ও৳ ৡৡৡ

ARMAS JÄRNEFELT was born in Viborg, Finland, on August 14, 1869. He studied music in Helsingfors with Ferruccio Busoni and Martin Wegelius; in Berlin with A. Becker; and in Paris with

Massenet. Beginning with 1898, and for several years thereafter, he conducted opera performances in Viborg and Helsingfors. In 1907 he settled in Sweden where three years later he became a citizen. There he became court composer and the conductor of the Royal Opera. After returning to Helsingfors in 1932, he directed the Opera for four years and the Helsingfors Municipal Theater for one. He also appeared as guest conductor of many important Finnish orchestras, distinguishing himself particularly in performances of music by Jean Sibelius (his brother-in-law). In 1940, Järnefelt received the official title of Professor. He died in Stockholm in June 1958.

Järnefelt wrote many works for orchestra, including suites, overtures, and shorter works. One of the last is *Berceuse* for two clarinets, one bassoon, two horns, violin solo and strings (1905), a moody and sensitive piece of music. The romantic main melody appears in solo violin after four introductory bars for muted strings.

His most popular composition is the *Praeludium* for chamber orchestra. It opens with a three-measure introduction for plucked strings. This is followed by a brisk march subject for oboe which is soon discussed by other winds, and after that by the violins over a drone bass. A passage for solo violin leads to the return of the march melody.

Dmitri Kabalevsky

DMITRI KABALEVSKY was born in St. Petersburg on December 30, 1904, and received his musical training in Moscow, at the Scriabin Music School and the Moscow Conservatory. He was graduated from the latter school in 1929, and in 1932 he was appointed instructor there. His first success as composer came in 1931 with his first symphony, commemorating the fifteenth anniversary of the Russian revolution; this was followed in 1934 by his second symphony, which enjoyed an even greater triumph both in and out of the Soviet Union.

In 1939 Kabalevsky was elected a member of the Presidium of the Organizing Committee of the Union of Soviet Composers; in 1940 he was given the Order of Merit; and in 1946 he received the Stalin Prize for the second string quartet. He has also written operas, concertos, additional symphonies, and piano music.

A composer who has always been partial to the more conventional means and techniques, and has relied heavily on broad and stately melodies and subjective feelings, Kabalevsky has managed to produce several compositions that have wide appeal. One is the sprightly *Colas Breugnon Overture. Colas Breugnon* was an opera adapted by V. Bragin from a novel by Romain Rolland; it was first performed in Leningrad on February 22, 1938. The central character is a 16th-century crafts-man—a jovial man who enjoys life and has a spicy sense of humor and a happy outlook on all things. The overture is essentially a study of that man, consistently gay and sprightly. There are two main melodies, both of them lively, and both derived from Burgundian folk songs.

Another popular work by Kabalevsky is *The Comedians*, op. 26 (1938), an orchestral suite made up of selections from the incidental music to a children's play, *The Inventor and the Comedians.* The play is about the varied and picaresque adventures of a group of wandering performers in various towns and at public fairs. There are ten episodes in the suite, each in a light, infectious style that makes for such easy listening that this work is often given at children's concerts. The ten sections are: Prologue, Galop, March, Waltz, Pantomime, Intermezzo, Little Lyrical Scene, Gavotte, Scherzo, and Epilogue.

Emmerich Kálmán

EMMERICH KÁLMÁN was born in Siófok, Hungary, on October 24, 1882. He studied composition in Budapest. In 1904 one of his symphonic compositions was performed by the Budapest Philharmonic, and in 1907 he received the Imperial Composition Prize. After settling in Vienna he abandoned serious composition for light music. From this time on he devoted himself to and distinguished himself in writing tuneful operettas. His first success came in 1909 with *Ein Herbstmanoever,* presented in New York as *The Gay Hussars.* Subsequent operettas made him one of Europe's leading composers for the popular theaters. The most famous are: *Sari* (1912), *The Gypsy Princess* (1915), *Countess Maritza* (1924) and *The Circus Princess* (1926). In 1938 he left Vienna, and after a period in Paris, he came to the United States where he remained until 1949. He completed his last operetta, *The Arizona Lady,* a few days before his death in Paris, on October 30, 1953; it was presented posthumously in Berne, Switzerland, in 1954.

Kálmán's forte in writing music for operettas was in combining the charm, *Gemuetlichkeit* and sentiment of Viennese music in general, and the Viennese waltz in particular, with the hot blood and sensual moods of Hungarian gypsy songs and dances.

The Circus Princess (Die Zirkusprinzessin)—first performed in Vienna in 1926, and in New York in 1927—was set in St. Petersburg and Vienna during the period immediately preceding World War I. When Fedora rejects the love of Prince Sergius by insisting she would sooner marry a circus performer, he seeks revenge by engaging a famous circus performer to pose as a member of nobility and woo and win Fedora. After their marriage, Fedora discovers the true identity of her husband, and leaves him. But she soon comes to the realization she is really in love with him and promises to come back if he in turn offers to give up his profession—a profession she now despises not from snobbery but because of fears for his safety. Two delightful waltz melodies—*"Leise schwebt das Glueck vorueber" "Im Boudoir der schoensten Frau"*—and an intriguing little melody that recurs throughout the operetta. *"Zwei maerchenaugen"* are the principal selections from this operetta.

Countess Maritza (Die Graefin Mariza) is Kálmán's most popular and successful operetta. It was first produced in Vienna in 1924, and in New York in 1926. The setting is Hungary in 1922. An impoverished count, Tassilo, finds employment on the estate of Countess Maritza under the assumed name of Torok. He falls in love with her, but when she learns of his real background she feels he is a fortune hunter interested only in her wealth. About to leave the employ of the countess and to bid her permanent farewell, Tassilo's fortune suddenly takes a turn for the better when his aunt, a Princess, comes to inform him that Tassilo is a wealthy man after all, due to her manipulations of his tangled business affairs. Now convinced that he loves her for herself alone, the Countess Maritza is only too happy to accept him as her husband.

This score contains some of Kálmán's finest and most beguiling music in a Hungarian-gypsy style. The most famous song is in this sensual, heart-warming idiom: "Play Gypsies, Dance Gypsies" (*"Komm Zigan, Komm Zigan, spiel mir was vor"*). This number begins with a languorous, romantic melody that soon lapses into a dynamic Hungarian-gypsy dance. Austrian waltz-music in a more sentimental manner is found in three winning songs: "Give My Regards to the Lovely Ladies of Fair Vienna" (*Gruess mir die reizenden Frauen im schoenen Wien"*), "I Would Like to Dance Once More" (*"Einmal moecht' ich wieder tanzen"*) and "Say, Yes!" (*"Sag ja, mein Lieb"*).

The Gypsy Princess (*Die Csárdásfuerstin*) was first performed in Vienna in 1915, and produced in New York in 1917 under the title of *The Riviera Girl*. The heroine is Sylvia Varescu, a performer in a Budapest cabaret, who is loved and pursued by Prince Edwin. But the Prince's father insists that he marry the Countess Stasi. Eventually the father's heart is softened and he becomes more tolerant towards having Sylvia as a daughter-in-law when he is discreetly reminded that once he, too, had been in love with a cabaret singer. The principal selections from his score include two soaring waltz melodies: *"Machen wir's den Schwalben nach"* and *"Tausend kleine Engel singen hab mich lieb."* The score also includes a dynamic Czardas, and a pleasing little tune in *"Ganz ohne Weiber geht die Chose nicht."*

Sari was introduced in New York in 1914. Pali is a gypsy violinist who has grown old and is eclipsed at one of his own concerts by his son, Laczi. Pali throws his beloved Stradivarius into the flames. Since both father and son have fallen in love with the same girl, the older man also renounces her. He wants Laczi to have her as well as his musical success. A bountiful score includes such delights as "Love Has Wings," "Love's Own Sweet Song," "My Faithful Stradivari," and "Softly Through the Summer Night."

Kéler-Béla

ᦞᧄᦞᧄ ᦞᧄᦞᧄ

K É L E R - B É L A was born Albert von Keler in Bartfeld, Hungary, on February 13, 1820. He studied law and worked as a farmer before turning to music in his twenty-fifth year. After studying in Vienna with Sechter and Schlesinger he played the violin in the orchestra of the Theater-an-der-Wien. In 1854 he went to Berlin where he became con-ductor of Gungl's Orchestra. He was soon back in Vienna to take over the direction of the famous Joseph Lanner Orchestra. From 1856 to 1863 he conducted an army band, and from 1863 to 1873 an orchestra in Wiesbaden. He died in that city on November 20, 1882.

Kéler-Béla wrote about one hundred and thirty compositions in the light Viennese style of Lanner and the two Johann Strausses. His works include waltzes, galops, and marches, a representative example of each being the waltz *Hoffnungssterne,* the *Hurrah-Sturm* galop, and the *Friedrich-Karl* march.

His most popular work is the *Hungarian Comedy Overture (Lust-spiel Ouverture).* It opens in a stately manner with forceful chords and a sustained melody in the woodwind. But the comedy aspect of this overture is soon made evident with two lilting tunes for the woodwind, separated by a dramatic episode for full orchestra. These two tunes receive extended enlargement. The overture ends with a succession of emphatic chords.

Jerome Kern

JEROME DAVID KERN was born in New York City on January 27, 1885. He first studied the piano with his mother. After being graduated from Barringer High School in Newark, New Jersey, he attended the New York College of Music where he was a pupil of Alexander Lambert, Albert von Doenhoff, Paolo Gallico and Austen Pearce. He received his apprenticeship as composer for the popular theater in 1903 in London, where with P. G. Wodehouse as his lyricist he wrote a topical song, "Mr. Chamberlain" that became a hit. After returning to the United States he worked in Tin Pan Alley and immediately became a prolific contributor of songs to the musical stage. In 1905 his song "How'd You Like to Spoon With Me?" was interpolated into *The Earl and the Girl* and became an outstanding success. From that time on, and up to the end of his life, he wrote over a thousand songs for more than a hundred stage and screen productions, thereby occupying an imperial position among American popular composers of his generation. His most famous Broadway musicals were: *The Girl from Utah* (1914), *Very Good, Eddie* (1915), *Oh, Boy!* (1917), *Leave it to Jane* (1917), *Sally* (1920), *Sunny* (1925), *Show Boat* (1927), *The Cat and the Fiddle* (1931), *Music in the Air* (1932), and *Roberta* (1933). His most significant motion pictures were *Swingtime* with Fred Astaire and Ginger Rogers, *You Were Never Lovelier* and *Cover Girl* both with Rita Hayworth, and *Centennial Summer*. Over a dozen of his songs sold more than two million copies of sheet music including "All the Things You Are," "They Didn't Believe Me," "Smoke Gets In Your Eyes," and "Look for the Silver Lining." Two of his songs received the Academy Award: "The Way You Look Tonight" from *Swingtime* and "The Last Time I Saw Paris" interpolated into *Lady Be Good*. Kern died in New York City on November 11, 1945.

Kern wrote two compositions for symphony orchestra which have entered the semi-classical repertory even though they are also performed by major symphony orchestras. These were his only ventures into the world of music outside the popular theater. One was *Mark Twain: A*

Portrait for Orchestra which he wrote on a commission from André Kostelanetz, who introduced it with the Cincinnati Symphony in 1942. This is a four movement suite inspired by the personality and life of Kern's favorite author, Mark Twain. The first movement, "Hannibal Days," describes a sleepy small town on a summer morning a century ago. The cry "Steamboat comin'!" pierces the silence. The town suddenly awakens. In the second movement, "Gorgeous Pilot House" Mark Twain leaves home to become a pilot's assistant on the Mississippi steamboat; this period in Mark Twain's life, which spans about nine years, ends with the outbreak of the Civil War. In "Wandering Westward," Twain meets failure as a Nevada prospector, after which he finally turns to journalism. The suite ends with "Mark in Eruption," tracing Twain's triumphant career as a writer.

Kern's second and only other symphonic work is *Scenario* in which he drew his basic melodic materials from his greatest and best loved musical production, *Show Boat*. Kern prepared *Scenario* at the behest of Artur Rodzinski, conductor of the Cleveland Orchestra, who felt that the music of *Show Boat* had sufficient artistic validity to justify its use in a major symphonic work. Rodzinski introduced *Scenario* in Cleveland with the Cleveland Orchestra in 1941, and since that time it has been performed by most of the major American orchestras.

A discussion of *Show Boat* is essential before *Scenario* can be commented upon. The libretto and lyrics are by Oscar Hammerstein II, based on the famous novel by Edna Ferber. *Show Boat,* in a lavish Florenz Ziegfeld production, was introduced in New York in 1927 and was an instantaneous box-office and artistic triumph. It has, to be sure, become a classic of the American stage, continually revived in all parts of the country, three times adapted for motion pictures, and has been given by an American opera company in its regular repertory. It proved a revolution in the American musical theater by avoiding the usual stilted routines and patterns of musical comedy—chorus girls, production numbers, synthetic humor, set dances and so forth—and arriving at an integrated musical play filled with authentic characterizations, backgrounds, atmosphere and dramatic truth. The story opens and closes on *Cotton Blossom,* a show boat traveling along the Mississippi to give performances at stops along the river. The principal love action involves Magnolia, daughter of Cap'n Andy (owner of the boat) and the gambler, Gaylord Ravenal. They run off and get married, but their happiness is short-lived. Magnolia, though pregnant, leaves her irresponsible husband. After the birth of Magnolia's daughter, Kim, the mother earns her living singing show boat songs in Chicago where she is found by her father and brought back to *Cotton Blossom*. Eventually, Magnolia and Ravenal are reconciled, and their daughter Kim becomes the new star of the show boat.

The most famous songs from this incomparable Kern score are: "Only Make Believe" and "Why Do I Love You?", both of them love duets of Magnolia and Ravenal; two poignant laments sung by the half-caste Julie, a role in which Helen Morgan first attained stardom as a torch-song performer, "Can't Help Lovin' That Man" and "Bill" (the latter with lyrics by P. G. Wodehouse); and a hymn to the Mississippi which has acquired virtually the status of an American folk song, "Ol' Man River."

Scenario makes extended use of these songs in an integrated piece of music. It opens with a sensitive passage for muted strings and continues with a theme for horn; both subjects are intended to portray the Mississippi River and are the motto subjects of the entire work. The main melody of this tone poem is "Ol' Man River," first given softly by violas and bass clarinet. Other major songs of the musical play follow, among them being "Only Make Believe" and "Why Do I Love You?", after which "Ol' Man River" is heard for the last time.

Many of Kern's more than a thousand popular songs are now classics in the popular repertory. They are so fresh and spontaneous in their lyricism, so inventive in the harmonic background, so filled with charm and grace that their survival seems assured. Two symphonic compositions by Robert Russell Bennett are constructed from one or more of Kern's best known songs. One is *Symphonic Study,* a tone poem introduced in 1946 by the NBC Symphony under Frank Black. This work presents several Kern songs in correct chronological sequence beginning with "They Didn't Believe Me." After that come "Babes in the Wood," "The Siren's Song," "Left All Alone Again Blues," "Who?", "Ol' Man River," "Smoke Gets In Your Eyes," and "All the Things You Are." The second of Bennett's symphonic compositions is the *Variations on a Theme by Jerome Kern,* written in 1934 and soon after that introduced in New York by a chamber orchestra conducted by Bernard Herrmann. The theme here used for an effective series of variations is "Once in a Blue Moon" from the Broadway musical *Stepping Stones.*

Albert Ketelby

ALBERT WILLIAM KETELBY was born in Birmingham, England, in or about 1885. Precocious in music he completed a piano sonata when he was only eleven. For six years he attended the Trinity College of Music in London where he captured every possible prize. When he was sixteen he became a church organist in Wimbledon, and at twenty-one he conducted a theater orchestra in London. He later distinguished himself as a conductor of some of London's most important theater orchestras, besides appearing as a guest conductor of many of Europe's major symphonic organizations, usually in performances of his own works. For many years he was also the music director of the Columbia Gramophone Company in England. He died at his home on the Isle of Wight on November 26, 1959.

A facile composer with a fine sense for atmospheric colors and for varied moods, Ketelby produced a few serious compositions among which were a *Caprice* and a *Concerstueck* (each for piano and orchestra), an overture and *Suite de Ballet* (both for orchestra) and a quintet for piano and woodwind. He is, however, most famous for his lighter compositions, two of which are known and heard the world over. *In a Monastery Garden* opens with a gentle subject describing a lovely garden populated by chirping birds. After that comes a religious melody—a chant of monks in a modal style. *In a Persian Garden* is effective for its skilful recreation of an exotic background through Oriental-type melodies, harmonies, and brilliant orchestral colors. Ketelby wrote several other compositions in an Oriental style, the best of which is *In a Chinese Temple Garden*.

Aram Khatchaturian

ARAM KHATCHATURIAN was born in Tiflis, Russia, on June 6, 1903. He was of Armenian extraction. He came to Moscow in 1920, and enrolled in the Gniessen School of Music. From 1929 to 1934 he attended the Moscow Conservatory. He first achieved recognition as a composer in 1935 with his first symphony, and in 1937 he scored a major success throughout the music world with his first piano concerto, still a favorite in the modern concert repertory. As one of the leading composers in the Soviet Union he has been the recipient of numerous honors, including the Order of Lenin in 1939, and the Stalin Prize in 1940 and 1942. In 1954 he visited London where he led a concert of his own music, and early in 1960 he toured Latin America.

Khatchaturian's music owes a strong debt to the folk songs and dances of Armenia and Transcaucasia. It is endowed with a sensitive and at times exotic lyricism, a compulsive rhythmic strength, and a strong feeling for the dramatic.

The most popular single piece of music by Khatchaturian comes from his ballet, *Gayne* (or *Gayaneh*), first performed in Moscow on December 9, 1942, and the recipient of the Stalin Prize. The heroine of this ballet is a member of a collective farm where her husband, Giko, proves a traitor. He tries to set the farm afire. The farm is saved by a Red Commander who falls in love with Gayne after Giko has been arrested.

Khatchaturian assembled thirteen numbers from his ballet score into two suites for orchestra. It is one of these pieces that has achieved widespread circulation: the "Saber Dance," a composition whose impact comes from its abrupt barbaric rhythms and vivid sonorities; midway, relief from these rhythmic tensions comes from a broad folk song in violas and cellos. "Saber Dance" has become popular in numerous transcriptions, including an electrifying one for solo piano. In 1948 Vic Schoen made a fox-trot arrangement that was frequently played in the United States.

Two other excerpts from these *Gayne* suites are also familiar. "Dance of the Rose Girls" presents a delightful Oriental melody in oboe

and clarinet against a pronounced rhythm. "Lullaby" has a gentle swaying motion in solo oboe against a decisive rhythm in harp and bassoon;
flutes take up this subject, after which the melody grows and expands
in full orchestra, and then subsides.

Masquerade is another of Khatchaturian's orchestral suites, this one
derived from his incidental music to a play by Mikhail Lermontov produced in 1939. Each of the five numbers of this suite is appealing either
for sensitive and easily assimilable melodies or for rhythmic vitality.
Gentle lyricism, of an almost folk-song identity, characterizes the second
and third movements, a "Nocturne" and "Romance." The first and the
last two movements are essentially rhythmic: "Waltz," "Mazurka," and
"Polka."

George Kleinsinger

GEORGE KLEINSINGER was born in San Bernardino,
California, on February 13, 1914, and came to New York City in his
sixth year. He was trained for dentistry, and only after he had left
dental school did he concentrate on music. His first intensive period
of music study took place with Philip James and Marion Bauer at New
York University where he wrote an excellent cantata, *I Hear America
Singing,* performed publicly and on records by John Charles Thomas.
Kleinsinger then attended the Juilliard Graduate School on a composition fellowship. In 1946 he scored a major success with *Tubby the
Tuba.* He later wrote several other works with humorous or satiric
content, often filled with unusual instrumental effects. Among these are
his *Brooklyn Baseball Cantata;* a concerto for harmonica and orchestra;
and the musical, *Archy and Mehitabel (Shinbone Alley),* which was
produced for records, on Broadway and over television. In a more serious vein are a symphony and several concertos.

Tubby the Tuba, for narrator and orchestra (1942) belongs in the class of Prokofiev's *Peter and the Wolf*. It serves to familiarize children with the instruments of the orchestra, but because of its wit and simple melodies it also makes for wonderful entertainment. It tells the story of a frustrated tuba who complains that he must always play uninteresting "oompahs oompahs" while the violins are always assigned the most beautiful tunes. In the end Tubby happily gets a wonderful melody of his own to enjoy and play. All the characters in this tale are instruments of the orchestra. In 1946 a recording of *Tubby the Tuba* sold over a quarter of a million albums. Paramount made a movie of it, and major orchestras throughout the country presented it both at children's concerts and in its regularly symphonic repertory.

Fritz Kreisler

FRITZ KREISLER, one of the greatest violin virtuosos of his generation, was born in Vienna, Austria, on February 2, 1875. He was a child prodigy at the violin. From 1882 to 1885 he attended the Vienna Conservatory, a pupil of Leopold Auer, winning the gold medal for violin playing. In 1887, as a pupil of Massart at the Paris Conservatory, he was recipient of the Grand Prix. In 1888, he toured the United States in joint concerts with the pianist, Moriz Rosenthal, making his American debut in Boston on November 9. Upon returning to Vienna, he suddenly decided to abandon music. For a while he studied medicine at the Vienna Academy. After that he entered military service as an officer in a Uhlan Regiment. The decision to return to the violin led to a new period of intensive training from which he emerged in March 1899 with a recital in Berlin. From 1901 on until his retirement during World War II he occupied a magistral place among the concert artists of his time.

As a composer, Kreisler produced a violin concerto and a string quartet. But his fame rests securely on an entire library of pieces for the violin now basic to that repertory and which are equally well loved in transcriptions for orchestra. The curious thing about many of these compositions is that for many years Kreisler presented them as the genuine works of the old masters, works which he said he had discovered in European libraries and monasteries, and which he had merely adapted for the violin. He had recourse to this deception early in 1900 as the expedient by which a still young and unknown violinist could get his own music played more frequently besides extending for his own concerts the more or less limited territory of the existing violin repertory. His deception proved much more successful than he had dared to hope. Violinists everywhere asked him for copies of these pieces for their own concerts. Publishers in Germany and New York sold these "transcriptions" by the thousands. As the years passed it became increasingly difficult for Kreisler to confess to the world that he had all the while been palming off a colossal fraud. Then, in 1935, Olin Downes, the music critic of the *New York Times,* tried to trace the source of one of these compositions—Pugnani's *Praeludium and Allegro* —now a worldwide favorite with violinists. Downes first communicated with Kreisler's New York publishers who were suspiciously evasive. After that Downes cabled Kreisler, then in Europe. It was only then that the violinist revealed that this piece was entirely his, and so were many others which he had been presenting so long as the music of Vivaldi, Martini, Couperin, and Francoeur among others.

It was to be expected that musicians and critics should meet such a confession with anger and denunciation. "We wish to apply the term discreditable to the whole transaction from start to finish," one American music journal said editorially. In England, Ernest Newman was also devastating in his attack. "It is as though Mr. Yeats published poems under the name of Herrick or Spenser," he said.

Yet, in retrospect, it is possible to suggest that musicians and critics should not have been taken altogether by surprise. For one thing, as Kreisler pointed out, numerous progressions and passages in all of these compositions were in a style of a period much later than that of the accredited composers, a fact that should have inspired at least a certain amount of suspicion. Also, when Kreisler presented his own *Liebesfreud, Liebesleid,* and *Schoen Rosmarin* as transcriptions of posthumous pieces by Joseph Lanner in a Berlin recital, and was vigorously assailed by a Berlin critic for daring to include such gems with "tripe" like Kreisler's own *Caprice Viennois,* Kreisler replied with a widely published statement that those pieces of Lanner were of his own composition. The reasonable question should then have arisen that if the three supposedly Lanner items were by Kreisler, how authentic were the other pieces of old masters played by the virtuoso?

Besides all this, Kreisler himself provided a strong clue to the correct authorship in the frontispiece of his published transcriptions. It read: "The original manuscripts used for these transcriptions are the private property of Mr. Fritz Kreisler and are now published for the first time; they are, moreover, so freely treated that they constitute, in fact, original works."

The furor and commotion caused by the uncovering of this fraud has long since died down. It has had no visible effect on Kreisler's immense popularity either as a violinist or composer. Since then, all this music has been published and performed as Kreisler's without losing any of its worldwide appeal.

Among the compositions by Kreisler which he originally ascribed to other masters in imitation of their styles were: *Andantino* (Martini); *Aubade provençale* (Couperin); *Chanson Louis XIII et Pavane* (Couperin); *Minuet* (Porpora); *Praeludium and Allegro* (Pugnani); *La Précieuse* (Couperin); *Scherzo* (Dittersdorf), *Sicilienne et Rigaudon* (Francoeur); *Tempo di minuetto* (Pugnani).

Perhaps the best loved pieces by Kreisler are those in the style of Viennese folk songs and dances in which are caught all the grace and Gemuetlichkeit of Viennese life and backgrounds. Some he originally tried to pass off as the works of other composers, as was the case with the already-mentioned *Liebesfreud, Liebesleid,* and *Schoen Rosmarin,* attributed to Lanner. Some were outright transcriptions. *The Old Refrain* is an adaptation of a song *"Du alter Stefanturm"* by Joseph Brandl taken from his operetta, *Der liebe Augustin,* produced in Vienna in 1887. Still others were always offered as Kreisler's own compositions and are completely original with him: *Caprice Viennois,* for example, and the *Marche miniature viennoise.*

Among other original Kreisler compositions which he always presented as his own are the following: *La Gitana,* which simulates an Arabian-Spanish song; *Polichinelle,* a serenade; *Rondino,* based on a theme of Beethoven; *Shepherd's Madrigal; Slavonic Fantasia,* based on melodies of Dvořák; *Tambourin Chinois;* and *Toy Soldiers' March.*

Édouard Lalo

❧❧ ☙☙

ÉDOUARD LALO was born in Lille, France, on January 27, 1823. After receiving his musical training at Conservatories in Lille and Paris, he became a member of the Armingaud-Jacquard Quartet, a renowned French chamber-music ensemble. In 1848–1849 he published some songs; in 1867 he received third prize in a national contest for his opera, *Fiesque;* and in 1872 he was acclaimed for his *Divertimento,* for orchestra, introduced in Paris. Two major works written for the noted Spanish violinist, Pablo de Sarasate, added considerably to his reputation: a violin concerto in 1872, and the celebrated *Symphonie espagnole,* for violin and orchestra, two years after that. One of his last major works was the opera, *Le Roi d'Ys,* introduced at the Opéra-Comique in Paris on May 7, 1888. In that same year he was made Officer of the Legion of Honor and sometime later he received the Prix Monbinne from the Académie des Beaux-Arts. In the last years of his life he was a victim of paralysis. He died in Paris on April 22, 1892.

A composer of the highest principles and aristocratic style, Lalo is essentially a composer for cultivated tastes. One of his works, however, makes for easy listening. It is the *Norwegian Rhapsody (Rapsodie norvégienne)*, for orchestra (1875). There are two sections. The first begins slowly and sedately, its main melody appearing in the strings. Here the tempo soon quickens and a sprightly passage ensues. The second part of the rhapsody, ushered in by a stout theme for trumpets, is vigorous music throughout.

Josef Lanner

᦮᧢᦮᧢   ᧢᦮᧢᦮

J O S E F   L A N N E R, the first of the great waltz kings of Vienna, was born in the Austrian capital on April 12, 1801. When he was twelve he played the violin in the band of Michael Pamer, a popular Viennese composer of that day. In 1818 Lanner formed a trio which played in smaller cafés and at the Prater. In 1819 the trio grew into a quartet with the addition of the older Johann Strauss (father of the composer of *The Blue Danube*), then only fifteen years old. Soon afterwards, the quartet was expanded into a quintet. By 1824, Lanner's ensemble was a full-sized orchestra popular throughout Vienna, heard in such famous café houses as the *Goldenen Rebbuhn,* and the *Gruenen Jager,* as well as at leading balls and other gala social events in Vienna. The call for Lanner's music was so insistent that to meet the demand it soon became necessary to create two orchestras; one led by Lanner, and the other by the elder Strauss. Lanner remained an idol of Vienna until his death, which took place in Oberdoebling, near Vienna, on April 14, 1843.

For his various ensembles and orchestras Lanner produced a wealth of popular Viennese music: quadrilles, polkas, galops, marches, and more than a hundred waltzes. It is in the last department that Lanner was most important, for he was one of the first composers to carry the waltz to its artistic fulfillment. With composers from Mozart to Schubert, the waltz was only a three-part song form with a trio. Johann Hummel and Karl Maria von Weber suggested a more spacious design by assembling several different waltz tunes into a single integrated composition. Lanner extended this form further. He prefaced each series of waltzes with an introduction in which the theme of the main melody was often suggested; after the waltz melodies had been presented, Lanner brought his composition to completion with a coda which served as a kind of summation of some of the ideas previously stated. Between the introduction and the coda came the succession of lilting, lovable, heart-warming waltz-melodies so remarkable for their grace, elegance, freshness and poignancy that Lanner has sometimes been described as "the Mozart of the dance." Nevertheless, Lanner always emphasized soaring lyricism where the elder Strauss was more partial to rhythm. The Viennese used to say: "With Lanner, it's 'Pray dance, I beg you.' With Strauss it's 'You must dance, I command you!' "

The form which Lanner finally crystallized, and the style with which his waltz music unfolded, were adopted by the two Johann Strausses, father and son, who were destined to bring this type of Viennese music to its ultimate development. Thus Lanner was the opening chapter of a musical epoch: He was the dawn of Vienna's golden age of waltz music.

Lanner's most famous waltz is *Die Schoenbrunner,* op. 200, his swan song. Other outstanding Lanner waltzes are: *Die Pesther,* op. 93, *Die Werber,* op. 103, *Hofballtaenze,* op. 161, *Die Romantiker,* op. 167, and *Abendsterne,* op. 180. "With Lanner," wrote H. E. Jacob, "the romantic epoch began for the waltz, and the flower-gardens and green leaves of Spring penetrated into the ballroom. Lanner's compositions are unsophisticated and unpretentious, but his waltzes could no more be commonplace than could a flower."

Charles Lecocq

❧❧ ❧❧

C H A R L E S L E C O C Q was born in Paris on June 3, 1832. For four years he attended the Paris Conservatory where, as a pupil of Bazin and Halévy, he received prizes in harmony and fugue. For a while he earned his living teaching the piano and writing church music. In 1857 he shared with Bizet the first prize in a competition for one-act operettas sponsored by Offenbach. This winning work, *Le Docteur miracle,* was successfully introduced in Paris that year. After that Lecocq wrote several light operas which were failures, before he enjoyed a major success with *Fleur de thé* in 1868, first in Paris and subsequently in England and Germany. His greatest successes came with two crowning works in the French light-opera repertory: *La Fille de*

Mme. Angot in 1872, and *Giroflé-Girofla,* in 1874. Between 1874 and 1900 he wrote over thirty more operettas. He died in Paris on October 24, 1918 after enjoying for almost half a century a place of signal honor among France's composers for the popular theater.

Lecocq is remembered today mainly for *La Fille de Mme. Angot* and *Giroflé-Girofla.* The first of these was introduced in Brussels on December 4, 1872. In Paris, where it was given on February 23, 1873, it enjoyed the formidable run of more than five hundred consecutive performances. The book—by Siraudin, Clairville and Koning—was set in Paris during the French Revolution. Clairette, daughter of Mme. Angot, must marry the barber Pomponnet even though she loves the poet, Pitou. To avoid an undesirable marriage, even at the risk of arrest, Clairette sings a daring song by Pitou about an illicit affair between Mlle. Lange (reputed a favorite of Barras, head of the Directory) and a young lover. When Pitou proves fickle, and is discovered in the boudoir of Mlle. Lange, Clairette stands ready to forget him completely and to take Pomponnet as her husband.

The sprightly overture, filled with vivacious tunes and dramatized by energetic rhythms, is a favorite of semi-classical orchestras. So are several dances from the operetta, including an electrifying Can-Can, and a sweeping *Grand Valse* with which the second act comes to an exciting close. The main vocal excerpts are Pomponnet's passionate avowal of Clairette's innocence, *"Elle est tellement innocente"* and the duet of Mlle. Lange and Clairette, *"Jours fortunes de notre enfance"* both from Act 2.

Giroflé-Girofla—book by Vanloo and Leterrier—was introduced in Brussels on March 21, 1874. Giroflé and Girofla are twin sisters. Giroflé is pressured by her parents to marry the banker, Marasquin; Girofla is in love with an impoverished fire-eating Moor, Mourzouk. When Girofla is secretly abducted by pirates, the Moor comes to her home demanding to see her, only to mistake Giroflé for Girofla. The complicated situation ensuing becomes resolved only after Girofla is rescued and brought back home.

The most frequently heard excerpts from this gay score are the Pirates' Chorus, *"Parmi les choses"*; the rousing drinking song, *"Le Punche scintille"*; the ballad, *"Lorsque la journée est finie"*; and the love duet, *"O ciel!"*

Ernesto Lecuona

E R N E S T O L E C U O N A was born in Havana, Cuba, on August 7, 1896. As a boy of eleven he published his first piece of music—an American two step still popular with some Cuban bands. While attending the National Conservatory in Cuba, from which he was graduated in 1911 with a gold medal in piano playing, he earned his living as a pianist in cafés and movie theaters. In 1917 he paid the first of several visits to the United States, at that time making some records and giving a piano recital. He then made concert tours throughout America and Europe playing the piano and conducting semi-classical and popular orchestras. His performances were largely responsible for popularizing in America both the conga and the rumba in the 1920's. He also made some successful appearances at the Capitol Theater, in New York, where he introduced his own music, including such outstanding successes as *Malagueña, Andalucia,* and *Siboney* (the last originally entitled *Canto Siboney,* which became an American popular-song hit in 1929). These and similar pieces made Lecuona one of the most successful exponents of Latin-American melodies and dance rhythms in the United States. Lecuona has written over five hundred songs, forty operettas, and numerous compositions both for orchestra and for piano solo.

From a piano suite entitled *Andalucia* come two of Lecuona's best known instrumental compositions. The first is also called *Andalucia,* a haunting South American melody set against a compulsive rhythm. It was made into an American popular song in 1955.

Another movement from *Andalucia* is even more familiar: the *Malagueña.* Since its publication as a piano solo in 1929, *Malagueña* has sold annually over a hundred thousand copies of sheet music each year; it has become a favorite of concert pianists; it is also often performed by salon and pop orchestras everywhere in orchestral transcriptions; and it has been adapted into a popular song, "At the Crossroads." It is in three sections, the first being in the malagueña rhythm dynamically projected in slowing expanding sonorities; a contrast comes in the middle part with a poignant Latin-American melody.

Andalucia, the single movement and not the suite as a whole, has been given a brilliant orchestral dress by Morton Gould who has also orchestrated two outstandingly popular Lecuona songs. One is "La Comparasa," a picture of a traditional parade during the Carnival season in which Negroes and muleteers play their native instruments and sing their sensual songs. The other is "Gitanerias," haunting gypsy music.

Franz Lehár

FRANZ LEHÁR was born in Komorn, Hungary, on April 30, 1870. His father, a bandmaster, was his first music teacher. When Franz was twelve, he entered the Prague Conservatory where he remained six years specializing in the violin with Bennewitz and theory with Foerster. His studies were completed in 1888, after which he played the violin in the orchestra of the Eberfeld Opera. He subsequently became an assistant bandleader of his father's ensemble and a director of Austria's foremost Marine bands. In 1896 he realized his first success as a composer of operettas with *Kukuschka,* produced in Leipzig. In 1902 he became conductor of the Theater-an-der-Wien, in Vienna, home of operettas. There, in the same year, he had produced *Viennese Women (Wiener Frauen).* The operetta after that was *The Gypsy (Der Rastelbinder),* seen in 1902 in one of Vienna's other theaters. With *The Merry Widow (Die lustige Witwe),* seen in 1905, Lehár achieved a triumph of such magnitude that from then on he was one of Austria's most celebrated operetta composers (and one of the wealthiest) since Johann Strauss II. He wrote about thirty more operettas (three of them in the single year of 1909–1910). The most famous were *The Count of Luxembourg (Der Graf von Luxemburg)* in 1909; *Gypsy Love (Zigeunerliebe)* in 1910; *Frasquita* in 1922; *Paganini* in 1925; *The Tsarevitch (Der Zarewitsch)* in 1927; and *The Land of Smiles (Das Land des Laechelns)* in 1929. During World War II Lehár lived in seclusion at his villa in Bad Ischl, Austria. After the war he became embittered by the widely publicized accusation that he had been pro Nazi, arising no doubt from the well-known fact that *The Merry Widow* was Hitler's favorite operetta. What was forgotten in this attack against Lehár was the fact that his wife had been classified by Nazis as non-Aryan and that on one occasion both and he and his wife were subjected by the Gestapo to house arrest. Lehár died in Bad Ischl, Austria, on October 24, 1948. He is one of the few composers to outlive the copyrights of some of his most famous works.

Lehár's popularity in the early part of this century gave the Viennese operetta a new lease on life at a time when its heyday was believed over. It was through the influence of Lehár's immense popularity and success that composers like Oscar Straus, Emmerich Kálmán, and Leo Fall began writing their own operettas. Lehár's best stage works have been described as "dance operettas" because of the emphasis placed on dance music, the waltz specifically. The dance usually becomes the climax, the focal point, of the production. Stan Czech further points out that Lehár's waltzes are "slower and sweeter than those of Johann Strauss, were definite prototypes of the modern slow waltz, and their Slav atmosphere gave them an exciting and individual character."

The Count of Luxembourg (Der Graf von Luxemburg)—text by Willner and Robert Bodanzky—was first given in Vienna on November 12, 1909. This operetta opens in an artist's studio in Paris where René, the impoverished Count of Luxembourg, is offered five hundred thousand francs by Prince Basil if René is willing to marry the singer Angele and let her share his title. The reason for this peculiar arrangement is that the Prince is himself in love with Angele, wants to marry her, but prefers that his wife have a title. After they get married, René and Angele discover they are in love with each other, a fact which eventually the Prince is willing to accept since he is ordered by the Czar to marry a legitimate Countess. As in most Lehár's operettas, the high musical moment comes with a waltz—the infectious duet of René and Angele, *"Bist du's, lachendes Glueck,"* which is also extremely popular in orchestral adaptations. Other appealing numbers are the second act duet, *"Lieber Freund, man greift nicht"* and the tenor aria, *"Maedel klein, Maedel fein."*

Frasquita, produced in Vienna on May 12, 1922, is remembered most often for one of Lehár's most beautiful vocal numbers, the nostalgic and romantic *Frasquita Serenade, "Hab ein blaues Himmelbett."* Fritz Kreisler made a fine transcription for violin and piano, and Sigmund Spaeth provided the melody with American lyrics.

Gypsy Love (*Zigeunerliebe*), had its world première in Vienna on January 8, 1910. The librettists (Willner and Bodanzky) provided a romantic storybook setting of Rumania, and a romantic central character in the form of the gypsy violinist, Jozsi. Zorika is ineluctably drawn to Jozsi though she is actually betrothed to his half-brother, Jonel. In a dream, she gets a foretaste of what her life would be with one so irresponsible and fickle as a gypsy violinist, with the result that she is more than happy to marry Jonel. The main waltz melody (one of Lehár's greatest) is *"Nur der Liebe macht uns jung"* and the most infectious Hungarian tune is Jozsi's soaring entrance gypsy melody to the accompaniment of his violin, *"Ich bin ein Zigeunerkind."*

From *The Land of Smiles* (*Das Land des Laechelns*) comes what is probably the best loved and most widely sung of all of Lehár's vocal numbers, "Dein ist mein ganzes Herz" ("Thine Is My Heart Alone") which opened not in Vienna but in Berlin, on October 10, 1929. This was actually a new version of an old Lehár operetta, originally called *The Yellow Jacket* (*Die gelbe Jacke*) which had been introduced in Vienna in 1923. The romantic plot of both operettas involved a Chinese diplomat, Prince Sou-Chong, and Lisa, daughter of an Austrian Count. They marry and settle in Peking in whose strange setting, Lisa's love for the Prince soon turns to hate. With great magnanimity—even though this is in violation of ancient Chinese traditions and customs— he allows Lisa to leave him and return home.

In *The Yellow Jacket,* "Thine Is My Heart Alone" is sung by Lisa, and at that time this number made little impression. The famous tenor, Richard Tauber, fell in love with it, and performed it so extensively in his recitals everywhere that he and the song became inextricably identified. When Lehár revised his operetta and renamed it *The Land of Smiles,* he cast the song "Thine Is My Heart Alone" as a major second-act aria for Prince Sou-Chong, Richard Tauber playing the part of the Prince. *The Land of Smiles* was a personal triumph for Tauber who appeared in it over 2,500 times all over the world. "Thine Is My Heart Alone" became with him something of a theme song. He rarely gave a concert anywhere without singing it either on the program itself or as an encore. When *The Land of Smiles* was given in New York City in 1946, with Tauber as the star, the operetta was renamed *Yours Is My Heart;* in this production Tauber sang the song four times in four different languages, French, Italian, German, and English.

There can be little question but that *The Merry Widow* (*Die lustige Witwe*) is one of the most famous operettas ever written. It was a sensation when first performed, in Vienna on December 28, 1905. It came both to London and New York in 1907, a major success in both places. In Buenos Aires it was performed simultaneously in five theaters in five different languages. Since 1907 there was hardly a time when *The Merry Widow* was not being performed in some part of the world. It has enjoyed in excess of six thousand performances, a thousand of these in Vienna alone. On several occasions it has been adapted for the screen.

Victor Léon and Leo Stein wrote the text. This is the usual operetta material involving a beautiful heiress from a mythical kingdom. She is Sonia from Marsovia, who is leading a gay life in Paris. Beautiful and wealthy, she is inevitably sought out by the most handsome men of Paris. The government of Marsovia is eager to get her to marry one of its native sons, the dashing Prince Danilo, thereby keeping her fortune at home. As she conducts her vivacious night life she is zealously watched over by the Marsovian Ambassador, Baron Popoff, who never loses an opportunity to further the interests of Danilo. Eventually, Sonia has had her fling and is ready to settle down with the Prince.

The *Merry Widow Waltz*, *"S'fluestern Geigen, Lippen schweigen,"* an eye-filling climax to the third act, is not only the most popular excerpt from this operetta but also one of the most celebrated waltzes ever written. A secondary waltz, "Vilia" is also highly beguiling, while a third musical favorite from this score is *"Da geh' ich zu Maxim"* ("The Girl at Maxim's").

What is one of Lehár's best waltzes, second in popularity only to that of *The Merry Widow,* does not come from any operetta. It is the *Gold and Silver Waltzes (Gold und Silber Waelzer)*, op. 79 which he wrote as a concert number.

Ruggiero Leoncavallo

RUGGIERO LEONCAVALLO was born in Naples, Italy, on March 8, 1858. He was graduated from the Bologna Conservatory, then spent several years traveling. He finally came to Paris where he earned his living playing the piano, singing, and writing music-hall songs. The powerful Italian publisher, Ricordi, commissioned him to write a trilogy of operas set in the Renaissance. Leoncavallo completed the first of these operas, *I Medici,* but it proved too expensive to mount and was shelved. This experience convinced him that he ought to write an opera of slighter dimensions, one which would not cost too much to produce, and which would be in the realistic style (*"Verismo"*) just made so popular by Mascagni's *Cavalleria Rusticana.* In four months' time, Leoncavallo completed *Pagliacci,* the opera through which his name survives. It received a triumphant première in Milan in 1892, with Toscanini conducting. Though Leoncavallo wrote many operas after that he never wrote one as good or as popular as the one that made him world famous. Only one of these later operas has retained interest, *Zaza,* introduced in 1900. A third opera, *La Bohème,* was well received when introduced in Venice in 1897, but was soon thrown into complete obscurity by a rival opera on the same subject, that of Puccini. In 1906 Leoncavallo toured the United States in performances of *Pagliacci.* The failures of his last operas made him a bitter, broken man in the last years of his life. He died in Montecatini, Italy, on August 9, 1919.

The composer prepared his own libretto for *Pagliacci,* a play within a play. A troupe of strolling players headed by Canio arrives for performances in a Calabrian village. Canio's wife, Nedda, falls in love with Silvio, one of the villagers, and she in turn is being pursued by the pathetic clown of the troupe, Tonio. Through Tonio, Canio discovers his wife has been unfaithful to him, but fails to learn the identity of his rival. At the troupe's evening performance—and in a play that closely resembles the actual happenings within the company—Canio kills Nedda when she fails to tell him who her lover is. But Silvio, in the audience, reveals himself by rushing on the stage to help Nedda. There Canio kills him.

Many of the selections from this opera are famous, but the most famous of all is the tenor aria, in which Canio speaks his immense grief on discovering that his wife has a lover, *"Vesti la giubba."*

The other familiar excerpts include the baritone prologue, *"Si può,"* in which Tonio explains to his audience that the incidents in the play about to be presented are true to life and that the players are not performers but human beings; Nedda's delightful ballatella, "The Bird Song" (*"Stridono lassù"*) where she tries to forget about Tonio's initial response of jealousy by watching and describing the casual and carefree

flight of birds overhead; the "Harlequin's Serenade" in the play within
the play sequence in the second act, *"O Columbina!"*; and a melodious
orchestral Intermezzo which separates the first and second acts, music
which hints darkly at impending tragedy through a poignant recall of
Tonio's prologue.

Anatol Liadov

ANATOL LIADOV was born in St. Petersburg, Russia, on
May 10, 1855, the son and grandson of eminent Russian conductors. He
was a pupil of Rimsky-Korsakov at the St. Petersburg Conservatory, but
was so derelict about attending classes that in 1876 he was expelled.
Reinstated two years later he now became fired with both ambition and
industry, proved a brilliant student, and was graduated with highest
honors. He was then appointed teacher of theory there, eventually becoming a renowned professor, a post he retained until the end of his
life. He died in Novgorod, Russia, on August 28, 1914.

Liadov was at his best in his fairy tales for orchestra (*The Enchanted
Lake, Baba Yaga* and *Kikimora*); in songs; and in smaller pieces for the
piano. He was a student of Russian folk music of which he made numerous adaptations, and whose styles and idioms percolated into many of
his compositions.

The *Eight Russian Folksongs*, a suite for orchestra, op. 58 (1906) is
one of Liadov's adaptations. There are eight movements. In the first,
"Religious Chant," the main song is that chanted by children in religious processions; it is heard in English horn and bassoons. This is followed by "Christmas Carol," its main theme presented by oboes and
clarinets. "Plaintive Melody" is a village song, and "I Danced With a
Mosquito," a humorous scherzo in which muted strings simulated buzzing mosquitoes. The fifth movement is "Legend of the Birds" where the
bird song is presented by the woodwind. "Cradle Song" is a tender

melody for strings. This is followed by a lively rhythmic section, "Round Dance." The suite ends with the "Village Dance Song," music that usually accompanies the crowning of the May Queen.

Liadov is also the composer of a delightful trifle called *The Music Box* in which the delicate little tune is the kind that lends itself gratefully to the tinkle of a music box. Liadov wrote this piece for the piano, op. 32, but it is better known in orchestral transcriptions.

Paul Lincke

❧❧ ☙☙

P A U L L I N C K E was born in Berlin, Germany, on November 7, 1866. After completing his music study he played the violin and bassoon in numerous theater orchestras. He later distinguished himself as a theater conductor. In 1897 he had his first operetta produced in Berlin. Thereafter he wrote many operettas, all originally given in Berlin; he became one of the foremost exponents of the light musical theater in Germany of his time. The most famous were *Frau Luna* (1899), *Fraeulein Loreley* (1900), *Lysistrata* (1902), *Prinzessin Rosine* (1905), and *Casanova* (1914). His last operetta was *Ein Liebestraum*, produced in Hamburg in 1940. From 1918 to 1920 he was conductor at the Folies-Bergère in Paris. He died in Klausthal-Zellernfeld, Germany, on September 3, 1946.

His most famous composition is a song from *Lysistrata* (1902): "The Glow Worm" (*"Gluehwuermchen"*), which achieved phenomenal popularity throughout the world independent of the operetta. It is still famous both as a vocal composition and in orchestral transcriptions. A new vocal version, with amusing lyrics by Johnny Mercer, was published and popularized in the United States in 1952.

Franz Liszt

ᴥᚖᴥᚖ ᚖᴥᚖᴥ

FRANZ LISZT was born in Raiding, Hungary, on October 22, 1811. A prodigy pianist who made an impressive debut in Hungary when he was nine, Liszt was financed by several Hungarian noblemen to study the piano with Czerny in Vienna. In 1822, Liszt made a sensational debut in that city, and in 1824, after a period of additional study in Paris, an equally momentous appearance in the French capital. For the next three years Liszt concertized throughout Europe, becoming an idol of music audiences everywhere. Then, in 1827, he decided to abandon music for what he regarded as nobler pursuits. He devoted himself in turn to religion, politics, literature, and philosophy without finding the satisfaction he sought. Then, in 1830, he went back to music. For about two years he worked industriously on his piano technique, reassuming an imperial position among the virtuosos of his generation beginning with 1833. He combined profound musicianship and a phenomenal technique with such a flair for showmanship and self-aggrandizement, that it can be said that the modern piano virtuoso (both in the best and worst sense of that term) was born with him.

In 1848, Liszt came to Weimar to fulfill duties as Kapellmeister to the Grand Duke. The eleven-year period of this office represented music-making of the highest order, as Liszt devoted himself to presenting the foremost operatic and symphonic music in the best possible performances. He was indefatigable in propagandizing the music of the avant-garde composers of his day, reviving Wagner's *Tannhaeuser* and presenting the world première of that master's *Lohengrin* at a time when Wagner was in disrepute in Germany because of his revolutionary activities.

Finding himself incapable of maintaining the high standards he had set, and disturbed by the prevailing antagonism to his espousal of new music, Liszt left Weimar in 1859. Once again he sought refuge in a career outside music. In 1865 he submitted to the tonsure and entered the Third Order of St. Francis of Assisi as abbé. But music was not abandoned. He taught the piano to gifted pupils who came to him from all parts of the world; and he wrote an abundant amount of music, mainly for the piano. He died in Bayreuth, Bavaria, on July 31, 1886, still at the height of his powers and fame as composer, pianist and teacher.

Liszt left a vast repertory of music, including tone poems, symphonies, piano concertos, songs, and a library of works for the piano. At his best he was a great innovator, and a creator of vast dramatic and poetic concepts. At worst, he was a showman shamelessly wooing his public with superficial effects and trivial material. Most of his works belong to the concert hall, but some of it has enormous popular appeal as salon music.

The most famous of the latter is the *Hungarian Rhapsody No. 2* in C-sharp minor (1847), originally for piano solo but subsequently orchestrated by the composer himself. This was one of nineteen compositions in which Liszt developed the form of the rhapsody and helped to make it popular; which he filled with strong national feelings and the individual traits of Hungarian folk music. One of the features of all these rhapsodies is their dynamic alternation of slow and sensual music (called *lassan*) with fast, dramatic, exciting passages (called *friskan*). The second *Hungarian Rhapsody* opens with a *lassan,* a slow, stately declamation. Then, after a clarinet cadenza, the *friskan* appears, a spirited melody for violins and woodwind. After that fast and slow passages, soft and loud dynamics, and rapidly changing meters and rhythm help to generate excitement and create drama. The drama and the excitement of this music never seem to lose their impact however many times this rhapsody is listened to.

Of Liszt's twelve tone poems for orchestra the most famous is *Les Préludes* (1850). The tone poem, or symphonic poem, is Liszt's creation in an attempt to bring to orchestral music the pictorial, dramatic and programmatic qualities of Wagner's music dramas. Thus Liszt conceived a one-movement composition, flexible in form, in which a story is told, picture described, or poem interpreted. The inspiration for *Les Préludes* is the *Méditations poétiques* of Lamartine, from which several lines are quoted in the published score to provide the music with its program:

"What is life but a series of Preludes to that unknown song of which death strikes the first solemn note? Love is the magic dawn of every existence; but where is the life in which the first enjoyment of bliss is not dispelled by some tempest; its illusions scattered by some fatal breath; its altar consumed as by a thunderbolt? What soul, this cruelly hurt, but seeks to repose with its memories in the sweet calm of pastoral life? Yet no man is content to resign himself for long to the mild, beneficent charms of Nature, and when the trumpet gives the alarm he hastens to the post of danger, on whatever field he may be called to fight, so that once more he may find in action full consciousness of himself and the possession of all his powers."

Les Préludes opens with a dignified subject in the basses which is subjected to considerable change and amplification before the main melody is introduced. This melody is an elegiac song expressing the happiness of love; its first entrance comes in four horns, strings, and harp. The music is carried to a climactic point, after which a frenetic mood is projected. Plaintively the oboe recalls the main melody; a country dance tune is offered by the horn; and the main melody reappears with opulent treatment. Another section of storm and stress follows before the final majestic statement of the main melody.

Of Liszt's voluminous writings for the piano, one composition above all others has won favor throughout the music world as a tender, and sentimental expression of love. It is the *Liebestraum,* "Love's Dream." Liszt actually wrote three *Liebesträume,* but it is the third of this set—in A-flat major (1850)—which is considered when we speak or hear of the *Liebestraum.* All of these three piano compositions are adaptations of songs by the same composer; the third *Liebestraum* originated as *"O Lieb', so lang du lieben kannst,"* words by Freiligrath.

Frederick Loewe

FREDERICK LOEWE was born in Vienna, Austria, on June 10, 1904. A musical prodigy, he began to study the piano when he was five; started composition at seven; at thirteen made a successful appearance as pianist with the Berlin Symphony; and at fifteen was the composer of a hit song, "Katrina," that sold over a million copies of sheet music in Europe. He received a thorough musical training from Busoni, Eugène d'Albert, and Emil Nikolaus Rezniček, winning the Hollander Medal for piano playing in 1923. One year after that he came to the United States. Unable to make any progress in his musical career, he spent the next decade traveling around the country and filling all sorts of odd jobs. He punched cattle, mined gold, served as a riding instructor, and even boxed professionally. Eventually he came back to New York where he found a job in a Greenwich Village café playing the piano. In 1938 four of his songs were heard in a Broadway musical, *Great Lady,* a failure. A meeting with Alan Jay Lerner, a young lyricist and librettist, brought him a gifted collaborator. They wrote a musical comedy that was produced by a stock company in Detroit, and another called *What's Up* that was seen on Broadway. Their first major success came with the Broadway musical, *Brigadoon,* in 1947. *My Fair Lady,* in 1956, was one of the greatest successes of the Broadway theater. They also helped make entertainment history further by writing songs for the motion picture musical, *Gigi,* the first to win nine Academy Awards, including one for Lerner and Loewe for the title song. In 1960, Lernei and Loewe wrote the Broadway musical *Camelot* based on King Arthur and the Knights of the Round Table.

Brigadoon was a whimsical Scottish fantasy which came to Broadway on March 13, 1947, book and lyrics by Lerner. Brigadoon is a mythical town in Scotland which comes to life for a single day once every hundred years. Two American tourists happen to come to Brigadoon during its one day of existence. They become a part of its quaint life, and one of them falls in love with a Scottish lass. The musical highlights include a song that became a hit in 1947, "Almost Like Being In Love," and several that have a charming Scottish flavor, including "Come to Me, Bend to Me," "The Heather on the Hill," and "I'll Come Home With Bonnie Jean."

My Fair Lady, produced on March 15, 1956, was Lerner's adaptation for the popular musical theater of Bernard Shaw's *Pygmalion.* Eliza Doolittle, an ignorant flower girl and daughter of a cockney, is transformed by the phonetician, Professor Henry Higgins, into a cultivated lady who is successfully palmed off upon high English society as a duchess. Higgins falls in love with her and, though a long confirmed bachelor, finds he can no longer live without her. *My Fair Lady* became one of the most highly acclaimed musical productions of recent memory; Brooks Atkinson called it "one of the best musicals of the century." It achieved a fabulous Broadway run and was brought by many touring countries to all parts of the civilized world, including the Soviet Union. It captured one third of the honors annually conferred on the theater by the Antoinette Perry Awards. The original-cast recording sold over three million discs. The principal numbers from Loewe's captivating score include three romantic songs, two of the Hit Parade variety ("I Could Have Danced All Night" and "On the Street Where You Live") and the third, "I've Grown Accustomed to Her Face"; two atmospheric numbers that evoke musically the place and setting of the play, "The Ascot Gavotte" and "The Embassy Waltz"; and the two cockney ditties of Eliza's father, "Get Me to the Church On Time" and "With a Little Bit of Luck."

Albert Lortzing

GUSTAV ALBERT LORTZING was born in Berlin on October 23, 1801. His parents were actors compelled to lead an itinerant life which made it impossible for Albert to obtain any systematic education. His mother taught him music, the study of which he later continued briefly in Berlin with Rungenhagen. His first effort at composition consisted of some songs, but in 1824 he completed his first opera, *Ali Pascha von Janina*. From 1833 to 1844 he was employed as a tenor at the Municipal Theater in Leipzig, for which he wrote the comic opera *Die beiden Schuetzen,* successfully produced in 1837. He achieved his greatest success the same year with the comic opera, *Zar und Zimmermann,* which within a few years' time became a favorite among theater audiences throughout Europe. His later operettas included *Der Wildschuetz* (*The Poacher*) in 1842 and *Der Waffenschmied* (*The Armourer*) in 1846, while one of his finest romantic operas was *Undine* in 1845. Lortzing also filled several engagements as conductor of operas and operettas in Leipzig, Vienna and Berlin, and as an opera impresario. He died in Berlin on January 21, 1851, one day after his last opera, *Die Opernprobe* (*The Opera Rehearsal*) was introduced in Frankfort.

Lortzing was one of the earliest and most successful exponents of German national comic opera; and *Czar and the Carpenter* (*Zar und Zimmermann*) was his masterwork. It was first produced in Leipzig on December 22, 1837. The music is consistently light and tuneful, frequently in the style of German folk songs. The libretto, by the composer, is a delightful comedy based on an actual historic episode: the escapade of Peter the Great of Russia in Holland where he worked as a carpenter. In the Lortzing comic opera, Peter the Great is a carpenter on a ship at Saardam where he meets a compatriot, also named Peter, who is a deserter. Temporarily they become rivals for the affection of Mary. After the arrival of the Ambassadors from France and England to seek out the Emperor, the latter quietly departs for his homeland, leaving behind him both money and an official pardon for the other Peter. The gay spirit of the comic opera as a whole is magically caught not only in its vivacious overture, but in several familiar excerpts. The most notable are: the Burgomaster's comic entrance song, *"O sancta justa";* in the second act, the Wedding Chorus, and the French Ambassador's beautiful air, *"Lebe wohl, mein flandrisch' Maedchen";* in the third act the vigorous *Clog Dance* (*Holzschutanz*), and the very famous air of Czar Peter, *"Sonst spielt' ich mit Zepter."*

Alexandre Luigini

ALEXANDRE LUIGINI was born in Lyons, France, on March 9, 1850. He was the son of the distinguished conductor of the Théâtre-Italien in Paris. After attending the Paris Conservatory—where he was a pupil of Massenet and Massart among others—the younger Luigini played the violin in his father's orchestra. In 1870 he began a successful career as ballet composer with *Le Rêve de Nicette,* given in

Lyons. His greatest success came with the *Ballet Égyptien,* first seen in Lyons in 1875. For twenty years Luigini was the conductor of the Grand Theater in Lyons and professor of harmony at the Lyons Conservatory. Until the end of his life he was the conductor of the Opéra-Comique in Paris. He died in Paris on July 29, 1906.

An orchestral suite derived from some of the most attractive pages of the *Ballet Égyptien* score is a favorite of bands and salon orchestras everywhere. This is music striking for its Oriental-type melodies and harmonies, and for its colorful orchestral hues. The first two movements are particularly popular. The first begins with a strong and stately theme, but midway comes a gayer section in an exotic Oriental style. The second movement highlights a capricious subject for the woodwind, once again in a recognizable Oriental style.

Hans Christian Lumbye

HANS CHRISTIAN LUMBYE was born in Copenhagen, Denmark on May 2, 1810. As a young man he played in military bands. He then formed an orchestra of his own which achieved extraordinary fame throughout Copenhagen (specifically at the Tivoli) with light musical programs. For these concerts Lumbye produced a library of light music: waltzes, galops, polkas, marches, and so forth. This music is so filled with infectious tunes and pulsating rhythms—and they are so light in heart and spirit—that they have won for their composer the sobriquet of "The Johann Strauss of the North" and the status of Denmark's foremost creator of semi-classical music. He died in Copenhagen on March 20, 1874.

Lumbye's dance pieces are played wherever there is a salon, pop or café-house orchestra. Among his best waltzes are *Amelie, Hesperus,* and *Sophie.* Other successful Lumbye compositions are the *Columbine Mazurka,* the *Champagne Galop, Concert Polka, Dream Pictures, An*

Evening at the Tivoli, King Frederick VII Homage March, and the *Railway Galop.*

Edward MacDowell

❧❧ ❧❧

EDWARD ALEXANDER MACDOWELL, one of America's most significant 19th-century composers, was born in New York City on December 18, 1861. After preliminary music study with private teachers, he attended the Paris Conservatory from 1876 to 1878, and the Frankfort Conservatory in Germany from 1879 to 1881. Maintaining his home in Germany, MacDowell joined the faculty of the Darmstadt Conservatory in 1881, and in 1882 he made an official bow as a composer by introducing his first piano concerto in Zurich, and his *Modern Suite* for piano in Germany. He returned to the United States in 1888, settling in Boston where a year later the Boston Symphony under Gericke introduced his now-famous Second Piano Concerto, the composer appearing as soloist. From then on, most of his important symphonic works were introduced by the Boston Symphony, placing him in the vanguard of American composers of that period. In 1896 he filled the first chair of music created at Columbia University in New York; at that time he was described as "the greatest musical genius America has produced." MacDowell resigned in 1904 after sharp differences with the trustees of the University over the way a music department should be run. The bitterness and frustrations suffered by MacDowell during this altercation with the University undermined and finally broke his always delicate health. His brain tissues became affected. From 1905 on he was a victim of insanity, spending his time in an innocent, childlike state, until his death in New York City on January 23, 1908. Shortly after his death the MacDowell Memorial Association was founded to establish a retreat for American creative artists on MacDowell's summer residence in Peterborough, New Hampshire, which MacDowell's widow had deeded to the Association.

A composer whose artistic roots lay deep in the soil of German Romanticism, MacDowell was a composer who filled his writing with noble poetic sentiments and the most sensitive emotions. His sense of style and his feeling for structure were the last words in elegance, and his lyricism and harmonic language were ever ingratiatingly inviting to the ear.

The *Indian Suite*, op. 48 (1892) is the second of MacDowell's suites for orchestra. It is one of several works in which MacDowell uses melodic and rhythmic material of the American Indian, blending this idiom with his usual sensitive and poetic style. This is one of Mac-Dowell's most popular works for orchestra. The first movement, "Legend," has a slow introduction in which the main melody is given by three unaccompanied horns in unison. The melody is taken over by other instruments and developed. Here the material comes from a sacred ceremony of Iroquois Indians. The second movement is "Love Song," whose principal subject is immediately given by the woodwind; this melody is derived from the music of Iowa Indians. "War Time" follows, a movement dominated by a melody to which Indians of the Atlantic Coast ascribed supernatural origin. This melody is heard in the first sixteen measures in two unison unaccompanied flutes. A subsidiary section follows. "Dirge," the fourth movement, is a woman's song of mourning for an absent song, come from the Kiowa Indians. The mournful melody is heard in muted violins. The suite ends with "Village Festival," in which two light and vivacious melodies from the Iroquois Indians are presented; the first is a woman's dance, and the second a war song.

The most familiar pieces of music written by MacDowell—*To a Water Lily* and *To a Wild Rose*—come from the *Woodland Sketches*, op. 51 (1896), a suite for solo piano made up of ten sections, each a descriptive poem in tones. In this suite MacDowell became one of the first American composers to interpret the beauty of American scenes and countrysides in delicate melodies. Both *To a Water Lily* and *To a Wild Rose* are exquisite tone pictures of Nature, and both have enjoyed numerous transcriptions. The other eight movements of the *Woodland Sketches* are: *Will o' the Wisp, At an Old Trysting Place, In Autumn, From an Old Indian Lodge, From Uncle Remus, A Deserted Farm, By a Meadow Brook,* and *Told at Sunset*.

Albert Hay Malotte

ALBERT HAY MALOTTE was born in Philadelphia, Pennsylvania, on May 19, 1895. The son of a choirmaster, he himself was a boy chorister, at the St. James Episcopal Church in his native city. After his music studies were completed in Paris and London, he served as organist in Chicago and London. In 1927 he opened a school for organists in Los Angeles, but when sound came to the screen he gave up the school to write music for the films. He subsequently joined the music staff at the Walt Disney studio, creating music for several of Disney's animated cartoons, including *Ferdinand the Bull*. He has written ballets, choral music, and songs besides scores for motion pictures, having received early in his career as composer important advice, guidance and encouragement from Victor Herbert.

Malotte is most famous for his song, "The Lord's Prayer," published in 1935, and since become a favorite of concert singers everywhere. Its deep religious sentiment, and the exciting dramatic thrust of its concluding measures, have an inescapable impact on audiences.

Gabriel Marie

GABRIEL MARIE was born in Paris, France, on January 8, 1852. After completing his music study at the Paris Conservatory he served for six years as chorusmaster of the Lamoureux Orchestra. Between 1887 and 1894 he conducted the concerts of the Société nationale de musique. He later led the orchestral performances in Bordeaux and Marseilles, and during the summers at the Vichy Casino. He was traveling in Spain when he died there suddenly on August 29, 1928.

Marie was a successful composer of light music for orchestra. The one composition which has survived is *La Cinquantaine,* a sentimental piece for orchestra which is also famous in adaptations for violin and piano, or cello and piano. Marie described this work as an "air in the old style." It is in three-part song form. The first and third parts consist of a light, delicate little air; the middle section is in a slower and statelier style.

Martini il Tedesco

JEAN PAUL ÉGIDE MARTINI — sometimes called "Il Tedesco" or "The German" to distinguish him from Padre Martini the famous 18th century Italian composer and theorist—was born in Freistadt, in the Palatinate, on September 1, 1741. His real name is Schwarzendorf. After completing the study of the organ and serving for a while as church organist, he won a prize for a military march for the Swiss Guard. For many years he was an officer of a Hussar regiment. During this military service he completed an opera, *L'Amoureux de quinze ans* (successfully introduced in Paris in 1771) and a considerable amount of band music. After leaving the army, he served as music director for the Prince of Condé and the Comte d'Artois; as conductor at the Théâtre Feydeau in Paris; and as Inspector and teacher of composition at the Paris Conservatory. He died in Paris on February 10, 1816.

The composer of twelve operas, some church music and many songs, Martini is today remembered for a single song—the eloquent and tender love melody, *"Plaisir d'amour,"* written originally for voice and harp, and arranged by Berlioz for voice and orchestra. Since Berlioz' time it has enjoyed numerous instrumental adaptations. Effective use of the song, as recurring theme music, was made in the American motion picture starring Irene Dunne and Charles Boyer, *Love Affair* (1939).

Pietro Mascagni

PIETRO MASCAGNI was born in Leghorn, Italy, on December 7, 1863. He studied music with private teachers in Leghorn, then for several years attended the Milan Conservatory. In 1884 he was appointed conductor of the municipal band in Cerignola. Meanwhile in 1880 he had completed his first opera, *Pinotta*. Success as composer came later in 1890 with the world première of the opera, *Cavalleria Rusticana* in Rome. A sensation when first introduced, *Cavalleria Rusticana* made the rounds of the world capitals to enjoy a triumph experienced by few operas before or since. Mascagni wrote many operas after that. Though he enjoyed varying degrees of success with *L'Amico Fritz* in 1891 and *Iris* in 1898, he never again duplicated the acclaim given *Cavalleria Rusticana;* and it is still the only one of his operas performed in the world's foremost opera houses. As he himself once said sadly: "It is a pity I wrote *Cavalleria* first. I was crowned before I became king." Mascagni made many tours as a conductor. He visited the United States in 1902 in performances of several of his operas, and South America in 1911. In 1929 he succeeded Toscanini as musical director of La Scala in Milan. Identifying himself closely with the Fascist regime—even to the point of writing an opera, *Nerone,* glorifying Mussolini—Mascagni was subjected to considerable abuse and attack after World War II. He was deprived of his property and other assets. The last year of his life was lived in poverty and disrepute in a small hotel room in Rome, where he died on August 2, 1945.

Cavalleria Rusticana is a one-act opera, libretto by Giovanni Targioni-Tozzetti and Guido Menasci based on a short story by Giovanni

Verga. The setting is Sicily in the latter part of the 19th century. Turiddu, a soldier, is in love with Lola, wife of Alfio, a teamster. But he has also conducted an illicit affair with Santuzza. When Turiddu rudely rejects Santuzza, she finds revenge by revealing to Alfio the love intrigue existing between Lola and Turiddu. In the duel that follows Alfio kills Turiddu.

The most celebrated single excerpt from the opera is the melodious Intermezzo for orchestra which accompanies the departing townspeople as they leave church after the Easter services. This music is radiant with the holiness and serenity of the Easter holiday.

Other popular excerpts include the lovely Siciliana, *"O Lola bianca"* a tenor aria which is sung offstage and breaks into the middle of the opening orchestral prelude; this is a serenade by Turiddu to Lola, sung to harp accompaniment. Santuzza's passionate aria, *"Voi lo sapete"* is the one in which she first discloses to Alfio that his wife and Turiddu are lovers. Turiddu's deeply emotional aria, *"Addio alla madre"* is his poignant farewell to his mother just before he engages in the duel in which he meets his doom.

Jules Massenet

J U L E S M A S S E N E T was born in Montaud in the Loire region of France on May 12, 1842. He entered the Paris Conservatory when he was nine, subsequently winning prizes in fugue and piano playing and, in 1863, the Prix de Rome. Four years later his first opera, *La Grand' Tante,* was produced in Paris. During the Franco-Prussian War he was a member of the National Guard. After the war, he achieved recognition as a composer with his incidental music to *Les Érynnies,* an oratorio *Marie Magdaleine,* and an opera *Le Roi de Lahore.* In 1878 he was elected to the Académie des Beaux-Arts, the youngest man ever to receive this honor, and was appointed professor of composition at the Paris Conservatory. He held the latter post until his death with out-standing distinction. His most significant operas appeared between 1880 and 1900, and included *Hérodiade* (1881), *Manon* (1884), *Le Cid* (1885), *Werther* (1892), *Thaïs* (1894) and *Sapho* (1897). He died in Paris on August 13, 1912.

A style that had lyrical charm, tender feelings, and poetic content placed Massenet with the foremost French composers for the lyric theater. The same qualities are found to a large degree in his instru-mental compositions, and endow them with their immense audience appeal. He had a vein of tenderness that was his uniquely, often con-trasting this with striking passion and intensity. A master of many dif-ferent moods and emotions, he was able to convey them in music that is suave and polished in the best French tradition.

Alsatian Scenes (*Scènes alsaciennes*) is one of Massenet's most popular orchestral compositions. It is the seventh of his suites for orchestra and was written in 1881. For each of its four movements the composer pro-vided an explicit program. About the first movement, "Sunday Morn-ing" ("*Dimanche matin*") the composer writes: "I recall with particular delight the Alsatian village Sunday morning at the hour of divine serv-ice; the streets deserted, the houses empty except for the elderly ones who sun themselves before their doors. The church is full, and the sacred hymns are heard at intervals in passing." "The Tavern" ("*Au cabaret*") is described as the happy meeting place of his friends "with its little windows framed with lead, garlanded with hops and roses. . . . 'Ho, Schmidt, some wine!' And the songs of the forest rangers going to shooting matches. Oh, the joyous life and the gay companions!" "Under the Linden Trees" ("*Sous les tilleuls*") depicts pictorially "the edge of the fields on a Sunday afternoon, the long avenue of linden trees, in the shadow of which, hand in hand, quietly talks a pair of lovers." The suite ends with "Sunday Evening" ("*Dimanche soir: Air alsacien, Retraite française*"). "In the market place, what noise, what movement! Everyone at the doorsteps, groups of young gallants in the streets, and dances which embody in rhythm the songs of the country. Eight o'clock! The noise of the drums, the blare of the trumpets—'tis the retreat! The French retreat! And when in the distance the sound of the drum died down, the women called their children in the street, the old men relighted their big old pipes, and to the sounds of violins the dance is joyously recommenced in smaller circles, with couples closer."

The ballet music for *Le Cid* is strikingly appealing for its exotic melodies and lambent orchestral colors. This opera, text by Louis Gallet and Edouard Blau, is based on Corneille's tragedy; its première performance took place in Paris on November 30, 1885. The setting is 12th century Burgos, in Spain, where Rodrigo called Le Cid, or The Conqueror, kills Chimene's father in a duel. She seeks vengeance but is unable to carry it out because she has fallen in love with him. The ballet music appears in the second scene of the second act. A public square is alive and colorful with dancing crowds, and six dances are performed in rapid succession, some with melodic and rhythmic material derived by Massenet from Spanish folk sources. These are the dances: *"Castillane,"* a highly rhythmic dance found in the Castille region of Spain; *"Andalouse,"* a sinuous, gypsy-like dance from Andalusia; *"Aragonaise,"* a dance popular in the Aragon district; *"Aubade,"* a gentle lyrical section; *"Catalane,"* a dance popular in Catalonia; *"Madrilène,"* a two-part dance from Madrid, the first quiet and introspective, the second dynamic; and *"Navarraise,"* a dance from Navarre.

The popular *"Élégie,"* a plangent melody muted in its grief, comes from the incidental music to *Les Érynnies* with which Massenet first won acclaim in 1873. The play, by Charles Marie Leconte based on Aeschylus, was produced with Massenet's music at the Odéon in Paris. Here the *"Élégie"* appeared as *"Invocation,"* scored for string orchestra. Later on Massenet arranged this section for cello and piano, and it was upon this occasion that he renamed the piece *Élégie*. It was later on also transcribed for violin and piano, and adapted into a song with lyrics by E. Gallet.

Three other sections from *Les Érynnies* have almost as much emotional appeal as the *Élégie,* but in varied moods. The "Entr'acte" is a passionate song for unison violins over a disturbed accompaniment. "Grecian Dance" begins with a vivacious dance tune for two flutes in thirds. A slow dialogue ensues between oboes and clarinets, in which the main subject has an Oriental identity. A fast section brings this movement to a close. *"Scène religieuse"* is a graceful, at times solemn, minuet in which a solo cello provides the main melody.

The famous opera *Manon* (1884) has two delightful dance episodes that are particularly well known, a gavotte and a minuet. *Manon* was based on the famous tale of Abbé Prévost, *L'Histoire du chevalier des Grieux et de Manon Lescaut,* adapted by Henri Meilhac and Philippe Gille. Its setting is France in the 18th century, and in the spirit of that place and time Massenet recreated two old-world dances, both of them appearing in the first scene of the third act, during a festival-day celebration in Paris. Before the curtain goes up, the graceful music of the minuet is heard in the orchestra as an entr'acte. After the rise of the curtain, and the appearance of Manon, she expresses her hedonistic philosophy of life in a gavotte (*"Obéissons quand leur voix appelle"*). This gavotte is often heard in an exclusively instrumental arrangement.

The *Phèdre Overture* (1876) is another of Massenet's frequently performed orchestral compositions. The music closely follows the action of the Racine tragedy, in which Phedre—daughter of King Minos and wife of Theseus—falls in love with Theseus' son, Hippolytus, who fails to respond to her passion. The overture begins in a gloomy mood, forecasting ominously the imminent tragedy awaiting Phedre and Hippolytus. Phedre's grief over her unreciprocated love is suggested by a passionate subject for clarinet; a second equally passionate melody brings us the picture of Hippolytus sent to his doom by an irate father. Violins in unison now bring us a rapturous melody speaking of Phedre's love, while a fiery dramatic section that follows tells of the doom awaiting Hippolyus at the hands of Neptune.

Picturesque Scenes (Scènes pittoresques) is the fourth of Massenet's suites for orchestra, completed in 1873. There are four short, tuneful sections: "March" (*"Marche"*), "Air de Ballet," "Angelus" and "Bohemian Festival" (*"Fête bohème"*). The religious music of the third movement, "Angelus," with its solemn tolling of bells, is the most popular section of this suite, frequently performed separately from the other movements.

Second only to the *"Élégie"* in popularity among Massenet's best-loved melodies is the "Meditation" which comes from the opera *Thaïs*. This excerpt is an orchestral entr'acte with violin obbligato heard just before the first scene of the second act. The opera, libretto by Louis Gallet based on the novel of Anatole France, describes the degradation of Athanaël, a Cenobite monk, because of his unholy passion for Thaïs, a courtesan. The radiant music of the "Meditation" describes Thaïs' renunciation of a life of pleasure for one of the spirit.

Robert McBride

ᴄᡦᵕᡦ ᢪᵕᢪᵕ

ROBERT GUYN McBRIDE was born in Tucson, Arizona, on February 20, 1911. As a boy he learned to play the clarinet and saxophone. He later played both instruments in various dance orchestras. In 1933 he was graduated from the University of Arizona, and a year after that received there his Masters degree. Having studied the oboe in college, he played that instrument with the Tucson Symphony for several years. Then, after additional study of the piano, composition and voice, he joined the music faculty of Bennington College in Vermont in 1935, holding this post eleven years. During this period he received a Guggenheim Fellowship. In 1942, the American Academy of Arts and Letters awarded him a prize for creating a "new idiom in American music." McBride has made successful use of jazz, popular and folk elements in serious chamber-music and orchestral compositions.

The *Mexican Rhapsody* (1936) is one of McBride's best known works for orchestra. He wrote it in Arizona while studying at the University. It was first presented in Tucson in a two-piano arrangement, then in its definitive orchestral version, and finally as a choreographic presentation. McBride here makes a colorful and freshly conceived presentation of four Mexican folk songs familiar to many: *"El Rancho Grande," "Jarabe"* (or "Hat Dance"), *"Cuatro Milpas,"* and *"La Cucaracha."*

McBride has written several interesting compositions in a jazz style. One of the best is the *Strawberry Jam* (1942). This is a caricature of a jazzband jam session, but with the utilization of modern harmonies and symphonic orchestration. *Stuff in G,* for orchestra (1942), is in the racy, tuneful style of Tin Pan Alley, while *Swing Stuff* (1941) brings to the symphonic orchestra the improvisational devices and techniques and the beat of Swing music.

Harl McDonald

❧❧ ❦❦

HARL McDONALD was born in Boulder, Colorado, on July 27, 1899. His music study took place in Redlands, California and at the University of Southern California. The winning of prizes from the American Federation of Music Clubs for two orchestral works enabled him to go to Europe and attend the Leipzig Conservatory. In Germany, his symphonic fantasy, *Mojave,* was successfully introduced by the Berlin State Opera Orchestra. After returning to the United States he was appointed in 1926 to the music faculty of the University of Pennsylvania, where he later became professor of music, and finally head of the music department. At the University he conducted various choral groups which appeared with the Philadelphia Orchestra. From 1939 until his death he was manager of the Philadelphia Orchestra, which introduced many of his orchestral compositions. McDonald wrote four symphonies, a two-piano concerto, a violin concerto, and various suites and tone poems for orchestra. He died in Princeton, New Jersey, on March 30, 1955.

The *Children's Symphony* was a work intended to teach children something about symphonic form through melodies they knew and loved. The form of the symphony is adhered to—in the presentation of two themes, their development, and recapitulation. Simple and unsophisticated, this symphony makes ideal listening for children, but there is enough charm here to provide considerable enjoyment to older people as well. In the first movement, McDonald uses for his two main themes, "London Bridge" and "Baa Baa Black Sheep." In the second movement we hear "Little Bo Peep" and "Oh, Dear, What Can the Matter Be?"; in the third, "Farmer in the Dell" and "Jingle Bells"; and in the finale, "Honey Bee" and "Snow Is Falling On My Garden."

Rhumba, for symphony orchestra, is the third movement of McDonald's Symphony No. 2 (1935). But this movement (which in the symphony displaces the conventional scherzo) is so popular that it is often played apart from the rest of the work. The symphony itself was inspired by the turbulent 1930's, with its labor conflicts, breadlines, unemployment, and depression. *Rhumba* injected a gay note into these somber proceedings, attempting to interpret "the passionate search after good times and diversions, and the restless pursuit of intoxicated pleasures,"as the composer explained. McDonald goes on to say that he here used the rumba rhythm because he liked it and because it seemed to him to be the pulse of those times.

Felix Mendelssohn

FELIX MENDELSSOHN-BARTHOLDY was born in Hamburg, Germany, on February 3, 1809. His grandfather was the famous philosopher, Moses Mendelssohn; his father, a successful banker. Both were of Jewish origin. When Felix was still a boy, however, his immediate family was converted to Protestantism, the occasion upon which they added the name of "Bartholdy" to their own to distinguish them from the other members of their family. A pupil of Ludwig Berger and Karl Friedrich Zelter, Felix was extraordinarily precocious in music. When he was seven and a half he made a successful appearance as pianist in Berlin; by the time he was twelve he had already written operas and symphonies; and in his seventeenth year he produced an unqualified masterwork in the *Overture to A Midsummer Night's Dream*. In 1827, one of his operas was produced in Berlin, but by that time he had already completed thirteen symphonies and a library of chamber music as well.

In 1829, Mendelssohn conducted in Berlin the first performance of Bach's *Passion According to St. Matthew* to be given since Bach's own day. This concert became a powerful influence in reviving interest in Bach's music, which at that time had been languishing in both neglect and obscurity. A few weeks after Mendelssohn had directed a repeat performance, he made his first trip to England where he led the première of a new symphony and was made honorary member of the Royal Philharmonic. A tour of Scotland that followed immediately was the inspiration for his overture, *Fingal's Cave*.

In 1833, Mendelssohn served as musical director of the city of Dues-seldorf. He held this post only six months. Much more significant was his engagement as the principal conductor of the Gewandhaus Orches-tra in Leipzig in 1835 which, during the five years of his leadership, was elevated to a position of first importance among the world's symphony orchestras.

In 1841, Mendelssohn became head of the music department of a projected Academy of Arts in Berlin. This appointment did not pre-vent him from visiting England where he was received with an adula-tion accorded to no foreign musician since Handel. Returning to Ber-lin he found that the Academy of Arts project had been abandoned. He was now made Kapellmeister to the King, an honorary post allow-ing him complete freedom of activity and movement. During the next few years he conducted concerts of the Gewandhaus Orchestra, and paid two more highly successful visits to England. He was also instru-mental in helping to found the Leipzig Conservatory in 1843. Always of delicate health and sensibilities, Mendelssohn collapsed at the news that his beloved sister, Fanny, died in 1847. He died in Leipzig soon after that, on November 4, 1847.

The finest qualities of German Romantic music can be found in Mendelssohn. He had the Romantic's partiality for fantasy and the supernatural, together with the lightness of touch with which to create such worlds through music. He had the Romantic's gift for translating natural scenes, landscapes and lyric poetry into sensitive tone pictures. He had a most winning lyricism and graceful harmonic and orchestral gift, and he never lacked the ability to charm and enchant his listeners with the most tender and lovable musical expression. Other composers may have written profounder or more emotionally stirring music than Mendelssohn; but no one could be more ingratiating, sensitive, or refined. Some of Mendelssohn's serious symphonic works are so full of the most wonderful melodies and beguiling moods that they have the universal appeal of semi-classics.

The concert overture, *Fingal's Cave,* or as it is also sometimes known, *Hebrides Overture,* op. 26 (1832) was inspired by the composer's visit to the Scottish Highlands in 1830. The opening theme in lower strings and bassoons suggests the roll of the waves at the mouth of a cave, a melody that came to the composer while visiting the caves of Staffa. This idea is developed, then a second beautiful melody unfolds in cellos and bassoons.

The orchestral suite, *A Midsummer Night's Dream,* op. 61 is derived from the incidental music comprising thirteen numbers which Mendelssohn wrote for a Potsdam production of the Shakespeare comedy in 1843; the Overture, however, was a fruit of the composer's youth, having been written in 1826. The magic world of fairies and elves which Mendelssohn projected so delicately in his youthful overture is preserved in many of the numbers he wrote seventeen years later. The Overture, op. 21, is initiated with four sensitive chords, and proceeds with fleeting, diaphanous music for strings with which we are suddenly plunged in fairyland. The main thematic material to follow comprises a haunting song for horn, a romantic episode for woodwind and strings, and a sprightly fairy dance for strings.

Three other musical sections from this incidental music, and basic to the orchestral suite, are famous. The "Nocturne" is a broad, moody song for horns. The "Scherzo"—like the Overture—is a picture of the world of fairies, gnomes and elves, though in a more energetic and spirited vein. The "Wedding March" is now one of the most frequently played pieces of wedding music, second in popularity only to Wagner's wedding music from *Lohengrin;* it first became popular as wedding music at the nuptials of the English Princess in London in 1858. A trumpet fanfare leads to the dignified march melody which is twice alternated with melodious trio sections.

"On Wings of Song" ("*Auf Fluegeln des Gesanges"*), op. 34, no. 2 (1834) is Mendelssohn's best-known song, a melody of incomparable loveliness and serenity. The poem is by Heine. Franz Liszt transcribed it for piano; Joseph Achron for violin and piano; Lionel Tertis for viola and piano. It has also enjoyed various orchestral transcriptions.

Ruy Blas, op. 95 (1839)—like *Fingal's Cave*—is a concert overture for orchestra; here the inspiration is the drama of Victor Hugo. Four solemn bars for wind instruments lead to the principal subject, first violins and flutes; clarinets, bassoons, and cellos later offer the second contrasting staccato theme.

The *Spinning Song* and the *Spring Song* are both instrumental favorites, and both come from the *Songs Without Words (Lieder ohne Worte),* for solo piano. The form of "song without words" is a creation of Mendelssohn: a brief composition of such essentially lyric character that it is virtually a "song" for the piano. Mendelssohn wrote forty-eight such pieces gathered in eight books. The *Spinning Song* in C major appears in op. 67 as the fourth number (1844). This is a tender melody placed against a rhythmic background suggesting the whirring of a spinning wheel. The *Spring Song* in A major is surely one of the most familiar tonal pictures of the vernal season to be found in the semi-classical literature; it appears in op. 62 (1842) as the concluding number. Both the *Spinning Song* and *Spring Song* appear in all kinds and varieties of transcriptions.

The stirring *War March of the Priests* is a number from the incidental music for Racine's drama, *Athalie*, op. 74 (1843); this incidental music was first performed with the Racine play in Berlin in 1845.

Giacomo Meyerbeer

GIACOMO MEYERBEER was born in Berlin, Germany, on September 5, 1791. His name, at birth, was Jakob Liebmann Beer. When Meyer, a rich relative, left him a legacy, he decided to change his name to Meyerbeer; some years later upon initiating a career as composer of Italian operas he Italianized his name. His music study took place with Clementi, Zelter, Anselm Weber and Vogler, the last of whom encouraged him to write his first opera, *Jephtha's Vow* (*Jephtha's Geluebde*), a failure when first performed in Munich in 1812. A second opera, performed in Stuttgart, was also a failure; Meyerbeer now seriously entertained the thought of abandoning composition altogether. The noted Viennese composer and teacher, Antonio Salieri, however, convinced him what he needed was more study. This took place in Italy where for several years Meyerbeer assimilated Italian traditions of opera. His first endeavor in this style was *Romilda e Costanza*, a success when introduced in Padua in 1817. During the next few years Meyerbeer wrote several more operas, some of them on commission, and became one of Italy's most highly regarded composers for the stage. In 1826, Meyerbeer settled in Paris where association with composers like Cherubini and Halévy, made him impatient with the kind of operas he had thus far created. In 1831, with *Robert le Diable*, he entered upon a new artistic phase in which Italian methods, procedures and traditions were discarded in favor of the French. *Robert le Diable,* produced at the Opera on November 21, 1831 was a sensation. Meyerbeer continued writing operas in the French style for the remainder of his life. These are the operas by which he is most often represented in the world's opera theaters: *Les Huguenots* (1836), *Le Prophète* (1849), and *L'Africaine* (1865). Meyerbeer died in Paris on May 2, 1864.

Meyerbeer was an exponent of drama in the grand style, his finest operas being filled with big climactic scenes, elaborate stage effects, and eye-filling visual displays. But he also had a pronounced dramatic gift, one which evoked from Wagner the highest admiration; and a pronounced expressiveness of lyricism.

L'Africaine (*The African*) is Meyerbeer's last opera, and many regarded it as his best. He completed it in 1864 just before his death, and its world première at the Paris Opera took place posthumously on April 28, 1865. The text, by Eugène Scribe, is set in Lisbon and Madagascar in the 15th century. The main action concerns the love of Selika, an African queen, for the Portuguese explorer, Vasco da Gama; Da Gama in turn is loved by Inez, daughter of Don Diego. Selika offers the explorer a secret route to the land of which she is queen, Madagascar, and with which Da Gama becomes enraptured. But when Inez appears, he abandons Selika for her, and leaves the magic island. Heartbroken, Selika kills herself by breathing the deadly fragrance of a manchineel tree.

The opera's most popular excerpt is Vasco da Gama's rapturous tenor aria from the fourth act in which he describes the beauty of Madagascar, *"O Paradis."* Another vocal favorite is the baritone ballad of Nelusko, slave of Selika, *"Adamastor, roi des vagues profondes";* as he steers the ship bearing Selika and Vasco da Gama to Madagascar he sings of Adamastor, monarch of the sea, who sends ships to their doom on treacherous reefs.

The *Coronation March* (*Marche du couronnement*)—music of pomp and circumstance—comes from the opera *Le Prophète,* first performed at the Paris Opéra on April 16, 1849. Eugène Scribe's libretto is based on an actual historical episode in 16th century Holland centered around the Anabaptist uprising, with John of Leyden, leader of the Anabaptists, as the principal character. In Act four, scene two, John is being crowned king outside the Muenster Cathedral. As a magnificent royal procession enters the Cathedral, the music of the *Coronation March* matches in splendor and grandeur the visual majesty of this scene. Another popular musical excerpt for orchestra from this opera is Prelude to Act 3, a colorful and rhythmic Quadrille that leads into the opening scene of that act, providing the lively musical background for a ballet and ice-carnival skating scene. Liszt made a technically brilliant transcription for the piano of this Quadrille music.

Les Huguenots (*The Huguenots*) was first performed at the Paris Opéra on February 29, 1836, the year it was completed; the libretto was by Eugène Scribe and Émile Deschamps. In 16th century Touraine and Paris, Raoul, a Huguenot nobleman, has saved the life of Valentine, daughter of the Catholic leader, St. Bris. She falls in love with Raoul, but the latter repudiates her, believing her to be the mistress of Count de Nevers. When he discovers he has been mistaken, Raoul risks his life to see her. During this visit he overhears a Catholic plot to massacre the Huguenots. After Raoul and Valentine get married, they are both murdered in the massacre—Valentine by her own father.

The Overture to *Les Huguenots* is built almost entirely from the melody of the famous Lutheran chorale, *Ein' feste Burg,* which in the opera itself served as the musical symbol for militant Protestantism. The outstanding individual excerpts from the opera include Raoul's beautiful romance from Act 1 describing the woman he has saved, *"Plus blanche que la blanche hermine";* the rhapsodic description in the second act of the Touraine countryside by Marguerite de Valois, betrothed to Henry IV of Navarre, *"O beau pays de la Touraine";* and in the fourth act the stirring "Benediction of the Swords," (*"Gloire au grand Dieu vengeur"*) with which the Catholics are blessed by three monks on the eve of their holy war against the Huguenots.

The exciting *Torch Dance,* No. 1, in B-flat is not from one of Meyerbeer's operas. It was written in 1846 for the wedding of the King of Bavaria, and originally was scored for brass band. It is now most frequently heard in orchestral adaptations. Meyerbeer subsequently wrote two other *Torch Dances:* the second in 1850 for the wedding of Princess Charlotte of Prussia, and the third in 1853 for the wedding of Princess Anne of Prussia.

Karl Milloecker

❧❧ ❦❦

KARL MILLOECKER was born in Vienna, Austria, on May 29, 1842. His father, a jeweler, wanted him to enter the family business, but from his childhood on, Karl was drawn to music. After studying music with private teachers, he attended the Conservatory of the Gesellschaft der Musikfreunde. Meanwhile, in his sixteenth year, he supported himself by playing the flute in a theater orchestra. When his music study ended, he became conductor of a theater in Graz in 1864; there his first operetta was produced one year later. In 1866 he was back in Vienna, and from 1869 to 1883 he was principal conductor at the Theater-an-der-Wien where most of his famous operettas were produced including *Countess Du Barry* (*Graefin DuBarry*) in 1879, *The Beggar Student* (*Der Bettelstudent*) in 1882, *Gasparone* in 1884, and *Poor Jonathan* (*Der arme Jonathan*) in 1890. Milloecker died in Baden, near Vienna, on December 31, 1899.

Milloecker's most famous operetta is *The Beggar Student* (*Der Bettelstudent*), which was first produced at the Theater-an-der-Wien in Vienna on December 6, 1882, and after that enjoyed highly successful performances at the Casino Theater in New York in 1883, and the Alhambra in London in 1884. The scene is Cracow, Poland; the time, 1704. General Ollendorf, spurned by Laura, evolves an elaborate plot to avenge himself. He finances the impoverished student, Symon, dresses him up as a lord, and sends him off to woo and win Laura. Only after the wedding does the General reveal the fact that Symon is a beggar. Just as disgrace faces the young man, he becomes involved in a successful maneuver to restore the rejected Polish king to his throne. Thus he acquires wealth and a title, and is welcomed with pride and love by Laura and her mother. Potpourris and selections from this tuneful operetta always include the principal waltz melody which comes as a first act finale, *"Ach ich hab' sie ja nur auf die Schulter gekuesst."* Other delightful excerpts include Symon's mazurka, *"Ich knuepfte manche zarte Bande,"* his lament *"Ich hab' kein Geld,"* and the second act duet of Symon and Laura, *"Ich setz den Fall."*

Moritz Moszkowski

ᴥᶾᴥᶾ ᶾᴥᶾᴥ

MORITZ MOSZKOWSKI was born in Breslau, Germany, on August 23, 1854. He received his musical training at three leading German Conservatories: the Dresden Conservatory, the Stern Conservatory and Kullak Academy in Berlin. He began a career as pianist in 1873, touring Europe with outstanding success. He also achieved recognition as a teacher of the piano at the Kullak Academy. In 1897, he went into retirement in Paris where he lived for the remainder of his life. In 1899 he was elected a member of the Berlin Academy. Towards the end of his life his financial resources were completely depleted, and his fame as composer, pianist, and teacher had long been eclipsed. He died in poverty and obscurity in Paris on March 4, 1925.

Though he wrote operas, ballets, suites, concertos and a symphony, Moszkowski was at his best—and is most famous today—for his lighter music in a Spanish idiom. Typical of his music in this style were the rhythmic *Bolero,* op. 12, no. 5, for piano solo; the languorous and haunting *Guitarre,* op. 45, no. 2, for piano solo (transcribed by Pablo de Sarasate for violin and piano); and the dashing *Malagueña,* from the opera *Boabdil.*

But his most celebrated compositions are the delightful *Spanish Dances,* opp. 12, and 65, two books of pieces for piano solo or piano duo, which have been arranged for orchestra. The most popular are the first in C major, the second in G minor, and the fifth (a bolero) in D major. While none of these dances can be accepted as authentic Spanish music —actually they are only a German Romantic's conception of what Spanish music is—they make most effective use of Spanish dance rhythms.

Wolfgang Amadeus Mozart

WOLFGANG AMADEUS MOZART was born in Salz-burg, Austria, on January 27, 1756. The son of Leopold, Kapellmeister at the court of the Salzburg Archbishop, Wolfgang Amadeus disclosed his remarkable musical powers at a tender age. He began composition at the age of five, completed a piano sonata at seven, and a symphony at eight. Taught the harpsichord, also very early in his childhood, he revealed such phenomenal abilities at improvisation and sight reading that he was the wonder and awe of all who came into contact with him. His ambitious father exhibited this formidable prodigy for several years before the crowned heads of Europe; and wherever he appeared the child was acclaimed. Goethe said: "A phenomenon like that of Mozart remains an inexplicable thing." In Milan in 1770 he was commissioned to write an opera *Mitridate, rè di Ponto,* successfully performed that year. In Bologna he became the only musician under the age of twenty to be elected a member of the renowed Accademia Filarmonica. And in Rome he provided dramatic evidence of his extraordinary natural gifts by putting down on paper the entire complex score of Allegri's *Miserere* after a single hearing.

As he outgrew childhood he ripened as a composer, gaining all the time in both technical and creative powers. But he was a prodigy no more, and though he was rapidly becoming one of the most profound and original musicians in Europe he was unable to attract the adulation and excitement that had once been his. Between 1772 and 1777, as an employee in the musical establishment of the Salzburg Archbishop, he was treated like a menial servant. The remarkable music he was writing all the time passed unnoticed. Finally, in 1782, he made a permanent break with the Archbishop and established his home in Vienna where he lived for the remainder of his life. Though he received some important commissions, and enjoyed several triumphs for his operas, he did not fare any too well in Vienna either. He had to wait several years for a court appointment, and when it finally came in 1787 he was deplorably underpaid. Thus he lived in poverty, often dependent for food and other necessities of life on the generosity of his friends. And yet the masterworks kept coming in every conceivable medium—operas, symphonies, sonatas, quartets, concertos, choral music and so forth. A few people in Vienna were aware of his prodigious achievements, and one of these was Joseph Haydn who called him "the greatest composer I know either personally or by name." During the last years of his life Mozart was harassed not only by poverty but also by severe illness. Yet his last year was one of his most productive, yielding his last three symphonies, the *Requiem,* the opera *The Magic Flute (Die Zauberfloete),* the *Ave Verum,* and a remarkable piano concerto and string quintet. He died in Vienna on December 5, 1791 and was buried in a pauper's grave with no tombstone or cross for identification.

Through his genius every form of music was endowed with new grandeur, nobility of expression and richness of thought. He was a technician second to none; a bold innovator; a creator capable of plumbing the profoundest depths of emotion and the most exalted heights of spirituality. Yet he could also be simple and charming and graceful, in music remarkably overflowing with the most engaging melodies conceived by man, and characterized by the most exquisite taste and the most consummate craftsmanship. Thus Mozart's lighter moods in music are often also endowed with extraordinary creative resources and original invention; yet they never lose their capacity to delight audiences at first contact.

The music Mozart wrote directly for popular consumption were the hundred or so *Dances* for orchestra: *Country Dances, German Dances, Minuets.* The greatest number of these consist of the *German Dances.* These are lively melodies in eight-measure phrases and with forceful peasant rhythms. Some of the best *German Dances* are those in which Mozart utilized unusual orchestral resources or instruments to suggest extra-musical sounds. The *Sleighride (Die Schlittenfahrt),* K. 605, in C major, simulates the sound of sleigh bells in the middle trio section, sounded in the tones A-F-E-C. *The Organgrinder (Der Leiermann),* K. 602, imitates the sound of a hurdy-gurdy. In *The Canary (Der Kanarienvogel),* K. 571, flutes reproduce the chirping of birds.

The *Country Dance,* or *Contretanze,* is sometimes regarded as the first modern dance, forerunner of the quadrille. Structurally and stylistically these are very much like *German Dances* with a peasant-like vitality and earthiness. Here, too, Mozart sometimes realistically imitates non-musical sounds as in *The Thunder Storm (Das Donnerwetter),* K. 534, in which the role of the timpani suggests peals of thunder.

Mozart's most popular Minuet—indeed, it is probably one of the most popular minuets ever written—comes from his opera *Don Giovanni,* libretto by Lorenzo da Ponte, and first performed in Prague in 1787. The hero of this opera is, to be sure, the Spanish nobleman of the 17th century whose escapades and licentious life finally bring him to doom at the hands of the statue of the Commandant come to life to consign him to the fires of hell. The Minuet appears in the fifth scene of the first act. Don Giovanni is the gracious host of a party held in his palace, and there the guests dance a courtly minuet while Don himself is making amatory overtures to Zerlina.

In a lighter mood, also, is the *Eine kleine Nachtmusik (A Little Night Music)*, K. 525, a serenade for string orchestra (1787). This work is consistently tuneful, gracious, charming. The first movement has two lilting little melodies, which are presented and recapitulated with no formal development to speak of. The second movement is a Romance, or Romanza, a poetic song contrasted by two vigorous sections; the main thought of this movement is then repeated between each of these two vigorous parts. After that comes a formal minuet, and the work ends with a brisk and sprightly rondo.

Mozart's popular *Turkish March*—in the pseudo Turkish style so popular in Vienna in his day—comes out of his piano Sonata in A major, K. 331 (1778), where it appears as the last movement. This march is extremely popular in orchestral transcription.

Modest Mussorgsky

MODEST MUSSORGSKY was born in Karevo, Russia, on March 21, 1839. When he was thirteen he entered the cadet school of the Imperial Guard in St. Petersburg, from which he was graduated to join the Guard regiment. In 1857 he met and befriended several important Russian musicians (including Balakirev and Stassov) under whose stimulus he decided to leave the army and become a composer. Until now his musical education had been sporadic, having consisted of little more than some piano lessons with his mother and a private teacher. He now began an intensive period of study with Balakirev, under whose guidance he completed a *Scherzo* for orchestra which was performed in St. Petersburg in 1860, as well as some piano music and the fragments of a symphony. Associating himself with Balakirev, Rimsky-Korsakov, Borodin, and Cui he now became a passionate advocate of musical nationalism, becoming the fifth member of a new school of Russian music henceforth identified as "The Mighty Five" or "The Russian Five." In 1863, with serfdom abolished in Russia, he lost the outside financial resources he had thus far enjoyed as the son of a landowner. To support himself he worked for four years as a clerk in the Ministry of Communications; in 1869 he found employment in the forestry department. During this period music had to be relegated to the position of an avocation, but composition was not abandoned. He completed the first of his masterworks, the orchestral tone poem, *A Night on the Bald Mountain,* in 1866. A lifelong victim of nervous disorders, melancholia and subsequently of alcoholism, his health soon began to deteriorate alarmingly; but despite this fact he was able to complete several works of crowning significance in 1874 including his folk opera, *Boris Godunov,* and his *Pictures at an Exhibition,* for piano. After 1874 his moral and physical disintegration became complete; towards the last months of his life he gave indications of losing his mind. He died in St. Petersburg on March 28, 1881.

As one of the most forceful and original members of the "Russian Five" Mussorgsky's greatest works certainly do not lend themselves to popular distribution. His writing is too individual in its melodic and harmonic construction; and his works show too great a tendency towards musical realism to make for palatable digest. However, several of the folk dances in his operas are strikingly effective for their rhythmic pulse and national colors and are by no means as elusive in their appeal as the rest of his production.

Mussorgsky's masterwork is his mighty folk opera, *Boris Godunov,* where we encounter one such delightful dance episode, the Polonaise. *Boris Godunov,* libretto by the composer based on a Pushkin drama, traces the career of the Czar from the years 1598 to 1605, from his coronation to his insanity and death. The Polonaise occurs in the first scene of the third act. At the palace of a Polish landowner, handsomely costumed guests perform this festive courtly dance in the adjoining garden. The première of *Boris Godunov* took place in St. Petersburg on February 8, 1874.

Two orchestral dances can also be found in another of Mussorgky's folk operas, *The Fair at Sorochinsk*, which was not introduced until October 26, 1917, in St. Petersburg. The libretto was by the composer based on Gogol's story, *Evenings on a Farm Near Dikanka*. Tcherevik, a peasant, wants his daughter to marry Pritzko, whereas the peasant's wife is partial to the pastor's son. However, when the pastor's son compromises the peasant's wife she realizes that Pritzko is, after all, the right man for her daughter. In the third act of this opera comes the lively *Hopak,* or *Gopak,* a folk dance with two beats to a measure.

Folk dances of a completely different nature—more oriental and exotic than the previously discussed Russian variety—will be found in *Khovanschina,* a musical drama with libretto by the composer and Stassov; this opera was first given, in an amateur performance, in St. Petersburg on February 21, 1886. Here the setting is Moscow during the reign of Peter the Great, and the plot revolves around the efforts of a band of radicals known as the Streltsy who try to overthrow the Czar. Prince Ivan Khovantsky, who is in league with the Streltsy, is murdered by assassins, and the insurrection is suppressed. But before the leaders of the Streltsy can destroy themselves they are given an official pardon by the Czar. A high moment in this opera comes with the *Dances of the Persian Slaves,* which takes place in the first scene of the fourth act. At the country house of Khovantsky, the Prince is being entertained by an elaborate spectacle, the main attraction of which is the sinuous, Corybantic dancing of the Persian slaves.

Almost as popular as these Persian dances are the Prelude to the first act and an entr'acte between the first and second scenes from this opera; these two episodes for orchestra are highly atmospheric, graphic in the pictures of Russian landscapes. The first act Prelude has been named by the composer, *Dawn on the Moskava River.* This is a subtle tone picture made up of a folk melody and five variations. The entr'acte offers another kind of landscape, this time a bleak one describing the vast, lonely plains of Siberia.

Ethelbert Nevin

۶۶ ۶۶

ETHELBERT WOODBRIDGE NEVIN was born in Edgeworth, Pennsylvania, on November 25, 1862. A precocious child in music, he wrote his first piano piece when he was eleven. A year later he wrote and had published a song that became exceedingly popular, "Good Night, Good Night Beloved." After studying music with private teachers, he went to Berlin in 1884, studying for two years with Hans von Buelow and Karl Klindworth. He returned to the United States in 1886. Soon after that he made his formal American concert debut as pianist with a program on which he included some of his own compositions. By 1890 he decided to give up his career as a virtuoso and to concentrate on being a composer. In 1891 he completed *Water Scenes,* a suite for the piano in which will be found one of the most popular piano pieces by an American, "Narcissus." In 1892 and again 1895 Nevin traveled extensively through Europe and Morocco. In 1897 he settled in New York City where he wrote one of the best-selling art songs by an American, "The Rosary." In 1900 Nevin went to live in New Haven. During the last year of his life he was a victim of depressions which he tried to alleviate through excessive drinking. He died of an apoplectic stroke in New Haven, Connecticut, on February 17, 1901.

"Mighty Lak a Rose" and "The Rosary" are Nevin's two most famous art songs; they are also among the most popular art songs written in America. "Mighty Lak a Rose" was one of Nevin's last compositions, written during the closing months of his life. He never lived to see the song published and become popular. The song is a setting of a poem by Frank L. Stanton, and is described by John Trasker Howard (Nevin's biographer) as "probably the simplest of all his songs . . . [with] a freshness and whimsical tenderness that make its appeal direct and forceful."

"The Rosary," words by R. C. Rogers, was an even greater success. From 1898 to 1928 it sold over two and a half million copies of sheet music. When Nevin had finished writing this song in 1898, he invited the singer Francis Rogers to dinner, after which he handed him a scribbled piece of music paper. "Here is a song I just composed," he told Rogers. "I want you to sing it at your concert next week." Rogers deciphered the notes as best he could while Nevin played the accompaniment from memory. The little audience listening to this first informal presentation of "The Rosary" was enthusiastic, but one of its members insisted it would be impossible for Rogers to memorize the song in time for the concert the following week. The guest bet Nevin a champagne supper for all present that the song would not be on Rogers' program. He lost the bet. The following week, on February 15, 1898, Rogers introduced the song at the Madison Square Concert Hall.

The *Water Scenes,* suite for piano, op. 13 is remembered principally because one of its movements is "Narcissus," often considered one of the most popular compositions ever written in this country. Nevin himself provided information about the origin of "Narcissus." "I remembered vaguely that there was once a Grecian lad who had something to do with the water and who was called Narcissus. I rummaged about my old mythology and read the story over again. The theme, or rather both themes, came as I read. I went directly to my desk and wrote out the whole composition. Afterwards, I rewrote it and revised it a little. The next morning I sent it to my publishers. Until the proofs came back to me I never tried it on the piano. I left almost immediately for Europe and was surprised when a publisher wrote to me of the astonishing sale of the piece." During Nevin's lifetime, the piece sold over 125,000 copies of sheet music, and was heard throughout America both in its original piano version (a favorite repertory number of piano students and budding piano virtuosos) and in transcriptions. It went on to circle the globe. As Vance Thompson wrote: "It was thrummed and whistled half around the world. It was played in Cairo as in New York and Paris; it was played by orchestras, on church organs, and on the mouth harps of Klondike miners; it became a mode, almost a mania."

The other movements of *Water Scenes* are: "Barcarolle," "Dragon Fly," "Water Nymph," "At Twilight," and "Ophelia." Each is a sensitive piece of tone painting, as lyrical and as unashamedly sentimental as the beloved "Narcissus."

Otto Nicolai

❧❧ ❧❧

OTTO NICOLAI was born in Koenigsberg, Germany, on June 9, 1810. After completing his music study with Zelter and Bernhard Klein, he came to Paris in 1830 where he remained three years. In Berlin he completed several works for orchestra, and some for chorus. In 1834 he went to Italy where he was organist in the Prussian Embassy at Rome and became interested in opera. From 1837 to 1838 he was principal conductor at the Kaerthnerthor Theater in Vienna. Then he returned to Italy to devote himself to the writing of operas, the first of which, *Rosmonda d'Inghilterra* was a failure when produced in Turin in 1838. His second opera, however, was a major success when first given in Turin in 1840: *Il Templario* based on Sir Walter Scott's *Ivanhoe;* it was produced in Naples and Vienna. In 1841 Nicolai came to Vienna to serve for six years as Kapellmeister to the court. During this period, in 1842, he helped to found the renowned Vienna Philharmonic Orchestra. In 1847 he came to Berlin to become conductor of the Domchor. It was here that he completed the work upon which his reputation rests, the comic opera, *The Merry Wives of Windsor (Die lustigen Weiber von Windsor)*. He died in Berlin of an apoplectic stroke on May 11, 1849, only two months after the première performance of his famous comic opera.

The Merry Wives of Windsor (Die lustigen Weiber von Windsor) is Nicolai's only opera to survive; and its overture is his only work for orchestra which retains its popularity. The opera received a highly successful première in Berlin on March 8, 1849. Its libretto, by Hermann Salomon Mosenthal, is based on Shakespeare's comedy and follows that play with only minor modifications. Falstaff's cronies (Bardolph, Pistol and Nym) are omitted; only slight reference is made to the love of Anne and Fenton; and considerable attention is paid to Falstaff's comical amatory overtures to Mistresses Ford and Page.

The overture opens with a slow introduction in which a flowing melody is given against a high C in the violins. This melody is repeated by several different sections of the orchestra, then treated in imitation.

The main part of the overture is made up of two vivacious melodies, the second of which, in the violins, is intended to depict Mistress Page. The development of both themes is in a gay mood, with a robust passage in F minor representing Falstaff. The overture concludes with an animated coda.

From the opera itself come three melodious vocal selections, prominent in all orchestral potpourris: Falstaff's drinking song, a long time favorite of German bassos, *"Als Bueblein klein";* Fenton's serenade to Anne Page, *"Horch, die Lerche singt in Haim";* and Mistress Page's third-act ballad of Herne the Hunter.

Siegfried Ochs

SIEGFRIED OCHS was born in Frankfort on the Main, Germany, on April 19, 1858. While studying medicine, he attended the Berlin High School for Music. Then deciding upon music as a life's career, he continued his music study with private teachers and became a protégé of Hans von Buelow. In 1882 he founded the Philharmonic Choir of Berlin, one of Germany's most celebrated choral groups. He remained its conductor even after it merged with the chorus of the Berlin High School for Music in 1920. Ochs died in Berlin on February 6, 1929.

Ochs wrote several comic operas, song cycles, and some choral music. A semi-classical favorite is the set of orchestral variations on the well-known German folk song, *"Kommt ein Vogel."* These variations are each in the style of a famous composer—Bach, Mozart, Beethoven. Wagner, Johann Strauss II, and so on; and each variation shows a remarkable skill, and a winning wit, in mimicking the individual creative mannerisms and idiosyncrasies of each composer.

Jacques Offenbach

⤚§⤚§ ⤙§⤙§

JACQUES OFFENBACH was born Jacques Oberst in Cologne, Germany, on June 20, 1819; his father was a cantor in one of the city synagogues. After attending the Paris Conservatory, Offenbach played the cello in the orchestra of the Opéra-Comique. Then, in 1849 he became conductor at the Théâtre Français. In 1850 he achieved his initial success as a composer with the song, *"Chanson de Fortunio"* interpolated into a production of the Alfred de Musset drama, *Chandelier.* Three years later his first operetta, *Pepito,* was produced at the Théâtre des Variétés. Between 1855 and 1866 he directed his own theater where operettas were given, Les Bouffes Parisiens, which opened on July 5, 1855 with a performance of one of his own works, *Les Deux aveugles.* For his theater Offenbach wrote many operettas including his masterwork in that genre, *Orpheus in the Underworld,* in 1858. After closing down the Bouffes Parisiens, Offenbach went to Germany and Austria where he had produced several more of his operettas. But in 1864 he was back in Paris. The première of *La Belle Hélène* at the Variétés that year enjoyed a spectacular success. Among his later operettas were *La Vie parisienne* (1866), *La Grande Duchesse de Gérolstein* (1867), and *La Périchole* (1868). In 1877 he toured the United States, an account of which was issued in America in 1957 under the title of *Orpheus in America.* Towards the end of his life Offenbach devoted himself to the writing of his one and only grand opera, *The Tales of Hoffmann (Les Contes d'Hoffmann).* He did not live to see it performed. He died in Paris on October 5, 1880, about half a year before the première of his opera at the Opéra-Comique on February 10, 1881.

Offenbach was the genius of the opéra-bouffe, or French operetta. His music never lacked spontaneity or gaiety, sparkle or engaging lyricism. His writing had the warmth of laughter, the sting of satire, and the caress of sincere and heartfelt emotion. His lovable melodies woo and win the listener. The lightness of his touch and the freshness of his humor give voice to the joy of good living. Like his celebrated Viennese contemporary, Johann Strauss II, Offenbach is a giant figure in semi-classical music. To the lighter musical repertory he brings the invention and imagination of a master.

The *Apache Dance* is the dashing music that invariably accompanies a performance of French Apache dances, though there are few that know Offenbach wrote it. Actually, the *Apache Dance* is an adaptation of the main melody of a waltz (*"Valse des Papillons"*) from Offenbach's comic opera, *Le Roi Carotte* (1872).

La Belle Hélène (Fair Helen), first performed in Paris on December 17, 1864, draws material for laughter and satire from mythology. Henri Meilhac and Ludovic Halévy prepared the text which is based on the love of Paris and Helen that led to the Trojan war. But this story is told with tongue-in-cheek frivolity, and the life of the Greeks is gaily parodied. One of the most familiar musical excerpts from *La Belle Hélène* is whirling Can-Can music—the Can-Can being the voluptuous French dance which first became popular in Paris in 1830 and which contributed to the quadrille high kicks, skirt-lifting and other suggestive and at times vulgar movements. (Offenbach also wrote brilliant Can-Can music for *Orpheus in the Underworld, Barbe-Bleue,* and *La Vie parisienne.*) Other delightful episodes from this operetta are Helen's invocation with chorus, *"Amours divins,"* and her highly lyrical airs, *"On me nomme Hélène," "Un mari Sage,"* and *"La vrai! je ne suis pas coupable."*

The Galop is almost as much a specialty with Offenbach as the Can-Can. This is a spirited, highly rhythmic dance of German origin introduced in Paris in 1829. Two of Offenbach's best known Galops appear respectively in *La Grande Duchess de Gérolstein* (1867) and *Genèvieve de Brabant* (1859).

It is perhaps not generally known that the famous "Marine's Hymn" familiar to all Americans as "From the Halls of Montezuma" also comes out of *Genèvieve de Brabant*. The Hymn was copyrighted by the Marine Corps in 1919. It is known that the lyric was written in 1847 by an unidentified Marine. The melody was taken from one of the airs in Offenbach's operetta, *Genèvieve de Brabant*.

Orpheus in the Underworld (Orphée aux enfers) is Offenbach's masterwork, first produced in Paris on October 21, 1858. This delightful comic opera, with book by Hector Crémieux and Ludovic Halévy, is a satire on the Olympian gods in general, and specifically on the legend of Orpheus and Eurydice. *Orpheus in the Underworld* was not at first successful since audiences did not seem to find much mirth in a satire on Olympian gods. But when a powerful French critic, Jules Janin, violently attacked it as a "profanation of holy and glorious antiquity," the curiosity of Parisians was aroused, and the crowds began swarming into the theater. Suddenly *Orpheus in the Underworld* became a vogue; it was the thing to see and discuss; its music (particularly the waltzes, galops, and quadrilles) were everywhere played. The operetta had a run of 227 performances.

The Overture is a perennial favorite of salon and pop orchestras throughout the world. It opens briskly, then progresses to the first subject, a light and gay tune for strings. The heart of the overture is the second main melody, a sentimental song first heard in solo violin, and later repeated by full orchestra.

The Can-Can music in *Orpheus in the Underworld* is also famous. Much of its effect is due to the fact that Offenbach presented the can-can immediately after a stately minuet in order to emphasize the contrast between two periods in French history. A contemporary described this Can-Can music as follows: "This famous dance . . . has carried away our entire generation as would a tempestuous whirlwind. Already the first sounds of the furiously playing instruments seem to indicate the call to a whole world to awake and plunge into the wild dance. These rhythms appear to have the intention of shocking all the resigned, all the defeated, out of their lethargy and, by the physical and moral upheaval which they arouse, to throw the whole fabric of society into confusion."

The Tales of Hoffmann (Les Contes d'Hoffmann) is Offenbach's only serious opera; but even here we encounter some semi-classical favorites. This opera, one of the glories of the French lyric theater, was based on stories by E. T. A. Hoffmann, adapted into a libretto by Jules Barbier and Michel Carré. It concerns the three tragic loves of the poet Hoffmann: Olympia, a mechanical doll; Giulietta, who is captive to a magician; and Antonia, a victim of consumption.

The "Barcarolle" from this opera is surely one of the most popular selections from the world of opera. It opens the second act. Outside Giulietta's palace in Venice, Hoffmann hears the strains of this music sung by his friend Nicklausse and Giulietta as they praise the beauty of the Venetian night. Harp arpeggios suggest the lapping of the Venetian waters in the canal, providing a soothing background to one of the most radiant melodies in French music. It is interesting to remark that Offenbach did not write this melody directly for this opera. He had previously used it in 1864 as a ghost song for an opera-ballet, *Die Rheinnixen.*

Two dance episodes from *The Tales of Hoffmann* are also frequently performed outside the opera house. One is the infectious waltz which rises to a dramatic climax in the first act. To this music Hoffmann dances with the mechanical doll, Olympia, with whom he is in love. The second is an enchanting little Minuet, used as entr'acte music between the first and second acts.

A collation of some of Offenbach's most famous melodies from various operettas can be found in *La Gaiete parisienne,* an orchestral suite adapted from a score by Manuel Rosenthal to a famous contemporary ballet. This one-act ballet, with choreography by Leonide Massine and scenario by Comte Étienne de Beaumont, was introduced in Monte Carlo by the Ballet Russe in 1938. The setting is a fashionable Parisian restaurant of the 19th century; and the dance offers a colorful picture of Parisian life and mores of that period, climaxed by a stunning Can-Can. Musical episodes are used from *Orpheus in the Underworld, La Périchole, La Vie parisienne,* and several other Offenbach opéra-bouffes. Beloved Offenbach melodies from various opéra-bouffes were adapted for the score of a Broadway musical produced in 1961, *The Happiest Girl in the World.*

Ignace Jan Paderewski

IGNACE JAN PADEREWSKI, one of the world's foremost piano virtuosos and one of Poland's most renowned statesmen, was born in Kurylówka, Podolia, on November 18, 1860. A child prodigy, he was given piano lessons from his third year on. Several patrons arranged to send him to the Warsaw Conservatory, from which he was graduated in 1878. Between 1881 and 1883 he studied composition and orchestration in Berlin, and from 1884 to 1887 piano with Leschetizky in Vienna. Paderewski's first major success as a pianist came in Vienna in 1889, a concert that was the beginning of a virtuoso career extending for about half a century and carrying him triumphantly to all parts of the world. In 1919 he temporarily withdrew from music to become the first Premier of the Polish Republic, but about a year later he resumed concert work. He made his American debut in New York in 1891, and his last American tour took place in 1939. During the early part of World War II he returned to political activity as President of the Parliament of the Polish Government in Exile. He died in New York on June 29, 1941. By order of President Roosevelt he was given a state burial in Arlington National Cemetery.

Paderewski produced many ambitious compositions, some in the style of Polish folk music; these included the opera *Manru,* a symphony, piano concerto, the *Polish Fantasy* for piano and orchestra and numerous shorter compositions for the piano. Ironically it is not for one of his ambitious works that he is most often recalled as a composer, but through a slight piece: the *Minuet* in G, or *Menuet à l'antique,* a graceful, well-mannered composition in an 18th-century style. This is one of the three most popular minuets ever written, the other two being by Mozart and Beethoven. Paderewski originally wrote it for the piano; it is the first of six pieces collectively entitled *Humoresques de concert,* op. 14. Fritz Kreisler transcribed it for violin and piano; Gaspar Cassadó for cello and piano. It has, of course, been frequently adapted for orchestra.

Gabriel Pierné

ᴖᶘᴖᶘ ᶘᴖᶘᴖ

GABRIEL PIERNÉ was born in Metz, France, on August 16, 1863. He attended the Paris Conservatory for eleven years, a pupil of Massenet and César Franck. He won numerous awards there including the Prix de Rome in 1882. After returning from Rome, he succeeded Franck as organist of the Ste. Clothilde Church in Paris, retaining this post until 1898. From 1903 until 1932 he was, first the assistant, and from 1910 on the principal, conductor of the Colonne Orchestra. He combined his long and fruitful career as conductor with that of composer, producing a vast library of music in virtually every form, including operas, oratorios, ballets, symphonic and chamber music. He achieved renown with the oratorio *The Children's Crusade (La Croisade des enfants)*, introduced in 1905 and soon after that winner of the City of Paris Award. Another major success came with the ballet, *Cydalise and the Satyr* in 1923. A conservative composer, Pierné utilized traditional forms with distinction, and filled them with beautiful lyricism, well-sounding harmonies, and a poetic speech. In 1925 Pierné was elected member of the Académie des Beaux-Arts. He died in Ploujean, France, on July 17, 1937.

The *Entrance of the Little Fauns (Marche des petites faunes)* is a whimsical little march for orchestra from the ballet, *Cydalise and the Satyr (Cydalise et le chèvre-pied)*, introduced at the Paris Opéra on January 15, 1923. A saucy tune for muted trumpet is juxtaposed against the wail of piccolos; all the while an incisive rhythm is projected not only by the snare drum and tambourine but also by the violinists tapping the wood of their bows on the strings. Within the ballet this march accompanies the appearance of a group of small fauns, led by their teacher, an old satyr, as they enter school to learn pan pipes.

The *March of the Little Lead Soldiers (Marche des petits soldats de plomb)* originated as a piano piece in the *Album pour mes petits amis,* op. 14 (1887), but was subsequently orchestrated by the composer. It opens with a muted trumpet call. A snare drum then establishes the rhythm and sets the stage for the appearance of the main march melody in solo flute.

Jean-Robert Planquette

JEAN-ROBERT PLANQUETTE was born in Paris on July 31, 1848. He attended the Paris Conservatory after which he supported himself by writing popular songs and chansonettes for Parisian *café-concerts*. He started writing operettas in 1874, and achieved world fame with *The Chimes of Normandy* in 1877. He wrote many more operettas after that, the most successful being *Rip Van Winkle* (1882), *Nell Gwynne* (1884) and *Mam'zelle Quat'Sous* (1897). He died in Paris on January 28, 1903.

The Chimes of Normandy (*Les Cloches de Corneville*) is one of the most famous French operettas of all time, and it is still occasionally revived. Introduced in Paris at the Folies Dramatiques on April 19, 1877, its success was so immediate and permanent that within a decade it had been given over a thousand times in Paris alone. It was first seen in New York in 1877, and in London in 1888, major successes in both places. The book by Clairville and Gabet presents the life of fishing and peasant folk in Normandy during the regime of Louis XV. Germaine is in love with the fisherman, Jean, but finds opposition in her miserly old uncle, Gaspard, who has other plans for her. To escape her uncle, Germaine finds employment with Henri, a Marquis, who has suddenly returned to his native village to take up residence in the family castle rumored to be haunted. The mystery of the haunted castle is cleared up when the discovery is made that Gaspard has used it to hide his gold; and the bells of the castle begin to ring out loud and clear again. Gaspard, after a brief siege with insanity, is made to sanction the marriage of Germaine and Jean at a magnificent festival honoring the Marquis; at the same time it is suddenly uncovered that Germaine is in reality a Marchioness.

This is an operetta overflowing with ear-caressing melodies. The most famous are Germaine's bell song, *"Nous avons, hélas, perdu d'excellence maîtres"*; the Marquis' lilting waltz-rondo, *"Même sans consulter mon coeur"*; and Serpolette's cider song, *"La Pomme est un fruit plein de sève."*

Eduard Poldini

EDUARD POLDINI was born in Budapest, Hungary, on June 13, 1869. His music study took place at the Vienna Conservatory. Poldini subsequently established his home in Vevey, Switzerland, where he devoted himself to composition. His most significant works are for the stage—both comic and serious operas that include *The Vagabond and the Princess* (1903) and *The Carnival Marriage* (1924). He was also a prolific composer of salon pieces for the piano, familiar to piano studies throughout the world. In 1935 Poldini received the Order of the Hungarian Cross and in 1948 the Hungarian Pro Arte Prize. He died in Vevey, Switzerland on June 29, 1957.

Poupée valsante (*Dancing Doll*) is Poldini's best known composition, a fleet, graceful melody contrasted by a sentimental counter-subject. The composer wrote it for solo piano. Fritz Kreisler adapted it for violin and piano, and Frank La Forge for voice and orchestra. It has also often been transcribed for orchestra.

Manuel Ponce

MANUEL MARIA PONCE was born in Fresnillo, Mexico, on December 8, 1882. His main music study took place in Europe where he arrived in 1905: composition with Enrico Bossi in Bologna; piano with Martin Krause in Berlin. After returning to Mexico he gave a concert of his own compositions in 1912. For several years he taught the piano at the National Conservatory in Mexico City, and from 1917 to 1919 he was the conductor of the National Symphony Orchestra there. During World War I he lived in Havana and New York. After the war he went to Paris for an additional period of study with Paul Dukas. From 1933 to 1938 he was professor of folklore at the University of Mexico. In 1941 he toured South America, and in 1947 he was the recipient of the first annual Mexican Arts and Sciences Award established by the President of Mexico. He died in Mexico City on April 24, 1948.

Ponce was a modernist who filled his orchestral compositions with the most advanced resources of modern harmony, counterpoint and rhythm. But in his songs he possessed a spontaneous and ingratiating lyricism, often of a national Mexican identity. It is one of these that has made him famous in semi-classical literature: *"Estrellita"* ("Little Star"), a song with such a strong Spanish personality of melody and rhythm that it was long believed to be a folk song. Ponce first published it in 1914 but it did not become universally popular until 1923 when it was issued in a new arrangement (by Frank La Forge) and translated into English.

Amilcare Ponchielli

ᵔᶜᵔᶜ ᶜᵓᶜᵓ

A M I L C A R E   P O N C H I E L L I   was born in Paderno Fasolaro, Italy, on August 31, 1834. For nine years he attended the Milan Conservatory where he wrote an operetta in collaboration with three other students. Following the termination of his studies, he became organist in Cremona, and after that a bandmaster in Piacenza. His first opera, *I Promessi sposi,* was introduced in Cremona in 1856, but it did not become successful until sixteen years later when a revised version helped to open the Teatro dal Verme in Milan. World renown came to Ponchielli with *La Gioconda,* first given at La Scala in Milan in 1876. Though Ponchielli wrote many other operas after that he never again managed to reach the high artistic level of this masterwork, nor to repeat its world success. From 1883 until his death he was professor of composition at the Milan Conservatory. He died in Milan, Italy, on January 16, 1886.

What is undoubtedly Ponchielli's most famous orchestral composition, "The Dance of the Hours" (*"Danza della ore"*) comes from his masterwork, the opera *La Gioconda.* This opera—first performed in Milan on April 8, 1876—was based on Victor Hugo's drama, *Angelo, tyran de Padoue,* adapted by Arrigo Boïto. The setting is 17th century Venice, and the principal action involves the tragic love triangle of Alvise, his wife Laura, and her beloved, Enzo.

"The Dance of the Hours" comes in the second scene of the third act. Alvise is entertaining his guests at a sumptuous ball in his palace, the highlight of which is a magnificent ballet, intended to symbolize the victory of right over wrong. The dancers in groups of six come out impersonating the hours of dawn, day, evening, and night. The music begins with a slight murmur, shimmering sounds passing through the violins and woodwind. Dawn appears. The music is carried to a dramatic climax with a strong rhythmic pulse as the day unfolds. When the music achieves mellowness and tenderness, the softness of evening touches the stage; and with the coming of night the music acquires a somber character. At midnight, the music is reduced to a sigh. The harp presents some arpeggios, and a broad melody unfolds. The mood then becomes excitable as all the twenty-four hours plunge into a spirited dance, as light conquers darkness.

The most familiar vocal excerpts from this opera are La Cieca's romanza from the first act, *"A te questo rosario"*; Barnaba's fisherman's barcarolle (*"Pescator, affonda l'esca"*) and Enzo's idyll to the beauty of the night (*"Cielo e mar"*) from the second act; and La Gioconda's dramatic narrative in which she plans to destroy herself (*"Suicidio"*).

Cole Porter

COLE PORTER was born in Peru, Indiana, on June 9, 1893 to an immensely wealthy family. Precocious in music, he began studying the violin when he was six, and at eleven had one of his compositions published. He pursued his academic studies at the Worcester Academy in Massachusetts and at Yale; music study took place at the School of Music at Harvard and subsequently in Paris with Vincent d'Indy at the Schola Cantorum. At Yale he participated in all its musical activities and wrote two football songs still favorites there, "Yale Bull Dog" and "Bingo Eli Yale." In 1916 he wrote the music for his first Broadway musical comedy, *See America First,* a failure. During the next few years he was a member of the French desert troops in North Africa, while during World War I he taught French gunnery to American troops at Fontainebleau. Just after the close of the war he contributed some songs to *Hitchy Koo of 1918,* and in 1924 five more songs to the *Greenwich Village Follies,* both of them Broadway productions. Success first came in 1928 with his music for *Paris* which included "Let's Do It" and "Let's Misbehave." For the next quarter of a century and more he was one of Broadway's most successful composers. His greatest stage hits came with *Fifty Million Frenchmen* (1929), *The Gay Divorce* (1932), *Anything Goes* (1934), *Leave It to Me* (1938), *Panama Hattie* (1940), *Let's Face It* (1941), *Kiss Me Kate* (1948), *Can-Can* (1953) and *Silk Stockings* (1955). From these and other stage productions came some of America's best loved popular songs, for which Porter wrote not merely the music but also the brilliant lyrics: "Night and Day," "Begin the Beguine," "Love for Sale," "You Do Something to Me," "My Heart Belongs to Daddy," and so forth. He was also a significant composer for motion pictures, his most successful songs for the screen including "I've Got You Under My Skin," "In the Still of the Night," "You'd Be So Nice to Come Home To," "Don't Fence Me In," and "True Love."

The most successful of all the Cole Porter musical comedies was *Kiss Me Kate* which began a Broadway run of over one thousand performances on December 30, 1948, then went on to be a triumph in Vienna, Austria, where it became the greatest box-office success in the history of the Volksoper where it was given. In Poland it was the first American music performed in that country. The text by Bella and Sam Spewack was based partly on Shakespeare's *Taming of the Shrew,* but it was really a play within a play. A touring company is performing the Shakespeare comedy in Baltimore, Maryland. The musical comedy moves freely from scenes of that production to the backstage complications in the private lives of its principal performers. In the end, the amatory problems of the two stars are resolved within a performance of the Shakespeare comedy. This was not only Cole Porter's most successful musical comedy but also the finest of his scores. Never before (or since) was he so prolix with song hits in a single production; never before was his style so varied. The repertory of semi-classical music has been enriched by a symphonic treatment given the best of these melodies by Robert Russell Bennett. Bennett's symphonic presentation of *Kiss Me Kate* opens with "Wunderbar," a tongue-in-cheek parody of a sentimental Viennese waltz. It continues with the sprightly measures of "Another Openin', Another Show," and after that come the plangent, purple moods of "Were Thine That Special Face," "I Sing of Love," and the show's principal love song, "So In Love."

Serge Prokofiev

SERGE PROKOFIEV was born in Sontzovka, Russia, on April 23, 1891. He was extraordinarily precocious in music. After receiving some training at the piano from his mother, he completed the writing of an opera by the time he was ten. Preliminary music study took place with Glière. In his thirteenth year he entered the Moscow Conservatory where he was a pupil of Rimsky-Korsakov and Liadov among others and from which he was graduated with the Rubinstein Prize for his first piano concerto. His advanced musical thinking was already evident in his first major work for orchestra, *The Scythian Suite,* introduced in St. Petersburg in 1916. He continued to develop his own personality, formulating his highly individual style and creative idiosyncrasies in works like the ballet *Chout,* the first violin concerto, and the *Classical Symphony,* all written during the era of World War I. In 1918 he toured the United States, making his American debut with a New York piano recital on November 20. While in the United States he was commissioned to write the opera *The Love for Three Oranges* for the Chicago Opera. From 1919 to 1933 Prokofiev made his home in Paris, but in 1933 he returned to his native land to stay there for the rest of his life. Though he was honored in the Soviet Union as one of its great creative figures—and was the recipient of the Stalin Prize for his monumental Seventh Piano Sonata inspired by World War II—he did not escape censure in 1948 when the Central Committee of the Communist Party denounced Soviet composers for their partiality towards experimentation, modernism and cerebralism, in their musical works. Nevertheless, Prokofiev soon recovered his high estate in Soviet music; in 1951 he received the Stalin Prize again, this time for his oratorio *On Guard for Peace* and the symphonic suite, *Winter Bonfire.* His sixtieth birthday, that year, was celebrated throughout the country with concerts and broadcasts. Prokofiev died of a cerebral hemorrhage in Moscow on March 5, 1953.

Prokofiev was one of the giants of 20th-century music. His seven symphonies, five piano concertos, nine piano sonatas, the opera *War and Peace,* ballets, chamber music, piano compositions and various shorter orchestral works are among the most significant contributions made in our time to music. The highly personal way of writing melodies, his unusual progressions, his harmonic vocabulary are all present in the few lighter and simpler works with which he made a significant contribution to the contemporary repertory of semi-classics.

The *March* so familiar to radio listeners throughout the United States as the theme music for the program "The F.B.I. in Peace and War" comes from the opera *The Love for Three Oranges* (1921). The libretto by the composer based on a tale of Carlo Gozzi is a charming fantasy in which a prince saves himself from death through gloom by means of laughter, and who then goes at once to rescue a princess from her prison in an orange. The march occurs in the second act where an effort is being made to get the Prince to laugh, for which purpose a festival is being arranged. The march music is played as the court jester drags the reluctant Prince to these festivities. The quixotic skips in the melody, the grotesquerie of the musical style, and the pert discords are all typical of Prokofiev's creative manner.

Peter and the Wolf, a "symphonic fairy tale" for narrator and orchestra op. 67 (1936) was intended by the composer to teach children the instruments of the orchestra. But the music is so consistently delightful for its sprightly lyricism and wit that it has proved a favorite at symphony and semi-classical concerts. The story here being told is about a lad named Peter who turns a deaf ear to his grandfather's warning and goes out into the meadow. There a wolf has frightened, in turn, a cat, bird, and duck. But Peter is not afraid of him. He captures the wolf, ties him up with a rope and takes him to the zoo.

The composition opens with the following explanation by the narrator: "Each character in the tale is represented by a different instrument in the orchestra: the bird by a flute; the duck by an oboe; the cat by a clarinet in the low register; grandpapa by the bassoon; the wolf by three French horns; Peter by the string quartet; and the hunter's rifle shots by the kettledrums and bass drums." Then, as the story of

Peter and the wolf unfolds, little melodies appear and reappear, each identifying some character in the story. Peter's theme is a lyrical folk song with a puckish personality for strings. Vivid and realistic little tunes represent the cat, bird, and duck, each tune providing an amusing insight into the personality of each of these animals.

Summer Day, opp. 65a and 65b (1935) is another of the composer's compositions for children which makes for delightful listening. It started out as a suite of twelve easy piano pieces for children called *Music for Children.* Later on the composer orchestrated seven of these sections and called the new work *Summer Day.* In the first movement, "Morning," a whimsical little tune is heard in first flute against a contrapuntal background by other woodwinds, strings, and bass drum. Midway a secondary melody is given by bassoons, horns and cellos. "Tag," the familiar child's game, is represented in a tripping melody for violins and flutes; the music grows increasingly rhythmic in the intermediary section. In the "Waltz," a saucy waltz tune with an unusual syncopated construction is presented by the violins, interrupted by exclamations from the woodwind with typical Prokofiev octave leaps. "Regrets" opens with a tender melody for cellos, but is soon taken over by oboes, and then the violins. This melody is then varied by violins and clarinets. "March" offers the main march melody in clarinets and oboes. "Evening" highlights a gentle song by solo flute, soon joined by the clarinet. As the violins take over the melody the pensive mood is maintained. The concluding movement, "Moonlit Meadows" is dominated by a melody for solo flute.

Giacomo Puccini

❧❧ ❧❧

GIACOMO PUCCINI was born in Lucca, Italy, on December 22, 1858, to a family which for several generations had produced professional musicians. As a boy, Giacomo attended the Istituto Musicale in his native city, played the organ in the local church, and wrote two choral compositions. A subsidy from Queen Margherita enabled him to continue his music study at the Milan Conservatory with Bazzini and Ponchielli. The latter encouraged Puccini to write for the stage. Puccini's first dramatic work was a one-act opera, *Le Villi*, given successfully in Milan in 1884, and soon thereafter performed at La Scala. On a commission from the publisher, Ricordi, Puccini wrote a second opera that was a failure. But the third, *Manon Lescaut*—introduced in Turin in 1893—was a triumph and permanently established Puccini's fame. He now moved rapidly to a position of first importance in Italian opera with three successive master-works: *La Bohème* (1896), *Tosca* (1900) and *Madama Butterfly* (1904). Puccini paid his first visit to the United States in 1907 to supervise the American première of the last-named opera; he returned in 1910 to attend the world première of *The Girl from the Golden West* which had been commissioned by the Metropolitan Opera. Puccini's subsequent operas were: *La Rondine* (1917), *Il Trittico*, a trilogy of three one-act operas (1918), and *Turandot* (1924), the last of which was left unfinished but was completed by Franco Alfano. Operated on for cancer of the throat, in Brussels, Puccini died of a heart attack in that city on November 29, 1924.

Though Puccini was an exponent of "Verismo," a movement in Italian opera which emphasized everyday subjects treated realistically, he poured into his operas such a wealth of sentiment, tenderness, sweetness of lyricism, and elegance of style that their emotional appeal is universal, and he has become the best loved opera composer of the 20th century. Selections from his three most popular operas are basic to the repertory of any semi-classical or "pop" orchestra.

La Bohème was based on Murger's famous novel, *Scènes de la vie de Bohème* adapted into an opera libretto by Giacosa and Illica. When first introduced (Turin, February 1, 1896) the opera encountered an apathetic audience and hostile critics. It had no big scenes, no telling climaxes, and most of its effects were too subtle emotionally to have an instantaneous appeal. But the third performance—in Palermo in 1896 —received an ovation. From that time on it never failed to move opera audiences with its deeply moving pathos and its vivid depiction of the daily problems and conflicts of a group of Bohemians in mid 19th-century Paris. The central theme is the love affair of the poet, Rodolfo, and a seamstress, Mimi. This love was filled with storm and stress, and ended tragically with Mimi's death of consumption in Rodolfo's attic. The following are some of the episodes heard most often in potpourris or fantasies of this opera: Rodolfo's celebrated narrative in the first act, *"Che gelida manina,"* in which he tells Mimi about his life as a poet; Mimi's aria that follows this narrative immediately, *"Mi chiamano Mimi,"* where she tells Rodolfo of her poignant need for flowers and the warmth of springtime; the first act love duet of Mimi and Rodolfo, *"O soave fanciulla";* Musetta's coquettish second-act waltz, *"Quando m'en vo' soletta,"* sung outside Café Momus in the Latin Quarter on Christmas Eve, informing her admirers (specifically Marcello the painter), how men are always attracted to her; Rodolfo's poignant recollection of his one time happiness with Mimi, *"O, Mimi, tu più"* in the fourth act; and Mimi's death music that ends the opera.

Madama Butterfly—libretto by Illica and Giacosa based on David Belasco's play of the same name, which in turn came from John Luther's short story—was first performed in Milan on February 17, 1904 when it was a fiasco. There was such pandemonium during that performance that Puccini had to rush on the stage and entreat the audience to be quiet so that the opera might continue. Undoubtedly, some of Puccini's enemies had a hand in instigating this scandal, but the opera itself was not one able to win immediate favor. The exotic setting of Japan, the unorthodox love affair involving an American sailor and a geisha girl ending in tragedy for the girl, and the provocatively different kind of music (sometimes Oriental, sometimes modern) written to conform to the setting and the characters—all this was not calculated to appeal to Italian opera lovers. But three months after the première the opera was repeated (with some vital revisions by the composer). This time neither the play nor the music proved shocking, and the audience fell under the spell of enchantment which that sensitive opera cast all about it. From then on, the opera has been a favorite around the world.

The most celebrated single excerpt from the opera is unquestionably Madame Butterfly's poignant aria, her expression of belief that her American lover, so long absent from Japan with his fleet, would some day return to her: *"Un bel di."* Other popular episodes include the passionate love music of Madame Butterfly and the American lieutenant with which the first act ends, *"Viene la sera";* the flower duet of the second act between Madame Butterfly and her servant in which the heroine excitedly decorates her home with cherry blossoms upon learning that her lover is back with his fleet (*"Scuoti quella fronda di ciliegio"*); the American lieutenant's tender farewell to Madame Butterfly and the scene of their love idyl from the third act (*"Addio fiorito asil"*); and Madame Butterfly's tender farewell to her daughter before committing suicide (*"Tu, tu piccolo iddio"*).

Tosca—based on the famous French drama of the same name by Sardou, the libretto by Giacosa and Illica—was introduced in Rome on January 14, 1900. It was a blood and thunder drama set in Rome at the turn of the 19th century; the dramatic episodes involved murder, horror, suicide, sadism. The heroine, Floria Tosca, is an opera singer in love with a painter, Mario Cavaradossi; she, in turn, is being pursued by Scarpia, the chief of police. To save her lover's life, she stands ready to give herself to Scarpia. The latter, nonetheless, is responsible for Cavaradossi's execution. Scarpia is murdered by Tosca, who then commits suicide.

Two tenor arias by Cavaradossi are lyrical highlights of this opera. The first is *"Recondita armonia,"* in the first act, in which the painter rhapsodizes over the beauty of his beloved Tosca; the second, *"E luce-van le stelle,"* comes in the last act as Cavaradossi prepares himself for his death by bidding farewell to his memory of Tosca. The third important aria from this opera is that of Tosca, *"Vissi d'arte,"* a monologue in which she reflects on how cruel life had been to one who has devoted herself always to art, prayer, and love. In addition to these three arias, the opera score also boasts some wonderful love music, that of Cavaradossi and Tosca (*"Non la sospiri la nostra casetta"*) and the first act stately church music (*"Te Deum"*).

Sergei Rachmaninoff

SERGEI RACHMANINOFF was born in Oneg, Novgorod, Russia, on April 1, 1873. He attended the St. Petersburg Conservatory for three years, and his musical training ended at the Moscow Conservatory in 1892 when he received a gold medal for a one-act opera, *Aleko*. In that same year he also wrote the Prelude in C-sharp minor with which he became world famous. His first piano concerto and his first symphony, however, were dismal failures. In 1901 he scored a triumph with his Second Piano Concerto which, since then, has been not only the composer's most celebrated composition in a large form but also one of the best loved and most frequently performed piano concertos of the 20th century. Rachmaninoff combined his success as composer with that as piano virtuoso. Beginning with 1900 he toured the world of music achieving recognition everywhere as one of the most renowned concert artists of his generation. The first of his many tours of America took place in 1909. He also distinguished himself as a conductor, first at the Bolshoi Theater between 1904 and 1906, and later with the Moscow Philharmonic. As a composer he enhanced his reputation with a remarkable second symphony, two more piano concertos, and sundry works for orchestra. He was a traditionalist who preferred working within the structures and with the techniques handed down to him by Tchaikovsky. Like Tchaikovsky whom he admired and emulated, he wore his heart on his sleeve, ever preferring to make his music the vehicle for profoundly felt emotions. His broad rhapsodic style makes his greatest music an ever stirring emotional experience. In 1917 Rachmaninoff left Russia for good, establishing his permanent home first in Lucerne, Switzerland, and in 1935 in the United States. All the while he continued to tour the world as concert pianist. His last years were spent in Beverly Hills, California, where he died on March 28, 1943.

The Prelude in C-sharp minor, op. 3, no. 2 (1892) is Rachmaninoff's most popular composition; the transcriptions and adaptations it has received are of infinite variety. He wrote it when he was nineteen and instantaneously the piece traveled around the globe. Unfortunately, the composer never profited commercially from this formidable success, having sold the composition outright for a pittance. The Prelude opens in a solemn mood with a theme sounding like the tolling of bells, or the grim pronouncement by some implacable fate. The second theme is agitated and restless, but before the composition ends the solemn first theme recurs. Numerous efforts have been made to provide this dramatic music with a program, including one which interpreted it in terms of the burning of Moscow in 1812.

The Prelude in G minor, op. 23, no. 5, for piano (1904), is almost as famous. The opening subject has the character of a brisk military march, while the contrasting second theme is nostalgic and reflective.

The *Vocalise*, op. 34, no. 14 (1912) is one of the composer's best known vocal compositions. This is a wordless song—a melody sung only on vowels, a "vocalise" being actually a vocal exercise. Rachmaninoff himself transcribed this work for orchestra, a version perhaps better known than the original vocal one. Many other musicians have made sundry other transcriptions, including one for piano, and others for solo instruments and piano.

Joachim Raff

JOSEPH JOACHIM RAFF was born in Lachen, on the Lake of Zurich, Switzerland, on May 27, 1822. He was mostly self-taught in music, while pursuing the career of schoolmaster. Some of his early compositions were published through Mendelssohn's influence, a development that finally encouraged Raff to give up schoolteaching and devote himself completely to music. An intimate association with Liszt led to the première of an opera, *King Alfred,* in Weimar in 1851. In 1863, his symphony, *An das Vaterland,* received first prize from the Vienna Gesellschaft der Musikfreunde. From 1877 until his death he was director of Hoch's Conservatory in Frankfort, Germany. He died in that city on June 25, 1882.

A prolific composer of symphonies, concertos, overtures, quartets, sonatas and sundry other works, Raff was a major figure in the German Romantic movement, highly regarded by his contemporaries, but forgotten since his death. Only some of his minor pieces are remembered. The most popular is the *Cavatina* in A-flat major, op. 85, no. 3, for violin and piano, a perennial favorite with violin students and young violinists, and no less familiar in various orchestral adaptations. A "cavatina" is a composition for an instrument with the lyric character of a song. Raff's broad and expressive melody has an almost religious stateliness.

Another popular Raff composition in a smaller dimension is the picturesque piano piece, *La Fileuse (The Spinner),* op. 157, no. 2, in which the movement of the spinning wheel is graphically reproduced.

Maurice Ravel

ↆↆ ↇↇ

MAURICE RAVEL was born in Ciboure, France, on March 7, 1875. After studying music with private teachers in Paris he entered the Paris Conservatory in 1889, remaining there fifteen years, and proving himself a brilliant (if at times an iconoclastic) student. While still at the Conservatory his *Menuet antique* for piano was published, and *Les Sites auriculaires* for two pianos was performed. By the time he left the Conservatory he was already a composer of considerable stature, having completed two remarkable compositions for the piano—*Pavane pour une Infante défunte* and *Jeux d'eau,* both introduced in 1902— and an unqualified masterwork, the String Quartet, first performed in 1904. The fact that a composer of such attainments had four times failed to win the Prix de Rome created such a scandal in Paris that the director of the Paris Conservatory, Théodore Dubois, was compelled to resign. But Ravel's frustrations from failing to win the Prix de Rome did not affect the quality of his music. In the succeeding years he produced a succession of masterworks: the ballet *Daphnis and Chloe,* its première by the Ballet Russe de Monte Carlo in Paris on June 8, 1912; the *Spanish Rhapsody (Rapsodie espagnole)* for orchestra; the suite *Miroirs,* for piano. During World War I, Ravel served at the front in an ambulance corps. After the war, he withdrew to his villa in Montfort l'Amaury where he lived in comparative seclusion, devoted mainly to creative work. Nevertheless, in 1928, he toured the United States, making his American debut in Boston with the Boston Symphony on January 12, 1929; Ravel died in Paris on December 28, 1937, following an unsuccessful operation on the brain.

One of the most significant of Impressionists after Debussy, Ravel was the creator of music that is highly sensitive in its moods, elegant in style, exquisite in detail, and usually endowed with the most stunning effects of instrumentation, rhythm, and harmony. Some of his best-known works derive their inspiration and material from Spanish sources. It is one of these that is probably his most popular orchestral composition, and one of the most popular of the 20th century, the

Bolero. A "bolero" is a Spanish dance in ¾ time accompanied by click-ing castanets. Ravel wrote his *Bolero* in 1928 as ballet music for Ida Rubinstein who introduced it in Paris on November 22, 1928. But *Bolero* has since then separated itself from the dance to become a con-cert hall favorite. When Toscanini directed the American première in 1929 it created a sensation, and set into motion a wave of popularity for this exciting music achieved by few contemporary works. It was per-formed by every major American orchestra, was heard in theaters and over radio, was reproduced simultaneously on six different recordings. It was transcribed for every possible combination of instruments (in-cluding a jazz band); the word "Bolero" was used as the title of a motion picture. Such immense appeal is not difficult to explain. The rhythmic and instrumental virtuosity of this music has an immediate kinaesthetic effect. The composition derives its immense impact from sonority and changing orchestral colors. The bolero melody has two sections, the first heard initially is the flute, then clarinet; the second is given by the bassoon, and then the clarinet. This two-part melody is repeated throughout the composition against a compelling rhythm of a side drum, all the while gradually growing in dynamics and continually changing its colors chameleon-like through varied instrumentation. A monumental climax is finally realized, as the bolero melody is pro-claimed by the full orchestra.

Another highly popular Ravel composition has a far different per-sonality—the *Pavane pour une Infante défunte* (*Pavane for a Dead Infante*). Where the appeal of the *Bolero* is strong, direct, immediate and on the surface, that of the Pavane is subtle, elusive, sensitive. A Pavane is a stately court dance (usually in three sections and in ⁴⁄₄ time) popular in France. Ravel's *Pavane* is an elegy for the death of a Spanish princess. Ravel wrote this composition for piano (1899) but he later transcribed it for orchestra. An American popular song was adapted from this haunting melody in 1939, entitled "The Lamp Is Low."

Emil von Reznicek

EMIL VON REZNIČEK was born in Vienna, Austria, on May
4, 1860, the son of a princess and an Austrian field marshal. For a time
he studied law, but then devoted himself completely to music study,
mainly at the Leipzig Conservatory. From 1896 to 1899 he was the conductor of several theater orchestras in Germany, Austria, and Switzerland. In 1902 he settled in Berlin where he founded and for several
years conducted an annual series of orchestral concerts. Subsequently
he was the conductor of the Warsaw Opera and from 1909 to 1911 of
the Komische Oper in Berlin. He also pursued a highly successful
career as teacher, principally at the Scharwenka Conservatory in Berlin
and from 1920 to 1926 at the Berlin High School of Music. He went
into retirement in 1929, and died in Berlin on August 2, 1945.

Reznicek was the composer of several operas, five symphonies, three
tone poems and various other compositions. His greatest success came
with the comic opera, *Donna Diana,* introduced in Prague on December 16, 1894, and soon thereafter heard in forty-three European opera
houses. The opera—libretto by the composer based on a Spanish comedy
by Moreto y Cabana—is consistently light and frothy. Carlos is in pursuit of Princess Diana, and to effect her surrender he feigns he is madly
in love with her. Princess Diana plays a game of her own. Coyly she
eludes him after seeming to fall victim to his wiles. In the end they
both discover they are very much in love with each other.

The opera is almost never heard any longer, but the witty overture
is a favorite throughout the world; it is the only piece of music by the
composer that is still often performed today. A sustained introduction
leads into the jolly first theme—a fast, light little melody that sets the
prevailing mood of frivolity. The heart of the overture is an expressive
melody shared by basses and oboe. It grows in passion and intensity as
other sections of the orchestra develop it. When this melody comes to a
climax, the passionate mood is suddenly dissipated, and the frivolous
first theme of the overture returns to restore a mood of reckless gaiety.

Nikolai Rimsky-Korsakov

NIKOLAI RIMSKY-KORSAKOV was born in Tikhvin, Russia, on March 18, 1844. Trained for a naval career, he was graduated from the Naval School in St. Petersburg in 1862, after which he embarked on a two-and-a-half-year cruise as naval officer. From earliest boyhood he had been passionately interested in music, especially the folk operas of Glinka and Russian ecclesiastical music. When he was seventeen, he was encouraged by Balakirev to essay composition. After returning to Russia in 1864, Rimsky-Korsakov associated himself with the national Russian school then being realized by Balakirev and Mussorgsky among others, and completed his first symphony, introduced in St. Petersburg in 1865. He plunged more deeply into musical activity after that by completing several ambitious works of national character, including the *Antar Symphony* and an opera, *The Maid of Pskov*. In 1873 he was relieved by the government of all his naval duties and allowed to devote himself completely to music. At that time the special post of Inspector of Military Orchestras was created for him. He soon distinguished himself as a conductor of the Free Music Society in St. Petersburg and as professor of composition and orchestration at the St. Petersburg Conservatory. He did not neglect composition, producing many significant operas and orchestral works. In his music he remained faithful to national ideals by filling his music with melodies patterned after Russian folk songs, harmonies derived from the modes of Russian church music, and rhythms simulating those of Russian folk dances. To all his writing he brought an extraordinary technical skill in structure, orchestration and harmony. He died of a heart attack in Liubensk, Russia, on June 21, 1908.

The exotic personality and harmonic and instrumental brilliance of Eastern music are often encountered in Rimsky-Korsakov. They are found in two extremely popular excerpts from his opera *Le Coq d'or* (*The Golden Cockerel*): "Bridal Procession" and "Hymn to the Sun."

Le Coq d'or is a fantasy-opera, introduced in Moscow on October 7, 1909; the libretto, by Vladimir Bielsky, is based on a tale by Pushkin.

A golden cockerel with the talent of prophecy is presented to King Dodon by his astrologer. In time the cockerel accurately prophesies the doom of both the astrologer and the King.

The oriental, languorous "Hymn to the Sun" (*"Salut à toi soleil"*) appears in the second act, a salute by the beautiful Queen of Shemaka. After the Queen has captured the love of King Dodon with this song, they marry. There are many transcriptions of this beautiful melody, including one for violin and piano by Kreisler and for cello and piano by Julius Klengel.

The third act of this opera opens with the brilliant music of the "Bridal Procession." The royal entourage passes with pomp and ceremony through the city accompanied by the cheers of the surrounding crowds.

In the vital "Dance of the Tumblers" or "Dance of the Buffoons" for orchestra, Rimsky-Korsakov skilfully employs folk rhythms. This dance comes from the composer's folk opera, *The Snow Maiden (Snegourochka)*. The third act opens with a gay Arcadian festival celebrated by the Berendey peasants during which this gay and exciting folk dance is performed.

The pictorial, realistic "Flight of the Bumble Bee" is an excerpt from still another of Rimsky-Korsakov's operas, *The Legend of Tsar Saltan*. This is an orchestral interlude in the third act describing tonally, and with remarkable realism, the buzzing course of a bee. This piece retains its vivid pictorialism even in transcriptions, notably that for solo piano by Rachmaninoff, and for violin and piano by Arthur Hartmann.

The "Hindu Chant" or "The Song of India" is also an operatic excerpt, this time from *Sadko*. It appears at the close of the second tableau of the second act. Sadko is the host to three merchants from foreign lands. He invites each to tell him about his homeland, one of whom is a Hindu who proceeds in an Oriental melody to speak of the magic and mystery of India.

The *Russian Easter Overture (La Grand pâque russe)*, for orchestra, op. 36 (1888) was one of the fruits of the composer's lifelong fascination for Russian church music. The principal thematic material of the overture comes from a collection of canticles known as the *Obikhod* from the Russian Orthodox Church. Two of these canticles are heard in the solemn introduction, a section which the composer said represented the "Holy Sepulcher that had shone with ineffable light at the moment of the Resurrection." The first is given loudly by strings and clarinets, the second quietly by violins and violas accompanied by woodwind, harps, and pizzicato basses. A brief cadenza for solo violin is the transition to the main body of the overture where the two canticles from the introduction are amplified and developed. A brilliant coda leads to the conclusion of the work where the second of the two melodies is given for the last time by trombones and strings.

Rimsky-Korsakov's most famous work for orchestra is the symphonic suite, *Scheherazade,* op. 35 (1888). Nowhere is his remarkable gift at pictorial writing, at translating a literary program into tones, more in evidence than here. This music describes episodes from the *Arabian Nights* in four movements which are unified by the recurrence of two musical motives. The first is that of the Sultan, a forceful, majestic statement for unison brass, woodwinds and strings; the second is a tender melody in triplets for strings depicting the lovely Scheherazade. The Sultan theme opens the first movement, entitled "The Sea and Sinbad's Ship." After quiet chords for the brass, the Scheherazade melody is heard in solo violin accompanied by harp arpeggios. The music later becomes highly dramatic as Sinbad's ship, represented by a flute solo, is buffeted about by an angry sea, the latter portrayed by rapid arpeggio figures. The poignant Scheherazade motive in solo violin introduces the second movement, "The Tale of the Kalendar." The tale is spun in a haunting song for bassoon, dramatically contrasted by a dynamic rhythmic section for full orchestra. The third movement, "The Young Prince and the Princess" is a tender love dialogue between violins and clarinets. After a recall of the Scheherazade melody there appears the finale: "The Festival at Bagdad; The Sea, The Ship Founders on the Rock." A brief recall of the Sinbad theme brings on an electrifying picture of a festival in Bagdad. The gay proceedings, however, are interrupted by a grim shipwreck scene, vividly depicted by the exciting music. This dramatic episode passes, and the suite ends with a final statement of the Scheherazade theme.

The *Spanish Caprice (Capriccio espagnol),* for orchestra, op. 34 (1887) is one of the composer's rare attempts at exploiting the folk music of a country other than his own. There are five parts. The first is a morning song, or "Alborada," in which two main subjects of Spanish identity are given by the full orchestra. This is followed by "Variations." A Spanish melody is here subjected to five brief variations. In the third part, the Alborada music returns in a changed tonality and orchestration. The fourth movement is entitled "Scene and Gypsy Dance" and consists of five cadenzas. The Capriccio ends with *"Fandango asturi-*

ano," in which a dance melody for trombones is succeeded by a contrast-ing subject in the woodwinds. A last recall of the main Alborada theme of the first movement brings the work to its conclusion.

Richard Rodgers

ᴇᴈᴇᴈ ᴈᴇᴈᴇ

R I C H A R D   R O D G E R S was born in Hammels Station, near Arverne, Long Island, on June 28, 1902. As a child he began studying the piano and attending the popular musical theater. He wrote his first songs in 1916, a score for an amateur musical in 1917, and in 1919 created the music for the Columbia Varsity Show, the first freshman ever to do so. Meanwhile he had initiated a collaborative arrangement with the lyricist, Lorenz Hart, that lasted almost a quarter of a century. Their first song to reach the Broadway theater was "Any Old Place With You" in *A Lonely Romeo* in 1919. Their first Broadway musical was *The Poor Little Ritz Girl* in 1920, and their first success came with *The Garrick Gaieties* in 1925 where the song, "Manhattan," was intro-duced. For the next twenty years, Rodgers and Hart—frequently with Herbert Fields as librettist—dominated the musical stage with some of the most original and freshly conceived musical productions of that period: *Dearest Enemy* (1925), *The Girl Friend* (1926), *Peggy-Ann* (1926), *A Connecticut Yankee* (1927), *On Your Toes* (1936), *Babes in Arms* (1937), *I'd Rather Be Right* (1937), *I Married an Angel* (1938), *The Boys from Syracuse* (1938), and *Pal Joey* (1940). From these and other productions came hundreds of songs some of which have since become classics in American popular music. The best of these were "Here In My Arms," "Blue Room," "My Heart Stood Still," "My Romance," "The Most Beautiful Girl in the World," "There's a Small Hotel," "Where or When," "My Funny Valentine," "Spring Is Here," "Falling in Love With Love," "I Could Write a Book" and "Be-witched, Bothered and Bewildered."

By Jupiter, in 1942, was the last of the Rodgers and Hart musicals.

Hart's physical and moral disintegration made it necessary for Rodgers to seek out a new collaborator. He found him in Oscar Hammerstein II, with whom Rodgers embarked on a new and even greater career as composer for the theater. Their first collaboration was *Oklahoma!* in 1943, an unprecedented box-office triumph, and a production that revolutionized the musical stage by crystallizing the concept and procedures of the musical play as opposed to the musical comedy. After that Rodgers and Hammerstein brought to the stage such classics as *Carousel, South Pacific,* and *The King and I.* Other Rodgers and Hammerstein productions were *Allegro* (1947), *Me and Juliet* (1953), *Pipe Dream* (1955), *The Flower Drum Song* (1958) and *The Sound of Music* (1959). Among the most famous songs by Rodgers from these productions—besides those from musical plays discussed below—were "A Fellow Needs a Girl," "No Other Love," "Everybody's Got a Home But Me," "All at Once You Love Her," "I Enjoy Being a Girl," "Do, Re, Mi," "The Sound of Music" and "Climb Every Mountain." The collaboration of Rodgers and Hammerstein ended in 1960 with the death of the lyricist.

Oklahoma!, Carousel, South Pacific, and *The King and I* have become enduring monuments in the American theater. They are continually revived, have been adapted for motion pictures, and are perpetually represented at semi-classical concerts and on records. In whatever form they appear they never fail to excite and inspire audiences. It is in these productions that Rodgers has reached the highest creative altitudes of his career, with music of such expressive lyricism, dramatic impact, consummate technical skill, and pervading charm and grace that its survival in American music seems assured. Robert Russell Bennett has made skilful orchestral adaptations of the basic melodic material from each of these musical plays, and it is most usually these adaptations that are most frequently performed by pop and semi-classical orchestras.

Carousel is the second of the Rodgers and Hammerstein masterworks, succeeding *Oklahoma!* by about two years. It is one of the most radiant ornaments of our musical stage. Oscar Hammerstein II here adapted Ferenc Molnar's play, *Liliom,* with changes in setting, time, and some basic alterations of plot. In the musical version the action takes place in New England in 1873. Billy Bigelow, a barker in an amusement park, falls in love and marries Julie Jordan. A charming but irresponsible young man, Billy decides to get some money in a holdup, when he learns his wife is pregnant. Caught, Billy eludes arrest by committing suicide. After a brief stay in Purgatory, Billy is permitted to return to earth for a single day to achieve redemption, the price for his admission to Heaven. On earth, he meets his daughter. Through her love, understanding and forgiveness he achieves his redemption. Thus the musical ends in a happy glow of love and compassion whereas Molnar's original play ended on the tragic note of frustration.

Carousel opened in New York on April 19, 1945. John Chapman described it as "one of the finest musical plays I have ever seen, and I shall remember it always." It received the Drama Critics Award and eight Donaldson Awards. Since then it has often been revived besides being adapted for the screen; in 1958 it was presented at the World's Fair in Brussels.

The heartwarming glow that pervades the play in Hammerstein's moving dialogue and lyrics was magically caught in the score, which begins with an extended waltz sequence for orchestra. In the play this music is heard under the opening scene which represents an amusement park dominated by a gay carousel. This waltz music is a self-sufficient composition that can be, and often is, played independently of the other excerpts. The other main musical episodes include the love duet of Billy and Julie, "If I Loved You"; Billy's eloquent and extended narrative, "Soliloquy," when he learns he is about to become a father; the spiritual "You'll Never Walk Alone"; the ebullient "June Is Bustin' Out All Over"; two vigorous choral episodes, "Blow High, Blow Low" and "This Was a Real Nice Clambake."

The King and I, presented on March 29, 1951, was adapted by Oscar Hammerstein II from Margaret Landon's novel *Anna and the King of Siam* (which had already been made into a successful non-musical motion picture starring Rex Harrison and Irene Dunne). Anna, played in the musical by Gertrude Lawrence, is an English schoolmistress come to Siam to teach Western culture to the royal princes and princesses. Her own strong will and Western independence comes into sharp conflict with the king, an Eastern despot enacted by Yul Brynner. But they are nonetheless drawn to each other, partly through curiosity, partly through admiration. Naturally, since they are of different social stations and cultures, a love interest is out of the question, but they are ineluctably drawn to each other, particularly after Anna has managed to save a critical political situation in Siam through her ingenuity. The king dies just before the final curtain; Anna remains on as a teacher of the children she has come to love.

Part of the attraction of Rodgers' music is its subtle Oriental flavoring. In the music—as in text, settings and costuming—*The King and I* is a picture of an "East of frank and unashamed romance," as Richard Watts, Jr., said, "seen through the eyes of . . . theatrical artists of rare taste and creative power." The Oriental element is particularly pronounced in the orchestral excerpt, "The March of the Royal Siamese Children," with its exotic syncopated structure and orchestration. Other popular excerpts from this score include Anna's lilting "I Whistle a Happy Tune"; her poignant ballad "Hello, Young Lovers"; Anna's duet with the king, "Shall We Dance?"; her amiable conversation with the children, "Getting to Know You"; the King's narrative, "A Puzzlement"; also two sensitive and atmospheric duets by the two Siamese lovers, Tuptim and Lun Tha, "We Kiss in the Shadow" and "I Have Dreamed."

Oklahoma!, the first of the Rodgers and Hammerstein musical plays —which opened on March 31, 1943—made stage history. Its run of 2,248 performances was the longest run of any Broadway musical up to then; a national company toured for ten years. It was successfully produced in Europe, Africa, and Australia. But beyond being a box-office triumph of incomparable magnitude, it was also an artistic event of the first importance. This was musical comedy no more, but a vital folk play rich in dramatic content, and authentic in characterization and background. The play upon which it was based was Lynn Riggs' folk play, *Green Grow the Lilacs,* adapted by Oscar Hammerstein II. In making his adaptation, Hammerstein had to sidestep long accepted formulas and clichés of the American musical stage to meet the demands of Riggs' play. Chorus-girl routines made way for American ballet conceived by Agnes De Mille. Set comedy routines were replaced by a humor which rose naturally from text and characters. Each musical incident was basic to the movement of the dramatic action. Even the plot was unorthodox for our musical theater. At the turn of the present century in West-Indian country, Laurey and Curly are in love, but are kept apart by their respective diffidence and a false sense of hostility. An ugly, lecherous character, Jud Fry, pursues Laurey. Laurey and Curly finally declare their love for each other. At their wedding Jud arrives inebriated, attacks Curly with a knife, and becomes its fatal victim when he accidentally falls upon the blade during a brawl. A hastily improvised trial exonerates Curly of murder and permits him and his bride to set off on their honeymoon for a land that some day will get the name of Oklahoma.

The play opens at once with its best musical foot forward, a simple song, "Oh, What a Beautiful Mornin'," which has the personality of American folk music. It is sung offstage by Curly. After that the principal musical episodes include the love song of Curly and Laurey, "People Will Say We're in Love"; several songs with a strong American national identity, including "Kansas City," "The Farmer and the Cowman," "The Surrey With the Fringe on Top," and the title number; and two highly expressive numbers, "Out of My Dreams" and "Many a New Day."

Slaughter on Tenth Avenue is one of Rodgers' most famous orchestral compositions, and one of the finest achievements of the school of symphonic-jazz writing. This music was used for a ballet sequence in the Rodgers and Hart musical, *On Your Toes,* first produced in 1936. Since *On Your Toes* dwelled in the world of ballet, with dancers as principal characters, ballet episodes played an important part in the unfolding of the story; these episodes were conceived by George Balanchine. The play reaches a dramatic climax with a jazz ballet, a satire on gangsters, entitled *Slaughter on Tenth Avenue.* This is a description of the pursuit by gangsters of a hoofer and his girl. Caught up in a Tenth Avenue café, the gangsters murder the girl and are about to kill the hoofer when the police come to his rescue. Rodgers' music for the ballet is an extended and integrated symphonic-jazz composition which has won its way into the permanent repertory of semi-classical music. It is constructed from two main melodic ideas. The first is an impudent little jazz tune, and the second is a rich and luscious jazz melody for strings.

South Pacific, produced on April 7, 1949, was both commercially and artistically of the magnitude of *Oklahoma!* Its Broadway run of 1,925 performances was only 325 less than that of its epoch-making predecessor. In many other respects *South Pacific* outdid *Oklahoma!:* In the overall box-office grossage; in sale of sheet music and records; in the capture of prizes (including the Pulitzer Prize for drama, seven Antoinette Perry and nine Donaldson awards). The book was adapted by Oscar Hammerstein II and Joshua Logan from *Tales of the South Pacific,* a series of short stories about American troops in the Pacific during World War II. In the adaptation two love plots are emphasized. The first involves the French planter, Emile de Becque, and the American ensign, Nellie Forbush; the other engages Liat, a Tonkinese girl, and Lieutenant Cable. The first ends happily, but only after complications brought on by the discovery on Nellie's part that Emile was once married to a Polynesian and is the father of two Eurasian children. The other love affair has a tragic ending, since Lieutenant Cable dies on a mission. With Ezio Pinza as De Becque and Mary Martin as Nellie, *South Pacific* was "a show of rare enchantment," as Howard Barnes reported, "novel in texture and treatment, rich in dramatic substance, and eloquent in song." Among its prominent musical numbers are De Becque and Nellie's love song, "Some Enchanted Evening"; De Becque's lament "This Nearly Was Mine"; Cable's love song "Younger Than Springtime"; three songs by Nellie, "I'm Gonna Wash That Man Right Outa My Hair," "A Cockeyed Optimist," and "I'm in Love with a Wonderful Guy"; two exotic numbers by the Tonkinese Bloody Mary, "Happy Talk" and "Bali Ha'i"; and a spirited and humorous choral number by the Marines, "There Is Nothing Like a Dame."

Victory at Sea is a nine-movement suite for symphony orchestra adapted by Robert Russell Bennett from the extended musical score for a series of documentary films on naval operations during World War II. These films were presented over NBC television in 1952 and received both the Sylvania and the George Foster Peabody Awards. Much of the acclaim accorded to these remarkable films belonged to Rodgers' background music which, as Otis L. Guernsey said, "suggested courage, self-sacrifice and the indomitable spirit of the free man." A *New Yorker* critic described Rodgers' music as a "seemingly endless creation, now martial, now tender, now tuneful, now dissonant . . . memorable and tremendously moving."

The first movement, "The Song of the High Seas," is a picture of ships menaced by Nazi U-boats on the seas during the early part of World War II. They finally get involved in battle. "The Pacific Boils Over" describes the beauty of Hawaii at peace in a melody suggesting Hawaiian song and dance. War comes, and this idyllic mood is shattered. A broad melody for strings ending in forceful chords tells about the tragedy of Pearl Harbor and the grim business of repairing the damage inflicted upon it by the Japanese. The third movement is one of the most famous in the suite, often performed independently of the other sections. It is stirring and dramatic march music of symphonic dimensions entitled "Guadalcanal March." This is followed by "D Day," its principal melody a broad, strong subject for brass telling of the gradual build-up of men and materials for the invasion of Fortress Europe. The fifth movement, "Hard Work and Horseplay" provides the lighter side of war. American soldiers find relief from grim realities in mischievous escapades and playtime. "Theme of the Fast Carrier" brings up the picture of a battle scene and ends with moving funeral music. In "Beneath the Southern Cross" we get an infectious tango melody which Rodgers later borrowed for his hit song, "No Other Love," for the Rodgers and Hammerstein musical play, *Me and Juliet*. "Mare Nostrum" recalls the harsh realities of war, first by presenting a serene Mediterranean scene, and then showing how it is torn and violated by the fierce naval attack on North Africa, Sicily, Salerno, and Anzio. The suite ends on a note of triumph with "Victory at Sea." A hymn of thanksgiving is sounded. Then we hear reminders of the "Guadalcanal March" and the seductive tango melody from "Beneath the Southern Cross." This tango is soon transformed into a rousing song of joy and triumph with which the suite comes to a magnificent culmination.

Sigmund Romberg

SIGMUND ROMBERG was born in Szeged, Hungary, on July 29, 1887. His boyhood and early manhood were spent in Vienna where he studied engineering and fulfilled his military service with the 19th Hungarian Infantry stationed in that city. In Vienna, Romberg's lifelong interest in and talent for music found a favorable climate. He heard concerts, haunted the city's leading music salons, was a devotee of Viennese operettas at the Theater-an-der-Wien. Vienna's influence led him to abandon all thoughts of becoming an engineer. In 1909 he came to the United States where he led salon orchestras in various restaurants and published his first popular songs. In 1912 he was engaged as staff composer for the Shuberts, for whose many and varied Broadway productions Romberg supplied all the music. Within a three-year period he wrote the scores for eighteen musicals, one of which was his first operetta in a European style, *The Blue Paradise* (1915) for which he created his first outstanding song hit, *"Auf Wiedersehen."* Though he continued writing music for many musical comedies, revues and extravaganzas—including some starring Al Jolson at the Winter Garden—it was in the field of the operetta that Romberg achieved significance in American popular music. His musical roots were so deeply embedded in the soil of Vienna that only in writing music for operettas in the manner and procedures of Vienna did he succeed in producing a lyricism that ran the gamut from sweetness and sentimentality to gaiety, masculine vigor and charm. His most successful operettas, which are discussed below, have never lost their capacity to enchant audiences however many times they are revived.

Romberg began writing music for motion pictures in 1930 with *Viennese Nights*. Out of one of his many scores for the screen came the poignant ballad, "When I Grow Too Old to Dream." His last huge success on Broadway was achieved not with an operetta but with an American musical comedy with American backgrounds, settings and characters—and songs in a pronounced American idiom. It was *Up in Central Park* in 1945. His last musical comedy was *The Girl in Pink Tights* produced on Broadway posthumously in 1954. Romberg died in New York City on November 9, 1951. Three years after his death his screen biography, *Deep in My Heart,* was released, with José Ferrer playing the part of the composer.

Blossom Time was first produced on Broadway on September 29, 1921 and proved so successful that to meet the demand for tickets a second company was formed to perform it at a nearby theater. There were also four national companies running simultaneously. This musical was derived from the successful German operetta, *Das drei Maederlhaus,* adapted by Dorothy Donnelly. The central character is the beloved Viennese composer of the early 19th century, Franz Schubert, and the plot is built around the composer's supposed frustrated love for Mitzi, who, in turn, falls in love with Schubert's best friend. The composer's anguish in losing her makes it impossible for him to finish the symphony he was writing for her—and it remains forever unfinished. This tragic episode, however, has no basis in biographical fact and is entirely the figment of a fertile operetta librettist's imagination.

Romberg's most famous songs were all based on Schubert's own melodies, and one became a hit of major proportions: "Song of Love" based on the beautiful main theme from the first movement of the *Unfinished Symphony*. Other popular selections include "Tell Me Daisy," "Lonely Hearts," "Serenade" and "Three Little Maids"—all possessed of that charm, grace and *Gemuetlichkeit* which we always associate with the city of Vienna and its popular music.

The Desert Song, produced on November 30, 1926, had for its background the colorful setting of French Morocco. There Margot Bonvalet is in love with the Governor's son but is being pursued by the bandit chief, The Red Shadow. In the end it turns out that the Governor's son and The Red Shadow are one and the same person. The principal musical excerpts include the romantic duet of Margot and The Red Shadow, "Blue Heaven"; the rapturous love song of The Red Shadow, "One Alone"; and two virile episodes, "Sabre Song" and "French Marching Song."

Unlike most Romberg operettas, *Maytime,* presented on August 16, 1917, did not have a foreign or exotic setting. The action takes place in Gramercy Park, New York, between 1840 and 1900. However, the tragic frustrations of the love affair of Ottilie and Richard belong inevitably in the make-believe world of the operetta. Otillie is forced to marry a distant relative. Many years later, Ottilie's granddaughter and Richard's grandson find each other, fall in love, and fulfil the happiness denied their grandparents. The most important musical number in this play is the sweet and sentimental waltz, "Will You Remember?", which is repeated several times during the course of the action. Other numbers include "Jump Jim Crow," "It's a Windy Day" and "Dancing Will Keep You Young."

The New Moon—which came to Broadway on September 19, 1928—was described by its authors (Oscar Hammerstein II, Frank Mandel, and Laurence Schwab) as a "romantic musical comedy." Its hero is a historical character, Robert Mission, an 18th-century French aristocrat who has come to New Orleans as a political fugitive. In the operetta he is a bondservant to Monsieur Beaunoir, with whose daughter, Marianne, he is in love. When the French police arrive to take him back to Paris for trial, Marianne boards his ship upon which a mutiny erupts on the high seas. The victorious bondservants now take possession of a small island off the coast of Florida where they set up their own government with Robert as leader, who then takes Marianne as his wife. This opulent score yields one of Romberg's most beautiful love songs, "Lover Come Back to Me," but it is significant to point out that its main melody was expropriated by Romberg from a piano piece by Tchaikovsky. Other delightful musical excerpts from this tuneful operetta include the tender ballads "Softly as in a Morning Sunrise," "One Kiss" and "Wanting You," and the stirring male chorus, "Stout-Hearted Men."

The Student Prince, like *Blossom Time,* was based on a successful

German operetta, *Old Heidelberg,* once again adapted for the American stage by Dorothy Donnelly. Its first performance took place on December 2, 1924. It has become one of the best loved operettas of the American theater; there is hardly a time when it is not revived somewhere in the United States. The setting is the romantic German University town of Heidelberg in 1860. Prince Karl Franz falls in love with Kathie, a waitress at the local inn. Their romance, however, is doomed to frustration, since the Prince must renounce her to marry a Princess. Romberg's music is a veritable cornucopia of melodic riches, including as it does the love duet of Kathie and the Prince, "Deep in My Heart," the Prince's love song "Serenade," and with them, "Golden Days" and a vibrant male chorus, "Drinking Song."

David Rose

DAVID ROSE was born in London, England, on June 15, 1910. His family came to the United States in 1914, settling in Chicago where Rose received his musical training at the Chicago Musical College. After working for radio and as pianist of the Ted Fiorito Orchestra, Rose came to Hollywood in 1938 where he became music director of the Mutual Broadcasting network. During World War II he served as musical director of, and composer for, *Winged Victory,* the Air Corps production by Moss Hart. After the war, Rose became outstandingly successful as musical director for leading radio and television programs (including the first Fred Astaire television show for which he received an "Emmy" Award), and as a composer of background music for many motion pictures. He has also appeared extensively in America and Europe as guest conductor of symphony orchestras.

Rose is the composer of several instrumental compositions in a popular style that have achieved considerable popularity. Indeed, it was with one of these that he first became famous as a composer. This was the *Holiday for Strings,* written and published in 1943, a three-part composition in which the flanking sections make effective use of plucked strings while the middle part is of lyrical character. *Holiday for Strings* received over a dozen different recordings and sold several million records. Fifteen years later, Rose wrote another charming composition in a similar vein, *Holiday for Trombones* in which virtuosity is contrasted with lyricism. Other instrumental works by Rose outstanding for either melodic or rhythmic interest are *Big Ben, Dance of the Spanish Onion, Escapade,* and *Our Waltz.*

Gioacchino Rossini

 torsion

GIOACCHINO ROSSINI was born in Pesaro, Italy, on February 29, 1792. He received his musical training at the Liceo Musicale in Bologna. In 1810 he wrote his first opera, *La Cambiale di matrimonio,* produced in Venice. Success came in 1812 with his third opera, *La Pietra del paragone,* given at La Scala in Milan. *Tancredi* and *L'Italiana in Algeri,* performed in Venice in 1813, further added to his fame and helped make him an adulated opera composer at the age of twenty-one. In 1815 Rossini was appointed director of two opera companies in Naples for which he wrote several successful operas. But his masterwork, which came during this period, was not written for Naples but for Rome: *The Barber of Seville* introduced in the Italian capital in 1816. In 1822 Rossini visited Vienna where he became the man of the hour. In 1824 he came to Paris to assume the post of director of the Théâtre des Italiens. Among the operas written for Paris was *William Tell,* introduced at the Paris Opéra in 1829. Though Rossini was now at the height of his fame and creative power—and though he lived another thirty-nine years—he never wrote another work for the stage. He continued living in Paris, a dominant figure in its social and cultural life. His home was the gathering place for the intellectual élite of the city, the scene of festive entertainments. He died of a heart attack in Paris on November 13, 1868.

Rossini was the genius of Italian comic opera (*opera buffa*). His melodies are filled with laughter and gaiety; his harmonies and rhythms sparkle with wit and the joy of life. He was at his best when he brought to his writing an infallible instinct for comedy, burlesque, and mockery. But he was also capable of a lyricism filled with poetry and infused with heartfelt sentiments. He was, moreover, a master of orchestral effect—especially in his dramatic use of the extended *crescendo*—and highly skilled in contrasting his moods through rapid alternation of fast and slow passages. He was also a daring innovator in his instrumentation.

He is a giant in opera, but with his infectious moods and endless fund of melodies he is also a crowning master in semi-classical music. His masterwork, *The Barber of Seville* (*Il Barbiere di Siviglia*) is as popular with salon orchestras through its merry overture and main selections as it is in the opera house. *The Barber of Seville* is based on two plays by Beaumarchais, *Le Barbier de Séville* and *Le Mariage de Figaro*, adapted by Cesare Sterbini. It is a vivacious comedy in which Count Almaviva, in love with Rosina (ward of Doctor Bartolo who is in love with her himself) tries to penetrate Bartolo's household by assuming various disguises. The Count and Rosina plan to elope, but Rosina reneges when Bartolo convinces her that the Count is unfaithful to her. Eventually, Rosina discovers that Bartolo has deceived her. She marries the Count, and Bartolo finds consolation in the fact that the Count is willing to renounce Rosina's dowry in his favor.

When this work was first performed in Rome on February 20, 1816 it was a dismal failure. This was largely due to a carefully organized uproar in the theater by admirers of another famous Italian composer, Paisiello, who had previously written an opera on the same subject. A sloppy performance did not help matters either. The furor in the auditorium was so great that it was impossible at times to hear the singers; and Rossini was in the end greeted with hisses and catcalls. But the second performance told a far different story. The singing and staging now went off much more smoothly, and Rossini's enemies were no longer present to do their damage. Consequently the opera was acclaimed. Five years later, a tour of the opera throughout Italy established its fame and popularity on a solid and permanent basis.

The deservedly famous overture is so much in the carefree and ebullient spirit of the opera as a whole—and so felicitously sets the tone for what is soon to follow on the stage—that it comes as a shock to discover that it was not written for this work. Rossini had actually created it for an earlier opera, and then used it several times more for various other stage works, tragedies as well as comedies. The overture opens with a slow introduction in which the violins offer a graceful tune. A transition of four chords leads to the main body in which strings doubled by the piccolo offer a spicy little melody. The same infectious gaiety is to be found in the second theme which is first given by oboe and clarinet. A dramatic crescendo now leads into the development of both themes, and the overture ends with a vivacious coda.

Besides the overture, some of the principal melodies from this opera are frequently given in various orchestral potpourris and fantasias: Count Almaviva's beautiful serenade, *"Ecco ridente in cielo"* and Figaro's patter song, *"Largo al factotum"* from the first act; in the second act, Rosina's coloratura aria, *"Una voce poco fa"* and Basilio's denunciation of slander in *"La Calunnia"*; and in the third act, Basilio's unctuous greeting *"Pace e gioia sia con voi"* and Figaro's advice to the lovers to get married in haste and silence, *"Zitti, zitti, piano, piano."*

La Gazza ladra (*The Thieving Magpie*), first produced at La Scala on May 31, 1817, is also a light comedy; libretto by Giovanni Gherardini, based on a French play. The central character is a servant girl falsely accused of having stolen a silver spoon; she is exonerated when the spoon is found in a magpie's nest just as the girl is about to be punished at the scaffold. The overture begins with an attention-arresting roll on the snare drum. This is followed by a brisk, march-like melody for full orchestra. In the main section, the principal themes consist of a sensitive little tune for strings and a pert melody for strings and woodwind.

L'Italiana in Algeri (*The Italian Lady in Algiers*) is, on the other hand, a serious opera. It was first produced in Venice on May 22, 1813, libretto by Angelo Anelli. In Algiers, Lindoro and Isabella are in love, but their romance is complicated by the fact that Isabella is sought after by the Mustafa. The lovers manage to effect their escape while the Mustafa is involved in complicated rites serving as his initiation into a secret society. The solemn opening of the overture has for its main thought a beautiful song for oboe. A crescendo then carries the overture to its principal section in which two lively melodies are heard, the first for woodwind, and the second for oboe.

La Scala di seta (*The Silken Ladder*) is an opera buffa which had its first performance in Venice on May 9, 1812. The libretto by Gaetano Rossi was based on a French farce involving a young girl who tries desperately to keep secret from her jealous guardian her marriage to the man she loves. A brief and electrifying opening for strings in the overture brings on a sentimental duet for flute and oboe. Two principal subjects in the main body of the overture include a gay and sprightly melody for strings, echoed by oboe, and a tender theme for flute and clarinet accompanied by strings.

Semiramide—introduced in Venice on February 3, 1823—is a serious opera based on Voltaire with libretto by Gaetano Rossi. Semiramis is the Queen of Babylon who is driven by her love for Asur to murder her husband. Her later love life is complicated when she discovers that the object of her passion, a Scythian, is actually her son. Semiramis is killed by a dagger which Asur directs at her Scythian son; Semiramis' son then murders Asur and assumes the throne. The overture opens dramatically with a gradual crescendo at the end of which comes a slow and solemn melody for four horns, soon taken over by woodwind against plucked strings. A short transition in the woodwind brings on a return of the opening crescendo measures. We now come to the main part of the overture in which the first theme is for strings, and the second for the woodwind.

The most famous of all Rossini's overtures, more celebrated even than that for *The Barber of Seville,* is the one for the tragic opera *William Tell (Guillaume Tell).* This is perhaps the most popular opera overture ever written. It is much more than merely the preface to a stage work but is in itself an elaborate, eloquent tone poem, rich in dramatic as well as musical interest, and vivid in its pictorial and programmatic writing.

William Tell, which had its première in Paris on August 3, 1829, is based on the drama of Friedrich Schiller, the libretto adaptation being made by Étienne de Jouy and Hippolyte Bis. The hero is, of course, the Swiss patriot who triumphs over the tyrant Gessler and helps bring about the liberation of his country.

In the early measures of the overture we get a picture of sunrise over the Swiss mountains, its beautiful melody presented by cellos and basses. A dramatic episode for full orchestra then depicts an Alpine storm. When it subsides we get a pastoral scene of rare loveliness evoked by a poignant Swiss melody on the English horn. Trumpet fanfares then bring on the stirring march music which, in our time and country, has been borrowed by radio for the theme melody of "The Lone Ranger." The overture ends triumphantly in telling of William Tell's victory over tyranny and oppression.

The contemporary British composer, Benjamin Britten, has assembled various melodies by Rossini into two delightful suites for orchestra. *Soirées musicales* (1936) is made up of five compositions by Rossini —from *William Tell* and from several pieces from a piano suite entitled *Péchés de vieillesse*. The five movements are marked; I. March; II. Canzonetta; III. Tyrolese; IV. Bolero; V. Tarantella. *Matinées musicales* (1941) also gets its material from *William Tell* and the piano suite. Here the movements are: I. March; II. Nocturne; III. Waltz; IV. Pantomime; V. Moto Perpetuo.

Anton Rubinstein

ANTON RUBINSTEIN was born in Viakhvatinetz, Russia, on November 28, 1829. He studied the piano with Alexandre Villoing after which, in 1839 he came to Paris with his teacher, deeply impressing Chopin and Liszt with his performances. Between 1841 and 1843 Rubinstein made a concert tour of Europe, but his career as a world-famous virtuoso did not begin until 1854 when his formidable technique and musicianship aroused the enthusiasm of Western Europe. After that he made many tours of the world, his reputation as pianist second only to that of Liszt; his first American appearance took place in 1872–1873 when he gave more than two hundred concerts. He also distinguished himself as conductor of the Russian Musical Society, and as director of the St. Petersburg Conservatory which he helped found in 1862. He was one of the most highly honored musicians in Russia of his generation. He resigned his post as director of the Conservatory in 1891, and on November 20, 1894 he died in St. Petersburg.

Rubinstein was an extraordinarily prolific composer, his works including many operas, symphonies, concertos, overtures, tone poems, chamber music together with a library of music for solo piano. About all that has survived from his larger works is his Fourth Piano Concerto which is flooded with Romantic ardor and is often in the recognizable style of Mendelssohn. Beyond this concerto, only a few of his smaller pieces for piano are still heard, so delightful in their melodic content and so charming in mood and atmosphere that they have lost little of their universal appeal.

Kamenoi-Ostrow, though best known as a composition for orchestra, originated as a piece for the piano. Actually the name *Kamenoi-Ostrow* belongs to a suite of twenty-four compositions for solo piano, op. 10. But the twenty-second number has become so popular independent of the suite, and in so many different guises, that its original title (*"Rêve angelique"*) has virtually been forgotten and it is almost always referred to now by the name of its suite. Kamenoi-Ostrow is a Russian town in which the Grand Duchess Helena maintained a summer palace. Rubinstein was its chamber virtuoso from 1848 on for a few years, and while there he wrote his piano suite, naming it after the Grand Duchess' residence. The solemn melody and its equally affecting countermelody have an almost religious character, emphasized in orchestral transcription by a background of tolling bells. Victor Herbert made an effective orchestral adaptation.

The *Melody in F* is one of the most popular piano pieces ever written. It is found in the first of *Two Melodies,* for solo piano, op. 3, but is most often heard in orchestral transcription, or adaptations for solo instrument and piano. The vernal freshness of its spontaneous lyricism has made it particularly appropriate describing Springtime; indeed, verses about Spring have been written for this melody.

The *Romance in E-flat* major is almost as well known as the *Melody in F.* This sentimental melody—filled with Russian pathos, yearning and dark brooding—is the first number in a set of six pieces for solo piano collectively entitled *Soirées de St. Petersbourg,* op. 44.

Camille Saint-Saëns

ಆಶಿಆಶಿ ಶಿ೭ಶಿ೭

CAMILLE SAINT-SAËNS was born in Paris on October 9, 1835. He was extraordinarily precocious. After some piano instruction from his aunt he gave a remarkable concert in Paris in his ninth year

A comprehensive period of study followed at the Paris Conservatory where he won several prizes, though never the Prix de Rome. In 1852 he received a prize for *Ode à Sainte Cécile,* and in 1853 the première of his first symphony attracted considerable praise. From 1858 to 1877 he was the organist of the Madeleine Church in Paris, a position in which he achieved renown as a performer on the organ. From 1861 to 1865 he was an eminent teacher of the piano at the École Niedermeyer, and in 1871 he helped organize the distinguished Société Nationale in Paris devoted to the introduction of new music by French composers. From 1877 his principal activity was composition in which, as in all the other areas in which he had been engaged, he soon became an outstanding figure. He was made Chevalier of the Legion of Honor in 1868; Officer in 1884; Grand Officer in 1900; and in 1913 the highest rank in the Legion of Honor, the Grand-Croix. He became a member of the Institut de France in 1881. Saint-Saëns paid his first visit to the United States in 1906, and made his first tour of South America in 1916 when he was eighty-one. He remained active until the end of his long life, appearing as pianist and conductor in a Saint-Saëns festival in Greece in 1920, and performing a concert of his own music in Dieppe a year later. He was vacationing in Algiers when he died there on December 16, 1921.

Though Saint-Saëns lived well into the 20th century and was witness to the radical departures in musical composition taking place all about him, he remained a conservative to the end of his days. He was, from a technical point of view, a master. There is no field of musical composition which he did not cultivate with the most consummate skill and the best possible taste. He was gifted not merely with a fine lyrical gift but also at other times with passion, intensity, and a sardonic wit. He wrote numerous compositions in a light style, but many of his most serious efforts are readily assimilable at first hearing and readily fall into the category of semi-classics.

The Carnival of Animals (*Le Carnaval des animaux*), for two pianos and orchestra (1886) finds the composer in a gay mood. This is witty, ironic and at times satiric music. The composer regarded the writing of this work as a lark, thought so little of the composition that he did not permit a public performance or a publication during his lifetime. Nevertheless it is one of the composer's most infectious compositions, one that never fails to enchant audiences young and old. It was described by the composer as "a grand zoological fantasy," and its fourteen sections represent pictures of various animals. The suite begins with a march ("Introduction and Royal March of the Lion," *"L'Introduction et marche royale du lion"*). After a brief fanfare, sprightly march music is heard. We can readily guess who is at the head of the parade by the lion's roar simulated by the orchestra. After this we are given a picture of a hen through the cackle in piano and strings, and of a cock through a clarinet call ("Hens and Cocks," *"Poules et coqs"*). This is followed by music for two unaccompanied pianos intended to depict "Mules" (*"Hémiones"*). Actually this portion was planned by the composer as a satire on pianists who insist on playing everything in a strict rhythm and unchanging dynamics. In the fourth movement, "Tortoises" (*"Tortues"*), two amusing quotations are interpolated from Offenbach's *Orpheus in the Underworld*. A cumbersome melody in a stately rhythm then introduces us to the "Elephant" (*"L'Eléphant"*). In this part the composer's fine feeling for paradox and incongruity asserts itself in contrasting a ponderous theme with a graceful waltz tune. In the halting music of the next movement, "Kangaroos" (*"Kangourous"*), the composer aims his satirical barbs not on these graceless animals but upon concert audiences who insist on talking throughout a performance. "Aquarium" consists of a sensitive melody for flute and violin against piano arpeggio figures. In "Personages With Long Ears" (*Personnages à longues oreilles"*) donkeys are represented by a melody with leaping intervals. The "Cuckoo in the Woods" (*"Le Coucou au fonds des bois"*) consists of a melody for clarinet. "Aviary" (*"Volière"*) reproduces the flight and singing of birds. "Pianists" (*"Pianistes"*), the composer feels, belongs to the animal kingdom; the attempt by embryo pianists to master his scales is here described amusingly. "Fossils" (*"Fossiles"*) quotes four popular themes from the classics: from Rossini's *The Barber of Seville*, Saint-Saëns' *Danse macabre*, and two French folk songs. Satire and wit are replaced by the most sensitive lyricism and winning sentiment in the thirteenth movement, a section so famous that it is most often heard apart from the rest of the suite, and in many different versions and arrangements. This is the movement of "The Swan" (*"Le Cygne"*), a beautiful melody for the cello in which the stately movement of the swan in the water is interpreted. A dance inspired by this music was made world famous by Anna Pavlova. The suite ends with the return of all the preceding characters in a section entitled "Finale." In the present-day concert hall, it is sometimes the practice to present *The Carnival of Animals* with an appropriate superimposed commentary in verse by Ogden Nash preceding each section.

Danse macabre, tone poem for orchestra, op. 40 (1874) is a musical interpretation of a poem by Henri Cazalis. The composition opens with a brief sequence in the harp suggesting that the hour of midnight has struck. Death tunes his violin and almost at once there begins a demoniac dance, its abandoned theme first presented by the flute. Another equally frenetic dance tune is given by Death, the xylophone simulating the rattle of bones. In the midst of the orgy the solemn refrain of the "Dies Irae" is sounded. Dawn is announced by the crowing of a cock. The wild dance dies down and the dancers disappear in the mist.

The Deluge (Le Déluge), op. 45 (1876), is an orchestral prelude to a Biblical poem, text by Louis Gillet. The inspiration for this music comes from a passage in the *Genesis:* "And God repented of having created the world." Solemn chords preface a fugal passage built from a theme in violas. After this a beautiful melody for solo violin unfolds symbolizing humanity in its original state of purity.

The *Havanaise,* op. 83 (1887) is a popular composition for violin and piano which makes effective use of a languorous Spanish melody set against the habanera rhythm. "Havanaise" is the French term for "Habanera," a popular Spanish dance in slow ⅔ time said to have originated in Cuba.

Henry VIII, an opera, is remembered for its effective ballet music. The opera, with libretto by Leonce Detroyat and Armand Sylvestre was first performed at the Paris Opéra on March 5, 1883. Since its setting is England during the Tudor Period, the popular ballet music is restrained, sensitive and graceful. It is heard in the second act during a festival given by the King of Richmond to honor the Papal Legate. Much of the material for these dances was acquired by the composer from a collection of Scottish and Irish tunes and dances provided him by the wife of one of his librettists. The Ballet Music is made up of five sections. The first is a restrained Introduction. Then comes "The Entry of the Clans." This music, it is amusing to remark, is English rather than Scottish in style because the composer confused the English Dee with the Scottish river of the same name and decided to use the English melody "The Miller of the Dee." The third movement is a "Scotch Idyll," this time a bright Scottish tune in the oboe. The Ballet Music continues with a "Gypsy Dance" in which a Hungarian-type melody for English horn is followed by brisker music whose main subject is offered by the violins. The suite concludes with "Gigue and Finale."

The *Introduction and Rondo Capriccioso,* op. 28 (1863) is for violin and orchestra. The main theme of the Introduction is found in the solo violin in the second measure, accompanied by the strings. A forceful chord for full orchestra brings on the Rondo Capriccioso section, whose main melody is presented by the solo violin. The solo instrument later on also introduces a contrasting second theme. After some embellishment of both ideas, the orchestra loudly interpolates a third subject which is repeated by the solo violin. All this material is amplified, often with brilliant virtuoso passages in the violin. A climactic point is reached when the first theme of the Rondo Capriccioso is pronounced by the orchestra against broken chords in the violin. This composition concludes with a coda marked by virtuoso passages for the solo instrument.

The *Marche heroïque,* for orchestra, op. 34 (1871) was originally written for two solo pianos but later the same year orchestrated by the composer himself. The composition is dedicated to one of Saint-Saëns' friends, the painter Alexandre Regnault, who served in the French army and was killed during the Franco-Prussian War. This music has a seven-bar introduction following which the principal march subject is given by the woodwind accompanied by plucked strings. In the middle trio section a contrasting theme is offered by the trombone against an accompanying figure taken from the earlier march melody. The march music returns in the closing section, but more vigorously than heretofore. The composition ends with a powerful coda.

Le Rouet d'Omphale (Omphale's Spinning Wheel), is an orchestral tone poem, op. 31 (1871), based on an old legend. Hercules is the slave of the Lydian queen. He disguises himself as a woman and is put to the task of spinning. The whirr of the spinning wheel is simulated by the violins at the beginning of the composition. The abused Hercules is then represented by a somber subject for the bass. Soon the whirr returns in an increased tempo to point up Hercules' return to the business of spinning.

The composer's most famous opera, *Samson and Delilah,* is represented on semi-classical programs with its colorful, exciting *Bacchanale.* The opera was first performed in Weimar in 1877, its libretto (by Ferdinand Lemaire) based on the famous Biblical story. The Bacchanale comes towards the end of the opera, the second scene of the third act. At the Temple of Dagon, the Philistines are celebrating their victory over Samson and the Hebrews with wild revelry in front of a statue of their god. A part of these festivities consists of a bacchanale to wild music Semitic in melodic content, orgiastic in tone colors, and barbaric in rhythms. The most celebrated vocal selection from this opera is Delilah's seductive song to Samson, "My Heart at Thy Sweet Voice" (*"Mon coeur s'ouvre à ta voix"*).

The *Suite algérienne,* for orchestra, op. 60, is a set of four "picturesque impressions of a voyage to Algeria," in the composer's own description. The opening movement is a prelude. The sea is here depicted in a swelling figure while brief snatches of melody suggest some of the sights of Algiers as seen from aboard ship. "Moorish Rhapsody" (*"Rapsodie mauresque"*) is made up of three sections. The first and last are brilliant in sonority and tonal colors, while the middle one is an Oriental song. "An Evening Dream at Blidah" (*"Rêverie du soir"*) is a dreamy nocturne picturing a famous Algerian fortress. The most popular movement of the suite is the last one, a rousing "French Military March" (*"Marche militaire française"*)—vigorous, at times even majestic, music representing the composer's delight and sense of security in coming upon a French garrison.

Pablo de Sarasate

PABLO DE SARASATE was born in Pamplona, Spain, on March 10, 1844. As a child prodigy violinist he made his debut in Spain when he was six, and soon thereafter toured the country. In 1859 he completed with honors a three-year period of violin study at the Paris Conservatory. He was only fifteen when he initiated a worldwide career as virtuoso which continued until the end of his life and placed him with the foremost violinists of his generation. In his concerts he featured prominently his own arrangements and fantasias of opera arias as well as his original compositions in all of which he could exhibit his phenomenal technique. Some of his compositions are now staples in the violin repertory. They include the *Gypsy Airs (Zigeuenerweisen), Caprice Basque, Jota aragonesa, Zapatadeo,* and the *Spanish Dances.*

The *Gypsy Airs* is a fantasia made up of haunting gypsy tunes and dance rhythms. The heart of the composition comes midway with a sad gypsy song which finds contrast in the electrifying dance melodies and rhythms that follow immediately.

Sarasate produced four sets of *Spanish Dances,* opp. 21, 22, 23, and 26, all for violin and piano. The identifiable Spanish melodies and rhythms of folk dances are here exploited most effectively. The most famous of these is the *Malagueña,* a broad and sensual gypsy melody followed by a rhythmic section in which the clicking of castanets is simulated.

Franz Schubert

FRANZ PETER SCHUBERT was born in Vienna, Austria, on January 31, 1797. He was extraordinarily precocious in music and was early trained to play the violin, viola and organ. From 1808 to 1813 he attended the Imperial Chapel School where he received a thorough musical background while preparing to be a chorister in the Chapel Choir. He showed such remarkable and natural gifts for music that one of his teachers, the renowned Antonio Salieri, did not hesitate to call him a "genius." When the breaking of his voice compelled him to leave the school in 1813, Schubert was encouraged by his father, a schoolmaster, to enter the field of education. For two years, from 1814 on, Schubert taught in the school owned and directed by his father. During this period he demonstrated phenomenal fertility as a composer by producing operas, symphonies, masses, sonatas, string quartets, piano pieces, and almost 150 songs including his first masterpiece, *The Erlking (Der Erlkoenig).* After 1817, Schubert devoted himself completely to composition. He remained singularly productive even though recognition failed to come. Few of his works were either published or performed—and those that were heard proved dismal failures. He managed to survive these difficult years only through the kindness and generosity of his intimate friends who loved him and were in awe of his genius. Combined with the frustration in failing to attract public notice with his music—and the humiliation of living on the bounty of friends —was the further tragedy of sickness brought on by a venereal disease. A concert of his works in Vienna on March 26, 1828 seemed to promise a turn in his fortunes. But it came too late. He died in Vienna on November 19, 1828—still an unrecognized composer. So completely obscure was his reputation that for many years some of his crowning master works lay forgotten and neglected in closets of friends and associates, none of whom seemed to realize that they were in the possession of treasures.

Schubert was undoubtedly one of the greatest creators of song the world has known. His almost five hundred art songs (*Lieder*) is an inexhaustible source of some of the most beautiful, most expressive, most poetic melodies ever put down on paper. He created beauty as easily as he breathed. The most inspired musical thoughts came to him so spontaneously that he was always reaching for quill and paper to get them down—whether at his home, or at the houses of his friends, in restaurants, café-houses, and even while walking through the country. "The striking characteristics of Schubert's best songs," wrote Philip Hale, "are spontaneous, haunting melody, a natural birthright mastery over modulation, a singular good fortune in finding the one inevitable phrase for the prevailing sentiment of the poem, and in finding the fitting descriptive figure for salient detail. His best songs have an atmosphere which cannot be passed unnoticed, which cannot be misunderstood." But far and beyond his natural gift at lyricism was his genius in translating the slightest nuances and suggestions of a line of poetry into tones. It is for this very reason that he is often described as the father of the *Lied*, or art song.

Because Schubert's melodies come from the heart and go to the heart they have been staples in semi-classical literature by way of orchestral transcription. Thus though they are as lofty and as noble a musical expression as can be found anywhere, Schubert's songs have such universality that they are as popular as they are inspired. These are a few of the Schubert songs that have profited from instrumental adaptations:

"*Am Meer*" ("By the Sea"), poem by Heinrich Heine. This stately melody seems to catch some of the vastness and mystery of the sea. This is the twelfth song from the song cycle *Schwanengesang* (1828).

"*An die Musik*" ("To Music"), poem by Franz von Schober (1817).

The glowing melody has caught the composer's wonder and awe at the magic of music.

"Auf dem Wasser zu singen" ("To Be Sung on the Water") poem by Stolberg. This gay, heartfelt tune expresses the composer's delight in floating on the water.

"Ave Maria," based on a poem by Sir Walter Scott (1825). This is a melody of exalted spiritual character touched with serenity and radiance. August Wilhelmj's transcription for violin and piano is a staple in the violin repertory.

"Du bist die Ruh' " ("You are Peace"), poem by Rueckert. An atmosphere of serenity is magically created by a melody of wondrous beauty.

"Der Erlkoenig" ("The Erlking"), poem by Goethe (1815). This is one of Schubert's most dramatic songs, describing the death of a child at the hands of the Erlking, symbol of death.

"Die Forelle" ("The Trout"), poem by Schubert (1817). This gay tune gives a lively picture of a trout leaping happily in and out of the water. Schubert used this melody for a set of variations in his piano quintet in A major, op. 114 (1819).

"Gretchen am Spinnrade" ("Marguerite at the Spinning Wheel"), poem by Goethe (1814). Against an accompaniment suggesting the whirr of the spinning wheel, comes Marguerite's haunting song as she thinks of her loved one.

"Hark, Hark, the Lark" (*"Horch, Horch, die Lerch"*), poem by Shakespeare (1826). The melody reflects the light-hearted mood of the famous Shakespeare verse from *Cymbeline*.

"Der Lindenbaum" ("The Linden Tree"), poem by Mueller is a poignant poem of unhappy love. It is the fifth song in the cycle *Die Winterreise* (1827).

"Staendchen" ("Serenade"), poem by Rellstab. This is probably one of the most famous love songs ever written. It is the fourth song in the cycle *Schwanengesang* (1828).

"Der Tod und das Maedchen" ("Death and the Maiden"), poem by Claudius (1817). This dramatic song consists of a dialogue between a young girl and Death, the words of death appearing in a solemn melody while that of the girl in a breathless entreaty. Schubert used this melody for a set of variations in his string quartet in D minor (1824).

Like Beethoven and Mozart Schubert wrote a considerable amount of popular dance music for solo piano, and also for orchestra: German Dances, Laendler, and Waltzes. All have a vigorous peasant rhythm and with melodies reminiscent of Austrian folk music. Schubert's waltzes are of particular interest since he was one of the first composers to unite several different waltz tunes into a single integrated composition. The Schubert waltzes, each a delight, are found in *Valses sentimentales*, op. 50 (1825) and *Valses nobles*, op. 77 (1827). Liszt adapted nine of the more popular of these waltz melodies in *Soirées de Vienne* for solo piano. The 20th-century French Impressionist composer, Maurice Ravel, was inspired by these Schubert waltzes to write in 1910 the *Valses nobles et sentimentales* in two versions, for solo piano, and for orchestra.

Marche militaire (Militaermarsch) is a popular little march in D major originally for piano four hands, the first of a set of three marches gathered in op. 41. This is one of Schubert's most popular instrumental numbers. Karl Tausig transcribed it for solo piano, and it has received many other adaptations including several for orchestra, in which form it is undoubtedly best known.

Moment musical is a brief composition for the piano. It is in song form and of an improvisational character, and is a *genre* of instrumental composition created and made famous by Schubert. He wrote many such pieces, but the one always considered when this form is designated is No. 3 in F minor, a graceful and lovable melody, the very essence of Viennese *Gemuetlichkeit*, although it is subtitled "Russian Air" (*Air Russe*). Fritz Kreisler transcribed it for violin and piano and it is, to be sure, familiar in orchestral adaptations including one by Stokowski, as well as versions for cello and piano, string quartet, clarinet quartet, four pianos, and so forth.

The incidental music to *Rosamunde* (1823) includes an often played overture and another of Schubert's universally loved instrumental numbers, the *Ballet Music*. When *Rosamunde* was introduced in Vienna on December 20, 1823 it was a failure, but this was due more to the insipid play of Helmina von Chézy than to Schubert's music. The overture heard upon that occasion is not the overture now known as *Rosamunde*. The latter is one which Schubert had written for an earlier operetta, *Die Zauberharfe*. A dignified introduction is dominated by a soaring melody for oboe and clarinet. The tempo changes, and a brisk little melody is given by the violins; a contrast is offered by a lyric subject for the woodwind.

The Entr'acte No. 2 in B-flat major from *Rosamunde* is one of Schubert's most inspired melodies, whose beauty tempted H. L. Mencken once to point to it as the proof that God existed. Schubert himself was fond of the melody for he used it twice more, in his String

Quartet in A minor (1824) and for a piano Impromptu in B-flat major (1827).

There are two musical episodes in *Rosamunde* designated as *Ballet Music*. The famous one is the second in G major, a melody so sparkling, infectious and graceful—and so full of the joy of life—that once again like the *Moment Musical* in F minor it embodies the best of what today we characterize as Viennese. Fritz Kreisler's transcription for violin and piano is famous.

Robert Schumann

ROBERT SCHUMANN was born in Zwickau, Germany, on June 8, 1810. Though he demonstrated an unusual gift for music from earliest childhood he was directed by his father to law. While attending the Leipzig Conservatory in 1828 he studied the piano with Friedrich Wieck. In 1829, in Heidelberg, where he had come to continue his law study, he completed the first of his works to get published, the *Abegg Variations* for piano. He returned to Leipzig in 1829, having come to the decision to make music and not law his lifework, and plunged intensively into study. His ambition was to become a great virtuoso of the piano. In his efforts to master his technique he so abused his hands that a slight paralysis set in, putting to rest all hopes of a career as pianist. He now decided on composition. After an additional period of study with Heinrich Dorn, he completed his first major work, the *Paganini Etudes* for piano, and started work on his first symphony. He became active in the musical life of Leipzig by helping found and editing the *Neue Zeitschrift fuer Musik,* which became a powerful medium for fighting for the highest ideals in music. He also formed a musical society called the *Davidsbuendler* made up of idealistic young musicians who attacked false values and philistinism in music. All the while his creative life was unfolding richly. He wrote two unqualified masterworks for piano between 1833 and 1835, the *Carnaval* and the *Études symphoniques*. In 1840 Schumann married Clara Wieck, daughter of his one-time piano teacher. Their love affair had been of more than five years' duration, but Clara's father was stubbornly opposed to their marriage and put every possible obstacle in their way. Schumann finally had to seek the sanction of the law courts before his marriage could be consummated. He now entered upon his most productive period as composer, completing four symphonies, three string quartets, a piano quartet, numerous songs, a piano concerto among other works. In 1843, he helped found the Leipzig Conservatory where for a while he taught the piano, and between 1850 and 1853 he was municipal music director for the city of Duesseldorf. After 1853 there took place a startling deterioration of his nervous system, bringing on melancholia, lapses of memory, and finally insanity. The last two years of his life were spent in an asylum at Endenich, Germany, where he died on July 29, 1856.

Schumann was a giant in German Romantic music. His works abound with the most captivating lyricism, heartfelt emotion, subtle moods, and an unrestricted imagination. There is not much in this wonderful literature that falls naturally within the category of semi-classics—only three piano pieces familiar in transcriptions, and a song.

Abendlied (*Evening Song*), a gentle mood picture in the composer's most rewarding Romantic vein, comes from *Twelve Four-Hand Pieces for Younger and Older Children*, op. 85 (1849) where it is the final number.

"*Die beiden Grenadiere*" (*The Two Grenadiers*) op. 49, no. 1 (1840) is probably the most familiar of Schumann's many songs. The poem is by Heine. The music describes with telling effect the reaction of two French grenadiers on learning that their Emperor Napoleon has been captured. The song reaches a powerful climax with a quotation from the *Marseillaise*.

The *Traeumerie* (*Dreaming*) is the seventh number in a set of thirteen piano pieces collectively entitled *Scenes from Childhood* (*Kinderscenen*), op. 15, (1838). Like the *Abendlied*, it is an atmospheric piece, perhaps one of the most popular compositions by Schumann.

Wild Horseman (*Wilder Reiter*) can be found in the *Album for the Young* (*Album fuer die Jugend*), op. 68, no. 3 (1848). It was made into an American popular song in the early 1950's by Johnny Burke.

Cyril Scott

❧❧ ❦❦

CYRIL MEIR SCOTT was born in Oxton, England, on September 27, 1879. His musical training took place at Hoch's Conservatory in Frankfort, Germany, and privately with Ivan Knorr. He went to live in Liverpool in 1898 where he taught piano and devoted himself to composition. Performances of several orchestral and chamber-music works at the turn of the century helped establish his reputation. He also distinguished himself as a concert pianist with performances throughout Europe and a tour of America in 1921. Though frequently a composer with *avant-garde* tendencies—one of the first English composers to use the most advanced techniques of modern music—Scott is most famous for his short pieces for the piano which have been extensively performed in transcription. His writing is mainly impressionistic, with a subtle feeling for sensitive atmosphere and moods. The best of these miniatures, each a delicate tone picture, are: *Danse nègre* (*Negro Dance*), op. 58, no. 3 (1908); and *Lotus Land*, op. 47, no. 1 (1905). The latter was transcribed for violin and piano by Kreisler and for orchestra by Kostelanetz.

Jean Sibelius

❧❧ ❦❦

JEAN SIBELIUS was born in Tavastehus, Finland, on December 8, 1865. Though he early revealed a pronounced gift for music he planned a career in law. After a year at the University of Helsinki he finally decided upon music. From 1886 to 1889 he attended the Helsinki Conservatory where one of his teachers was Ferruccio Busoni, after which he studied in Berlin with Albert Becker and in Vienna with Robert Fuchs and Karl Goldmark. He was back in his native land in 1891, and one year after that conducted in Helsinki the première of his first work in a national style, *Kullervo*. From then on, he continued producing works with a pronounced national identity with which he became not only one of Finland's leading creative figures in music but also its prime musical spokesman. In 1897 he was given the first government grant ever bestowed on a musician which enabled him to give up his teaching activities for composition. He now produced some of his greatest music, including most of his symphonies. In 1914 he paid his only visit to the United States, directing a concert of his works in Norfolk, Connecticut. After World War I, he toured Europe several times. Then from 1924 on he lived in comparative seclusion at his home in Järvenpää, which attracted admirers from all parts of the world. Sibelius wrote nothing after 1929, but by then his place in the world's music was secure as one of the foremost symphonists since Brahms. In Finland he assumed the status of a national hero. He died at his home in Järvenpää on September 20, 1957.

Some of the compositions by Sibelius enjoying popularity as semi-classics are in the post-Romantic German style which he had assumed early in his career; only one or two are in the national idiom for which he is so famous.

In the former category belongs a slight, sentimental piece called *Canzonetta*, for string orchestra, op. 62a (1911). As its name implies it is a small and simple instrumental song for muted strings, deeply emotional in feeling, at times with deeply somber colorations.

Finlandia, for symphony orchestra, op. 26 (1900) is one of Sibelius' earliest national compositions, and to this day it is the most famous. Both in and out of Finland this music is as much an eloquent voice for its country as its national anthem. One can go even further and say that more people in the world know the melodies of *Finlandia* than the Finnish anthem. So stirring are its themes, so indentifiably Finnish in personality and color, that for a long time it was believed Sibelius had utilized national folk tunes; but the music is entirely Sibelius'. It opens with a proud exclamation in the brass. After this comes a sensitive melody for the woodwind, and a prayer-like song for the strings. The music now enters a dramatic phase with stormy passages. But there soon arrives the most famous melody in the entire work, a beautiful supplication sounded first by the woodwind and then by the strings.

A forceful climax ensues with a strong statement which seems to be speaking in loud and ringing tones of the determination of the people to stay free.

Performances of *Finlandia* played a prominent role in the political history of Finland. When performed in its first version, in 1899, it was used to help raise funds for a Press Pension fight against the suppression of free speech and press by the Russians. Within the next two years (following a radical revision of the music in 1900) the work was given under various titles: In France it was first performed as *Suomi* and then as *La Patrie;* in Germany, as *Vaterland.* In Finland the music proved so inflammatory in arousing national ardor that Russia suppressed its performances in that country, while permitting it to be played in the Empire so long as the title *Impromptu* was used. When, in 1905, Russia made far-reaching political concessions to Finland, Sibelius' tone poem was once again permitted performances. For the next twelve years it became the national expression of a people stubbornly fighting for its independence. Performances kept alive the national fire to such an extent that it has been said that they did more to promote the cause of Finland's freedom than all the propaganda of speeches and pamphlets.

When the Soviets invaded Finland in the first stages of World War II, *Finlandia* once again acquired political importance. In the free world, particularly in the United States, the music was used to speak for the spirit of a people refusing to accept oppression and defeat.

Another piece of stirring national music that has become a lighter classic comes out of the *Karelia Suite* for orchestra, op. 11 (1893), the *Alla Marcia* section. This work was written for a historical pageant presented by the students of Viborg University and consists of an overture, two melodious sections (*Intermezzo* and *Ballade*) and the *Alla marcia,* march music of dramatic surge and sweep, in which effective use is made of abrupt key changes.

Sibelius wrote several delightful *Romances* in the German-Romantic idiom of his early *Canzonetta.* One of these was originally for solo piano, in D-flat major, op. 24, no. 9 (1903); another for violin and piano, F major, op. 78, no. 2 (1915). The former has become popular in transcriptions for salon orchestra; the latter, for violin and orchestra, and cello and piano. Perhaps the most famous of Sibelius' *Romances* is that in C major, for string orchestra, op. 42 (1903). It begins with an unorthodox opening, unusual in harmonic structure and varied in inflections, but its principal melody—a soulful song—is in the traditional idiom of an uninhibited Romanticist.

The best known of Sibelius' Romantic compositions, a universal favorite with salon orchestras, is the *Valse Triste*, for orchestra, op. 44 (1903). This is a section from the incidental music for *Kuolema*, a play by Sibelius' brother-in-law, Arvid Jaernefelt; but it is the only one from this score to get published. This slow and lugubrious melody, bathed in sentimentality, is a literal musical interpretation of the following program, translated by Rosa Newmarch: "It is night. The son who has been watching by the bedside of his sick mother has fallen asleep from sheer weariness. Gradually a ruddy light is reflected through the room; there is a sound of distant music; the glow and the music steal nearer until the strains of a valse melody float distinctly to our ears. The sleeping mother awakens, rises from her bed, and, in her long white garment which takes the semblance of a ball dress, begins to move slowly and silently to and fro. She waves her hands and beckons in time to the music, as though she were summoning a crowd of invisible guests. And now they appear, these strange visionary couples, turning and gliding to an unearthly valse rhythm. The dying woman mingles with the dancers, she strives to make them look into her eyes, but the shadowy guests one and all avoid her glance. Then she seems to sink exhausted on her couch, and the music breaks off. But presently she gathers all her strength and invokes the dance once again with more energetic gestures than before. Back come the shadowy dancers, gyrating in a wild, mad rhythm. The weird gaiety reaches a climax; there is a knock at the door, which flies wide open; the mother utters a despairing cry; the spectral guests vanish; the music dies away. Death stands on the threshold."

Christian Sinding

CHRISTIAN SINDING was born in Kongsberg, Norway, on January 11, 1856. After attending the Leipzig Conservatory from 1877 to 1881 he settled in Oslo as a teacher of the piano. His first published composition was a piano quintet in 1884, and in 1885 he directed a concert of his own music in Oslo. Though he wrote in large forms, including symphonies, concertos, suites, tone poems and various chamber-music compositions, he is best known for his smaller pieces for the piano. In 1890 he received an annual subsidy from his government to enable him to devote himself completely to composition. One of Norway's most significant composers, he was given a handsome life pension in 1915, and in 1916 an additional government gift of 30,000 crowns. In 1921–1922 he visited the United States when he served for one season as a member of the faculty of the Eastman School of Music. He died in Oslo on December 3, 1941.

His smaller pieces for the piano include etudes, waltzes, caprices, intermezzos and various descriptive compositions. It is by one of the last that he is most often remembered, a favorite of young pianists throughout the world, and of salon and pop orchestras in instrumental adaptations. This is the ever-popular *Rustle of Spring (Fruehlingsrauschen)*, probably the most popular piece of music describing the vernal season. This is the second of *Six Pieces,* for solo piano, op. 32 (1896). The rustle can be found in the accompaniment, against which moves a soft, sentimental song filled with all the magic of Nature's rebirth at springtime. In this same suite, a second number of markedly contrasting nature, has also become familiar—the first number, played in a vigorous and picaresque style, the *Marche grotesque.*

Leone Sinigaglia

✥✥✥ ✥✥✥

LEONE SINIGAGLIA was born in Turin, Italy, on August 14, 1868. His preliminary music study took place at the Liceo Musicale of his native city and was completed with Mandyczewski in Vienna and Dvořák in Prague. The latter encouraged him to write music in a national Italian idiom. It was in this style that he created his earliest significant compositions, the first being *Danze piemontesi,* introduced in Turin in 1905, Toscanini conducting. Later works included *Rapsodia piemontese* for violin and orchestra; *Piemonte,* for orchestra; a violin concerto; and various works for chamber music groups, solo instruments and orchestra. He died in Turin on May 16, 1944.

His best known and most frequently played composition is a gay, infectious little concert overture, *Le Baruffe chiozzotte* (*The Quarrels of the People of Chiozzo*), op. 32 (1907). It was inspired by the Goldoni comedy of the same name which offers an amusing picture of life in the little town of Chiozzo. There Lucietto and Tita are in love, quarrel, and become reconciled through the ministrations of the magistrate. A loud theme for full orchestra provides the overture with a boisterous beginning. A passing tender thought then comes as contrast. After some elaboration of these ideas, a delightful folk song is heard first in the oboe, and then in violins. The tempo now quickens, the mood becomes restless, and the music grows sprightly. An amusing little episode now appears in woodwind and violins after which the folk song and the loud opening theme are recalled.

Piemonte, a suite for orchestra, op. 36 is a charming four-movement composition in which the folk melodies and dances of Piedmont are prominently used. The first movement, "Over Woods and Fields," opens with a folk tune, which the composer repeats in the finale. Two other delightful ideas follow: the first in the horn, repeated by the cellos; the second in muted first violins. In the second movement, "A Rustic Dance," the principal Piedmont dance tune is heard in solo violin and oboe; a second subject occurs after the development of the first in lower strings and woodwind. The heart of the third movement, "In the Sacred Mountain," is a folk song first offered by the horns, accompanied by cellos and double basses. The suite ends with a picture of a festival, "Piedmontese Carnival," its two vigorous ideas heard respectively in full orchestra, and in trumpet and first violins.

Bedřich Smetana

❧❧ ☙☙

BEDŘICH SMETANA was born in Leitomischl, Bohemia, on March 2, 1824. Though he was interested in music from childhood on, he received little training until his nineteenth year when he came to Prague and studied with Josef Proksch. For several years after the completion of his music study he worked as teacher of music for Count Leopold Thun. He soon became active in the musical life of his country; in 1848 he was a significant force in the creation of Prague's first music school. In 1849, Smetana was appointed pianist to Ferdinand I, the former Emperor of Austria residing in Prague. From 1856 to 1861 Smetana lived in Gothenburg, Sweden, where he was active as conductor, teacher, and pianist. After returning to his native land in 1861 he became one of its dominant musical figures. He served as director of the music school, conducted a chorus, wrote music criticisms, founded and directed a drama school, and organized the Society of Artists. He also wrote a succession of major works in which the cause of Bohemian nationalism was espoused so vigorously and imaginatively that Smetana has since become recognized as the father of Bohemian national music. His most significant works are the folk opera, *The Bartered Bride,* and a cycle of orchestral tone poems collectively entitled *My Country (Má Vlast).* Smetana was stricken by deafness in 1874, despite which he continued creating important works, among them being operas and an autobiographical string quartet called *From My Life (Aus meinem Leben).* Total deafness was supplemented by insanity in 1883 which necessitated confinement in an asylum in Prague where he died on May 12, 1884.

The rich folk melodies and pulsating folk rhythms of native dance music overflow in Smetana's music, providing it with much of its vitality and popular interest. Smetana's gift at writing music in the style, idiom, and techniques of Bohemian folk dances is evident in many of his compositions, but nowhere more successfully than in his delightful folk comic opera, *The Bartered Bride (Prodaná nevešta).* This little opera, first performed in Prague on May 30, 1866, is the foundation on which Bohemian national music rests securely. It is a gay, lively picture of life in a small Bohemian village. The principal action involves the efforts of the village matchmaker to get Marie married to Wenzel, a dim-witted, stuttering son of the town's wealthy landowner. But Marie is in love with Hans who, as it turns out, is also the son of the same landowner, though by a previous marriage. Through trickery, Hans manages to win Marie, though for a while matters become complicated when Marie is led to believe that Hans has deserted her.

In its first version, *The Bartered Bride* was presented as a play (by Karel Sabina) with incidental music by Smetana. Realizing that this work had operatic possibilities, Smetana amplified and revised his score, and wrote recitatives for the spoken dialogue. In this new extended form the opera was heard in Vienna in 1892 and was a sensation; from then on, and to the present time, it has remained one of the most lovable comic operas ever written.

There are three colorful and dynamic folk dances in this opera which contribute powerfully to the overall national identity, but whose impact on audiences is by no means lost when heard apart from the stage action. "The Dance of the Comedians" appears in the third act, when a circus troupe appears in the village square and entertains villagers with a spirited dance. The "Furiant"—a fiery type of Bohemian dance with marked cross rhythms—comes in the second act when villagers enter the local inn and perform a Corybantic dance. The "Polka," a favorite Bohemian dance, comes as an exciting finish to the first act as local residents give vent to their holiday spirits during a festival in the village square.

The effervescent overture which precedes the first act is as popular as the dances. The merry first theme is given by strings and woodwind in unison against strong chords in brasses and timpani. This subject is simplified, at times in a fugal style, and is brought to a climax before a second short subject is stated by the oboe. Still a third charming folk tune appears, in violins and cellos, before the first main subject is recalled and developed. The coda, based on this first theme, carries the overture to a lively conclusion. Gustav Mahler, the eminent music director of the Vienna Royal Opera which gave this opera its first major success outside Bohemia, felt this overture was so much in the spirit of the entire work, and so basic to its overall mood and structure, that he preferred using it before the second act so that latecomers into the opera house might not miss it.

Smetana's most famous work for orchestra comes from his cycle of six national tone poems entitled *My Country* (*Má Vlast*), which he wrote between 1874 and 1879 in a tonal tribute to his native land. Each of the tone poems is a picture of a different facet of Bohemian life, geography, and background. The most famous composition of this set is *The Moldau* (*Vltava*), a portrait of the famous Bohemian river. This is a literal tonal representation of the following descriptive program interpolated by the composer in his published score:

"Two springs gush forth in the shade of the Bohemian forest, the one warm and spouting, the other cold and tranquil. Their waves, gayly rushing onward over their rocky beds, unite and glisten in the rays of the morning sun. The forest brook, fast hurrying on, becomes the river Vltava, which, flowing ever on through Bohemia's valleys, grows to be a mighty stream; it flows through thick woods in which the joyous noise of the hunt and the notes of the hunter's horn are heard ever nearer and nearer; it flows through grass-grown pastures and lowlands where a wedding feast is celebrated with song and dancing. At night the wood and water nymphs revel in its shining waves, in which many fortresses and castles are reflected as witnesses of the past glory of knighthood and the vanished warlike fame of bygone ages. At St. John Rapids the stream rushes on, winding in and out through the cataracts, and hews out a path for itself with its foaming waves through the rocky chasm into the broad river bed in which it flows on in majestic repose toward Prague, welcomed by time-honored Vysehrad, whereupon it vanishes in the far distance from the poet's gaze."

The rippling flow of the river Moldau is portrayed by fast figures in the strings, the background for a broad and sensual folk song representing the river itself heard in violins and woodwind. Hunting calls are sounded by the horns, after which a lusty peasant dance erupts from the full orchestra. Nymphs and naiads disport to the strains of a brief figure in the woodwind. A transition by the wind brings back the beautiful Moldau song. A climax is built up, after which the setting becomes once again serene. The Moldau continues its serene course towards Prague.

John Philip Sousa

JOHN PHILIP SOUSA, America's foremost composer of march music, was born in Washington, D. C., on November 6, 1854. The son of a trombone player in the United States Marine Band, John Philip early received music instruction, mainly the violin from John Esputa. When he was about thirteen, John enlisted in the Marine Corps where he played in its band for two years. For several years after that he played the violin in and conducted the orchestras of various theaters; in the summer of 1877 he played in an orchestra conducted by Jacques Offenbach at the Philadelphia Centennial Exposition. Between 1880 and 1892 he was the musical director of the Marine Band. It was during this period that he wrote his first famous marches. In 1892 he formed a band of his own with which he toured Europe and America for many years, and with which he gave more than a thousand concerts. His most popular marches (together with his best transcriptions for band of national ballads and patriotic airs) were always the highlights of his concerts. Besides the marches, Sousa wrote the music for numerous comic operas, the most famous being *El Capitan* (1896) and *The Bride Elect* (1898). In 1918 Sousa and his band were heard in the Hippodrome extravaganza, *Everything*. He published his autobiography, *Marching Along*, in 1928, and died in Reading, Pennsylvania, on March 6, 1932.

In the closing years of the 19th century, and in the first part of the 20th, America was undergoing expansion in many directions: art, science, literature, commerce, finance, world affairs. Hand in hand with this development and growth came an aroused patriotism and an expanding chauvinism. Sousa's marches were the voice of this new and intense national consciousness.

As Sigmund Spaeth has pointed out, most of Sousa's famous marches follow a similar pattern, beginning with "an arresting introduction, then using a light, skipping rhythm for his first melody, going from that into a broader tune," then progressing to the principal march melody. A massive climax is finally realized with new, vibrant colors being realized in the main march melody through striking new combinations of instruments.

The following are some of Sousa's most popular marches:

El Capitan (1896) was adapted from a choral passage from the comic opera of the same name. This music was played aboard Admiral Dewey's flagship, *Olympia*, when it steamed down Manila Bay for battle during the Spanish-American War. And it was again heard, this time performed by Sousa's own band, when Dewey was welcomed as a conquering hero in New York on September 30, 1900.

King Cotton (1895) was written on the occasion of the engagement of the Sousa Band at the Cotton States Exposition. *Semper Fideles* (1888) was Sousa's first famous composition in march tempo, and to this day it is still one of his best known marches, a perennial favorite with parades of all kinds. Since Sousa sold this march outright for $35.00 he never capitalized on its immense popularity.

Sousa's masterpiece—and probably one of the most famous marches ever written—was the *Stars and Stripes Forever,* completed on April 26, 1897. In 1897 Sousa was a tourist in Italy when he heard the news that his friend and manager had died in the United States. Sousa decided to return home. Aboard the *Teutonic* a march melody kept haunting him. As soon as he came home he put the melody down on paper, and it became the principal subject of "The Stars and Stripes Forever." This principal melody achieves an unforgettable climax in the march when it is proudly thundered by the full orchestra to figurations in the piccolo.

The Thunderer and *The Washington Post March* were written in 1889. The latter was commissioned by the *Washington Post* for the ceremonies attending the presentation of prizes in a student essay contest.

Among Sousa's other marches are *The Bride Elect* (1897) from the comic opera of the same name; *The Fairest of the Fair* (1908); *Hands Across the Sea* (1899); *Invincible Eagle* (1901); and *Saber and Spurs* (1915) dedicated to the United States Cavalry.

It was long maintained that Sousa was the composer of the famous hymn of the Artillery branch of the United States armed services, "The Caisson Song." Sousa played this march in his own brilliant new band arrangement at a Liberty Loan Drive at the Hippodrome, in New York, in 1918. For some time thereafter Sousa was credited as being the composer. But further research revealed the fact that the words and music had been written in 1908 by Edmund L. Gruber, then a lieutenant with the 5th Artillery in the Philippines.

Oley Speaks

❦❦ ❦❦

OLEY SPEAKS was born in Canal Winchester, Ohio, on June 28, 1874. He received his musical training, principally in voice, from various teachers including Armour Galloway and Emma Thursby. He then filled the post of baritone soloist at churches in Cleveland, Ohio, and New York City, including the St. Thomas Church in New York from 1901 to 1906. He also filled numerous engagements in song recitals and performances of oratorios. He died in New York City on August 27, 1948.

Speaks was the composer of more than 250 published art songs which have placed him in a front rank among American song composers. Three have become outstandingly popular; there is hardly a male singer anywhere who has not sung such all-time favorites as "Morning," "On the Road to Mandalay" and "Sylvia," each of which is among the most widely circulated and most frequently heard art songs by an American. "Morning," words by Frank L. Stanton, was published in 1910. Where "Morning" is lyrical, "On the Road to Mandalay" (published in 1907) is dramatic, a setting of the famous poem by Rudyard Kipling. The persistent rhythmic background suggesting drum beats, and the effective key change from verse to chorus, have an inescapable effect on listeners. "Sylvia," poem by Clinton Scollard, published in 1914, is in a sentimental mood, and like "Morning" reveals the composer's marked gift for sensitive lyricism.

Robert Stolz

❧❧ ❦❦

ROBERT STOLZ was born in Graz, Austria, on August 25, 1882. His parents were musical, his father being a successful conductor and teacher, and his mother a concert pianist. Robert's music study took place first with his father, then with Robert Fuchs in Vienna and Humperdinck in Berlin. In 1901 he assumed his first post as conductor, at an opera house in Brunn. When he was twenty-five he was appointed conductor of the Theater-an-der-Wien in Vienna where he remained twelve years, directing most of the masterworks in the field of Austrian and German operettas. His own career as composer of operettas had begun in 1903 with *Schoen Lorchen* produced in Salzburg. Since then Stolz has written music for about sixty operettas, scores for more than eighty films, and a thousand songs in all. His music is in the light, graceful, ebullient style that has characterized Viennese operetta music since the time of Johann Strauss II. His most famous operettas are: *Die lustigen Weiber von Wien* (1909), *Die Gluecksmaedel* (1910), *Die Tanzgraefin* (1921), *Peppina* (1931), *Zwei Herzen in dreiviertel Takt* (1933), *Fruehling im Prater* (1949) and *Karneval in Wien* (1950). In 1938 Stolz came to the United States where for several years he worked in Hollywood. After the end of World War II he returned to Vienna, remaining active as a composer not only in that city but also in Berlin and London.

Stolz' most famous song is *"Im Prater bluehn wieder die Baeume"* ("In the Prater the Trees Are Again Blooming"), a glowing hymn not only to a district in Vienna famous for its frolic and amusement but even more so to the city of Vienna itself.

A waltz from his operetta, *Two Hearts in Three-Quarter Time* (*"Zwei Herzen in dreiviertel Takt*) is perhaps one of the most celebrated pieces in three-quarter time written in Vienna since Lehár, and it is loved the world over. This operetta originated in 1931 as a German motion-picture which won accolades around the world for its charm and freshness, for which Stolz wrote a score that included his famous waltz. It was then adapted for the stage by Paul Knepler and J. M. Willeminsky and introduced in Zurich, Switzerland, in 1933. This delightful text concerns the trials and tribulations of producing an operetta.

That operetta is accepted for production on the condition that a good waltz melody is written for it, and the composer Toni Hofer gets his inspiration for that tune from lovely Hedi, the young sister of the librettist. This waltz, of course, is the title number, which, in its lilt and buoyancy and Viennese love of life, is in the best tradition of Viennese popular music.

Oscar Straus

OSCAR STRAUS was no relation to any of the famous Viennese Strausses; nevertheless in the writing of light, gay music in waltz tempo and spirited melodies for the operetta stage he was certainly their spiritual brother. He was born in Vienna on March 6, 1870, and studied music with private teachers in Vienna and Berlin, including Max Bruch. In 1901 he settled in Berlin where he became conductor at a famous cabaret, *Ueberbrettl*, for whose productions of farces he wrote a number of scores. Soon after that he turned to writing operettas, becoming world famous with *The Waltz Dream* in 1907 and *The Chocolate Soldier* in 1908, both introduced in Vienna. He wrote about thirty operettas after that, many heard with outstanding success in the music centers of the world. The best of these were *Der letzte Walzer* (1920), *Die Teresina* (1921), *Drei Walzer* (1935), and *Bozena* (1952). He was at his best writing waltz melodies but he was also skilful in interpolating satirical elements into his musical writing through the exploitation of ragtime, jazz, and the shimmy. Straus lived in Berlin until 1927, and for a decade after that he made his home in Vienna and Paris. In 1939 he became a French citizen, and from 1940 to 1948 he lived in the United States, filling some assignments in Hollywood. He returned to his native land in 1948, and died at Bad Ischl, Austria, on January 11, 1954.

The Chocolate Soldier (*Der tapfere Soldat*) was the operetta adaptation of Bernard Shaw's comedy, *Arms and the Man*, by R. Bernauer and L. Jacobsen. Its première took place in Vienna on November 14, 1908, with the first American performance taking place a year later at the Casino Theater in New York. The setting is Serbia in 1885 where the hero, Lieutenant Bumerli, gains the nickname of "chocolate soldier" because of a sweet tooth. While escaping from the enemy, he finds refuge in the bedroom of Nadina, daughter of Colonel Popoff. Nadina becomes the instrument by means of which the lieutenant is now able to effect his escape, disguised in the coat of Colonel Popoff. But before the final curtain Bumerli and Nadina also become lovers.

The waltz, "My Hero," (*"Komm, Komm, Held meiner Traeume"*) Nadina's waltz of love to the chocolate soldier, is the most celebrated excerpt from this operetta. Other familiar pages include the lovely first act duet of Nadina and Bumerli, "Sympathy"; the little orchestral march in the second act, a satirical take off on military pomp and circumstance; and Nadina's "Letter Song" in the third act.

A Waltz Dream (*Ein Walzertraum*), book by Felix Doermann and Leopold Jacobsen, was introduced in Vienna on March 2, 1907, and in New York in April 1908. Lieutenant Niki of the Austrian army is ordered by the Austrian Emperor to marry Princess Helen, but he falls in love with Frantzi, a violinist in a girl's orchestra. This love affair becomes frustrated when Niki must return to Vienna to become Prince Consort.

The main musical selection from this operetta is the title number, a waltz which first appears as a duet between Niki and a fellow officer in the first act, then recurs throughout the operetta, and finally brings it to a close. Two sprightly march excerpts, from the second and third acts respectively, and the duet, "Piccolo, piccolo, tsin, tsin tsin" are also popular.

Eduard Strauss

EDUARD STRAUSS, the younger brother of Johann Strauss II, was born in Vienna on March 15, 1835. He studied music in Vienna with G. Preyer following which he made his café-house debut in 1862 by conducting his father's orchestra at the Dianasaal. He continued to lead his father's orchestra at the Volksgarten and Musikverein as well as at various leading café-houses in Vienna. He also made many tours, including two of the United States in 1892 and 1901. In 1902 he dissolved the musical organization which his father had founded three-quarters of a century earlier and which all that time had dominated the musical life of Vienna. Besides conducting this orchestra, he also substituted from time to time for his famous brother, Johann Strauss II, and in 1870 he succeeded him as conductor of the court balls. Eduard Strauss died in Vienna on December 28, 1916.

Eduard wrote over three hundred popular instrumental compositions in the style of his celebrated brother but without ever equalling his remarkable creative freshness and originality. But there is a good deal of pleasurable listening in Eduard's waltzes and polkas. In the former category belongs the *Doctrinen* (*Faith*) Waltzes, op. 79; in the latter, the gay *Bahn Frei* (*Fast Track*) Polka, op. 45. In collaboration with his two brothers, Johann and Josef, Eduard wrote the *Trifolien-walzer* and the *Schuetzenquadrille*.

Johann Strauss I

JOHANN STRAUSS I was one of the two waltz kings of Vienna bearing that name. The more famous one, the composer of "The Blue Danube" was the son. But the father was also one of Vienna's most popular composers and café-house conductors. He was born in Vienna on March 14, 1804, and as a boy he studied both the violin and harmony. His love for music, combined with the decision of his parents to make him a bookbinder, led him to run away from home. When he was fifteen he joined Michael Pamer's orchestra which played at the Sperl café; another of its members was Josef Lanner, soon also to become a major figure in Vienna's musical life. As Lanner's star rose, so did Johann Strauss'. First Strauss played in the Lanner Quartet at the *Goldenen Rebbuhn* and other cafés; after that he was a member of the Lanner Orchestra which appeared in Vienna's leading cafés. When Lanner's mounting success made it necessary for him to create two orchestras, he selected Johann Strauss to conduct one of them. Then, in 1826, Johann Strauss formed an orchestra of his own which made its debut at the Bock Café. For the next two decades he was the idol of Vienna, Lanner's only rival. By 1830 he had two hundred musicians under him. His major successes as a café-house conductor came at the Sperl and the Redoutensaal. But his fame spread far beyond Vienna. In 1833 he toured all Austria, and in 1834 he appeared in Berlin. After that he performed in all the major European capitals, achieving formidable successes in London and Paris. Meanwhile, in 1833, he had become bandmaster of the first Vienna militia regiment, one of the highest honors a performer of light music could achieve in Austria. In 1845 he was appointed conductor of the Viennese court balls. He died in Vienna on September 25, 1849.

Like Lanner, Strauss wrote a considerable amount of dance and café-house music, over 250 compositions. His first composition was the *Taeuberlwalzer,* named after the café *Zwei Tauben* where he was then appearing. After that he wrote waltzes, galops, polkas, quadrilles, cotillons, contredanses, and marches—which Vienna came to love for their rhythmic vitality and appealing lyricism. People in Vienna used to say that the waltzes of the first Johann Strauss were *made* for dancing because their rhythmic pulse excited the heart and made feet restless.

Not much of the father Strauss' library of music has survived. The exceptions are the following waltzes: *Caecilien, Donaulieder,* the *Kettenbruecken,* and the *Lorelei Rheinsklaenge.* To the waltz, the older Johann Strauss brought a symphonic dimension it had heretofore not known, particularly in his spacious introductions of which the thirty-bar prelude of the *Lorelei Rheinsklaenge* is an outstanding example. He also carried over to the waltz a variety of mood and feeling and a lightness of touch new for this peasant dance. "This demon of the ancient Viennese folk spirit," wrote Richard Wagner after hearing Strauss perform one of his own waltzes in Vienna, "trembled at the beginning of a new waltz like a python preparing to spring, and it was more the ecstasy produced by the music than the drinks among the enchanted audience that stimulated that magical first violin to almost dangerous flights."

Of his other music the most famous is the *Radetzky March.* Count

Radetzky was an Austrian military hero, victor over the Italians in 1848–1849. In honor of his Italian triumphs and suppression of the Italian nationalist movement, Strauss wrote the spirited, sharply accented march in 1848 which almost at once became the musical symbol of Hapsburg Vienna and Austrian military power. The following programmatic interpretation of this music by H. E. Jacob is of interest: "Drunk with triumph, the Generalissimo's battalions hurl themselves down into Lombardy. They are close on the heels of the fleeing troops of King Albert, the King of Sardinia. And then comes a new phase of the march to accompany the victorious troops. A different sun shines down on this, a memory of Vienna, a lingering trace of the feel of girls' arms; scraps of a dance song with a backward glance at three-quarter time. But on they go, still forward. There are no more shots, there is laughter. The trio follows. The . . . superdominant . . . hoisted as if it were a flag. . . . Finally comes the return of the principal theme with the laurels and gaiety of victory."

Johann Strauss II

JOHANN STRAUSS II, son of the first Johann Strauss, was born in Vienna on October 25, 1825. Though he showed an unmistakable bent for music from his childhood on, he was forbidden by his father to study music or to indulge in any musical activity whatsoever. The young Johann Strauss, encouraged by his mother, was forced to study the violin surreptitiously with a member of his father's orchestra. Only after the father had deserted his family, to set up another home with his mistress, did young Johann begin to devote himself completely and openly to music. After studying the violin with Kohlmann and counterpoint with Joseph Drechsler, he made his debut as a café-house conductor and composer at Dommayer's Casino in Hietzing, near Vienna, on October 15, 1844. The event was widely publicized and dramatized in Vienna, since the son was appearing as a rival to his father. For this momentous debut, the son wrote the first of his waltzes —the *Gunstwerber* and the *Sinngedichte*—which aroused immense enthusiasm. He had to repeat the last-named waltz so many times that the people in the café lost count. "Ah, these Viennese," reported the editor of *The Wanderer*. "A new waltz player, a piece of world history. Good night, Lanner. Good evening, Father Strauss. Good morning, Son Strauss." The father had not attended this performance, but learned of his son's triumph from one of his cronies.

Thus a new waltz king had arisen in Vienna. His reign continued until the end of the century. For fifty years Johann Strauss II stood alone and unequalled as the musical idol of Vienna. His performances were the talk of the town. His own music was on everyone's lips. After the death of father Strauss in 1849, he combined members of the older man's orchestra with his own, and toured all of Europe with the augmented ensemble. From 1863 to 1870 he was conductor of the Viennese balls, a post once held by his father. In 1872 he made sensational appearances in Boston and New York. All the while he was writing some of the most famous waltzes ever written, as well as quadrilles and polkas and other dance pieces. And in 1871, with the première in Vienna of *Indigo* he entered upon a new field, that of the operetta, in which once again he was to become a dominating figure. He was admired not merely by the masses but also by some of the greatest musicians of his generation—Brahms, Wagner, Verdi, Hans von Buelow, Offenbach, Goldmark, Gounod, all of whom expressed their admiration for his music in no uncertain terms. In 1894, Vienna celebrated the 50th anniversary of his debut with a week of festive performances; congratulations poured into Vienna from all parts of the civilized world. He died five years after that—in Vienna on June 3, 1899—and was buried near Schubert, Beethoven, and Brahms.

It is perhaps singularly fitting that Johann Strauss should have died in 1899. A century was coming to an end, and with it an entire epoch. This is what one court official meant when he said that "Emperor Francis Joseph reigned until the death of Johann Strauss." History, with its cold precision, may accurately record that the reign of Francis Joseph actually terminated in 1916. But its heyday had passed with the 19th century. The spirit of old Vienna, imperial Vienna of the Hapsburgs, the Vienna that had been inspiration for song and story, died with Johann Strauss. After 1900, Vienna was only a shadow of its former self, and was made prostrate by World War I.

If the epoch of "old Vienna" died with Johann Strauss, it was also born with him. After 1825, the social and intellectual climate in the imperial city changed perceptibly. The people, always gay, now gave themselves up to frivolity. For this, political conditions had been responsible. The autocratic rule of Francis I brought on tyranny, repression, and an army of spies and informers. As a result, the Viennese went in for diversions that were safe from a political point of view: flirtation, gossip, dancing. They were partial to light musical plays and novels. Thus, an attitude born out of expediency, became, with the passing of time, an inextricable part of everyday life in Vienna.

Of the many light-hearted pleasures in which the Viennese indulged none was dearer to them than dancing. It has been recorded that one out of every four in Vienna danced regularly. They danced the polka, and the quadrille; but most of all they danced the waltz.

Johann Strauss II was the genius of the Viennese waltz. More than anybody before him or since he lifted the popular dance to such artistic importance that his greatest waltzes are often performed at symphony concerts by the world's greatest orchestras under the foremost conductors. Inexhaustible was his invention; richly inventive, his harmonic writing; subtle and varied his gift at orchestration; fresh and personal his lyricism; aristocratic his structure. To the noted 20th century German critic, Paul Bekker, the Strauss waltz contained "more melodies than a symphony of Beethoven, and the aggregate of Straussian melodies is surely greater than the aggregate of Beethoven's."

Actually the waltz form used by Strauss is basically that of Lanner and of Strauss' own father. A slow symphonic introduction opens the waltz. This is followed by a series of waltz melodies (usually five in number). A symphonic coda serves both as a kind of summation and as a conclusion. But here the similarity with the past ends. This form received from the younger Strauss new dimension, new amplification. His introductions are sometimes like tone poems. The waltz melodies are incomparably rich in thought and feeling, varied in mood and style. A new concept of thematic developments enters waltz writing with Strauss. And his codas, as his introductions, are symphonic creations built with consummate skill from previously stated ideas, or fragments of these ideas. No wonder, then, that the waltzes of Johann Strauss have been described as "symphonies for dancing."

The following are the most popular of the Johann Strauss waltzes:

Acceleration (*Accelerationen*), op. 234, as the title indicates, derives its effect from the gradual acceleration in tempo in the main waltz melody. Strauss had promised to write a waltz for a ball at the Sofiensaal but failed to deliver his manuscript even at the zero hour. Reminded of his promise, he sat down at a restaurant table on the night of the ball and hurriedly wrote off the complete *Acceleration Waltz* on the back of a menu card, and soon thereafter conducted the première performance.

Artist's Life (Kuenstlerleben), op. 316, opens in a tender mood. A transition is provided by an alternation of soft and loud passages, after which the first waltz melody erupts zestfully as a tonal expression of the lighthearted gaiety of an artist's life. A similar mood is projected by the other waltz melodies.

The Blue Danube (An der schoenen blauen Donau), op. 314, is perhaps the most famous waltz ever written, and one of the greatest. It is now a familiar tale how Brahms, while autographing a fan of Strauss' wife, scribbled a few bars of this waltz and wrote underneath, "alas, not by Brahms." Strauss wrote *The Blue Danube* at the request of John Herbeck, conductor of the Vienna Men's Singing Society; thus the original version of the waltz is for chorus and orchestra, the text being a poem by Karl Beck in praise of Vienna and the Danube. Strauss wrote this waltz in 1867, and it was introduced on February 15 of the same year at the Dianasaal by Strauss' orchestra, supplemented by Herbeck's singing society. The audience was so enthusiastic that it stood on the seats and thundered for numerous repetitions. In the Spring of 1867, Strauss introduced his waltz to Paris at the International Exposition where it was a sensation. A tremendous ovation also greeted it when Strauss performed it for the first time in London, at Covent Garden in 1869. When Johann Strauss made his American debut, in Boston in 1872, he conducted *The Blue Danube* with an orchestra numbering a thousand instruments and a chorus of a thousand voices! Copies of the music were soon in demand in far-off cities of Asia and Australia. The publisher, Spina, was so deluged by orders he had to have a hundred new copper plates made from which to print over a million copies.

It is not difficult to see why this waltz is so popular. It is an eloquent voice of the "charm, elegance, vivacity, and sophistication" of 19th century Vienna—so much so that it is second only to Haydn's Austrian National Anthem as the musical symbol of Austria.

Emperor Waltz (Kaiserwalz), op. 437, was written in 1888 to celebrate the 40th anniversary of the reign of Franz Joseph I. This is one of Strauss' most beautiful waltzes. A slow introduction spanning seventy-four bars that has delicacy and grace, and is of a stately march-like character, is Viennese to its very marrow. A suggestion of the main waltz tune then appears quickly but is just as quickly dismissed by a loud return of the main introductory subject. Trombones lead to a brief silence. After some preparation, a waltz melody of rare majesty finally unfolds in the strings. If this wonderful waltz melody can be said to represent the Emperor himself then the delightful waltz tunes that follow—some of almost peasant character—can be said to speak for the joy of the Austrian people in honoring their beloved monarch. An elaborate coda then comes as the crown to the whole composition.

Morning Journals (Morgenblaetter), op. 279, was written for a Viennese press club, the Concordia. Offenbach had previously written for that club a set of waltzes entitled *"Evening Journals."* Strauss decided to name his music *Morning Journals*. The Offenbach composition is today remembered only because it provided the stimulus for Strauss' title. But Strauss' music remains—the four waltzes in his freshest and most infectious lyric vein, and its introduction highlighted by a melody of folk song simplicity.

Roses from the South (Rosen aus dem Sueden), op. 388, is a potpourri of the best waltz tunes (each a delight) from one of the composer's lesser operettas, *Spitzentuch der Koenigen (The Queen's Lace Handkerchief)*. The "south" in the title refers to Spain, the background of the operetta, but there is nothing Spanish to this unmistakably Viennese music.

Tales from the Vienna Woods (G'schichten aus dem Wiener Wald), op. 325—performed for the first time by the Strauss orchestra at the *Neue Welt* café in 1868—is a bucolic picture of Nature's beauty in the forests skirting Vienna. The beauty of Nature is suggested in the stately introduction with its open fifths and its serene melody for cello followed by a flute cadenza. All the loveliness of the Vienna woods is then represented by a waltz melody (originally scored for zither, but now most often presented by strings), a loveliness that is carried on with incomparable grace and charm by the ensuing waltz tunes.

Vienna Blood (Wiener Blut), op. 354, like so many other Strauss waltzes, is a hymn of praise to Strauss' native cities; but where other waltzes are light and carefree, this one is more often moody, dreamy, and at times sensual. After the introduction come four waltz melodies, the first full of fire and the last one touched with sentimentality. The second and third waltz tunes are interesting for their rhythmic vitality and marked syncopations.

Voices of Spring (Fruehlingsstimmen), op. 410—dedicated to the renowned Viennese pianist, Albert Gruenfeld—is (like the *Tales from the Vienna Woods*) an exuberant picture of the vernal season, the joy and thrill that the rebirth of Nature always provides to the Viennese.

Wine, Woman and Song (*Wein, Weib und Gesang*), op. 333, opens with an eloquent mood picture that is virtually an independent composition, even though it offers suggestions of later melodies. This is a spacious ninety-one bar introduction that serves as an eloquent peroration to the four waltz melodies that follow—each graceful, vivacious, and at times tender and contemplative. Richard Wagner, upon hearing Anton Seidl conduct this music, was so moved by it that at one point he seized the baton from Seidl's hand and conducted the rest of the piece himself.

Strauss wrote other dance music besides waltzes. He was equally successful in bringing his wonderful melodic invention, fine rhythmic sense, and beautiful instrumentation to the Polka, the native Bohemian dance in duple quick time and in a lively mood. The best of the Strauss polkas are: *Annen-Polka*, op. 117; *Electrophor Polka*, op. 297 dedicated to the students of a Vienna technical school, its effect derived from its breathless tempo and forceful dynamics; *Explosions Polka*, op. 43, written when Strauss was only twenty-two and characterized by sudden brief crescendos; *Pizzicato Polka*, written in collaboration with the composer's brother Josef, and, as the name indicates, an exercise in plucked strings; and the capricious *Tritsch-Tratsch* (or *Chit-Chat*) *Polka*, op. 214.

Of Strauss' other instrumental compositions, the best known is a lively excursion in velocity called *Perpetual Motion,* op. 257, which the composer himself described as a "musical jest."

Beyond being Vienna's waltz king, Johann Strauss II was also one of its greatest composers of operettas. Indeed, if a vote were to be cast for the greatest favorite among all Vienna operettas the chances are the choice would fall on Strauss' *Die Fledermaus* (*The Bat*), first produced in Vienna on April 5, 1874, book by Carl Haffner and Richard Genée based on a French play by Meilhac and Halévy. This work is not only a classic of the light theater, but even a staple in the repertory of the world's major opera houses. It is a piece of dramatic intrigue filled with clever, bright and at times risqué humor, as well as irony and gaiety. The plot, in line with operetta tradition, involves a love intrigue: between Rosalinda, wife of Baron von Eisenstein, and Alfred. The Baron is sought by the police for some slight indiscretion, and when they come to the Baron's home and find Alfred there, they mistake him for the Baron and arrest him. Upon discovering he is supposed to be in jail, the Baron decides to take full advantage of his liberty by attending a masked ball at Prince Orlovsky's palace and making advances there to the lovely women. But one of the masked women with whom he flirts is his own wife. Eventually, the identity of both is uncovered, to the embarrassment of the Baron, and this merry escapade ends when the Baron is compelled to spend his time in jail.

The overture is a classic, recreating the effervescent mood that prevails throughout the operetta. It is made up of some of the principal melodies of the opera: Rosalinda's lament, *"So muss allein ich bleiben"* first heard in the woodwind; the chorus, *"O je, o je, wie ruhrt mich dies"* in the strings; and most important of all, the main waltz of the operetta and the climax of the second act, also in the strings.

Other delightful episodes frequently presented in instrumental versions include the lovely drinking song, *"Trinke, Liebchen, trinke schnell";* the laughing song of the maid, Adele, *"Mein Herr Marquis";* the blood-warming czardas of the "Hungarian countess" who is actually Rosalinda in disguise, *"Klaenge der Heimat";* the stirring hymn to champagne, *"Die Majistaet wird anerkannt";* and the buoyant waltz, *"Du und du."*

The Gypsy Baron (Die Ziguenerbaron) is almost as popular as *Die Fledermaus.* This is an operetta with libretto by Ignaz Schnitzer, introduced in Vienna on October 24, 1885. Sandór Barinkay returns to his ancestral home after having left it as a child. He finds it swarming with gypsies who have made it their home, and he falls in love with one of them, Saffi.

The overture is made up of material from the concerted finales, beginning with the entrance of the gypsies in the first finale; continuing with Saffi's celebrated gypsy air, *"So elend und treu";* and culminating with the celebrated waltz music of the second act, the *Schatz,* or *Treasure,* waltzes.

Other familiar excerpts include Sandór's exuberant aria with chorus from the first act *"Ja, das alles auf Ehr,"* probably the most celebrated vocal excerpt from the entire operetta; and the *Entry March (Einzugmarsch)* from the third act—for chorus and orchestra in the operetta, but often given by salon ensembles in an orchestral version.

Josef Strauss

❧❧ ❦❦

JOSEF STRAUSS, like Eduard, is a younger brother of Johann Strauss II, and son of Johann Strauss I. He was born in Vienna on August 22, 1827. He was an extremely talented young man not only in music but even as architect and inventor. Of more serious and sober disposition than either of his two brothers, he long regarded café-house music condescendingly, his musical preference being for the classics. His famous brother, Johann Strauss II, needing someone to help him direct his orchestra, finally prevailed on Josef to turn to café-house music. Josef made his debut as café-house conductor and composer simultaneously on July 23, 1853, his first waltz being *Die Ersten*. After that he often substituted for brother Johann in directing the latter's orchestra in Vienna and on extended tours of Europe and Russia. Josef died in Vienna on July 21, 1870.

Josef Strauss wrote almost three hundred dance compositions. Though certainly less inspired than his brother, Johann, he was also far more important than Eduard. Josef's best waltzes have much of the lyrical invention, and the harmonic and instrumental invention of those by Johann Strauss II. Perhaps his greatest waltz is the *Dorfschwalben aus Oesterreich* (*Swallows from Austria*), op. 164, a nature portrait often interrupted by the chirping of birds. Here Josef's outpouring of the most sensitive lyricism and delicate moods is hardly less wondrous than that of Johann Strauss II. H. E. Jacob went so far as to say that "since Schubert's death there has been no such melody. It is in the realm of the Impromptus and Moments Musicaux. It breathes the sweet blue from which the swallows come."

Another Josef Strauss classic in three-quarter time is *Sphaerenklaenge* (*Music of the Spheres*), op. 285, equally remarkable for its spontaneous flow of unforgettable waltz tunes. Among Strauss' other delightful waltzes are the *Aquarellen*, op. 258; *Delirien*, op. 212; *Dynamiden*, op. 173; *Marienklaenge*, op. 214. A theme from *Dynamiden* waltzes was used by Richard Strauss in his famous opera *Der Rosenkavalier*.

In collaboration with his brother, Johann, Josef wrote the famous

Pizzicato Polka and several other pieces including the *Monstrequadrille* and *Vaterlandischer March*. With Johann and Eduard he wrote the *Schuetzenquadrille* and the *Trifolienwalzer*.

Sir Arthur Sullivan

SIR ARTHUR SEYMOUR SULLIVAN — musical half of the comic-opera team of Gilbert and Sullivan—was born in London, England, on May 13, 1842. The son of a bandmaster, Sullivan was appointed to the Chapel Royal School in 1854. One year after that his first published composition appeared, an anthem. In 1856 he was the first recipient of the recently instituted Mendelssohn Award which entitled him to attend the Royal Academy of Music where he studied under Sterndale Bennett and Goss. From 1858 to 1861 he attended the Leipzig Conservatory. After returning to London in 1862, he achieved recognition as a serious composer with several ambitious compositions including the *Irish Symphony*, a cello concerto, a cantata, and an oratorio. Meanwhile, in 1866, he had become professor of composition at the Royal Academy, and in 1867 he completed his first score in a light style, the comic opera *Cox and Box*, libretto by F. C. Burnand, which enjoyed a successful engagement in London.

In 1871, a singer introduced Sullivan to W. S. Gilbert, a one-time attorney who had attracted some interest in London as the writer of burlesques. An enterprising impresario, John Hollingshead of the Gaiety Theater, then was responsible for getting Gilbert and Sullivan to work on their first operetta. This was *Thespis,* produced in London in 1871, and a failure. It was several years before librettist and composer worked together again. When they did it was for a new impresario, Richard D'Oyly Carte, for whom they wrote a one-act comic opera, *Trial by Jury,* a curtain raiser to a French operetta which Carte was producing in London on March 25, 1875. *Trial by Jury*—a stinging satire on court trials revolving around a breach of promise suit—inaugurates the epoch of Gilbert and Sullivan. D'Oyly Carte now commissioned Gilbert and Sullivan to create a new full length comic opera for a company he had recently formed. The new light opera company made a successful bow with *The Sorcerer,* on November 17, 1877. *Pinafore,* a year later on May 25, 1878, made Gilbert and Sullivan a vogue and a passion both in London and in New York. In 1879 Gilbert and Sullivan came to the United States where on December 31 they introduced a new comic opera, *The Pirates of Penzance,* that took the country by storm. Upon returning to London, Gilbert and Sullivan opened a new theater built for them by D'Oyly Carte—the Savoy—with *Patience,* a tumultuous success on April 25, 1881. After that came *Iolanthe* (1882), *Princess Ida* (1884), *The Mikado* (1885), the *Yeomen of the Guard* (1888) and *The Gondoliers* (1889).

Gilbert and Sullivan came to the parting of the ways in 1890, the final rift precipitated by a silly argument over the cost of a carpet for the Savoy Theater. But the differences between them had long been deep rooted. An attempt to revive the partnership was made in 1893 with *Utopia Limited,* and again with *The Grand Duke* in 1896. Both comic operas were failures.

After 1893, Sullivan wrote a grand opera, *Ivanhoe,* and several operetta scores to librettists other than Sullivan. None of these were successful. During the last years of his life he suffered from deterioration of his health, and was almost always in acute pain. He died in London on November 22, 1900. Gilbert died eleven years after that.

Of Sullivan's other achievements in the field of music mention must be made of his importance as a conductor of the concerts of the London Philharmonic from 1885 to 1887, and of the Leeds Festival from 1880 to 1898. Between 1876 and 1881 he was principal of, and professor of composition at, the National Training School for Music. In recognition of his high estate in English music, he was the recipient of many honors. In 1878 he was made Chevalier of the Legion of Honor, and in 1883 he was knighted by Queen Victoria.

It is irony fitting for a Gilbert and Sullivan comic opera that the music on which Sullivan lavished his most fastidious attention and of which he was most proud has been completely forgotten (except for one or two minor exceptions). But the music upon which he looked with such condescension and self apology is that which has made him an immortal—in the theater if not in the concert world. For where Sullivan was heavy-handed, pretentious, and often stilted in his oratorios, serious operas, and orchestral compositions, he was consistently vital, fresh, personal, and vivacious in his lighter music. In setting Gilbert's lyrics to music, Sullivan was always capable of finding the musical *mot juste* to catch every nuance of Gilbert's wit and satire. So neatly, even inevitably, does the music fit the words that it is often difficult to think of one without the other. Like Gilbert, Sullivan was a master of parody and satire; he liked particularly to mock at the pretensions of grand opera, oratorio, and the sentimental ballad, pretensions of which he himself was a victim when he endeavored to work in those fields. Like Gilbert, he had a pen that raced with lightning velocity in the writing of patter music to patter verses. Sullivan, moreover, had a reservoir of melodies seemingly inexhaustible—gay tunes, mocking tunes, and tunes filled with telling sentiment—and he was able to adapt the fullest resources of his remarkable gift at harmony, rhythm and orchestration to the manifold demands of the stage. He was no man's imitator. Without having recourse to experimentation or unorthodox styles and techniques, his style and manners were so uniquely his that, as T. F. Dunhill has said, "his art is always recognizable. . . . The Sullivan touch is unmistakable and can be felt instantly."

Of the universality of the Gilbert and Sullivan comic operas, Isaac Goldberg wrote: "They [Gilbert and Sullivan] were not the rebels of an era, yet as surely they were not the apologists. Their light laughter carried a pleasant danger of its own that, without being the laughter of a Figaro, helped before the advent of a Shaw to keep the atmosphere clear. Transition figures they were, in an age of transition, caught between the personal independence of the artist and the social imperatives of their station. They did not cross over into the new day, though they served as a footbridge for others. Darwin gave them . . . only a song for *Princess Ida,* their melodious answer to the revolt of woman against a perfumed slavery; Swinburne and Wilde . . . characters for *Patience.* They chided personal foibles, and only indirectly social abuses. They were, after all, moralists not sociologists. It was in their natures; it was of their position. Yet something vital in them lives beyond their time. From their era of caste, of smug rectitude, of sanctimoniousness, they still speak to an age that knows neither corset nor petticoat, that votes with its women, and finds Freud insufficiently aphrodisiac. Perhaps it is because they chide individuals and not institutions that their work, so admirably held in solution by Sullivan's music, has lived through the most critical epoch in modern history since the French Revolution. For, underneath the cataclysmic changes of history remain the foibles that make us the fit laughter of the gods."

Overtures to and potpourris from the principal Gilbert and Sullivan comic operas are integral to the repertory of salon and pop orchestras everywhere. In all cases, the overture is made up of the opera's main melodies, and in most cases these overtures were written by others.

The Gondoliers was the last of the Gilbert and Sullivan comic operas to survive in the permanent repertory. It was produced on December 7, 1889. After the operatic pretension of the *Yeomen of the Guard* which had preceded it, *The Gondoliers* represented a welcome return by the authors to the world of paradox, absurdity, and confusion. It has aptly been described as a "farce of errors." The setting is Venice in the middle of the 18th century. The Duke and Duchess of Plaza-Toro come to Venice accompanied by their daughter, Casilda, and a drummer boy, Luiz, who loves her. In her childhood, Casilda had married the infant heir to the throne of Barataria. This heir had then been stolen and entrusted to the care of a gondolier who raised him as one of his two sons. In time the gondolier himself has forgotten which of his two boys is of royal blood. To complicate matters even further, the two gondolier boys, Marco and Giuseppe, are married. Thus it seems impossible to solve the problem as to who really is the heir to Barataria's throne and by the same token Casilda's husband. But when this problem is finally unscrambled it turns out that the heir is neither Marco nor Giuseppe, but none other than Luiz.

The following are the principal selections from *The Gondoliers:* Antonio's song, "For the Merriest Fellows Are We"; the duet of Marco and Giuseppe, "We're Called Gondolieri"; the autobiographical chant of the Duke of Plaza-Toro, "The Duke of Plaza-Toro"; the duet of Casilda and Luiz, "There Was a Time"; the song of the Grand Inquisitor, "I Stole the Prince"; Tessa's song, "When a Merry Maiden Marries"; the duet of Marco and Giuseppe, "For Everyone Who Feels Inclined"; Giuseppe's patter song, "Rising Early in the Morning"; Marco's serenade, "Take a Pair of Sparkling Eyes"; and the song of the Duchess, "On the Day that I was Wedded."

Iolanthe, introduced on November 25, 1882, carried Gilbert's love of paradox, confusion and absurdity into the fairy kingdom. To Isaac Goldberg, this comic opera, both as words and as music is "a peer among its kind. It is surprisingly complete. It is, indeed, of Gilbert and of Sullivan, all compact. The Gilbertian conflict between reality and fantasy is mirrored in details great and small—in scene, costume, in line, in gesture. . . . It would be difficult to find among the remaining thirteen comic operas one that reveals the collaborators playing so neatly into each other's hands—responding so closely to the conscious and unconscious demands of the reciprocal personality." The heroine, Iolanthe, is a fairy who has married a mortal and thus has been banished to the bottom of a stream by the Queen of her kingdom. But the Queen eventually forgives Iolanthe. Upon returning to her fairy kingdom, Iolanthe discovers she is the mother of a son, Strephon, who is half fairy and half mortal; and Strephon is in love with the mortal, Phyllis, who, in turn, is being pursued not only by her guardian, the Lord Chancellor, but even by the entire House of Peers. When Phyllis finds Strephon with Iolanthe she suspects him of infidelity, since she has no idea that Iolanthe is Strephon's mother. Immediately she begins to bestow her kindly glances upon two members of the House of Peers. Summoned for help, Iolanthe reveals that Strephon is, indeed, her son, and that his father is none other than the Lord Chancellor. By this time the other fairies of the kingdom have succumbed to the charms and appeal of the Peers. Iolanthe is saved from a second punishment when the Lord Chancellor helps change fairy law to read that any fairy *not* marrying a mortal is subject to death.

Leading numbers from *Iolanthe* include the following: the opening chorus of the fairies, "Tripping Hither, Tripping Thither"; Strephon's song, "Good Morrow, good Mother"; the love duet of Phyllis and Strephon, "Thou the Tree and I the Flower"; Entrance, chorus, and march of the Peers, "Loudly Let the Trumpet Bray" followed immediately by the Lord Chancellor's monologue, "The Law is the True Embodiment"; the Lord Chancellor's personal credo, "When I Went to the Bar"; the song of Willis, the sentry, "When All Night Long a Chap Remains"; Lord Mount Arrat's chauvinistic hymn, "When Britain Really Ruled the Waves"; the Fairy Queen's song, "Oh, Foolish Fay"; the Lord Chancellor's patter song about a nightmare, "When You're Lying Awake"; the trio of the Lord Chancellor, Mount Ararat and Tolloler, "If You Go In"; Strephon's song, "Fold Your Flapping Wings"; and the finale, "Soon as We May."

The Mikado was a sensation when first performed in London on March 14, 1885; and with many it is still the favorite of all Gilbert and Sullivan comic operas. By 1900, it had received over one thousand performances in London and five thousand in the United States. Since then these figures have multiplied. It has been adapted for motion pictures, and in New York it has been given in two different jazz versions (*The Hot Mikado* and *Swing Mikado*). In 1960 it was presented over television with Groucho Marx as the Lord High Executioner.

In its own day much of its appeal was due to its exotic setting of Japan and strange Japanese characters. Such a novelty for the English stage was the strong spice that endowed the play with much of its succulent flavor. Gilbert's inspiration had been a miniature Japanese village set up in the Knightsbridge section of London which aroused and stimulated the interest of the English people in all things Japanese. Gilbert was one of those who became fascinated by this Oriental exhibit, and his fascination led him to conceive a comic opera with a Japanese background.

But while the Japanese are certainly no longer curiosities in the theater—have, indeed, become a vogue on Broadway since the end of World War II—*The Mikado* has never lost its tremendous popularity. For *The Mikado* represents Gilbert and Sullivan at their creative peak. The whimsical characters, absurd situations, the savage malice of the wit and satire, and the strange and paradoxical deviations of the plot find Gilbert at the height of his whimsical imagination and skill; and at every turn, Sullivan was there with music that captured every subtle echo of Gilbert's fancy.

The thought of having to marry the unattractive Katisha proves so distasteful to Nanki-Poo, son of the Mikado, that he puts on the disguise of a wandering minstrel and flees. After coming to the town of Titipu, he meets and falls in love with Yum-Yum who, in turn, is being sought after by her own guardian, Ko-Ko, the Lord High Executioner. The Lord High Executioner faces a major problem. The ruler of Japan has sent a message to Titipu stating that since no execution has taken place there for many years the office of Lord High Executioner will be abolished if somebody is not executed shortly. When Ko-Ko discovers that Nanki-Poo is about to commit suicide, rather than live without Yum-Yum, he finds a solution to his own problem. Ko-Ko is willing to allow Nanki-Poo to marry Yum-Yum and live with her for a month if at the end of that time he allows himself to be beheaded. The wedding takes place, but before the beheading can be consummated the Mikado arrives on the scene with Katisha. Only then is the discovery made in Titipu that Nanki-Poo is the Mikado's son and that anyone responsible for his death must boil in oil. The news that Nanki-Poo is alive saves Ko-Ko from this terrible fate; but he soon confronts another in the form of Katisha, whom he must now marry to compensate her for her loss of Nanki-Poo.

Many of the excerpts from *The Mikado* are known to anyone who has ever heard or whistled a tune. These are the most significant: the opening chorus of the Japanese nobles, "If You Want to Know Who We Are"; Nanki-Poo's self-introductory ballad, "A Wandering Minstrel I"; Pish-Tush's description of the Mikado's decree against flirtation, "Our Great Mikado"; Ko-Ko's famous patter song, "I've Got a Little List"; the song of Yum-Yum's companions, "Three Little Maids"; the affecting duet of Nanki-Poo and Yum-Yum, "Were You Not to Ko-Ko Plighted"; Yum-Yum's radiant song, "The Sun Whose Rays"; Ko-Ko's allegorical song, "Tit Willow"; the madrigal of Yum-Yum, Pitti Sing, Nanki-Poo and Pish Tush, "Brightly Dawns Our Wedding Day"; the sprightly trio of Yum-Yum, Nanki-Poo and Ko-Ko, "Here's a How-de-do"; the song of the Mikado, "My Object All Sublime"; the duet of Nanki-Poo and Ko-Ko, "The Flowers That Bloom in the Spring."

Patience in 1881 directed its well aimed satirical pricks and barbs at the pre-Raphaelite movement in England with its fetish for simplicity and naturalness; and with equal accuracy at poets and esthetes like Oscar Wilde and Algernon Swinburne, leaders of an esthetic movement that encouraged postures, poses, and pretenses. Twenty maidens are turned into esthetes through their common love for the "fleshly poet" Bunthorne. Because of this love they hold in disdain their former sweethearts, the officers of the Heavy Dragoon. Bunthorne, however, is in love with the simple, unselfish milkmaid Patience, who dotes after the idyllic poet of heavenly beauty, Grosvenor. Since Patience is unselfish she cannot hope to win Grosvenor's love, for to be loved by one so beautiful is the most selfish thing in the world. She decides to accept Bunthorne. Now the twenty love-sick maidens fall in love with Grosvenor and through his influence abandon estheticism for simplicity. Unaware of this new direction in their loved ones, the Dragoons desert their uniforms for esthetic garb, substitute their former practical everyday behavior for extravagant postures and poses. Weary of the demands made upon him by the doting maids, Grosvenor (with a push from Bunthorne) becomes commonplace. But, unfortunately for Bunthorne, since it is no longer selfish to be loved by a commonplace man, Patience returns to Grosvenor. The maidens, now interested in the commonplace, can now return to their Dragoons. But poor Bunthorne is left alone with nothing but a lily in his hand to console him.

The following are the principal selections from *Patience:* the opening female chorus, "Twenty Lovesick Maidens We"; Patience' simple query about the nature of love, "I Cannot Tell What This Love May Be"; the chorus of the Dragoons, "The Soldiers of Our Queen" followed immediately by the Colonel's patter song, "If You Want a Receipt"; Bunthorne's recipe for success in the business of being an esthete, "If You're Anxious For to Shine"; Grosvenor's duet with Patience, "Prithee, Pretty Maiden"; Jane's soliloquy, "Silvered is the Raven Hair" with which the second act opens; Grosvenor's fable to the lovesick maidens, "The Magnet and the Churn"; Patience's ballad, "Love is a Plaintive Song"; and the gay duet of Bunthorne and Grosvenor, "When I Go Out of Doors."

Pinafore was the first of the successful Gilbert and Sullivan comic operas in which we encounter that strange topsy-turvy world over which Gilbert and Sullivan ruled; that we confront the accidents, coincidences, paradoxes, and mishaps that beset its hapless inhabitants. *Pinafore* is a devastating satire on the Admiralty in general and William H. Smith, its First Lord, in particular. But it also makes a mockery of social position. Ralph Rackstraw, a humble seaman, is in love with Josephine, daughter of Captain Corcoran, commanding officer of the *H.M.S. Pinafore*. But the first Lord of the Admiralty, Sir Joseph Porter, is also in love with her. Since Josephine's father would never consent to have his daughter marry one so lowly as Ralph, the lovers decide to elope. But the plans are overheard by the seaman, Dick Deadeye, who reports them to the Captain with the result that Ralph is put in irons. An impasse is thus reached until Little Buttercup, a "Portsmouth Bumboat woman," reveals an incident of the distant past. Entrusted the care of two infants she mixed them up with the result that the lowly born child, Corcoran, was mistaken for the one of high station and was thus able to rise to the station of Captain; but the child of high station believed to have been of lowly origin, Ralph, had been forced to become a seaman. By order of Sir Joseph, Ralph now becomes the master of the ship and can claim Josephine as his bride. The proud Captain, now reduced to a seaman, must content himself with Little Buttercup.

Pinafore was a sensation when introduced in London in 1878, enjoying seven hundred consecutive performances. But it proved even more sensational in the United States, following its première there at the Boston Museum on November 25 of the same year. Ninety different companies presented this comic opera throughout the country in that first season, with five different companies operating simultaneously in New York. *Pinafore* was given by colored groups, children's groups, and religious groups. It was widely parodied. Some of its catch phrases ("What never? No never!" and "For he himself has said it") entered American *argot*.

As a bountiful source of popular melodies, the score of *Pinafore* is second only in importance to that of *The Mikado*. Here are the main ones: the opening chorus of the sailors, "We Sail the Ocean Blue"; Buttercup's forthright self-introduction, "I'm Called Little Buttercup"; Ralph's madrigal, "The Nightingale," and ballad, "A Maiden Fair to See"; the Captain's colloquy with his crew, "I Am the Captain of the *Pinafore*"; Josephine's poignant ballad, "Sorry Her Lot"; Sir Joseph's exchange with his sisters, cousins, and aunts, "I am the Monarch of the Sea," and his autobiographical, "When I Was a Lad"; the Captain's sad reflection, "Fair Moon to Thee I Sing"; the choral episode, "Carefully on Tip-Toe Stealing" followed by the tongue-in-the-cheek paean to England and Englishmen, "He Is an Englishman."

The Pirates of Penzance was the only Gilbert and Sullivan comic opera to receive its world première outside England. This took place in New York at the Fifth Avenue Theater in 1879. (There was a single hastily prepared performance in Paignon, England, on December 30, 1879 but this is not regarded as an official première.) The reason why *The Pirates* was introduced in New York was due to the presence there of its authors. Numerous pirated versions of *Pinafore* were then being given throughout the United States in about a hundred theaters, and Gilbert and Sullivan decided to come to America for the dual purpose of exploring the conditions under which they might protect their copyright and to offer an authorized version of their opera. In coming to the United States, they brought with them the manuscript of their new work, *The Pirates of Penzance,* and arranged to have its première take place in New York.

The Pirates of Penzance is a blood relative of *Pinafore*. Where *Pinafore* made fun of the British Navy, *The Pirates* concentrates on the British Army and constabulary. In *Pinafore* two babies are mixed up in the cradle for a confusion of their identities; in *The Pirates* it is the future professions of babies which are confounded in the cradle. In *Pinafore* the secret is divulged by Buttercup, in *The Pirates* by Ruth. *Pinafore* boasts a female chorus of cousins, sisters and aunts while *The Pirates* has a female chorus made up of the Major General's daughters.

The hero is young Frederic, apprenticed to a band of pirates by his nurse Ruth, who mistakes the word "pilot" for "pirate." Frederic falls in love with Mabel, one of the many daughters of Major General Stanley and looks forward eagerly to his freedom from his apprenticeship to the pirate band, which arrives on his twenty-first birthday. But Frederic discovers that since he was born on leap year the year of his freedom—his twenty-first *birthday*—is many, many years off; that by the calendar he is still only a little boy of five. As a pirate he must join his confederates in exterminating Mabel's father and the constables attending him. But all turns out happily when the pirates actually prove to be ex-noblemen, and are thus found highly acceptable as husbands for the daughters of Major General Stanley. The Major General is also in favor of the union of Mabel and Frederic.

The following are the leading musical selections: the opening chorus of the pirates, "Pour, Oh Pour, the Pirate Sherry"; the Pirate king's hymn to his profession, "For I am a Pirate King"; the chorus of the Major General's daughters, "Climbing Over Rocky Mountain"; Frederic's plaintive plea for a lover, "Oh, Is There Not One Maiden Breast"; the Major General's autobiographical patter song, "I Am the Very Pattern of a Modern Major General"; the rousing chorus of the constabulary, "When the Foeman Bares His Steel"; the tripping trio of Ruth, Fred and the Pirate King on discovering Fred is only a child of five, "A Paradox, a Most Ingenious Paradox"; Mabel's haunting ballad, "Oh, Leave Me Not to Pine"; the Police Sergeant's commentary on his profession, "When a Felon's Not Engaged in His Employment"; the Pirates' chorus, "Come Friends Who Plough the Sea," a melody expropriated by an American, Theodore Morse, for the lyric "Hail, Hail the Gang's All Here"; and the General's idyllic ballad, "Sighing Softly To the River."

Ruddigore, a travesty on melodrama, was first performed on January 22, 1887. Because the Murgatroyd family has persecuted witches, an evil spirit had fated it to commit a crime a day. Ruthven Murgatroyd tries to flee from this curse by assuming the identity of simple Robin Oakapple. He meets and falls in love with Rose who is being sought after by Ruthven's foster brother, Richard. Since Ruthven as Robin Oakapple has the upper hand with Rose, Richard avenges himself by revealing the fact that his brother is really a member of the Murgatroyd family and like all of them is the victim of the ancient family curse. Back in his ancestral home, Ruthven must fulfil his quota of crimes, a job he bungles so badly that his ancestors suddenly come alive out of the picture frames on the wall, to condemn him. But after numerous convolutions of typically Gilbertian logic and reasoning, the curse is broken and Ruthven can live happily with his beloved Rose.

From *Ruddigore* come the following familiar sections: the opening chorus of the bridesmaids, "Fair Is Rose as the Bright May Day"; Hannah's legend, "Sir Rupert Murgatroyd"; Rose's ballad, "If Somebody There Chanced to Be"; the extended duet of Robin and Rose, "I Know a Youth Who Loves a Little Maid"; Richard's ballad, "I Shipped, D'ye See, in a Revenue Sloop"; Robin's song, "My Boy You May Take it From Me"; the chorus of the bridesmaids, "Hail the Bride of Seventeen Summers" followed by Rose's madrigal, "Where the Buds Are Blossoming"; the duet of Robin and Adam, "I Once Was As Meek as a New Born Lamb"; Rose's ballad, "In Bygone Days"; the chorus of the family portraits, "Painted Emblems of a Race"; Sir Roderic's patter song, "When the Night Wind Howls"; and Hannah's ballad, "There Grew a Little Flower."

The Sorcerer, the first successful Gilbert and Sullivan comic opera, was introduced in 1877. Alexis, in love with Aline, wishes to spread around the blessings of love. For this purpose he enlists the cooperation of John Wellington Wells, the creator of a love brew. In an effort to perpetuate Aline's love for him, Alexis has her drink this potion, only to discover that his beloved has fallen for the vicar, Dr. Daly, he being the first man she sees after drinking the draught. Since Alexis is not the only one to suffer from this now-general epidemic of loving, a serious effort must be made to offset the effects of this magic: a human sacrifice. Naturally that sacrifice becomes none other than John Wellington Wells who is driven to self immolation before things can once again be set normal.

The music of *The Sorcerer* is not so well known as that of the other famous comic operas, but it does contain several Gilbert and Sullivan delights. Among them are: the song with which Wells introduces himself and his black art, "Oh! My Name Is John Wellington Wells," the first of the Gilbert and Sullivan patter songs; the vicar's haunting ballad, "Time Was When Love and I Were Well Acquainted"; and the romantic duet of Aline and Alexis, "It Is Not Love."

In the *Yeomen of the Guard,* produced on October 3, 1888, the topsy-turvy world of Gilbert and Sullivan is temporarily sidestepped for another of operatic pretensions. Of all the Gilbert and Sullivan plays this one comes closest to resembling an opera. The immediate stimulus for the writing of the text came to Gilbert from an advertisement in a railway station depicting a Beefeater. Out of this acorn grew the oak of Gilbert's play in which Colonel Charles Fairfax is falsely accused by his kinsman, Poltwhistle, of sorcery. For this he must be condemned to death in the Tower of London. Since Fairfax is not married, his fortune will pass on to his accuser. But Charles thwarts such evil designs by marrying Elsie Maynard, a strolling player—if only for an hour. Then he manages to escape from the Tower disguised as a yeoman of the guard. When the execution is to take place there is no victim. Eventually, a reprieve enables Charles to live permanently with Elsie.

The most important selections from the *Yeomen of the Guard* are: Phoebe's song with which the opera opens, "When Maiden Loves"; the chorus of the yeomen, "In the Autumn of Our Life"; Fairfax' ballad, "Is Life a Boon?"; the extended duet of Point and Elsie, "I Have a Song to Sing, O"; Phoebe's ballad, "Were I Thy Bride"; Point's patter song, "Oh, a Private Buffoon Is a Light-Hearted Loon"; the quartet of Elsie, Fairfax, Dame Carruthers and Meryll, "Strange Adventure"; the trio of Fairfax, Elsie and Phoebe, "A Man Who Would Woo a Fair Maid"; the quartet of Elsie, Fairfax, Phoebe and Point, "When a Wooer, Goes a-Wooing"; and the finale, "Oh, Thoughtless Crew."

Besides his music for the comic operas there exists a vast repertory of serious music by Sullivan. Of this hardly more than two songs have retained their popularity. One is "The Lost Chord," lyric by Adelaide Proctor, written by Sullivan in December 1876 at the deathbed of his brother, Fred. From Charles Willeby we get an account of how this deeply moving piece of music came itno being: "For nearly three weeks he watched by his bedside night and day. One night—the end was not very far off then—while his sick brother had for a time fallen into a peaceful sleep, and he was sitting as usual by the bedside, he chanced to come across some verses by Adelaide Proctor with which he had some five years previously been struck. He had then tried to set them to music, but without satisfaction to himself. Now in the stillness of the night he read them over again, and almost as he did so, he conceived their musical equivalent. A stray sheet of music paper was at hand, and he began to write. Slowly the music took shape, until, becoming quite absorbed in it, he determined to finish the song. Even if in the cold light of day it were to prove worthless, it would at least have helped to while away the hours of watching. So he worked on at it. As he progressed, he felt sure this was what he had sought for, and failed to find on the occasion of his first attempt to set the words. In a short time it was complete and not long after in the publisher's hands. Thus was written "The Lost Chord," perhaps the most successful song of modern times."

"Onward Christian Soldiers," words by Sabine Baring-Gould, is the most celebrated of Sullivan's more than fifty religious hymns. It is effective not merely for its religious mood but also for its martial spirit. "The music," says Isaac Goldberg, "has the tread of armies in it, and a broad diatonic stride." Sullivan wrote it in 1873 upon being appointed editor of the *Hymnal,* a collection of hymns published by Novello for the Society for the Promotion of Christian Knowledge and the Hymnary.

Franz von Suppé

❦❦ ❦❦

FRANZ VON SUPPÉ was born Francesco Suppé-Demelli in Spalato, Yugoslavia, on April 18, 1819. He played the flute at eleven, at thirteen started the study of harmony, and at fifteen completed a Mass. Nevertheless, for a while he entertained the idea of becoming either a physician or a teacher of Italian. When he finally decided upon music as a profession he attended the Vienna Conservatory. After serving an apprenticeship as conductor of operettas in Pressburg and Baden, he was appointed principal conductor at Theater-an-der-Wien in Vienna. In 1862 he assumed a similar post with the Karlstheater, and from 1865 until his death at the Leopoldstadttheater. While absorbing the influence and traditions of the opéra-bouffe of Offenbach, he began writing operettas of his own in a style uniquely his, setting and establishing many of the traditions and clichés which would henceforth identify the Viennese operetta. He had an unusual gift for light, caressing tunes, a gay and infectious spirit, and a direct emotional appeal. His first operetta was *Jung lustig in alter traurig* in 1841. Success came with his incidental music to *Poet and Peasant (Dichter und Bauer),* introduced on August 24, 1846; its overture is still his best known composition and a classic in the musical literature in a lighter vein. A succession of popular operettas, over twenty-five in number, made him one of Europe's most celebrated composers for the stage. His most famous operettas were: *Das Maedchen vom Lande* (1847), *Die schoene Galatea,* or *Beautiful Galathea* (1865), *Leichte Cavallerie,* or *Light Cavalry* (1866), *Fatinitza* (1876), *Boccaccio* (1879), and *Donna Juanita* (1880). Suppé died in Vienna on May 21, 1895.

The overture to *The Beautiful Galathea* (*Die schoene Galatea*) opens with brisk music. Horns and woodwind lead into an extended portrayal of exaltated character by strings. Once again horns and woodwind appear, this time providing a transition to a caressing melody that soon develops into a fulsome song. After a theatrical passage, the overture's main melody is heard in the strings, with harmonies filled in by the woodwind; this is a graceful dance tune which, towards the end of the overture, is repeated with harmonic and tonal amplitude by the full orchestra.

The *Light Cavalry* Overture (*Leichte Cavallerie*) is, as its name indicates, stirring music of martial character. Horn calls and forceful chords in full orchestra provide at once the military character of this music. A vivacious tune for the violins follows this forceful introduction after which comes the brisk melody for woodwind followed by the full orchestra that has made this overture so famous; the gallop of the cavalry is here simulated in a brisk rhythm. The agitation is dissipated by a sensitive transition in strings and clarinet to a spacious melody in strings in a sensual Hungarian style. The brisk military music and the open horning calls then give the overture a dynamic conclusion.

Morning, Noon and Night in Vienna (*Ein Morgen, ein Mittag ein Abend in Wien*) is one of the composer's famous concert overtures. A dramatic introduction—with forceful chords in full orchestra—leads to a beautiful and fully realized song for solo cello against plucked strings, one of Suppé's most inspired flights of melody. The song ended, the dramatic opening is recalled to serve as a transition to two buoyant and graceful Viennese tunes in the strings, the second repeated vigorously and amplified by full orchestra. The overture ends in a robust rather than lyrical vein.

The *Pique Dame* (*Queen of Spades*) Overture begins with a murmuring passage for strings that grows in volume and changes character before an expressive melody unfolds in lower strings against an accompanying figure borrowed from the opening passage. A vigorous interlude of strong chords and a vigorous pronouncement by the brass lead into the most famous theme of the composition, a vivacious and jaunty melody for strings and woodwind. This subject is developed at some length before a melodic episode is offered by the lower strings as a preface to a soft, idyllic interlude for the woodwind. The conclusion of the overture is in a vigorous manner with an energetic restatement of earlier thematic material.

Of all the Suppé overtures, whether for the stage or the concert hall, the most famous undoubtedly is the *Poet and Peasant* (*Dichter und Bauer*). After a stately introduction there arrives a gentle song for the strings. This is succeeded by a more robust theme. The main melody of the overture is a pulsating melody in 3⁄8 time. Indicative of the enormous popularity of this overture in all parts of the world is that it has been adapted for almost sixty different combinations of instruments.

Johan Svendsen

JOHAN SVENDSEN was born in Oslo, Norway, on September 30, 1840. The son of a bandmaster, he dabbled in music for many years before receiving formal instruction. When he was twenty-three he embarked for the first time on a comprehensive musical education by attending the Leipzig Conservatory where he was a pupil of Ferdinand David, Reinecke, and others. After that he toured Europe as a concert violinist and lived for a while in Paris where he played in theater orchestras. In 1870 he visited the United States where he married an American woman whom he had originally met in Paris. Following his return to his native land he was the conductor of the Christiana Musical Association from 1872 to 1877 and again from 1880 to 1883. In 1883 he settled in Copenhagen where for sixteen years he was court conductor, and part of that time conductor at the Royal Theater as well. As a composer Svendsen distinguished himself with major works for orchestra in a pronounced Norwegian style, the most famous being four Norwegian Rhapsodies and the *Carnaval des artistes norvégiens,* in all of which Norwegian folk melodies are used extensively. He also produced many works not of a national identity, among which were symphonies, concertos, chamber-music works, and the highly popular *Carnival in Paris,* for orchestra. Svendsen died in Copenhagen on June 14, 1911.

The Carnival in Paris (*Carnaval à Paris*), for orchestra, op. 9 (1873) is one of Svendsen's best-known works, even though it is not in his characteristic Norwegian style. His early manhood in Paris had been one of the composer's happiest experiences in life, and some of that joy and feeling of excitement is found in this music describing a Mardi Gras in Paris. The full orchestra enters after a swelling trumpet tone over drum rolls. There is then heard an exchange among the wind instruments and a quickening of the tempo to lead into the first main theme, a delicate subject for flutes and clarinets. This theme is twice repeated after which the music becomes stormy. Divided violins then bring on the second theme, which like the first is quiet and gentle. In the development, in which much is made of the first subject, there are effective frequent alternations of tempo. A rhapsodic section, with a subject for divided strings, followed by extended drum rolls and calls for muted horns, precede the concluding section.

Deems Taylor

JOSEPH DEEMS TAYLOR was born in New York City on December 22, 1885. He received his academic education in New York, at the Friends School, Ethical Culture School, and New York University. All the while he studied music with private teachers. Following his graduation from college, Taylor appeared in vaudeville, worked for several magazines, and from 1921 to 1925 was the music critic of the New York *World*. He first distinguished himself as a composer in 1919 with the orchestral suite, *Through the Looking Glass*. In 1925 he resigned from the *World* to concentrate on composition. In the next half dozen years he completed two operas, each successfully performed at the Metropolitan Opera: *The King's Henchman* (with libretto by Edna St. Vincent Millay) in 1927, and *Peter Ibbetson* in 1931. Since 1927, Taylor has followed several careers besides that of one of America's most important serious composers. He was editor of *Musical America*, music critic for the *New York American*, master of ceremonies on radio and television, program annotator, intermission commentator for broadcasts of opera and orchestral music, and author of several best-selling books on music. A highly sophisticated composer with a consummate technical skill, Taylor's works are not for popular consumption. But he did write one composition in a popular style, *Circus Day;* and a second of his works, *Through the Looking Glass,* while intended for symphonic concerts, has enough wit and charm to fall gracefully into the semi-classical category.

Circus Day is a fantasy for orchestra, op. 18 (1925) written on commission from Paul Whiteman and his Orchestra. When Whiteman and his orchestra introduced it that year, the work was orchestrated by Ferde Grofé, but since then Taylor has prepared his own symphonic adaptation. Subtitled "eight pictures from memory" this fantasy strives "to convey one's early impressions of a day at the circus." The composer has provided his own program notes for the eight movements. The first, entitled "Street Parade," describes the circus parade as it "passes on down the street." "The playing of the band grows fainter and dies away in the distance. "The Big Tops" tells in musical terms about "peanuts, popcorn, pink lemonade, bawling side-show barkers." This is followed by "Bareback Riders." "As the ringmaster cracks his whip, the riders perform the miraculous feats . . . that make horseback riders the objects of such awe and admiration." The fourth movement is in three parts. The first is devoted to "The Lion's Cage." "The roar of the lions is blood curdling, but they go through their tricks with no damage to any of us." The second speaks about "The Dog and the Monkey Circus." "Into the ring dash a whole kennel full of small dogs guised as race horses, ridden by monkeys dressed as jockeys." In the third, we get a picture of "The Waltzing Elephants." "The great beasts solemnly waltz to a tune that is a pachydermous version of the theme of the bareback riders." In the fifth movement, "Tight-Rope Walker," the performer "balances his parasol; he pirouettes and slips and slides as he makes his perilous way along the taut wire." "The Jugglers," in the sixth movement, "juggle little balls and big ones, knives, dishes, hats, lighted candles. . . ." Even the orchestra is seized by the contagion and finally juggles its main theme, keeping three versions of it in the air. In "Clowns," two of them "come out to play us a tune. . . . Finally, after a furious argument, the entire clown band manages to play the tune through, amid applause." The finale, the composer goes on to explain, "might better be called 'Looking Back.' For the circus is over, and we are back at home, trying to tell a slightly inattentive family what we saw and heard. The helpful orchestra evokes recollections of jugglers, clowns, bareback riders, tight-rope walkers, trained animals."

Through the Looking Glass, a suite for orchestra (1919) is a musical setting of episodes from Lewis Carroll's delightful tale of the same name. Taylor's suite is in four movements, for which he has provided his own program. The first movement, "Dedication; The Garden of Live Flowers," consists of "a simple song theme, briefly developed," which leads immediately to the brisk music of "The Garden of Live Flowers." In the second movement, "Jabberwocky," the theme of the frightful beast, the Jabberwock, "is first announced by the full orchestra. The clarinet then begins the tale [with] the battle with the monsters recounted in a short and rather repellant fugue." The third movement, "Looking Glass Insects" tells of "the vociferous *diptera* that made such an impression on Alice—the Bee-elephant, the Gnat, the Rockinghorse fly, and the Bread-and-butter fly." The last movement, "The White Knight" has two themes. "The first is a sort of instrumental prance, being the knight's own conception of himself as a slashing daredevil. The second is bland, mellifluous, a little sentimental—much more like the knight as he really was."

Peter Ilitch Tchaikovsky

PETER ILITCH TCHAIKOVSKY was born in Votkinsk, Russia, on May 7, 1840. Serious music study began comparatively late, since he prepared for a career in law and then for three years served as clerk in the Ministry of Justice. He had, however, revealed unusual sensitivity for music from earliest childhood, and had received some training on the piano from the time he was five. Intensive music study, however, did not begin until 1861 when he became a pupil of Nicholas Zaremba, and it was completed at the St. Petersburg Conservatory. His professional career began in 1865, the year in which he was appointed professor of harmony at the newly founded Moscow Conservatory. This was also the year when one of his compositions was performed for the first time: *Characteristic Dances,* for orchestra, introduced by Johann Strauss II in Pavlovsk, Russia. Tchaikovsky's first symphony was introduced in Moscow in 1868; his first opera, *The Voivoda,* in Moscow in 1869; and his first masterwork—the orchestral fantasy *Romeo and Juliet*—in Moscow in 1870. During the next half dozen years he reached maturity as composer with the completion of his second and third symphonies, first two string quartets, famous Piano Concerto No. 1, and the orchestral fantasy, *Francesca da Rimini.*

In 1877, Tchaikovsky embarked precipitously on a disastrous marriage with Antonina Miliukova. He did not love her, but was flattered by her adoration of his music. In all probability he regarded this marriage as a convenient cloak with which to conceal his sexual aberration which was already causing some talk in Moscow and of which he was heartily ashamed. In any event, this marriage proved a nightmare from the beginning. Always hypersensitive, he now became a victim of mental torment which led him to try suicide. Failing that, he fled from his wife to find refuge in his brother's house where he collapsed physically. For a year after that he traveled about aimlessly in Europe.

This strange relationship with his wife was followed by another one, even more curious and unorthodox, with the woman whom he admired and loved above all others. She was the wealthy patroness and widow, Nadezhda von Meck, with whom he maintained a friendship lasting thirteen years. But during all that time he never once met her personally, their friendship being developed through an exchange of often tender at times even passionate letters. She had written him to speak of her admiration for his music and he had replied in gratitude. Before long, she endowed him with a generous annual subsidy to allow him full freedom to write music. From then on, they wrote each other frequently, with Tchaikovsky often baring his heart and soul. The reason why they never met was that Mme. von Meck had firmly established that condition for the continuation of their friendship and her financial generosity. Why this strange request was made, and why she adhered to it so tenaciously, has never been adequately explained. She may have been influenced by their different stations in life, or by her excessive devotion to her children, or even by a knowledge of the composer's sexual deviation.

Now financially independent—and strengthened by the kindness, affection and sympathy of his patroness—Tchaikovsky entered upon one of his richest creative periods by producing one masterwork after another:

the fourth and fifth symphonies, the opera, *Eugene Onegin;* the violin concerto; the *Capriccio italien,* for orchestra; a library of wonderful songs. Inevitably he now assumed a rank of first importance in Russian music. In 1884 he was honored by the Czar with the Order of St. Vladimir, and in 1888 a life pension was conferred upon him by the Russian government.

In 1890, while traveling in the Caucasus, Tchaikovsky heard from Mme. von Meck that she had recently suffered financial reverses and was compelled to terminate her subsidy. The composer replied that he was no longer in need of her financial help but that he hoped their friendship might continue. To this, and to all subsequent letters by Tchaikovsky, Mme. von Meck remained silent. Upon returning to Moscow, Tchaikovsky discovered that his patroness was in no financial difficulties whatsoever, but had used this as an excuse to terminate a relationship of which she had grown weary. The loss of his dearest friend, and the specious reason given for the termination of their relationship, was an overwhelming blow, one largely responsible for the fits of melancholia into which Tchaikovsky lapsed so frequently from this time on.

In 1891, Tchaikovsky paid his only visit to the United States where he helped open Carnegie Hall in New York by directing a performance of his own *Overture 1812.* After returning to Russia, he became so morbid, and succumbed so helplessly to fits of despair, that at times he thought he was losing his mind. In such a mood he wrote his last symphony, the *Pathétique,* one of the most tragic utterances in all music; there is good reason to believe that when Tchaikovsky wrote this music he was creating his own requiem. He died in St. Petersburg on November 6, 1893, a victim of cholera contracted when he drank a glass of boiled water during an epidemic.

The qualities in his major serious works that made Tchaikovsky one of the best loved and most frequently performed composers in the world are also the traits that bring his lesser works into the permanent semi-classical repertory: an endless fund of beautiful melody; an affecting sentiment that at times lapses into sentimentality; a lack of inhibitions in voicing his deepest emotions and most personal thoughts.

The *Andante Cantabile* is a gentle, melancholy song in three-part form which comes from one of the composer's string quartets, in D major, op. 11 (1871). This is the second movement of the quartet, and the reason why this work as a whole is still occasionally performed. This famous melody, however, is not original with the composer, but a quotation of a Russian folk song, "Vanya Sat on the Divan," which the composer heard a baker sing in Kamenka, Russia. Tchaikovsky himself adapted this music for orchestra. In 1941, this melody was adapted into the American popular song, "On the Isle of May."

Chanson Triste is another of the composer's soft, gentle melodies that is filled with sentiment. This is the second of twelve children's pieces for the piano "of moderate difficulty," op. 40 (1876–1877).

Humoresque, op. 10, no. 2 (1871)—a "humoresque" being an instrumental composition in a whimsical vein—finds Tchaikovsky in a less familiar attitude, that of grotesquerie. This sprightly little tune is almost as celebrated as the very popular *Humoresque* of Dvořák; and like that of Dvořák, it originated as a composition for the piano, a companion to a *Nocturne* which it follows. Fritz Kreisler made a fine transcription for violin and piano, while Stokowski was one of several to adapt it for orchestra.

The *Marche Slav,* for orchestra, op. 31 (1876) was intended for a benefit concert in St. Petersburg for Serbian soldiers wounded in the war with Turkey. At that performance, the work aroused a "whole storm of patriotic enthusiasm," as the composer himself reported. The work opens with a broad Slavic march melody which Tchaikovsky borrowed from a Serbian folk song. The middle trio section is made up of two other folk tunes. The composition ends with a triumphant restatement of the opening march melody, now speaking for the victory of the Serbs over the Turks.

The *Melodie,* in E-flat major, op. 42, no. 3 (1878) is a simple and haunting little song that originated as a piece for violin and piano. It appears in a set of three such pieces entitled *Souvenir d'un lieu cher,* of which it is the closing number. This melody was used in 1941 for the American popular song, "The Things I Love."

The Months, op. 37b (1876) is a suite for piano out of which come several compositions exceedingly popular in transcriptions. Each movement of this suite is devoted to a month of the year. The sixth movement is *June,* a little barcarolle, or Venetian boat song. The tenth, for October, is *Autumn Song,* a gentle melody lightly touched by sadness. The eleventh, for November, is by contrast a lively piece entitled *Troika en Traneaux,* or *The Troika.*

"None But the Lonely Heart" is one of Tchaikovsky's most famous songs, a melancholy setting of Goethe's poem. This is the last of a set of six songs, op. 16 (1872) which is extensively performed in transcriptions of all sorts.

The *Nutcracker Suite,* or *Casse-Noisette,* op. 71a (1892) is a suite for orchestra adapted from a ballet score. The ballet (introduced in St. Petersburg in 1892) tells about a nutcracker, received as a Christmas gift by a little girl, which in her dreams becomes a handsome prince. He leads toys into battle against mice, and conducts the little girl to Jam Mountain, Arabia, where she is delighted with all kinds of games and dances. Those accustomed to associate the name of Tchaikovsky with lugubrious music will find this suite a revelation, for it is filled with the most enchanting moods, and is consistently light of heart and spirit. The highly popular suite for orchestra is made up of eight little movements. "Miniature Overture" is built from two lively tunes. The main subject of the "March" is a pert melody for clarinet, horn, and two trumpets; the trio section consists of a vivacious staccato melody for the woodwind and strings. "The Dance of the Sugarplum Fairy" is a sensitive melody for the celesta, the "Trepak" is a vigorous, rhythmic Russian dance, the "Arabian Dance" is an exotic melody for the clarinet, and the "Chinese Dance" an Oriental subject for flute and piccolo. The two last movements are the "Dance of the Flutes" in which a sensitive melody for flutes is contrasted by a more robust section for trumpets, and the "Waltz of the Flowers," where the waltz tune in horns and then in clarinets is followed by two more important ideas, the first in the strings, and the second in flutes and oboe.

The *Overture 1812* is a concert overture for orchestra, op. 49 (1880) commissioned for the consecration of a temple built as a memorial to Napoleon's defeat in Russia in 1812. This overture was intended by the composer to describe the historic events of Napoleon's invasion of and flight from Russia. An introductory section quotes the well-known Russian hymn, "God Preserve Thy People." In the main body of the overture, the Battle of Borodino is dramatically depicted, the two opposing armies represented by quotations from the *Marseillaise* and the Russian national anthem. A climax is reached with a triumphant restatement of the Russian national anthem.

The *Polonaise* is one of two celebrated dance episodes in the opera *Eugene Onegin.* (The other is the Waltz discussed below.) This three-act opera is based on a poem by Pushkin, adapted by Konstantin Shilovsky and the composer himself, and was introduced in Moscow on March 29, 1879. The setting is St. Petersburg in or about 1815, and its central theme concerns the frustrated love affair of Eugene Onegin and Tatiana. The brilliant music of the Polonaise is heard in the first scene of Act 3. In the palace of Prince Gremin there takes place a reception during which the guests dance to the vital strains of this courtly Polish dance, its vigor derived from sharp syncopations and accents on the half beat.

Romance, in F minor, op. 5 (1868) is a composition for piano written by the composer when he believed himself in love with the singer, Désirée Artôt, to whom the piece is dedicated. This music gives voice to a romantic ardor.

The *Sérénade mélancolique* in B-flat minor, op. 26 (1875) is a work for violin and orchestra. As the title indicates it is a sentimental rather than romantic effusion. Here a brief subject leads to a soaring three-part song for the violin.

Serenade for Strings, in C major, op. 48 (1880) is particularly famous for its second and third movements. The second is a Waltz, perhaps the most popular of this composer's many well loved waltzes. This is a graceful, even elegant, dance movement, the waltz of the Parisian salon rather than the more vital and earthy dance of Vienna. Such a light-hearted mood is instantly dispelled by the gloom of the third movement, an eloquent *Elegy,* in which the sorrow is all the more poignant because it is so subdued and restrained.

Solitude, op. 73, no. 6 (1893)—sometimes known as Again as Before—is a song set to a poem by D. M. Rathaus. This is the last of a set of six songs. Stokowski made an effective arrangement for orchestra.

Song Without Words (Chanson sans paroles), in F major is the third of a set of three pieces for the piano collectively entitled *Souvenir de Hapsal,* op. 2 (1867). This tender melody is far more familiar in transcriptions than it is in its original version.

Tchaikovsky wrote three Suites for orchestra. From two of these come movements which must be counted with the composer's most popular works. The Suite No. 1 in D minor, op. 43 (1880) is famous for its fourth movement, a *Marche Miniature.* The inclusion of this section into the suite was something of an afterthought with the composer, since it was interpolated into the work only after it had been published, placed as a fourth movement between an intermezzo and a scherzo. This march is in the grotesque, fantastic style of the piano *Humoresque.* The main subject is heard in the piccolo against plucked-string accompaniment. A transitory episode in strings and bells leads to a development of this melody.

The third movement from this same suite, *Intermezzo,* has two main melodies: the first appears in first violins, violas, bassoons and flute; the second, in cellos and bassoon. The coda is based on the first theme.

The suite No. 3 in G major, op. 55 (1884) is a four-movement work of which the second is particularly celebrated. This is a *Valse mélancolique* for full orchestra, highly expressive and emotional music in the composer's identifiable sentimental style.

There are several other waltzes by Tchaikovsky familiar to all lovers of light music. The *Valse sentimentale,* op. 51, no. 6 comes from a set of six pieces for the piano (1882) where it is the final number. The opera *Eugene Onegin* (commented upon above for its Polonaise) is also the source of a remarkable waltz episode. This music, the essence of aristocratic style and elegance, appears in the first scene of the second act. Tatiana's birthday is celebrated with a festive party during which the guests dance to its infectious strains. Two other famous Tchaikovsky waltzes come from his famous ballets—*Sleeping Beauty* and *Swan Lake*. In the orchestral suite derived from the score of *Sleeping Beauty,* the waltz appears as the fourth and concluding movement and consists of a lilting melody for strings which is carried to an overpowering climax. The *Swan Lake* consists of thirty-three numbers, various combinations of its most popular sections serving as orchestral suites for concert performance. The suave waltz music serves in the ballet for a dance of the swans at the lakeside in the second act.

Ambroise Thomas

AMBROISE THOMAS was born in Metz, France, on August 5, 1811. Between 1828 and 1832 he attended the Paris Conservatory where he won numerous prizes including the Prix de Rome. After his three-year stay in Rome, where he wrote some orchestral and chamber music, he returned to Paris in 1836 and devoted himself to writing operas. The first was *La double échelle,* produced at the Opéra-Comique in 1837. His first success was realized in 1843 with *Mina,* and in 1866 the opera by which he is remembered, *Mignon,* was triumphantly introduced at the Opéra-Comique. Later operas included *Hamlet* (1868) and *Françoise de Rimini* (1882). In 1851, Thomas was elected member of the French Academy. In 1871 he was appointed director of the Paris Conservatory, and in 1894 he was the recipient of the Grand Cross of the Legion of Honor. He died in Paris on February 12, 1896.

Mignon represents the French lyric theater at its best, with its graceful melodies, charming moods, and courtly grace of style. Its world première took place at the Opéra-Comique on November 17, 1866. In less than a century it was given over two thousand performances by that company besides becoming a staple in the repertory of opera houses the world over. The opera is based on Goethe's novel, *Wilhelm Meister*, adapted by Michel Carré and Jules Barbier. Mignon is a gypsy girl purchased by Wilhelm Meister. She falls in love with him and is heartbroken to discover how he is attracted to the actress, Philine. She tells the demented Lothario of her sorrow and of her wish that Meister's castle be burned to the ground. Lothario then proceeds to set Meister's castle aflame. Mignon, caught therein, is saved by Meister and then gently nursed back to health. Meister now realizes he is in love with her and her alone. When the demented Lothario regains his sanity we learn that Mignon is in actuality his daughter and that the castle he has burned is not Meister's but his own.

Parts of this opera are better known than the whole, and through these parts *Mignon* remains deservedly popular on semi-classical programs. The Overture makes extended use of two of the opera's main melodies. The first is *"Connais-tu le pays,"* *("Knowest Thou the Land?")*, Mignon's poignant first-act aria in which she recalls her childhood in some distant land; the melody is given in the wind instruments after a brief introduction. The second aria is Philine's polonaise, *"Je suis Titania"* ("I am Titania") from the second scene of the second act.

Another delightful orchestral episode from this opera is a suave, graceful little gavotte heard as entr'acte music just before the rise of the second-act curtain.

The *Raymond* Overture is even more popular than that to *Mignon*. *Raymond* was first performed at the Opéra-Comique on June 5, 1851. The overture opens with a spirited section punctuated with dashing chords. A serene transition, highlighted by a passage for solo cello, brings on a light, tuneful air in the violins against sharply accented plucked strings; a graceful countermelody for the woodwind follows. This appealing material is repeated at some length with embellishments and amplifications until a new thought is asserted: a brisk, march-like melody that slowly gains in sonority and tempo until a climactic point is reached in which this march melody is forcefully given by the full orchestra. The strings then offer a sentimental melody by way of temporary relief. But the overture ends in a dramatic and spirited mood with a finale statement of the march tune.

Enrico Toselli

ENRICO TOSELLI was born in Florence, Italy, on March 13, 1883. After studying with Sgambati and Martucci, Toselli toured Italy as a concert pianist. But he achieved renown not on the concert stage but with the writing of several romantic songs. One of these is the *"Serenata,"* No. 1, op. 6, through which his name survives. He also wrote some orchestral music and an operetta, *La Principessa bizzarra* (1913) whose libretto was the work of the former Crown Princess Luisa of Saxony whom he married in 1907 thereby creating an international sensation. Toselli died in Florence, Italy, on January 15, 1926.

The *"Serenata"* (*"Rimpianto"*) with Italian words by Alfred Silvestri and English lyrics by Sigmund Spaeth was published in the United States in 1923. This romantic, sentimental, Italian melody, as well loved in this country as in Europe, was for many years used by Gertrude Berg as the theme music for her radio and television program, *The Goldbergs.* It was also used as the theme music for an early talking picture, *The Magic Flame,* in which Ronald Colman and Vilma Banky were starred.

Sir Paolo Tosti

SIR FRANCESCO PAOLO TOSTI, one of Italy's best known song composers, was born in Ortona sul Mare, Abruzzi, Italy, on April 9, 1846. His musical education took place at the Royal College of San Pietro a Maiella in Naples. He left Naples in 1869 after serving for a while as teacher of music. Returning to his native city he now initiated his career as a composer of songs. Though a few of these early efforts became popular he failed for a long time to find a publisher. Success first came to him in Rome at a song recital in which he featured some of his own compositions. He scored an even greater success as singer-composer in London in 1875. He now settled permanently in London, serving as a singing master to the royal family, and as professor of singing at the Royal Academy of Music. In 1908 he was knighted. In 1913 he returned to his native land. He died in Rome on December 2, 1916.

Tosti had a remarkable lyric gift that was Italian to its very core in the ease, fluidity, and singableness of his melodies. This talent was combined with an elegant style and a sincere emotion. His best songs are among the most popular to emerge from Italy. The most famous and the most moving emotionally is without question *"Addio"* ("Goodbye, Forever"). Almost as popular and appealing are *"Ideale"* ("My Ideal"), *"Marechiare,"* *"Mattinata,"* *"Segreto,"* *"La Serenata,"* and *"Vorrei morire."*

Giuseppe Verdi

❧❧ ❧❧

GIUSEPPE VERDI, the greatest of the Italian opera composers, was born in Le Roncole, Italy, on October 10, 1813. He demonstrated such unmistakable gifts for music in his boyhood that his townspeople created a fund to send him to the Milan Conservatory. In 1832 he appeared in Milan. Finding he was too old to gain admission to the Conservatory, he studied composition privately with Vincenzo Lavigna. For several years Verdi lived in Busseto where he conducted the Philharmonic Society and wrote his first opera, *Oberto,* produced in Milan in 1839. Now settled in Milan, he continued writing operas, achieving his first major success with *Nabucco* in 1842. During the next eight years he solidified his position as one of Italy's best loved opera composers with several important works among which were *Ernani* (1844), *Macbeth* (1847) and *Luisa Miller* (1849). A new era began for Verdi in 1851 with *Rigoletto,* an era in which he became Italy's greatest master of opera, and one of the foremost in the world. *Il Trovatore* and *La Traviata* came in 1853, to be followed by *I Vespri Siciliani* (1855), *Simone Boccanegra* (1857), *Un ballo in maschera* (1859), *La Forza del destino* (1862), and *Aida* (1871). Now a man of considerable wealth (as well as fame), Verdi bought a farm in Sant' Agata where he henceforth spent his summers; after the completion of *Aida,* he lived there most of the time in comparative seclusion, tending to his crops, gardens, and live stock. When Cavour initiated the first Italian parliament, Verdi was elected deputy. But Verdi never liked politics, and soon withdrew from the political arena; however, in 1874, he accepted the honorary appointment of Senator from the King.

As a composer, Verdi remained silent for about fifteen years after *Aida.* By the time the world became reconciled to the fact that Verdi's life work was over, he emerged from this long period of withdrawal to produce two operas now generally regarded as his crowning achievements: *Otello* (1887) and *Falstaff* (1893). During the last years of his life, Verdi lived in a Milan hotel. His sight and hearing began to deteriorate, and just before his death—in Milan on January 27, 1901—he suffered a paralytic stroke. His death was mourned by the entire nation. A quarter of a million mourners crowded the streets to watch his bier pass for its burial in the oratory of the Musicians Home in Milan—accompanied by the stately music of a chorus from *Nabucco,* conducted by Toscanini.

Verdi's profound knowledge of the theater and his strong dramatic sense, combined with his virtually incomparable Italian lyricism, made him one of the greatest composers for the musical theater of all time. But it is his lyricism—with all its infinite charm and variety—that makes so much of his writing so popular to so many in such widely scattered areas of the world. Selections from his most famous operas are favorites even with many who have never seen them on the stage, because their emotional appeal is inescapable.

Aida is an opera filled not only with some of the most wonderful melodies to be found in Italian opera but also with scenes of pomp, ceremony, with exotic attractions, and with episodes dynamic with dramatic interest. This was the opera that brought Verdi's second creative period to a rich culmination; and it is unquestionably one of the composer's masterworks. He wrote it on a commission from the Egyptian Khedive for ceremonies commemorating the opening of the Suez Canal. However, Verdi took so long to complete his opera that it was not performed in Cairo until about two years after the canal had been opened, on December 24, 1871. The libretto—by Antonio Ghislanzoni—was based on a plot by Mariette Bey. Radames, captain of the Egyptian guard, is in love with Aida, the Ethiopian slave of Amneris. The latter, daughter of the King of Egypt, is herself in love with Radames. When an invading Ethiopian force comes to threaten Egypt, Radames becomes the commander of the army and proves himself a hero. Lavish festivities and ceremonies celebrate his victorious return, during which the king of Egypt offers him the hand of Amneris as reward. But Radames is still in love with Aida. Since Aida is actually the daughter of the Ethiopian king, she manages to extract from Radames the secret maneuvers of the Egyptian army, information enabling the Ethiopian army to destroy the Egyptians. For this treachery, Radames is buried alive; and Aida, still in love with him, comes within his tomb to die with him.

The brief overture opens with a tender melody in violins suggesting Aida. After an effective development we hear a somber and brooding motive of the Priests of Isis, which soon receives contrapuntal treatment. The Aida motive is dramatized, brought to a magnificent climax, then allowed to subside.

The Ballet Music is famous for its brilliant harmonic and orchestral colors, exotic melodies, and pulsating rhythms. In Act 2, Scene 1 there takes place the *Dance of the Moorish Slaves,* an oriental dance performed before Amneris by the Moorish boys. The *Ballabile* is another oriental dance which appears in Act 2, Scene 2, performed by the dancing girls during the celebration attending the arrival of the triumphant Egyptian army headed by Radames. In this scene there is also heard the stirring strains of the *Grand March.* This march begins softly but soon gathers its strength and erupts with full force as the king, his attendants, the Priests, the standard bearers, Amneris and her slaves appear in a brilliant procession. The people raise a cry of praise to the king and their Gods in *"Gloria all' Egitto."* After this comes the dramatic march music to which the Egyptian troops, with Radames at their head, enter triumphantly into the square and file proudly before their king.

Of the vocal excerpts the most famous is undoubtedly Radames' ecstatic song of love to Aida in the first act, first scene, *"Celeste Aida,"* surely one of the most famous tenor arias in all opera. Two principal arias for soprano are by Aida. The first is her exultant prayer that Radames come back victorious from the war, *"Ritorna vincitor"* in Act 1, Scene 1; the other, *"O Patria mia,"* in Act 3, is her poignant recollection of her beloved homeland in Ethiopia. Amneris' moving aria in Act 2, Scene 1, *"Vieni amor mio"* where she thinks about her beloved Radames, and the concluding scene of the opera in which Radames and Aida bid the world farewell, *"O terra, addio"* are also famous.

La Forza del destino (The Force of Destiny) has a popular overture. This opera was first performed in St. Petersburg, Russia on November 10, 1862—libretto by Francesco Piave based on a play by the Duke de Riva. Leonora, daughter of the Marquis of Calatrava, is in love with Don Alvaro, a nobleman of Inca origin. When they plan elopement, Leonora's father intervenes and is accidentally killed in the ensuing brawl. Leonora's brother, Don Carlo, swears to avenge this death by killing Don Alvaro. On the field of battle, Don Alvaro saves Don Carlo's life. Not recognizing Don Alvaro as his sworn enemy, Don Carlo pledges eternal friendship; but upon discovering Don Alvaro's true identity, he challenges him to a duel in which Don Carlo is wounded. Aware that he has brought doom to two people closest and dearest to his beloved Leonora, Don Alvaro seeks sanctuary in a monastery where many years later he is found by Don Carlo. In the sword duel that follows, Don Alvaro kills Don Carlo, whose last act is to plunge a fatal knife into his sister's heart.

A trumpet blast, creating an ominous air of doom, opens the overture. An air in a minor key then leads to a gentle song for strings; this is Leonora's prayer for help and protection to the Virgin in the second scene of the second act, "*Madre pietosa.*" A light pastoral tune, depicting the Italian countryside in the third act, is now heard. Leonora's song of prayer is now forcefully repeated by the full orchestra, after which the overture ends robustly.

Rigoletto, introduced in Venice on March 11, 1851, is based on the Victor Hugo play, *Le Roi s'amuse* adapted by Francesco Piave. Rigoletto is the hunchbacked jester to the Duke of Mantua who jealously guards his daughter, Gilda, from the world outside their home. Disguised as a student, the Duke woos Gilda and wins her love. Since the Duke's courtiers hate the jester, they conspire to abduct Gilda and bring her to the ducal court to become the Duke's mistress. Distraught at this turn of affairs, the jester vows to kill the Duke and hires a professional assassin to perform this evil deed. But since his own sister loves the Duke, the assassin decides to spare him and to kill a stranger instead. The stranger proves to be none other than Gilda, disguised as a man for a projected flight to Verona. The body is placed in a sack for delivery to Rigoletto who, before he can get rid of the body, discovers that it is that of his beloved daughter.

The following are the best loved and most widely performed excerpts from this tuneful opera: the Ballata, "*Questa o quella*" from the first act in which the Duke flippantly talks of love and his many conquests; the graceful Minuet to which the courtiers dance during a party at the Ducal palace in the same act; Gilda's famous coloratura aria, "*Caro nome*" from the second act, in which she dreams about the "student" with whom she has fallen in love; the light and capricious aria of the Duke, "*La donna è mobile*" from the third act, in which the Duke mockingly comments on fickle womanhood, and one of the most celebrated tenor arias in the repertory; the quartet "*Bella figlia dell' amore*"—as celebrated an ensemble number as "*La donna è mobile*" is as an aria—in which each of the four principal characters of the opera (Gilda, Rigoletto, the Duke, and Maddalena) speaks of his or her inner turmoil, doubts, and hatreds in the third act.

La Traviata (The Lost One) is Francesco Maria Piave's adaptation of Alexandre Dumas' celebrated romance, *La Dame aux camélias.* Its central theme is the tragic tale of the courtesan, Violetta, who falls in love with and is loved by Alfredo Germont. After they live together for a blissful period, Alfredo's father is instrumental in breaking up the affair by convincing Violetta she must give up her lover for his own good. She does so by feigning she has grown tired of him. Only too late does Alfredo learn the truth; when he returns to Violetta, she is dying of tuberculosis.

The première of *La Traviata* in Venice on March 6, 1853 was a dismal failure. The public reacted unfavorably to a play it regarded immoral, and to the sight of a healthy prima donna seemingly wasting away with tuberculosis; it also resented the fact that the opera was given in contemporary dress. At a revival, a year later in Venice, the opera was performed in costume and settings of an earlier period. Profiting further from a carefully prepared presentation, the opera now cast a spell on its audience. From this point on, *La Traviata* went on to conquer the opera world to become one of the most popular operas ever written.

The orchestral preludes to the first and third act are celebrated. The Prelude to Act 1 begins softly and slowly with a poignant melody suggesting Violetta's fatal sickness; this is followed by a broad, rich song for the strings describing Violetta's expression of love for Alfredo. The Prelude to Act 3 also begins with the sad, slow melody speaking of Violetta's illness. The music then becomes expressive and tender to point up the tragedy of her life; this prelude ends with a succession of broken phrases as Violetta's life slowly ebbs away.

The following are the principal vocal selections from *La Traviata:* the opening drinking song, or Brindisi *("Libiamo, libiamo")*; Violetta's world-famous aria, *"Ah, fors è lui"* in which she reveals her love for Alfredo followed immediately by her determination to remain free and pleasure-loving *("Sempre libera")* also in the first act; Alfredo's expression of joy that Violetta has come to live with him, *"De' miei bollenti spiriti"* and the elder Germont's recollection of his happy home in the Provence, *"Di Provenza il mar"* from the second act; Violetta's pathetic farewell to the world, *"Addio del passato,"* and Alfredo's promise to the dying Violetta to return together to their happy home near Paris, *"Parigi, o cara"* from the fourth act.

Il Trovatore (The Troubadours) is so full of familiar melodies that, like a play of Shakespeare, it appears to be replete with "quotations." It was first performed in Rome on January 19, 1853. The libretto by Salvatore Commarno, based on a play by Antonio Garcia Gutiérrez, is complicated to a point of obscurity, and filled with coincidences and improbabilities; but this did not prevent Verdi from creating one of his most melodious scores, an inexhaustible reservoir of unforgettable arias and ensemble numbers. The story involves Count di Luna in a frustrated love affair with Leonora; his rival is Manrico, an officer of a rival army with whom Leonora is in love. The gypsy Azucena convinces Manrico, her foster son, that Count di Luna had been responsible for the death of Manrico's father, and incites him on to avenge that murder. Later in the play, Azucena and Manrico are captured by Di Luna's army. To help free Manrico, Leonora promises to marry the Count. Rather than pay this price, Leonora takes poison and dies at Manrico's feet. Manrico is now sentenced to be executed. After his death, Azucena, half-crazed, reveals that Manrico is really Count di Luna's half brother.

The long list of favorite selections from *Il Trovatore* includes the following: Manrico's beautiful serenade to Leonora in Act 1, Scene 2, *"Deserto sulla terra";* Leonora's poignant recollections of a mysterious admirer in the second scene, *"Tacea la notte placida";* the ever popular *Anvil Chorus* of the gypsies with which the second act opens, *"Vedi! le fosche";* Azucena's stirring recollection of the time long past when her mother had been burned as a witch, *"Stride la vampa,"* and Count di Luna's expression of love for Leonora, *"Il balen"* also in the second act; in the third act, Manrico's dramatic aria, *"Di quella pira"* and the rousing soldier's chorus of Manrico's troops, *"Squilli, echeggi la tromba guerriera";* Leonora's prayer for her beloved Manrico *"D'amor sull' ali rosee"* followed immediately by the world-famous *Miserere* (*"Ah, che la morte ognora"*), a choral chant asking pity and salvation from the prisoners, all in the first scene of the fourth act; and the poignant duet of Manrico and Azucena in the final scene, a fervent, glowing hope that some day they can return to their beloved mountain country in peace and love, *"Ai nostri monti."*

While *I Vespri siciliani,* or *Les Vêpres siciliennes* (*Sicilian Vespers*) is one of Verdi's less familiar operas, its overture is one of his most successful. The opera-libretto by Eugène Scribe and Charles Duveyrier— was first performed at the Paris Opéra on June 13, 1855. Its setting is 13th-century Sicily where the peasants rise in revolt against the occupying French. The overture is constructed from some basic melodies from the opera. The first *Allegro* theme speaks of the massacre of the French garrison. A second melody—a beautiful lyrical passage *pianissimo* against tremolos—is taken from the farewell scene of the hero and the heroine who are about to die.

Richard Wagner

WILHELM RICHARD WAGNER, genius of the music drama, was born in Leipzig, Germany, on May 22, 1813. In his academic studies (at the Kreuzschule in Dresden, the Nikolaischule in Leipzig, and the University of Leipzig) he was an indifferent, lazy, and irresponsible student. But his intensity and seriousness of purpose where music was concerned were evident from the beginning. He studied theory by memorizing a textbook and then by receiving some formal instruction from Theodor Weinlig. In short order he completed an overture and a symphony that received performances between 1832 and 1833; in 1834 he completed his first opera, *Die Feen,* never performed in his lifetime. In 1834 he was appointed conductor of the Magdeburg Opera where, two years later, his second opera, *Das Liebesverbot,* was introduced. Between 1837 and 1838 he conducted opera in Riga. Involvement in debts caused his dismissal from this post and compelled him to flee to Paris, where he arrived in 1839. There he lived for three years in extreme poverty, completing two important operas, *Rienzi* in 1840, and *The Flying Dutchman* in 1841. His first major successes came with the first of these operas, introduced at the Dresden Opera on October 20, 1842. This triumph brought Wagner in 1843 an appointment as Kapellmeister of the Dresden Opera which he held with considerable esteem for six years. During this period he completed two more operas: *Tannhaeuser,* introduced in Dresden in 1845, and *Lohengrin,* first performed in Weimar under Liszt's direction, in 1850.

As a member of a radical political organization, the Vaterlandsverein, Wagner became involved in the revolutionary movements that swept across Europe in 1848–1849. To avoid arrest, he had to flee from Saxony. He came to Weimar where he was warmly welcomed by Liszt who from then on became one of his staunchest champions. After that Wagner set up a permanent abode in Zurich. He now began to clarify and expound his new theories on opera. He saw opera as a drama with music, a synthesis of many arts; he was impatient with the old clichés and formulas to which opera had so long been enslaved, such as formal ballets, recitatives and arias, production scenes, and so forth. And he put his theories into practice with a monumental project embracing four dramas, collectively entitled *The Nibelung Ring (Der Ring des Nibelungen)* for which, as had always been his practice, he wrote the text as well as the music; the four dramas were entitled *The Rhinegold (Das Rheingold), The Valkyries (Die Walkuere), Siegfried,* and *The Twilight of the Gods (Goetterdaemmerung).* It took him a quarter of a century to complete this epic. But during this period he was able to complete several other important music dramas, including *Tristan and Isolde* in 1859 and *The Mastersingers (Die Meistersinger)* in 1867.

In 1862, Wagner was pardoned for his radical activities of 1849 and permitted to return to Saxony. There he found a powerful patron in Ludwig II, king of Bavaria, under whose auspices premières of Wagner's mighty music dramas were given in Munich beginning with *Tristan and Isolde* in 1865. In 1876 there came into being one of Wagner's most cherished dreams, a festival theater built in Bayreuth, Bavaria, according to his own specifications, where his music dramas could be presented in the style and manner Wagner dictated. This festival opened in August 1876 with the first performance anywhere of the entire *Ring* cycle. Since then Bayreuth has been a shrine of Wagnerian music drama to which music lovers of the world congregate during the summer months. Wagner's last music drama was the religious consecrational play, *Parsifal,* first performed in Bayreuth on July 26, 1882. Wagner died in Venice on February 13, 1883, and was buried in the garden of his home, Wahnfried, in Bayreuth.

Of his turbulent personal life which involved him in numerous and often complex love affairs, mention need here be made only of his relations with Cosima, daughter of Liszt, and wife of Hans von Buelow. Wagner and Cosima fell in love while the latter was still von Buelow's wife. They had two illegitimate children before they set up a home of their own at Lake Lucerne; and one more (Siegfried) before they were married on August 25, 1870.

Wagner's creative career divides itself into two phases. In the first he was the composer of operas in more or less a traditional style. To the accepted formulas of operatic writing, however, he brought a new dimension—immense musical and dramatic power and invention. In the second phase he was the prophet of a new order in music, the creator of the music drama. It is from the works of his first phase that salon or pop orchestras derive selections that have become universal favorites— sometimes overtures, sometimes excerpts. For these earlier works abound with such a wonderful fund of melody, emotion, expressiveness and dramatic interest that they have become popular even with those operagoers to whose tastes the later Wagner is perhaps too subtle, complex, elusive, or garrulous.

From *The Flying Dutchman* (*Der fliegende Hollaender*) comes a dramatic overture. This opera—text by the composer based on an old legend adapted by Heinrich Heine—was first performed at the Dresden Opera on January 2, 1843. "The Flying Dutchman" is a ship on which the Dutchman must sail until he achieves redemption through the love of a faithful woman. Only once in every seven years is he permitted to go ashore to find that love. He finally achieves his redemption through Senta. They both meet their final doom together in a raging sea which swallows up the ship.

Turbulent music, intended to describe a storm at sea, opens the overture. We then hear the theme of the Dutchman in the horns and bassoons. The stormy music returns and subsides as a motive from Senta's beautiful second-act ballad, *"Traft ihr das Schiff"* is presented. This motive brings up the image of Senta herself. A vigorous sailors' chorus is followed by a return of the Senta motive in full orchestra.

Three selections from *The Flying Dutchman* are of particular appeal: Senta's spinning song, *"Summ und brumm"* and her famous ballad, both from the second act; and the chorus of the sailors in the third act, a rousing chantey, *"Steuermann! lass die Wacht."*

Lohengrin was Wagner's last "opera." After that he confined himself to music dramas. He completed it in 1848. After its première in Weimar on August 28, 1850 it became one of the most successful operas in Germany of that period. The text, by the composer, was adapted from medieval legends. Lohengrin is a knight of the Holy Grail who becomes Elsa's champion against Telramund when Elsa is unjustly accused of having murdered Gottfried. Lohengrin arrives on a swan and extracts from Elsa the promise that she must never try to uncover his true identity. After defeating Telramund, Lohengrin marries Elsa who, provoked by Telramund's wife, cannot stifle her curiosity about her husband's background and source. He finally must reveal to her that he is a knight of the Holy Grail. Having made that revelation he must leave her forever.

The two familiar orchestral preludes, from the first and third acts, are opposites in mood, texture, and dynamics. The Prelude to Act 1 has spiritual content, a portrait of a heavenly vision wherein the Holy Grail is carried by angels. The main theme is heard quietly in the upper registers of the violins, then repeated by other instruments. This theme is developed into a *crescendo* and culminates in an exultant statement by trumpets and trombones. Now the theme is given in a *decrescendo,* and the prelude ebbs away *pianissimo,* once again in the strings in the upper register.

The Prelude to Act 3 is more robust in character, since it depicts the joy of Elsa and Lohengrin on the eve of their wedding. A forceful melody is pronounced by the full orchestra, succeeded by a second strong theme for the cellos, horns, bassoons in unison; a march-like episode for the wind instruments follows.

What is probably the most famous wedding march ever written comes out of *Lohengrin.* Its strains are heard after the rise of the curtain for Act 3, Scene 1, as a procession enters the bridal chamber. The chorus hymns a blessing to the marriage couple (*"Treulich gefuert"*). From one side ladies conduct Elsa, while from the other the King and his men lead Lohengrin. The two processions then meet midstage and Elsa joins Lohengrin to be blessed by the King. The two columns of the procession then refile and march out of the two sides of the stage.

The Mastersingers (Die Meistersinger), while written after Wagner had set forth on his operatic revolution, is the only one of his music dramas with a recognizable operatic ritual: big arias, huge production numbers, even dances. For *The Mastersingers* is a comedy, the only one Wagner ever wrote. For purposes of comedy some of the traditions of opera still prove useful to Wagner, even if fused with techniques, approaches and esthetics of the music drama. Wagner completed *The Mastersingers* in 1867—eight years after *Tristan and Isolde* and more than a decade following the first two dramas of the *Ring* cycle. The first performance took place in Munich on June 21, 1868. The libretto, by the composer, was set in Nuremberg in the middle 16th century, and its plot revolves around a song contest conducted by the Mastersingers, its winner to receive the hand of lovely Eva, daughter of the cobbler-philosopher, Hans Sachs. Walther von Stolzing, a knight, and Beckmesser, a contemptible town clerk, are the main rivals for Eva. At a magnificent ceremony at the banks of the Pognitz River the contestants sing their offerings. It is Walther's eloquent "Prize Song" that emerges victorious.

This "Prize Song" (*"Morgenlich leuchtend"*) is one of Wagner's most famous melodies, the pivot upon which the entire opera gravitates. It is first heard in the first scene of the third act, where Walther comes to tell Hans Sachs of a song come to him in a dream. The song is repeated in the closing scene of the opera during the actual contest. This "Prize Song" is used by Wagner symbolically. Its victory over the dull and stilted creation of Beckmesser represents the triumph of inspiration and freedom of expression over hackneyed rules and procedures. August Wilhelmj made a famous transcription of the "Prize Song" for violin and piano.

Rienzi, an early Wagner opera, is today remembered primarily for its overture. But in its own day it was extremely popular. Immediately after its première performance in Dresden on October 20, 1842, *Rienzi* made Wagner's name known throughout all of Germany for the first time, appearing in the repertory of virtually every major German opera house at the time. The novel from which the composer derived his libretto is that of Bulwer-Lytton. The central character, Rienzi, is a Roman ruler of the 14th century who meets his destruction at the hands of his enemies who set the Capitol aflame in which Rienzi perishes. Trumpet calls in the opening measures of the overture lead to a slow section in which is prominent an affecting melody for strings, Rienzi's prayer for the Roman people. In the main section of the overture, the first main theme is the battle hymn of the first act (in the brass) set against Rienzi's prayer-melody. The opening slow section returns and is succeeded by the stirring music from the first act finale. In the coda, the battle-hymn music is powerfully projected for the last time.

Tannhaeuser boasts many popular selections beyond its very famous overture. The opera was first performed in Dresden on October 19, 1845. The libretto is by the composer. Tannhaeuser is a minstrel-knight who has grown weary of the carnal delights on the Hill of Venus and longs for his own world. By invoking the name of the Virgin Mary, in whom he places his trust, Tannhaeuser is transported to a valley near the Wartburg Castle, where he is recognized and welcomed back by Wolfram, a companion minstrel-knight. Joyously, Tannhaeuser returns with Wolfram to the Hall of the Minstrels in the Wartburg Castle to find that his beloved Elisabeth is still in love with him. But only he who can come out triumphant in a song contest on the subject of love can win Elisabeth. The song Tannhaeuser presents, glorifying sensual pleasure, horrifies the audience. Contrite, Tannhaeuser offers to atone for his sins by joining pilgrims to Rome and seeking absolution from the Pope. Elisabeth promises to pray for his soul. After several months have passed, Elisabeth is awaiting the return of the Roman pilgrims, and Wolfram beseeches heaven to guide Elisabeth and protect her. Suddenly Tannhaeuser—haggard and decrepit—makes his appearance. He confesses to Wolfram that his soul will not be redeemed until the staff in the Pope's hands sprouts leaves. Only after Elisabeth has died of grief in despair of ever seeing Tannhaeuser again, do the tidings come from Rome that the Pope's staff has, indeed, blossomed with foliage.

The Overture is built from some of the principal melodies of the opera; in a sense it traces the main events of the story. The religious chant of the Pilgrims (in clarinets, bassoons and horns) is heard at once. This is followed by music suggesting Tannhaeuser's repentance, a touching melody for strings. After both these ideas have been discussed we hear in the strings the voluptuous music of Venusberg, a picture of the carnal life led by Tannhaeuser with Venus on Venus Hill. The music is brought to a compelling climax with a loud statement of Tannhaeuser's passionate hymn to carnal love with which he so horrified the minstrel-knights at Wartburg Castle. The chant of the pilgrims, which had opened the overture, also brings it to conclusion.

The Prelude to Act 3 is solemn music that bears the title, "Tannhaeuser's Pilgrimage." Two themes are set forth at once, that of Tannhaeuser's repentance, and that suggesting Elisabeth's intercession. Tannhaeuser's suffering is then portrayed by a poignant melody for strings. Suggestions of the Pilgrim's Chorus and a motive known as "Heavenly Grace" are then offered. The prelude ends quietly and sensitively, as Tannhaeuser at long last achieves salvation.

The sensual, even lascivious, music of the *Bacchanale* in the opening scene (recreating the revelry enjoyed by Tannhaeuser and Venus on Venus Hill) is often performed in conjunction with the Overture, sometimes independently. Another orchestral episode extremely popular is the stately *March* of the second act with which the minstrel-knights of the Wartburg file into the Castle, followed by the nobles, ladies, and attendants, as they chant the strains of *"Freudig begruessen wir die edle Halle."*

The most popular vocal excerpt from *Tannhaeuser* is Wolfram's "Ode to the Evening Star" (*"O du mein holder Abendstern"*) in the last act. This atmospheric music, a hymn to the mystery and beauty of the night, is Wolfram's prayer to the evening star that it guide and protect Elisabeth. Elisabeth's second-act song of praise to the Hall of Wartburg Castle in which she speaks of her joy in learning of Tannhaeuser's return (*"Dich, teure Halle"*) and her eloquent third-act prayer for Tannhaeuser's forgiveness (*"Allmaecht'ge Jungfrau"*) are also deservedly celebrated for their affecting lyricism.

Wagner did not write much music not intended for the stage. Of this meager repertory one or two items deserve attention in the semi-classical repertory. One is *"Traeume"* ("Dreams") a song often heard in transcriptions, particularly for orchestra. This is one of five poems by Mathilde Wesendonck which Wagner set to music in 1857–1858, and it appears as the last song of the cycle. This gentle nocturne derives some of its melody from the famous love-duet of the second act of *Tristan and Isolde* (*"O sink hernieder, Nacht der Liebe"*) but the overall effect of the song is one of gentle revery rather than sensual love. Wagner himself arranged *"Traeume"* for small orchestra. On Mathilde Wesendonck's birthday on December 23, 1857, he conducted eighteen musicians in a performance of the song under Mathilde's window.

The *Kaiser March* was another of Wagner's compositions not intended for the stage. He wrote it in 1871 to celebrate Germany's victory over France. A proud, exultant theme is first offered by the full orchestra. A transition in the brasses and timpani brings on a second theme of contrasting character in the woodwind. There follows a brief statement of Martin Luther's famous chorale, *"Ein feste Burg."* After dramatic music depicting the fever of battle, the Luther chorale is repeated triumphantly by the brasses. The first theme returns loudly in full orchestra after a fanfare to end the march.

Emil Waldteufel

EMIL WALDTEUFEL, waltz-king of France, was born in Strasbourg on December 9, 1837. His father, a professor of music at the Strasbourg Conservatory, gave him his first music instruction. After that Emil attended the Paris Conservatory, but he never completed his course of study there, leaving the schoolroom to take on a job with a piano manufacturer. He published his first waltzes at his own expense in 1860, *Joies et peines* and *Manola*. The latter so enchanted the Prince of Wales that he willingly accepted the dedication of Waldteufel's next waltz, *Bien aimé*, a fact that played no small part in establishing Wald-teufel's reputation in England. Waldteufel now decided to sidestep all other activities to concentrate on the writing of waltz music. In short order he became the idol of Paris in the same way that Johann Strauss II was of Vienna. For a period, Waldteufel's fame throughout Europe was second only to that of the Viennese waltz king. Waldteufel made many tours of the European capitals conducting his own compositions, scor-ing triumphs in Covent Garden in 1885, and in Berlin in 1889. In 1865 he became chamber musician to the Empress Eugénie and director of the court balls. He died in Paris on February 16, 1915.

Waldteufel published over 250 waltzes. A comparison with Johann Strauss is perhaps inevitable. The French waltz king never equalled Strauss' remarkable melodic invention, original approaches in harmony and orchestration, and overall inspiration. Most of Waldteufel's waltzes are functional pieces, and make far better dance music than concert music. But a handful of his waltzes are classics, and deservedly so. They are buoyant and inviting in their spirit, aristocratic in style, spontane-ous in expression. Waldteufel's most famous waltzes include the fol-lowing: *España,* op. 236, which utilizes for its waltz melodies the basic themes from Chabrier's rhapsody of the same name; and *The Skaters* (*Les Patineurs*), op. 183, in which the main elegant melody has the lightness of foot and the mobility of motion of facile figure skaters. Other popular Waldteufel waltzes include the *Acclamations,* op. 223; *Dolores,* op. 170; *Estudiantina,* op. 191; *Mon rêve,* op. 151; *Les Sirènes,* op. 154; *Toujours ou jamais,* op. 156; and *Violettes,* op. 148.

Karl Maria von Weber

KARL MARIA VON WEBER was born in Eutin, Olden-burg, Germany, on November 18, 1786. His father, who played the violin in small theaters, was determined to make his son a musical prodigy, subjecting him from childhood on to severe discipline, and to intensive study with Karl's stepbrother, J. P. Heuschkel and Michael Haydn. Weber made public appearances as pianist in early boyhood. His first opera was written when he was only thirteen, and at fourteen his second opera was performed in Chemnitz, Freiberg, and Vienna. An even more comprehensive period of study than heretofore followed in Munich with Abbé Vogler. After that, in 1804, Weber was appointed conductor of the Breslau City Theater. In 1806 he became Musik Intendant to the Duke of Wuerttemberg, and in 1807 private secretary and music master to Duke Ludwig in Stuttgart. From 1813 to 1816 he was the music director of German Opera in Prague and in 1817 musical director of German Opera in Dresden. It was in this last post that he created the first of his unqualified masterworks, the opera *Der Freischuetz,* introduced with phenomenal success in Berlin on June 18, 1821. It was with this work that German Romantic opera was born, grounded in Germanic nationalism, filled with the German love for the legendary and the supernatural, and characterized by its use of German landscapes and backgrounds. Weber wrote two more masterworks with which his high station in opera was solidified: *Euryanthe,* introduced in Vienna on October 25, 1823, and *Oberon,* first heard in London, on April 12, 1826. In London, attending the première of the latter opera, Weber succumbed to his last sickness on June 5, 1826. His body was transferred to Dresden where it was buried to special ceremonies at which Wagner delivered the eulogy.

Weber's monumental contributions to opera in general, and German opera, in particular, do not fall within the scope of this volume; neither do the three masterworks with which he gained immortality. In music in a lighter vein he was most significant for being one of the first to create waltz music within an extended structure. The most popular of these compositions was the *Invitation to the Dance (Aufforderung zum Tanz),* written in 1819 as a "rondo brilliant" in D-flat major, for piano solo. It has since become celebrated in several orchestral transcriptions, notably those by Berlioz and Felix Weingartner. This work is one of the first in music history in which several different waltz tunes are combined into a single cohesive composition, preceded by an introduction and concluding with an epilogue. The introduction consists of a subdued, well-mannered melody, simulating the request to a lady by a young man for a dance, and the acceptance. Several waltz melodies follow, to which this couple dance. The epilogue consists of a return of the introduction, this time with the gentleman thanking the lady for having danced with him.

The *Jubilee Overture (Jubel)*, op. 59, for orchestra is another of Weber's more popular creations, this time in a stirring style. He wrote it in 1818 on the occasion of the 50th anniversary of the ascension to the throne by the King of Saxony. A slow introduction leads to the main body of the overture in which the main theme is forcefully stated by the full orchestra. By contrast there later appears a light-hearted tune, soon given considerable prominence in the development section. When both ideas have been repeated, a climax is reached with a statement of the English anthem, "God Save the King" in the wind instruments accompanied by the strings.

Kurt Weill

᪥᪥ ᪥᪥

K U R T   W E I L L was born in Dessau, Germany, on March 2, 1900. A comprehensive musical training took place first with private teachers in Dessau, then at the Berlin High School of Music, and finally for three years with Ferruccio Busoni. Weill started out as a composer of avant-garde music performed at several important German festivals. His first opera, *The Protagonist,* with a text by Georg Kaiser, was produced in 1926. From this point on Weill continued writing operas in which the texts were realistic or satiric, and the music filled with popular idioms, sometimes even those of jazz. The most important were *The Royal Palace* in 1927; *The Three-Penny Opera,* a sensation when first produced in 1928; *The Czar Has Himself Photographed,* also in 1928; and *The Rise and Fall of Mahagonny,* in 1930, one of whose numbers, "The Alabamy Song," was a leading song hit in Germany that year. With these works Weill became one of the leading exponents of the cultural movements then sweeping across Germany under the banners of *Zeitkunst* (Contemporary Art) and *Gebrauchsmusik* (Functional Music). In the fall of 1935, Weill established permanent residence in the United States, becoming an American citizen in 1943. He soon

assumed a position of first importance in the Broadway theater by virtue of a succession of outstanding musicals: *Johnny Johnson* (1936);
Knickerbocker Holiday (1938) in which Walter Huston starred as Peter
Stuyvesant and out of which came one of Weill's most popular musical
numbers, "September Song"; Moss Hart's musical about psychoanaly-
sis and the dream life, *Lady in the Dark* (1941) in which Gertrude Lawrence was starred; *One Touch of Venus* (1943), with Mary Martin;
Street Scene (1947), a trenchant musical play based on Elmer Rice's
realistic drama of New York; *Love Life* (1948), book and lyrics by Alan
Jay Lerner, its main musical number being another all-time Weill song
favorite, "Green-Up Time"; and *Lost in the Stars* (1949), a powerful
musical drama adapted from Alon Paton's novel, *Cry, the Beloved
Country*. Weill died in New York City on April 3, 1950.

The Three-Penny Opera (*Die Dreigroschenoper*) is one of the most
important musical productions of the post-World War I era in Europe;
and since its première it has lost little of its initial popularity. This
musical play (or opera, if you will) was based on the historic 18th-cen-
tury ballad opera of John Gay, *The Beggar's Opera*. The text was re-
written and modernized by Berthold Brecht, in whose hands the comic
opera became a brilliant, though often bitter, satire of Germany in the
late 1920's, with penetrating satirical comments on crime and corrup-
tion in this post-war era. Weill's opera was introduced in Berlin on
August 31, 1928 and scored a sensation with few parallels in contemporary German theater. Over one hundred theaters gave it four thousand performances throughout Germany in its initial year. It was made
into a motion-picture by G. W. Pabst (the first of several screen adaptations). It was introduced in the leading theatrical centers of the world;
the American première—in New York on April 13, 1933—was, however,
a dismal failure. It has since been revived frequently in all parts of the
civilized world. An off-Broadway presentation in 1954—with a new
modernized text by Marc Blitzstein, but with the Weill music un-
touched—made history by accumulating a run of more than five years;
a national company was then formed to tour the country in 1960. During this long Broadway run, the principal musical number, "Moritat"
(or "Mack the Knife") became an American hit song on two different
occasions. In 1955 it was given over twenty different recordings and was
often represented on the Hit Parade; revived in 1959 by Bobby Darin,
it sold over a million discs.

Weill's score is a mixture of opera and musical comedy, of European
stage traditions and American idioms. It opens with a blues and con-

cludes with a mock chorale, while in between these opposite poles there can be heard a shimmy, a canon in fox-trot, popular tunes, formal ballads, light airs, choruses, and ensemble numbers. The style ranges freely from Tin Pan Alley clichés to atonality, from mock romanticism to dissonance. Each number was basic to the plot; principal numbers often became penetrating psychological commentaries on the characters who presented them. "Moritat" (or "Mack the Knife") is the main musical number. But several others are also of outstanding interest including "Love Song" ("*Liebeslied*"), "The Ballad of Pleasant Living" ("*Ballade vom angenehmen Leben*"), the Canon-Song, *Barbarasong*, and the Bully's Ballad ("*Zuhaelterballade*").

Jaromir Weinberger

❧❧ ☙☙

JAROMIR WEINBERGER was born in Prague, Czechoslovakia, on January 8, 1896. After completing his music study at the Prague Conservatory, and privately with Max Reger in Berlin, he came to the United States in 1922, teaching for one season at the Ithaca Conservatory in Ithaca, New York. Following his return to Europe he held various posts as teacher and conductor. He achieved international renown as a composer with a Bohemian folk opera, *Schwanda, der Dudelsackpfeifer* first performed in Prague on April 27, 1927, then successfully heard throughout Europe and in the United States. Weinberger wrote many operas after that, and a considerable amount of orchestral music. Up to 1937 his home was in Prague, but since 1939 he has lived in the United States. One of his most successful works for orchestra was introduced in the United States soon after his arrival, *Under the Spreading Chestnut Tree*.

Among the numerous works by Weinberger are two that can be said to have a more popular appeal than the others. One is in an American idiom and manner which Weinberger assumed for many of his major works after coming to this country; the other is in the Bohemian style with which he first became famous.

That in the American style and spirit (but technically in a fugue idiom) is a delightful treatment of the popular American tune by Dan Emmett, "Dixie." "Dixie" had originated as a minstrel-show tune, being written by Emmett as a "walk-around" (or closing number) for a minstrel-show production at the Bryant Theater in New York in November 1859. It became an immediate favorite with minstrel troupes throughout the country. During the Civil War it became the Southland's favorite battle hymn, despite the fact that it was the work of a Northerner. The charge at Gettysburg by General George Pickett was made to the strains of this music. After the surrender at Appomattox, President Lincoln invited a band outside the White House to play the tune for him maintaining that since the North had conquered the Southern army it had also gained its favorite song as a spoils of war. In 1940 Weinberger wrote the *Prelude and Fugue on Dixie* for symphony orchestra. The prelude devotes itself to a simple statement of the melody, after which comes the lively fugal treatment of its main theme. The treatment is throughout so skilful and musical that we never feel any sense of contradiction in the use of a popular minstrel-show tune within a soundly classical structure and through soundly classical means.

Out of the composer's most famous opera, *Schwanda, der Dudelsackpfeifer (Schwanda, the Bagpipeplayer)* comes a *Polka and Fugue* for orchestra that is undoubtedly the most familiar excerpt from the opera. The vivacious *Polka*—which has a lusty peasant vitality in its marked accentuations—comes from Act 2, Scene 2; the fugue (whose main theme is suggested in the polka) is used in the opera's closing scene. Just before the end of the fugue, the polka melody is heard again, set contrapuntally against the fugue tune in a powerful climax in which the full orchestra, as well as an organ, is utilized.

Henri Wieniawski

෯෯෯ ෯෯෯

HENRI WIENIAWSKI was born in Lublin, Poland, on July 10, 1835. When he was eight he entered the Paris Conservatory, from which he was graduated three years later with first prize in violin-playing, the first time this institution conferred such an honor on one so young. Sensational appearances as child prodigy followed throughout Europe. After an additional period of study at the Paris Conservatory between 1849 and 1850, he initiated his career as a mature performer, and as one of the world's foremost violinists, with performances in Europe and Russia. In 1872 he toured the United States with the pianist, Anton Rubinstein. Meanwhile, in 1859, he was appointed solo violinist to the Czar of Russia, and from 1862 to 1867 he was professor of the violin at the St. Petersburg Conservatory. In 1874 he succeeded Vieuxtemps as professor of the violin at the Brussels Conservatory where he remained fourteen years. He suffered a heart attack while performing in Berlin in 1878, and died in Moscow on March 31, 1880.

Wieniawski produced a rich repertory of music for the violin which is still performed extensively. This includes the famous Concerto in D minor and many smaller compositions. Among the latter can be found pieces which have become favorites with salon orchestra in transcription. These, like other major works by the composer, are characterized by broad and expressive melodies and brilliant technical effects.

The *Kujawiak,* in A minor, op. 3 is a brilliant rhythmic number—a spirited mazurka which derives its name from the fact that it has come out of the Kuawy district of Poland. The *Légende,* op. 17, on the other hand, is outstanding for its sentimental lyricism. This piece is an eloquent song, originally for violin and orchestra, that seems to be telling a romantic tale. The *Polonaise brilliante,* in D major, op. 4, like the *Kujawiak,* is a successful attempt to incorporate within a concert work the characteristics of a popular Polish dance. This composition is appealing for its sharp accentuations on the half beat, syncopations, and brilliant passage work. The *Souvenirs of Moscow (Souvenirs de Moscou),* op. 6, is a fantasia on famous Russian airs, the most important of which is "The Red Sarafin."

Ralph Vaughan Williams

ໆຈໆຈ ຈໆຈໆ

RALPH VAUGHAN WILLIAMS was born in Down Ampney, England, on October 12, 1872. After attending the Royal College of Music, he studied composition privately with Max Bruch in Berlin. In 1901 he was appointed organist of the St. Barnabas Church in London. For the next few years he devoted himself mainly to church music. His interest in the English folk songs of the Tudor period, first stimulated in 1904, proved for him a decisive turning point. Besides dedicating himself henceforth to intensive research in English folk music (much of which he helped to revive from neglect and obscurity through his editions and adaptations) he found a new direction as composer: in the writing of music with a national identity, music absorbing the melodic, harmonic and modal techniques—at times even the actual material—of these old songs and dances. This new trend first became evident in 1907 with his *Norfolk Rhapsodies*. After an additional period of study with Maurice Ravel in Paris, Vaughan Williams embarked upon the writing of his first major works which included the famous *Fantasia on a Theme by Thomas Tallis, London Symphony,* and the opera *Hugh the Drover.* Subsequent works in all fields of composition placed him with the masters of 20th-century music. These compositions included symphonies, operas, concertos, fantasias, choral and chamber music. For more than thirty years, Vaughan Williams taught composition at the Royal College of Music in London; from 1920 to 1928 he was the conductor of the Bach Choir, also in that city. He paid two visits to the United States, the first time in 1922 to direct some of his works at a music festival in Connecticut, and the second time a decade later to lecture at Bryn Mawr College. He received the Order of Merit in 1935 and the Albert medal of the Royal Society of Arts in 1955. He died in London on August 26, 1958.

Only a meagre number of Vaughan Williams' compositions have popular appeal. One of these is the *Fantasia on Greensleeves,* for orchestra. "Greensleeves" is an old English folk song dating from the early 16th century, and mentioned in Shakespeare's *The Merry Wives of*

Windsor. In the 17th century it became the party song of the Cavaliers. Americans know it best through a popular-song adaptation in 1957. Vaughan Williams' delightful fantasia appears as an orchestral inter-lude in his opera *Sir John in Love* (1929), based on *The Merry Wives of Windsor.* A brief episode for flute leads to "Greensleeves," which is harmonized opulently for strings. Two brief variations follow. Then the opening flute episode is recalled as is the folk song itself—the main melody in lower strings with embellishments in the upper ones.

The March of the Kitchen Utensils is an amusing little episode for orchestra, part of the incidental music prepared by the composer for a production of Aristophanes' *The Wasps* in Cambridge in 1909. This march opens with a humorous little theme for the wind instruments in the impish style of Prokofiev. The theme is taken over by the strings. The middle section is much more in the identifiable national style of Vaughan Williams with a melody that resembles an old English folk dance.

Jacques Wolfe

JACQUES WOLFE, composer of songs in the style of Negro Spirituals familiar in the repertory of most American baritones, was born in Botoshan, Rumania on April 29, 1896. He was trained as a pianist at the Institute of Musical Art. While serving in the army dur-ing World War I, a member of the 50th Infantry Band, he was stationed in North Carolina where he first came into contact with Negro folk songs. This made such a profound impression on him that he devoted himself to research in this field. After the war he made many appear-ances on the concert stage both as a solo performer and as an accom-panist. For several years he was also a teacher of music at New York City high schools.

Wolfe's two best known songs in the style of Negro folk songs appeared in 1928. One is "De Glory Road," words by Clement Wood, a work of such extraordinary fervor and dramatic character that it has proved a sure-fire number with concert baritones throughout the country, and notably with Lawrence Tibbett with whom it was a particular favorite. The other was "Short'nin' Bread," to Wolfe's own words. The latter in all probability is not original with Wolfe but an adaptation of one of the melodies he discovered in North Carolina. Several Negro composers have been credited with being its composer; one of them was Reese d'Pres who is said to have written the melody in or about 1905.

Among Wolfe's other familiar songs are "God's World," "Goin' to Hebb'n" and "Hallelujah Rhythm."

Ermanno Wolf-Ferrari

❦❦ ❧❧

E R M A N N O W O L F - F E R R A R I was born in Venice, Italy, on January 12, 1876. Originally planning to make art his career he went to Rome, but while there became so fascinated by opera that then and there he decided to become a musician. He completed his musical training in Munich in 1895 with Josef Rheinberger. In 1899 he returned to his native city where his first major work—an oratorio, *La Sulamite*—was successfully performed. His first opera, *Cenerentola (Cinderella)* was introduced in Venice in 1900. His first comic opera (or opera buffa) came to Munich in 1903: *Le Donne Curiose.* He achieved world renown with still another comic opera, *The Secret of Suzanne,* first performed in Munich in 1909. This distinguished achievement was followed by an equally significant achievement in a serious vein, the grand opera, *The Jewels of the Madonna,* first heard in Berlin in 1911. One year later Wolf-Ferrari paid his first visit to the United States to attend in Chicago the American première of *The Jewels of the Madonna.* He wrote many operas after that, both in a comic and serious style, but his fame still rests securely on *The Secret of Suzanne* and *The Jewels of the Madonna*. From 1902 to 1912 he was director of the Benedetto Marcello Conservatory in Venice. He died in that city on January 21, 1948.

From *The Jewels of the Madonna* (*I Gioielli della Madonna*) have come several familiar orchestral episodes. This tragedy—libretto by the composer with verses by Carlo Zangarini and Enrico Golisciani—was successfully introduced in Berlin on December 23, 1911. Rafaele, leader of the Camorrists, and Gennaro, a blacksmith, are rivals for the love of Maliela. After Rafaele appears to have won Maliela's love, Gennaro wins her away from his rival by stealing for her the jewels decorating the image of the Madonna. Maliela confesses to Rafaele and other Camorrists about this theft, then rushes off into a raging sea to meet her death. After Gennaro has returned the jewels to the Madonna, he plunges a dagger into his own breast.

Two melodious intermezzos for orchestra are often played by salon and pop orchestras. The first comes between the first and second acts and is in a languorous mood. The second, heard between the second and third acts, opens with a light subject and continues with a broadly lyrical episode. A third popular orchestral excerpt from this opera is the dramatic "Dance of the Camorristi" during a revel in the Camorristi hideout in the opening of the third act.

As an opera *The Secret of Suzanne* (*Il Segreto di Susanna*) is a trifle. The libretto by Enrico Golisciani concerns a terrible secret harbored by the heroine, Suzanne: she is addicted to smoking. Since her husband finds cigarette butts in their house he suspects her of entertaining a lover during his absence. Spying on her through the window, one day, he learns about his wife's secret to his infinite relief, and does not hesitate to join her in a smoke. Light, breezy, infectious, and unpretentious, this little opera has been a favorite with operagoers everywhere since its world première in Munich on December 4, 1909.

The overture is as gay and as capricious as this merry tale. It begins vivaciously with the main theme in first violins and the woodwind. After this idea has been elaborated upon, a second melody is heard in the flute and clarinet accompanied by strings. The two melodies are soon merged contrapuntally, with the first theme heard in woodwinds and trumpet and the second in the strings.

Sebastián Yradier

ᵥᵍᵥᵍ ᵍᵥᵍᵥ

SEBASTIÁN YRADIER was born in Sauciego, Álava, Spain on January 20, 1809. Little is known of his career beyond the fact that his music instruction took place with private teachers; that in 1851 he was appointed singing master to the Empress Eugénie in Paris; and that for a period he lived in Cuba. He died in Vitoria, Spain, on December 6, 1865. He was a successful composer of Spanish songs. The most famous is *"La Paloma,"* which is in the habanera rhythm, its melody in the sensual, sinuous style of a flamenco song. *"El Arreglito,"* also a habanera, was borrowed by Bizet for his opera *Carmen* where it re-emerges as the world-famous "Habanera"; Bizet made only minor changes in the melody while retaining Yradier's tonality and accompaniment. A third popular Yradier song, in a style similar to *"La Paloma,"* is *"Ay Chiquita!"*

Carl Zeller

ᵥᵍᵥᵍ ᵍᵥᵍᵥ

CARL ZELLER was born in St. Peter-in-der-Au, Austria on July 19, 1842. Music, the study of which he had pursued since boyhood with private teachers, was an avocation. He earned his living as an official in the Ministry of Education in Austria. Nevertheless, he managed to write many operettas, two of which were among the most successful written in Austria during his time. Among his first works for the stage were *Joconde* (1876), *Die Carbonari* (1880), and *Der Vagabund* (1886).

His first major success came with *Der Vogelhaendler* in 1886, still a great favorite on the Continent. The second of his operetta classics, *Der Obersteiger,* was introduced in 1894. A later successful, though less well known, operetta, *Der Kellermeister,* was produced posthumously in 1901. Zeller died in Baden near Vienna on August 17, 1898.

Der Obersteiger (The Master Miner)—book by M. West and L. Held —received its première in Vienna on January 5, 1894. The setting is a salt-mining district of Austria in or about 1840. Martin instigates a strike among the miners, for which he is deprived of his job. To support himself he organizes a band of musicians from among the miners and tours the country. Eventually Martin returns to his mining town where he finally manages to regain his job and to win Nelly, with whom he has always been in love. The most popular song in the operetta is Martin's air with chorus, *"Wo sie war, die Muellerin,"* and its most delightful waltz is *"Trauet nie dem blossen schein."*

Der Vogelhaendler (The Bird-Seller), once again with a book by M. West and L. Held, was first heard in Vienna on January 10, 1891; but in 1933 it was presented in a new version in Munich adapted by Quedenfelt, Brugmann and Bauckner. In the Rhine Palatinate in the 18th century, Adam, a wandering bird-seller, is in love with Christel, but she refuses to consider marriage unless he gets a permanent job. He gets that job on the estate of the Elector Palatine at which point Christel is all too willing to give up a projected marriage with Count Stanislaus for the sake of her beloved Adam. The lovable melodies from this operetta—in the best traditions of Suppé and Johann Strauss II— have made it a favorite not only in Germany and Austria, but also throughout the rest of Europe, in North and South America, and in South Africa. Among the musical highlights of this operetta are the waltz *"Schau mir nur recht ins Gesicht";* the "Nightingale Song" (*"Wie mein Ahn'l zwanzig Jahr"*); the pert march tune *"Kaempfe nie mit Frau'n";* and Christel's sprightly air, *"Ich bin die Christel von der Post."*

Karl Michael Ziehrer

꿍ᤱᤳᤳᤳ ᤳᤳᤳᤳᤳ

KARL MICHAEL ZIEHRER, beloved Viennese composer
of waltzes and operettas, was born in Vienna on May 2, 1843. He was
completely self-taught in music. In 1863 he formed a café-house orchestra with which he toured Austria and Germany, often featuring his
own dance pieces and marches. He later expanded this orchestra into
an ensemble numbering fifty players with which he gave a series of successful concerts of semi-classical music in Vienna. In 1907 he became
music director of the court balls. After World War I he suffered extreme poverty, his personal fortune having been lost with the collapse
of the Hapsburg monarchy. He died in want and obscurity in Vienna
on November 14, 1922.

Ziehrer wrote more than five hundred popular pieces for orchestra,
including numerous marches and waltzes. His waltzes were particularly
favored, many of these in the style of Johann Strauss II. Some are still
extensively played. Probably the most famous of all his waltzes is
Wiener Maedchen ("Vienna Maidens"), which must rank with Lehár's
"Merry Widow Waltz" as one of the most popular such dances produced in Vienna since the time of Johann Strauss II. Its first melody
sounds like a Schubert Laendler, with the peasant vigor of its rhythm
and its robust tune; but the main subject is a soaring waltz in the finest
traditions of Viennese café-house music. The following are other
famous Ziehrer waltzes: *"Alt Wien"* ("Old Vienna"), *"Faschingskinder"*
("Carnival Children"), and *"Wiener Buerger"* ("Viennese Citizens"),
all three of which come closest among his works in assuming the structural outlines and the melodic identity of the Johann Strauss waltz
classics. Also popular are the *"Donauwalzer"* ("Waltzes from the Danube") and *"Evatochter"* ("Daughter of Eve").

Ziehrer's most famous operetta is *Die Landestreicher (The Vaga-
bonds)*—book by L. Krenn and C. Lindau, first performed in Vienna on
July 26, 1899. In upper Bavaria two tramps—Fliederbusch and his wife
Bertha—manage to live by their wits. Disguised respectively as Prince
Gilka and a dancer they visit a famous resort hotel and are involved in

numerous adventures. By managing to retrieve a supposedly valuable lost necklace for the Prince they finally win his favor and enter his service. Of particular interest is the captivating waltz at the end of the first act, *"Sei gepriesen, du lauschige Nacht."*

From several of Ziehrer's other operettas there come other delightful waltzes, notably *"Samt und Seide"* from *Der Fremdenfuehrer* (1902) and *"Hereinspaziert"* from *Der Schatzmeister* (1904).

An Alphabetical Listing
of the Lighter Classics in Music

❦❦ ❧❧

"*Abendlied*" (Schumann)

Abendsterne (Lanner)

Acceleration Waltzes (Johann Strauss II)

Acclamations (Waldteufel)

"*Ach, ich hab' sie ja nur die Schulter gekuesst*" (Milloecker), see *The Beggar Student*

Adagio pathétique (Godard)

"*Addio*" (Tosti)

"*Addio all madre*" (Mascagni), see *Cavalleria Rusticana*

"*Addio del passato*" (Verdi), see *La Traviata*

"*Addio fiorito asil*" (Puccini), see *Madama Butterfly*

Adoration (Borowski)

L'Africaine: Selections (Meyerbeer)

Agnus Dei (Bizet)

"*Ah! che la morte ognora*," or "*Miserere*" (Verdi), see *Il Trovatore*

"*Ah, fors è lui*" (Verdi), see *La Traviata*

"*Ah Sweet Mystery of Life*" (Herbert), see *Naughty Marietta*

Aida: Overture, Ballet Music, and Selections (Verdi)

"*Ai nostri monti*" (Verdi) see *Il Trovatore*

Air, or *Air on the G String* (Bach)

Al fresco (Herbert)

"*Allia marcia*" (Sibelius), see *Karelia Suite*

"*Allmaecht'ge Jungfrau*," or "*Elisabeth's Prayer*" (Wagner), see *Tannhaeuser*

Alley Tunes (Guion)

"*Almost Like Being in Love*" (Loewe), see *Brigadoon*

Alsatian Scenes (Massenet)

"*Als Bueblein klein*" (Nicolai), see *The Merry Wives of Windsor*

Alt Wien (Godowsky)

Alt Wien (Ziehrer)

Amelia (Lumbye)

American Fantasia (Herbert)

American Salute: "When Johnny Comes Marching Home" (Gould)

American Suite (Cadman)

American Symphonette No. 2 (Gould)

"*Am Meer*" (Schubert)

An American in Paris (Gershwin)

Andalucia (Lecuona)

Andaluza (Granados), see *Spanish Dances*

Andante cantabile (Tchaikovsky)

Andante religioso (Halvorsen)

Andantino (Kreisler)

An der schoenen blauen Donau (Johann Strauss II), see *The Blue Danube*

"*An die Musik*" (Schubert)

"The Angelus" (Herbert)

Anitra's Dance (Grieg), see *Peer Gynt Suite, No. 1*

Annen-Polka (Johann Strauss II)

Anvil Chorus (Verdi), see "*Vedi, le fosche notturne spoglie*," *Il Trovatore*

Apache Dance (Offenbach)

"*Après un rêve*" (Fauré)

Aquarellen (Josef Strauss)

Arabian Dance (Tchaikovsky), see *Nutcracker Suite*

Arkansas Traveler (Guion)

L'Arlésienne, Suite Nos. 1 and 2 (Bizet)

"*El Arreglito*" (Yradier)

Artist's Life (Johann Strauss II)

Ascot Gavotte (Loewe), see *My Fair Lady*

Ase's Death (Grieg), see *Peer Gynt Suite, No. 1*

"Liebeslied" (Weill), see *The Three-Penny Opera*
Liebestraum (Liszt)
A Life for the Tsar: Overture, Mazurka and Waltz (Glinka)
"Life's Garden" (Bond)
Light Cavalry Overture (Suppé)
"Der Lindenbaum" (Schubert)
Lohengrin: Prelude to Acts 1 and 3, Wedding March (Wagner)
London Suite (Coates)
"Londonderry Air," see *Irish Tune from County Derry* (Grainger)
"Lonely Hearts" (Romberg), see *Blossom Time*
"The Lord's Prayer" (Malotte)
Lorelei Rheinsklaenge (Johann Strauss I)
"The Lost Chord" (Sullivan)
Lotus Land (Scott)
"Loudly Let the Trumpet Bray" (Sullivan), see *Iolanthe*
Love for Three Oranges: March (Prokofiev)
"Love is a Firefly" (Friml), see *The Firefly*
"Love is a Plaintive Song" (Sullivan), see *Patience*
"Lover Come Back to Me" (Romberg), see *The New Moon*
"Love Song" (Weill), see *The Three-Penny Opera*
Lucia di Lammermoor: Selections (Donizetti)
Lullaby (Khatchaturian), see *Gayane*
Die lustige Witwe (Lehár), see *The Merry Widow*
Lyric Suite (Grieg)

"Mack the Knife" (Weill), see *The Three-Penny Opera*
Madama Butterfly: Selections (Puccini)
"Madre pietosa" (Verdi), see *La Forza del destino*
"Mad Scene" (Donizetti), see *Lucia di Lammermoor*
"Maedel klein, Maedel fein" (Lehár), see *The Count of Luxembourg*
"The Magnet and the Churn" (Sullivan), see *Patience*
"A Maiden Fair to See" (Sullivan), see *Pinafore*
"Die Majistaet wird anerkannt" (Johann Strauss II), see *Die Fledermaus*
Malambo (Ginastera), see *Dances from Estancia*
Malagueña (Lecuona)
Malagueña, from Boabdil (Moszkowski)
Malagueña (Sarasate)
Manhattan Masquerade (Alter)

Manhattan Moonlight (Alter)
Manhattan Serenade (Alter)
Manon: Gavotte, Minuet (Massenet)
"A Man Who Would Woo a Fair Maid" (Sullivan), see *Yeomen of the Guard*
"Many a New Day" (Rodgers), see *Oklahoma!*
March, from *Tannhaeuser* (Wagner)
March of the Gladiators (Fučik)
March of the Little Fauns (Pierné)
March of the Little Lead Soldiers (Pierné)
March of the Royal Siamese Children (Rodgers), see *The King and I*
March of the Smugglers (Bizet), see *Carmen*
March of the Toys (Herbert), see *Babes in Toyland*
Marche miniature (Tchaikovsky), see *Suite for Orchestra, No.* 1
Marche Slav (Tchaikovsky)
"Marechiare" (Tosti)
Marienklaenge (Josef Strauss)
Mark Twain: A Portrait for Orchestra (Kern)
Masaniello (Auber), see *The Mute of Portici*
Masquerade (Khatchaturian)
"Massa's in De Cold, Cold Ground" (Foster)
The Mastersingers: "Prize Song" (Wagner)
Matinées musicales (Rossini-Britten), see *Rossini*
"Mattinata" (Tosti)
Maytime: Selections (Romberg)
Mazurka (Delibes), see *Coppélia*
Mazurka (Glinka), see *A Life for the Tsar*
Mazurkas (Chopin)
Meditation, from Thaïs (Massenet)
"Mein Herr, Marquis" (Johann Strauss II), see *Die Fledermaus*
Die Meistersinger (Wagner), see *The Mastersingers*
Mélodie (Tchaikovsky)
Melody in F (Rubinstein)
Menuet à l'antique (Paderewski), see *Minuet*
Merrie England: Selections (German)
Merrymaker's Dance (German), see *Nell Gwynn*
The Merry Widow: Selections (Lehár)
The Merry Widow Waltz: "S'fuersten Geigen" (Lehár), see *The Merry Widow*
The Merry Wives of Windsor: Overture, Selections (Nicolai)
Mexican Rhapsody (McBride)
"Mi chiamano Mimi" (Puccini), see *La Bohème*
Midsommarvaka (Alfvén), see *Midsummer Vigil*
A Midsummer Night's Dream, Suite (Mendelssohn)

"Wanting You" (Romberg), see *The New Moon*

"A Wandering Minstrel I" (Sullivan), see *The Mikado*

War March of the Priests (Mendelssohn)

Warsaw Concerto (Addinsell)

Washington Post (Sousa)

Water Music (Handel)

Water Scenes (Nevin)

Waves of the Balaton (Hubay), see *Hungarian Czardas Scenes*

Waves of the Danube (Ivanovici)

Wedding March (Mendelssohn), see *A Midsummer Night's Dream,* Suite

Wedding March (Wagner), see *Lohengrin*

Wein, Weib, Gesang (Johann Strauss II), see *Wine, Women, and Song*

"*Im weissen Roessl*" (Benatzky), see *The White Horse Inn*

"We Kiss in the Shadow" (Rodgers), see *The King and I*

Welsh Rhapsody (German)

Die Werber (Lanner)

"We're Called Gondolieri" (Sullivan), see *The Gondoliers*

"Were I Thy Bride" (Sullivan), see *Yeomen of the Guard*

"Were Thine That Special Face" (Porter), see *Kiss Me Kate*

"Were You Not to Ko-Ko Plighted" (Sullivan), see *The Mikado*

"We Sail the Ocean Blue" (Sullivan), see *Pinafore*

"What God Hath Done Is Rightly Done" (Bach), see *The Wise Virgins*

"When a Felon's Not Engaged in his Employment" (Sullivan), see *Pirates of Penzance*

"When All Night Long a Chap Remains" (Sullivan), see *Iolanthe*

"When a Maiden Loves" (Sullivan), see *Yeomen of the Guard*

"When a Merry Maiden Marries" (Sullivan), see *The Gondoliers*

"When a Wooer Goes a-Wooing" (Sullivan), see *Yeomen of the Guard*

"When Britain Really Ruled the Waves" (Sullivan), see *Iolanthe*

"When I Go Out of Doors" (Sullivan), see *Patience*

"When I Was a Lad" (Sullivan), see *Pinafore*

"When I Went to the Bar" (Sullivan), see *Iolanthe*

"When Johnny Comes Marching Home," see *The American Salute* (Gould)

"When the Foeman Bares His Steel" (Sullivan), see *Pirates of Penzance*

"When the Night Wind Howls" (Sullivan), see *Ruddigore*

"Where the Buds are Blossoming" (Sullivan), see *Ruddigore*

The White Horse Inn: Selections (Stolz)

"*Wiegenlied*" (Brahms), see "Cradle Song"

"*Wie mein Ahn'l zwanzig Jahr,*" the "Nightingale Song" (Zeller) see *Der Vogelhaendler*

Wiener Buerger (Ziehrer)

Wiener Maedchen (Ziehrer)

Wild Horsemen (Schumann)

William Tell: Overture (Rossini)

Wine, Women and Song (Johann Strauss II)

"Wintergreen for President" (Gershwin), *Of Thee I Sing*

The Wise Virgins (Bach-Walton), see Bach

"With a Little Bit of Luck" (Loewe), see *My Fair Lady*

"A Woman is a Sometime Thing" (Gershwin), see *Porgy and Bess*

Woodland Dance (German), see *As You Like It*

Woodland Fancies (Herbert)

"*Wunderbar*" (Porter), see *Kiss Me Kate*

"Why Do I Love You?" (Kern), see *Show Boat*

Yankee Doodle Went to Town (Gould)

Yeomen of the Guard: Selections (Sullivan)

"You'll Never Walk Alone" (Rodgers), see *Carousel*

"Younger than Springtime" (Rodgers), see *South Pacific*

Youthful Suite (Grainger)

Zampa: Overture (Hérold)

Zapateado (Sarasate)

Zar und Zimmermann (Lortzing), see *Czar and Carpenter*

"*Zigeuner*" (Coward), see *Bitter Sweet*

Zigeunerbaron (Johann Strauss II), see *Gypsy Baron*

Zigeunerliebe (Lehár), see *Gypsy Love*

Die Zirkusprinzessin (Kálmán), see *The Circus Princess*

"*Zitti, Zitti, piano, piano*" (Rossini), see *The Barber of Seville*

"*Zorike, kehre zurueck*" (Lehár), see *Gypsy Love*

"*Zuhaelterballade*" (Weill), see "The Bully's Ballad," *The Three-Penny Opera*

"*Zwei Herzen in drei-viertel Takt*" (Stolz), see *Two Hearts in Three-Quarter Time*